The Progressive Yankees

The Progressive Yankees

Republican Reformers
in New Hampshire, 1906-1916

James Wright

Published for Dartmouth College by
University Press of New England
Hanover and London, 1987

*F
39
W75
1987*

Printed in the United States of America

LIBRARY OF CONGRESS CATALOGING-IN-PUBLICATION DATA
Wright, James Edward, 1939–
    The progressive Yankees.

    Bibliography: p.
    Includes index.
    1. New Hampshire—Politics and government—1865–1950.
2. Progressivism (United States politics) 3. Social
reformers—New Hampshire—History—20th century.
I. Title.
F39.W75 1987   974.2′041   86–40553
ISBN 0–87451–409–6

5 4 3 2 1

For My Children
Ann, Jim, and Michael

Contents

Illustrations

Foreword

Some twelve years ago, in a history of New Hampshire that I was writing with my wife, Elizabeth Forbes Morison, I described the state in the late nineteenth century as a place where "nothing much was really happening." The evidence appeared to support this view: A diary entry explained that in the "upright, unenterprising" towns, "today's report is yesterday's" as life goes on in its "smooth, even placid" way; a sardonic political observer suggested that the platform for the next campaign was made from the planks used in the last election; another judged that succeeding governors were so much alike that "it was hard to distinguish one from another"; the Bureau of Labor reported that the "leading industry" was the tourist trade—people in search of unchanging scenery and the old-time pleasures; and so on.

Now James Wright comes forward to demonstrate that the suggestive evidence was sometimes wrong (as in the case of the Bureau of Labor report) and quite frequently deceiving. He has searched with care beneath surface appearances and has concluded that New Hampshire at the turn of the century, far from being a "bucolic sanitarium," was on its way to "becoming a modern, urban, industrial state."

As a modern state, New Hampshire confronted a modern problem, one which Theodore Roosevelt had defined very clearly: "Big business was here to stay," Roosevelt noted, and it held out, in about equal parts, the promise of a more interesting world than had ever existed before and the possibility of disaster. Left unregulated, Roosevelt argued, the technological energies would produce no more than a new kind of "barbarism." "It behooves us," therefore, he said, "to look ahead and plan out the right kind of civilization as that which we intend to develop from these wonderful new conditions of industrial growth."

In New Hampshire in the first decade of this century, a significant group of individuals earnestly turned to the task of shaping the "right kind" of society. They tried to find a good answer to the question of "how to get your *state* to sum up the right reason of the community, on such matters as the regulation of coal, iron, and railroads." In so doing, those people left behind many of their attachments to the past, at least for a season. Describing New Hampshire in 1910, William Allen White concluded that it had become an "ultra radical" community committed to a "clear, strong, uncompromising fight" for a more just and decent future.

And now this penetrating and level-headed study tells how New Hampshire arrived at this point. These pages reveal—fully, fairly, and in telling detail—the process by which forces released by this "modern, urban, industrial state" jarred loose many of the settled connections that held the old structure of society together. The rising tension between the customary procedures and the new opportunities generated conflicts of interest, collisions of attitude, and continuing uncertainty in the areas of purpose and of choice.

The way in which New Hampshire worked its way through this exciting and confusing time to an acceptable program of specific objectives—how for a splendid moment those whom Wright calls the progressive Yankees got the state to sum up the right reason of the community—is absorbing and still instructive. Part of New Hampshire's success was, no doubt, a consequence of scale; the place was small enough so that well-considered, specific causes could produce general effects. Part of it also was no doubt due to the fact that the processes the reformers sought to control were made up of simple machinery; it was still possible to think of managing them in the interests of "the right kind of civilization." And a large part of it, as revealed in these pages, was a consequence of the fact that certain gifted men were prepared to come forward with their views of a just and decent society.

In the beginning there was William E. Chandler. An arresting and eccentric character, he spent the closing fifteen years of the last century explaining, as a senator and newspaper publisher, how much damage the Boston and Maine railroad could do the community. He prepared the ground; he made people think about the need to regulate industrial enterprise; and he liked to think of himself as the "first Progressive."

Building on this foundation, Winston Churchill, a novelist of distinction, put forward a more general program, vividly defining issues and proposing remedies. By his labors he brought an increasing number of citizens together on a ground of common understanding and mutual purpose.

Churchill was followed by Robert P. Bass who, more clearly than many of those around him, seemed to have understood that the only way to be sure that the state would sum up the right reason of the community was to get elected. In 1910 he successfully ran for governor, and his well-organized campaign produced an impressive number of like-minded supporters in the legislature. For the next two years Bass conducted a series of masterful negotiations and obtained a body of legislation that set a standard for all other states. What in 1910 had seemed "ultra radical" in New Hampshire became in passing years commonplace throughout the nation.

It should be clear that James Wright has written a very good book. In this reconstruction of New Hampshire's significant experience he has also rendered a larger and more general historical service. There has been a continuing debate over the meaning of what is called the progressive movement: Who were the progressives? What did they think they were doing? How did they try to do it? Why, after the great moment of 1912, as described in these pages, did they fail? Or looking beyond the election returns, in the long run did they succeed? For such questions all kinds of answers have been proposed, ranging from the claim that progressivism was the last best hope of the Republic to the assertion that its objectives were so disparate and ill-defined that it could not possibly be said to deserve the label of a formal "movement." In the pages that follow, the meticulous description of the play of the progressive impulse through New Hampshire's political process in the years from 1900 to 1916 will yield much solid information on what progressivism really was, how it really worked, and why, finally, it lost its power to sustain itself.

Elting E. Morison

Preface

While researching and writing this book, I generally responded to inquiries about my work by describing the project as a study of progressive reform in New Hampshire. Occasionally such descriptions would generate, from historians and nonhistorians alike, responses that ranged from incredulity to sarcastic humor. The prevailing image of New Hampshire is not one that always links the state with political reform movements. This book demonstrates that at least for one significant period, historically this image is incorrect. But this accomplishment was incidental to my purpose. My concern was more with the process than with the context. New Hampshire provided a convenient case study for examining some broader questions about political parties and reform politics. Specifically I was interested in understanding better the politics of progressivism. I believe I have accomplished that understanding, but only through a recognition and reminder of the importance of context in shaping the process of American politics.

In 1915 Benjamin Parke DeWitt published a book entitled *The Progressive Movement*. DeWitt began his study with the observation that "the term 'progressive movement' has been so widely used, so much discussed, and so differently interpreted that any exposition of its meaning and principles, to be adequate, must be prefaced by careful definition." DeWitt's definition of progressivism was composed of three elements: (1) "the insistence by the best men in all political parties that special, minority, and corrupt influence in government—national, state, and city—be removed"; (2) "that the structure or machinery of government, which has hitherto been adapted to control by the few, be so changed and modified that it will be more difficult for the few, and easier for the many, to control"; and (3) "the rapidly growing conviction that the functions of government at present are too restricted and that they must be increased and extended to relieve social and economic distress."[1]

DeWitt's definition of progressivism continues to be useful, but not as a set of rigorous criteria against which phenomena can be objectively tested. His understanding of "careful" did not, unfortunately, include characteristics such as specificity and thoroughness; nor did his definition, which he revealingly qualified as "tendencies," have the precise limits that permit easy determination of which phenomena fell within, and without, their scope. His categories have an elastic quality which invites subjective judgments. And finally, his definition excluded progressive reforms that were not related to politics and government.

Those who have in later years shared with DeWitt an interest in explaining progressivism can sympathize with his problems. They would certainly agree with him that the concept of a progressive movement has been "so widely used, so much discussed, and so differently interpreted." Historians of progressivism in the seventy years after DeWitt's book appeared have encountered many of the same problems of definition that he had. Most historians likely would agree with the statement that the period from the 1890s down to the April 1917 entry of the United States into the First World War was a time of sweeping changes in American life. These changes included an expanded understanding of both public and private responsibilities. A concomitant of this process was a number of innovations and modifications in the legal, organizational, and institutional frameworks that shaped and monitored these responsibilities. This abstracted proposition does not define "the progressive period," the label customarily attached to these years, but it may well approach the limits of scholarly consensus.[2]

Any general survey of the progressive years includes the peripatetic and energetic Theodore Roosevelt and the moralizing and learned Woodrow Wilson, their presidencies (1901–9, and 1913–21, respectively) sandwiching and usually eclipsing the term of the cautious William Howard Taft (1909–13). The image is one of a new, aggressive, presidential government, casting off nineteenth-century constraints and challenging trusts, regulating business activities, and generally flexing muscles at home and abroad. Some scholars question this image, both in terms of its substance and in terms of the role and objectives of these presidents. The quandary of progressive scholarship, however, is not simply one of differing interpretations of presidential leadership: national political activities themselves often seemed incidental or at best merely responsive to more basic forces driving these changes.

Beginning with Benjamin DeWitt, students of political progressivism have located these changes in cities and states as well as at the national level. Perhaps the most productive scholarship on progressivism has focused on its manifestation in specific localities. Hiram Johnson in California, Robert La Follette in Wisconsin, and

Charles Evans Hughes in New York represent paradigmatic progressive governors. There were others, in perhaps a score of states; while particular forms vary, the general theme is one of reformers challenging established party and governmental leadership, opening processes of government, bringing recalcitrant corporations into line, providing for more equitable revenue sources and collection processes, and instituting new programs ranging from conservation of natural resources to labor protection laws. Historians have also described progressivism in its urban context, where mayors such as Hazen Pingree in Detroit, Mark Fagan in Jersey City, and Tom Johnson in Cleveland worked with others to fight political "machines," restructure their governments, challenge utility and transportation companies, and introduce new welfare and social service programs. In the South as well as the West, the Northeast as well as the Midwest, cities as well as states, progressives contributed new public policies.[3]

It is in the interpretation of these policies, in the identification of distinctly progressive values, and in their understanding of the class or group base of support for progressivism, that historians disagree. Scholars have variously argued that progressive reforms derived from demands from business elites, from labor organizations, from agrarian interests, from the new middle class, from the old middle class; from probusiness and antibusiness attitudes; from nineteenth-century values and from new bureaucratic values; from a moralistic, crusading ideology and from an amoral quest for efficiency in public life. Progressives were Democrats, were Republicans, were nonpartisan, were bipartisan, and were partisan innovators in the form of Theodore Roosevelt's new Progressive party in 1912. Progressives were process oriented or were result oriented; they were humanitarians seeking new social policy or they were committed opponents of any policy that seemed to favor a specific group no matter how disadvantaged. They were enthusiastic supporters of new, large, corporate organizations or they were opponents of these enterprises who sought to stem them through antitrust action. Progressives might be found in public life, as either elected or appointed officials; alternatively progressives might be found in private life, acting to reenergize professional associations, working to broaden the scope of charitable or philanthropic activities, or seeking to maximize efficiency—and profit—in their business enterprises.

To concede elements of truth in all of these contradictory components is to confront the essential dilemma of the historiography of progressivism. Terms such as *change,* or even *reform,* at the least implicit concepts in most descriptions of the progressive era, are too flexible and subjective in their use to yield an unambiguous product. Many activities and many individuals could represent a plausible case for inclusion within the scope of progressivism. Plausibility, however, resembles but does not establish a cogent argument. The recognition that progressivism represented many things does not lead to the conclusion that it represented everything, or concurrently nothing. Examples of progressive "reforms" that turned out to have had effects inconsistent with their stated purpose, of "reformers" who upon closer examination appear to have been shams, or of progressives who in the era of the First World War and thereafter appear to have become reactionary opponents of their own earlier principles, may qualify but do not negate the accomplishments of the progressive period. The United States was significantly different in April 1917 from what it had been at the beginning of the twentieth century. Surely the same could be said of any comparable period in recent history. But this was not just any period; it was the dawn of the twentieth century, and the changes at this time, quantitatively and qualitatively significant, had few antecedents and many consequences. It was an era of transition marked by profound organizational changes; some scholars use the concept of modernization to explain the progressive years.[4]

My interest is in political progressivism; this is not to discount the important developments in other spheres of activity during this same period. It is a statement of focus rather than of order. Political activity and debate over public policy ultimately reflected most aspects of the progressive movement. Nonetheless, many major reforms in American thought and education, in private charity and welfare activities, in labor unions, in professional associations, and in business organization and practices often only tangentially had political reflections. The forces driving these changes were part of the context, the weltanschauung of progressivism, that helped define political reform; nonpolitical activities and accomplishments were sufficiently important in their own right and should not be forced into a political equation, whether as dependent or independent variables.

The focus of this book is on the progressive Republicans in New Hampshire. Much of their activity followed patterns found in other states—indeed Theodore Roosevelt's *Outlook* considered New Hampshire "well to the front among Republican progressive States"—but they never received the attention of some of their more publicized contemporaries to the south and to the west. A *Collier's* article noted in 1911 that the New Hampshire reform effort was "as hearty as any western insurrection." Yet, the author conceded, it was the "progress of the other big Insurgent waves [that] has been recorded in the newspapers."[5] Except for an occasional reference, the same pattern of omission has persisted in most of the major scholarly literature on progressivism.[6]

The Republican reformers in New Hampshire were not all-inclusive of the state's progressives; on the other hand they represented or at least had elements of contiguity with other reform efforts in the state. These included the Democratic progressives and the relatively minor, in New Hampshire, nonpolitical and nonpartisan reformers. Initially these Republican progressives focused essentially on state politics and government. The dynamic urban or local progressivism that was an important catalytic and sustaining element in reform politics elsewhere had no real counterpart in New Hampshire. On the other hand, the progressive Republican movement in the Granite State had important connections with national politics. These connections had a significant and complicated impact on the fortunes of the state movement.

Progressive Republicans in New Hampshire were largely Yankees, by which I mean most of the identifiable progressives were old-stock, native, and Protestant New Englanders. Needless to say, they were male. Partisan political activity remained a distinctly male enterprise until passage of the Nineteenth Amendment to the United States Constitution in 1920. *Yankee*, however, is a descriptive rather than a differentiating quality. The progressives' opponents in the Republican party and most of the Democratic progressives as well tended to be Yankees. And some key progressive leaders were born outside of New England.[7]

Republican progressivism in the Granite State was not a mass movement. To be certain, electoral politics, an arena in which the reformers had some successes, depended upon popular appeal. When I began the research for this study it was the nature of this appeal that interested me; I hoped to determine, largely through an analysis of popular voting behavior, the demographic base and the attitudes that shaped the progressive movement. These analyses indicated that no characteristics distinguished the progressive voters; the latter represented a cross section of the Republican party.[8] Progressive successes resulted from the skills and objectives of their leaders rather than from palpable voter pressure. Even these leaders were not of one mind on some important issues. Progressives seemed to shout the same principles and then shout at each other over specific policy matters and their implementation.

In 1911 progressive governor Robert Perkins Bass invited Henry Hale of The Balsams resort to be the state delegate to a convention planned by the "See Europe if you will, but see America First" group. Hale replied that "nothing would suit me better than to give this all the support that I can"; unfortunately he had to decline the appointment because he would be traveling abroad when the conclave was in session.[9] The convention was not equivalent to progressive legislation, of course, but Governor Bass must have felt that he had been in that verbal maze before, a feeling that resonates in the scholarly enterprise of trying to understand the shared values and common characteristics that marked the reformers and their movement.

The elusiveness of these shared values and common characteristics may well reflect asking the wrong questions of the progressive movement or of using inappropriate standards to examine the answers. A political movement such as progressivism in New Hampshire, or in any other state or locality, need not necessarily display qualities of intellectual or of social coherence in order to establish its legitimacy. To the extent that such consonance was present, it likely related to the local situation and provides a limited base for predicting its shape elsewhere. One of the problems of progressive scholarship has been the recognition that this reform impulse pervaded American politics and society and yet the case studies of it are sufficiently contradictory to frustrate efforts to develop good generalizations about this phenomenon.

If U.S. state government has historically occupied a pivotal role in the federal system of government, U.S. state politics has tended to play an equivocal role in the federal system of politics. Political federalism has not been the subject of empirical or of theoretical studies to the extent that governmental federalism has.[10] Part of the difficulty has been the particularity of state and local politics. The national political parties have been the cohering institutions, but they have seldom had the means—or the inclination to try—to impose ideological or organizational uniformity on these constituent parts. Historical intraparty disagreement, often quite intense, on issues of public debate is both cause and consequence of this condition. In the early twentieth century national parties expected of their state counterparts little more than campaign and electoral support for congressional and presidential elections. Consensus tended to center around abstract or rhetorical principles that permitted significant freedom on specific matters of policy. For example, at the turn of the century New England and midwestern Republicans could agree with their party's traditional tariff principles and fight with each other about specific schedules on hides or finished textiles.

New Hampshire progressive Republicanism emerged in this context of semiautonomy from the national party and in an environment marked by a long tradition of party leadership squabbles and competition for offices. National reform, meaning that occurring in other areas as well as that at the federal level, influenced but did not determine the shape of the New Hampshire variant on progressivism. The state's own political traditions and culture, its own historical conflicts, and its particular agenda and distribution of power at the turn of the century all provided conformation for Granite State progressivism. But the progressive movement was more than broad theme harmonizing with local circumstance. The equation outlines but hardly describes the energy and personality that marked the reform impulse. New Hampshire proved more than a convenient case study.

In the first years of the twentieth century some New Hampshire Republicans became convinced that their party had lost its ideals and that the party leadership had become too responsive to corrupt influence. They determined to challenge this state of affairs and to redirect their party. The nature of their challenge to the old party leadership was influenced by the national reform mood; the rhetoric, the stated principles, the sense of purpose and efficacy of the New Hampshire challengers, the progressives, were not inconsistent with those characteristics of reformers elsewhere. And the nature of their challenge was equally the product of New Hampshire's political traditions and styles. But the essence of their challenge was more complicated than these factors. The progressive reformer leadership group was not large, and within this group individual personalities and ambitions and ideals could be quite influential. The same was true of their opponents in the party leadership. The latter, the old guard, and the progressives engaged in public debate about party principles and about public policy; if rhetoric stretched the differences from time to time, the latter were nonetheless real. New Hampshire progressivism cannot be understood simply in terms of contending ideas, however; at its core it represented, as politics often does, contending individuals. The old guard was basically comfortable with the nineteenth-century party structure and philosophy; the progressives sought to change these. Individual leaders were critical in shaping this conflict.

This conflict had some deep roots and complicated causes, but it essentially began in 1906 when a group of Republican insurgents calling themselves Lincoln Republicans organized to advance the gubernatorial candidacy of novelist Winston Churchill. This group rallied to challenge the Republican "machine" in the state, particularly its association with the Boston and Maine railroad. Failure in the 1906 campaign spurred the reformers to broaden their scope and their agenda; by 1908 a young Peterborough legislator, Robert Bass, had begun to exercise leadership in the progressive Republican movement. Bass participated in the expansion of the group's demands to include a more comprehensive set of governmental reforms. In 1910, taking advantage of the state's direct-primary law that he had helped write and pass, Robert Bass was elected governor, a major Republican victory in the Northeast in that year of Democratic sweep. As governor, Bass accomplished most of the progressive goals even as he was articulating a vision of greater state responsibility for social welfare. At the peak of their power and influence, the Republican progressives split in 1912, with many following Bass into Theodore Roosevelt's camp for the presidential primary challenge to the incumbent William Howard Taft. When Roosevelt failed, some of his followers, including Bass, joined him in the third-party Bull Moose Progressive effort. This effectively ended the Republican progressive interlude, despite continuing individual activities and accomplishments, but the progressive legacy was a state political and governmental system significantly different from that which had existed at the turn of the century.

This study is concerned with this struggle for control of the Republican party in New Hampshire. If much of their bickering was gossipy and personal, the issues were nonetheless real and the implications were significant for the nature of politics and for the direction of the New Hampshire state government. This book follows a chronological organization. Chapters 1 and 2 provide context and introduction for this conflict. Chapter 1 is a survey of the nature of New Hampshire life at the turn of the century, while chapter 2 outlines the state political system. Chapters 3 and 4 describe the progressive challenge as it evolved from 1906 to victory in 1910. Chapter 5 is a study of the administration of Robert Bass, from apogean legislative success to the frustration of the failed Roosevelt candidacy in 1912. Chapter 6 focuses on the post–1912 struggles of the Republican reformers, while chapter 7 sums up their contributions to public life in New Hampshire.

I have incurred many debts in the course of this study. The project was first suggested to me by the late Louis Morton. He encouraged me to make use of the rich Bass and Churchill collections at the Dartmouth College Library. Elting Morison also encouraged the study, and he has been a patient and good critic over the years. The children of Robert P. Bass have been most supportive of this study. Perkins Bass and Robert P. Bass, Jr., have shared with me materials and photographs relating to their father. Their insights and recollections were most helpful, and their generous hospitality and good humor have sustained me. They read this book in an earlier draft and helped with factual and family information. They and their sisters, Edith Bass Bonsal and Joanne Bass Bross, and their brother, Jeremiah Bass, provided gifts to Dartmouth College which supported some of my research activity. John Bass III of Englewood, Florida, allowed me to examine his grandfather's manuscripts and provided a genial and hospitable environment for research. The late Creighton Churchill allowed me unrestricted access to his father's papers at Dartmouth College.

A year as a John Simon Guggenheim fellow gave me the freedom and support I needed to initiate this study. Dartmouth has been continually supportive of my scholarship, providing financial support and released time. The Charles Warren Center at Harvard University furnished a stimulating and delightful setting for writing. It is hard to exaggerate the supportive attitude of the staff of the Dartmouth College Library. Kenneth Cramer, Phillip Cronenwett, Robert Jaccaud, and Virginia Close deserve special mention, as do all of the patient circulation desk staff. Steven Cox and his associates in the manuscript division of the New Hampshire Historical Society were always helpful.

Jo Malin Roodman worked as my research assistant in the early phase of this study. She completed a thorough and professional bibliography, and she assisted in the collection and coding of data. Betty Olson, Virginia Page, Laurie Geary, and Katherine Singleton assisted me with various phases of my research. I am indebted to them and to all of the Dartmouth students who have helped and prodded me along in my understanding of progressivism. Among these students several assisted me directly on this project: Peter Marsden, Peter Fowler, Robert Schpoont, Ronald Cima, Nicholas Theodorou, Lisa Mendelson, James Hokans, Donald Bourassa, and Michael Moody. Patricia Denault at Harvard and Nancy Blake and Gail Patten at Dartmouth typed parts of the manuscript. Larry Levine patiently assisted me as I learned the intricacies of word processing.

I am obligated to several historians for their generosity and graciousness in reading this in manuscript form. Ballard Campbell, Jere Daniell, and Elting Morison have patiently offered suggestions at several draft stages. Their criticisms and questions, along with those of Roger Daniels, Richard L. McCormick, and Harry N. Scheiber, all of whom read and commented on the manuscript, have assisted me greatly. Daniels and Allan Bogue encouraged me over the years and always proved an inspiration. On behalf of all readers and critics, I offer the standard disclaimer that any remaining errors of fact or interpretation as well as intractable stylistic inelegance are my responsibility. On my behalf, I would record that they have aided me considerably in understanding and explaining New Hampshire progressivism.

Charles Backus and Mary W. Crittendon and their associates at

the University Press of New England have smoothed and speeded
along the whole process of transforming my manuscript into this
book. I have enjoyed working with them. Kathryn Gohl has been a
superb copyeditor. Her careful reading and thoughtful suggestions
have made it a better book.

Finally, Susan DeBevoise Wright helped me through the tough
times and never let me think this would not be completed. Thanks
to her support, it is.

Hanover, New Hampshire   J.W.
February 1987

1

New Hampshire and the New Century: An Introduction

As the twentieth century began, New Hampshire was not in a state of crisis or even of palpable tension. The sharp divisions and profound changes that would mark the state's politics in the next dozen years were not rooted in erupting social and economic demands. Nonetheless the state was continuing to shift from its earlier nineteenth-century moorings of agriculture and rural, homogeneous communities. This process was ongoing rather than sudden, one that steadily altered the nature of the state and set a framework and influenced the agenda for the political upheaval that would follow.

Some residents of New Hampshire debated whether January 1, 1900, really was the start of a new century. Nineteen hundred and one, they argued, seemed the more logical point to mark the beginning of the twentieth century. The debate served as useful filler for newspaper editors, but, one concluded, "really what does it all amount to?" After all, "the division of time into years and centuries is purely arbitrary."[1]

The choice of a time to profile a state is arbitrary as well. New Hampshire has never been static. Nonetheless it is useful to understand some of the major themes of New Hampshire life as the twentieth century began. The late nineteenth and early twentieth centuries were a time of great change. This generation of Granite Staters did not need the perspective of the historian or the careful indexes of the social scientist to tell them things were changing: they knew it; they could feel it, and most were optimistic about the consequences of change. As the governor of the state beamed in a New Year's message, "You will hear from the old Granite State more than once during 1900." A year later his successor would tell the state

1

legislature that the new century "promises beyond what we can think or ask. Prosperity is on every hand."[2]

As the century turned, some Granite Staters looked backward and expressed regret about things that now seemed lost. The governor of the state in 1900, Frank Rollins, was one of these. Governor Rollins remembered, or thought he did, "the rugged, down-right, straight-going belief, free from guesswork or uncertainty, of those good old days." He was uneasy with what he perceived as the modern style of "easy-going indifference, an all-accepting optimism ready to throw down all customs, rules, and bars in order to preserve our own comfort." This was the same governor whose New Year's message promised a year of "prosperity and progress."[3]

Rollins was unintentionally engaging in irony. And of course he was not exceptional in his bifurcated view of the world. He could thrill in the promise of the future and mourn the loss of the past. The transitions that marked New Hampshire life at this time, from agricultural to industrial, from rural to urban, from relative cultural homogeneity to pluralism, seemed generally positive. Clearly most would have agreed that they constituted progress, at least in a material sense, but the tensions rubbed by these changes often involved basic values and life-styles. The tensions seldom flared, however, as old and new coexisted.

Life and death hinted at these patterns of change. Measles, typhoid, consumption, and smallpox still claimed lives in this modern state. These were diseases responsible for uncounted granite markers in the burying grounds of hillside farm and valley town, and they only now were coming under the control of new vaccines, diagnoses, and treatment.[4] Accidents involving animals, wagons, and logging still killed and crippled the careless and the unlucky. No more beneficent, the new industrial order brought engines, boilers, and elevators that could maim or kill in the trauma of steel and steam.[5] Disease and accident, old and new forms, cut a wide and tragic swath in the Granite State. Only Rhode Island had a higher death rate than New Hampshire among the New England states in 1900. Infant mortality figures suggest a great variation in death rates and causes among immigrants and natives. Nearly one in eight of the children born in New Hampshire to native parents in 1900 would die before their first birthday. Among children of immigrants, the figure was slightly more than one in five.[6]

Natural forces still touched the lives of people as they had in the past. A January blizzard isolated some communities and many farms, but failed to relieve a continuing drought that dried water supplies and closed mills and power plants, even slowing the harvest of ice haulers from the lakes and ponds. Fire was a constant concern, particularly with old and combustible wooden structures standing close together and heated by flammable kerosene or gas.[7]

New comforts often compensated for traditional inconveniences. Electric lighting had reached the streets and homes of larger towns. Water and sewage systems provided individual service and community protection.[8] The twentieth century seemed to promise no end to such technological improvement and economic growth. Only a few seemed explicitly concerned with the social costs of growth and technology. Antimodernization was not a popular or even a viable ideology. Nostalgia for a remembered past and acceptance of the comforts of the present seemed in functional balance. It was quite possible to have it both ways.

On August 29, 1899, some former residents returned to Henniker, a hill town west of the Merrimack River valley. This was Old Home Week in New Hampshire, a program initiated by Governor Rollins to call back for a visit the sons and daughters of the state who had sought their opportunities elsewhere. Sixty towns sponsored this activity in 1899; in 1900 seventy-two towns participated. In Henniker the 1899 program motto struck a common theme: "Be it a weakness, it deserves some praise; we love the play-place of our early days."[9] This concept of "play-place" as well as the general nostalgia explicit in these 1899 and 1900 celebrations symbolized well some contrasts in New Hampshire at the turn of the century.

By 1900 New Hampshire had become a tourist state and a focus of organized, commercial nostalgia in New England. The commissioner of the New Hampshire Bureau of Labor reported that the summer trade had become by 1900 "undoubtedly the leading industry of the state."[10] His adverb was not a hedge, but neither can his argument be demonstrated. The figures, as we shall see later, do not verify this conclusion. On the other hand, in the still informal cash-for-services tourist economy the figures are not fully reliable. Certainly rural New Hampshire was slowly learning how to profit from the seasonal visitors, but the commercialization of culture was not all to the good. To be sure, the good roads movement received a boost from tourist needs, and forest conservation and fish and wildlife management took on a greater urgency, but tourism involved as well a nostalgic emphasis on the old rural Yankee culture and the necessary concession that something important had passed. Governor Rollins spoke euphorically of that life where children were "brought up with their ears to the ground where they can hear Nature whisper her secrets." Alas, said the governor, New Hampshire had been "sapped" of the "best of our life blood." Now, at least, the state had a new role as "one vast sanitarium from June to December."[11]

New Hampshire was not dead or sapped as the twentieth century began. The population of the rural areas had declined, both in absolute and in relative terms, but this largely reflected the growth of the state's cities. New Hampshire was not simply a bucolic sanitarium, a "play-place" fixed in time; rather it was becoming a modern, urban, industrial state. By 1900 natives born of native parents composed less than 60 percent of the state population, and rural dwellers had become a minority.[12]

Contrasting population patterns had marked New Hampshire for much of the nineteenth century. Some towns had peaked in population in the early nineteenth century; by the time of the Civil War, most had begun a century-long pattern of decline, at the very time other communities were growing rapidly. Between 1890 and 1900 the urban population had increased 35.9 percent while the rural population had declined 44.9 percent.[13] It was the latter that captured attention and caused concern. Governor Rollins ignored urban growth, except to condemn cities as "forced, artificial, unreal, unhealthful," and said in Old Home Week remarks in his family home of Rollinsford that "New Hampshire has suffered greatly from the drifting away of its best-bred stock to build up and open up the more arable lands of the West. She has been a prolific mother."[14] This concern over a population drain to the West was an old one in New England, and, setting aside Rollins's unprovable qualitative judgment about the types of people who migrated, the numbers of New Hampshirites who had relocated to the West were not that significant at the turn of the century relative to other emigrant targets. Of the 124,048 New Hampshire natives who were living outside the state in 1900, 27,300 lived in the Midwest and West. On the other hand 94,934 (76.5 percent of the total) lived in other New England states, in New York, in New Jersey, or in Pennsylvania. Over half of the emigrants lived in Massachusetts.[15]

In 1900, 80,435 New Hampshire residents had been born in other states. The contiguous states of Massachusetts (26,587), Vermont (19,647), and Maine (16,650) provided the vast majority of these immigrants. In 1900 New Hampshire's cumulative net loss due to internal migration was down 15,000 from the 1890 figure and marked the lowest number recorded in the 1850–1900 period. New Hampshire was becoming more object than source for population relocation.[16]

Swelling New Hampshire's population at the turn of the century were over 88,000 foreign-born residents, over one-half of whom were natives of French Canada. This group had increased in numbers over the previous thirty years, pushing ahead of the Irish and British immigrants. In 1900 immigrants, particularly French Canadians, were not deeply rooted in New Hampshire. Forty-one percent of the total had arrived in the previous decade; only 38 percent of the 72,340 foreign-born in the state in 1890 remained in 1900.[17]

Manchester had become easily the dominant city in New Hampshire. With a 1900 population of 56,987, it was 34,000 people larger than the second city, Nashua, down the Merrimack River. Concord, the state capital, had fewer than 20,000 people. A direct comparison of Manchester with the aggregate rural areas of the state reveals Manchester to have been more female (53.4 percent as compared to 48.3 percent in rural areas) and more foreign (42.6 percent as compared to 11.7 percent in the rural areas). Home of the giant Amoskeag mills, Manchester was a vibrant, polyglot city with a majority of its population of foreign stock, led by the French Canadians but including Irish, Germans, Greeks, Poles, and Swedes as well as members of several other nationalities. Among cities in the United States, Manchester in the late nineteenth century had one of the highest proportions of residents who could not speak English. Nonetheless, the foreign-born were not the sole basis for the city's population growth: New Hampshire natives in Manchester increased in the 1890s while they were declining in the remainder of the state.[18]

Manchester was quantitatively unique in New Hampshire, but the same general patterns and distributions were evident in a score of cities from Nashua in the south to Berlin in the north, Rochester in the east and Lebanon in the west. One small mill in Newport had a work force that included "Americans, Irish, French and Finlanders."[19] Valley cities, located by water power and along railroad lines, witnessed the greatest growth in this period. Here foreign- and native-stock workers joined in textile mills, shoe factories, tanneries, and granite works. The hill country rural population was leaving farm and village; many were not traveling far.

Not endowed with a good growing season, rich deep soil, convenient topography, or substantial mineral deposits, New Hampshire from the colonial period had been marked by a practical and adaptive economy. Semisubsistence agriculture, forest products exploitation, and small-scale manufacturing and processing plants were common activities for much of the eighteenth and nineteenth centuries. These patterns were seldom static, a condition perhaps best illustrated by New Hampshire agriculture.

To understand agricultural evolution—indeed broader economic changes—it is useful to consider a judgment made by the editor of the Concord *Independent Statesman* in 1883:

New Hampshire is to a certain extent a dependent state. While we have within our borders a diversity of interests, we are largely dependent upon

Massachusetts for our market in which both to buy and sell. London is no more the centre of England than is Boston the centre of all that portion of New England east of the Connecticut River. All our railroads centre in that city.[20]

In general terms this point was true: New Hampshire was a dependent state, and Boston was the hub. But Boston in turn was dependent upon national and international market turns. New Hampshire early provided cereal and livestock for the Northeast because these were the major market demands, not because the Granite State was particularly well adapted to this type of production. Then as eastern (and European) demands as well as western production changed, New Hampshire successively was a wool and mutton producer, a poultry and dairy products producer, and, by the turn of the century, a raw milk and truck producer. These patterns were by no means uniform throughout the state. Southern New Hampshire always responded more immediately to changes in the eastern market. Raw milk did not flow from the northern hill country into Boston until later in the twentieth century.[21]

As New Hampshire agriculture went through these stages, there was always a rippling social effect. Small, semi-independent farms were aggregated into larger operations; the family and nonfamily agricultural labor force declined; local communities became more fully integrated into broader economic, social, and cultural networks. Those who mourned the passing of New Hampshire rural and agrarian life in 1900 were only partially correct. Traditional routines and patterns had declined, but the state of agriculture in New Hampshire was not nearly so threadbare as these observers believed. Population decline was a wholly rational process in economic terms; by the end of the nineteenth century New Hampshire farmers apparently were earning a per capita income far greater than that enjoyed by the previous generation.[22]

While agrarian prosperity may have depended upon a declining rural population, industrial growth relied upon an increasing urban work force. Large manufacturing complexes, especially in textiles but as well in shoes, symbolized the modern city as the dairy barn symbolized the modern farm. Smaller early manufacturing activities often went the way of the merino sheep which had dominated New Hampshire hills before the Civil War. Symbolically, in 1900 when the mills in Manchester were expanding to where they comprised the largest textile complex in the world, upriver in Concord a group of creditors took over the assets of the venerable old Abbot-Downing company, makers of the distinguished "Concord" coach.[23]

Any discussion of industrial New Hampshire at the turn of the century must begin with the Amoskeag mills. Organized in 1831 by the Boston group of investors that financed textile mills at Lowell, Nashua, and Waltham, Amoskeag early recruited female operatives from rural New Hampshire and followed the prevailing paternalistic system. Manchester was essentially a company town, an Amoskeag town, but the company seldom defined its interests narrowly. It provided land for churches and civic buildings, helped design a livable and attractive city, and encouraged commercial development—even to the point of selling land and water rights to other textile mills. By the turn of the century the corporation remained the most influential force in the city but perhaps not the dominating, controlling institution it might have been. In the years between 1900 and World War I, Amoskeag integrated other major city mills under its control.[24]

Successive technological developments in energy production from water power to steam to electricity gave New Hampshire mills and factories some greater flexibility in location; few took advantage of it. The Merrimack River valley remained the most industrial part of the state, with significant other complexes along the Connecticut, the Cocheco, the Winnipesaukee, and the Ashuelot rivers and at Salmon Falls. Smaller high-volume streams as well as the prevalence of earlier cottage manufacturing had nonetheless given a ubiquitous quality to early nineteenth-century manufacturing. The combination of railroad access with water resources concentrated more the post–Civil War manufacturing centers. Some older manufacturing towns suffered aborted development due to railroad location decisions.[25]

At the turn of the century the railroad in New Hampshire was a single system, the Boston and Maine, commonly referred to simply as The Railroad. In 1900, with the leasing of the Fitchburg railroad, the Boston and Maine controlled 1,136 miles of track in New Hampshire, all but 52 miles of the state's railroad mileage. Reaching this dominant position had been a lengthy and difficult process, one marked by economic and political skirmishes, and one resolved ultimately by lease, acquisition, and the approbation of the New Hampshire state legislature. The integrated system included some old and powerful Northeastern lines: the Eastern railroad, the Northern railroad, the Manchester and Lawrence railroad, and the Boston, Concord, and Montreal system. Chartered as a Massachusetts corporation and headquartered in Boston, the Boston and Maine provided New Hampshire with connections to eastern cities and to the west. It served all regions of the state and all communities of any substantial size.[26]

As was the case elsewhere, the railroad proved a mixed blessing in New Hampshire. Towns with no railroad service inevitably stagnated.[27] Communities within the railroad network enjoyed the fruits of economic, social, and cultural integration within a broader regional structure. Commerce, passenger traffic, and mail and newspaper delivery broke down many of the illusions of community self-sufficiency. But corporate decisions on track and station location, service quantity and quality, and rate structure had a major impact upon the towns served by the railroad.

In 1897, when railroads were carrying products to and from every part of New Hampshire, the industrialized Merrimack River valley witnessed the annual log drive. It would be the last on that river.[28] Lumbering had been important in the state's economy since the colonial period. The end of the Merrimack drives did not mark the close of the industry. Bridges, dams, and mill races had simply rendered this process of shipment an anachronism. Railroad tracks into the northern forest made most river drives inefficient. And the growth of major wood products companies such as the Berlin Mills Company and the International Paper Company meant that it was no longer necesary to ship logs elsewhere for processing. Centering around Berlin, the lumber and lumber products industry had become the dominant nonagricultural force in the north country of New Hampshire.[29] The great spruce, fir, and pine stands of the state fell at a rate that was alarming to some. In February of 1900, at the winter meeting of the state board of agriculture, a young U.S. Department of Agriculture official, Gifford Pinchot, made an impassioned plea for the adoption of modern forest management concepts. These, he insisted, had nothing to do with "shade trees" and apple orchards. They did not aim at "the beautifying of public parks." Rather, the young forester insisted, "forestry is altogether a business proposition." Pinchot's audience was receptive to this argument.[30] Not all Granite Staters, however, agreed with his assumptions. Parks and shade and beauty, the aesthetics of nature, had become important to many whose interests would be represented by the Society for the Protection of New Hampshire Forests, founded in 1901.[31]

Society members as well as others in New Hampshire recognized the relationship between forest conservation and the summer tourist industry. In 1899 New Hampshire realized an estimated $6.6 million in direct income from the 174,280 tourists who came to the state.[32] As an industry tourism was still at a rudimentary—and literal—cottage level. Large numbers of tourists came and stayed in rooms made available in private farms. There were more luxurious accommodations, of course, such as the Glen House at the foot of Mount Washington. Some summer visitors were more than brief vacationers. Northeastern city dwellers purchased old, often "abandoned," farms and established summer homes. Places like Peterborough, Cornish, and Jaffrey boasted of their "colonies." Lake resorts like Winnepesaukee, Sunapee, and Newfound attracted both short- and long-term visitors. By the turn of the century most New London manufacturing companies, for example, had ceased operation due to their inability to compete with larger industries now enjoying regular access to the New London market. On the other hand, the eighteen summer tourist establishments in New London registered over twelve hundred guests in 1900; this was in addition to the growing ownership of summer homes in the area by nonresidents.[33] For the tens of thousands of summer people who visited the state, the natural and picturesque ambience was important. Forest conservationists recognized this fact.

In 1899 the commissioner of the Bureau of Labor reported that the New Hampshire tourist industry employed 12,354 people.[34] Most of these workers undoubtedly were part-time employees; nevertheless this new industry provided at the least an important supplemental income source for a substantial and growing number of Granite Staters. Table 1.1 provides a more complete picture of employment in selected occupational categories in 1900. It is important to note that all agricultural activities, including logging and gardening, occupied only 22 percent of the New Hampshire work force in 1900. Manufacturing occupations employed nearly twice as many people. The breakdown by gender reveals that women worked disproportionately in manufacturing, especially in the state's cotton mills. In Manchester, women provided 37 percent of the manufacturing work force. The professional classes, with the significant exception of schoolteachers, were male dominated.

Certainly wage work was not an exclusively male activity in New Hampshire in 1900. Nor did women workers represent only the young, single women of the traditional New England mill system. The 1900 census revealed that 20.4 percent of the married women in Manchester were "breadwinners," that is, major wage earners. This was one of the highest ratios in the country among cities with greater than 50,000 population. For comparison the New England average was 8.1 percent and the national average was 5.8 percent. Outside of Manchester this breadwinner status was less common among married women in New Hampshire, but even here the 7.6 percent figure was exceeded only in the states of the deep South and in the Arizona territory.[35] Among all females over ten years of age in Manchester, 41.2 percent were designated by the Census Bureau as breadwinners; this was the highest rate in the country for cities with greater than 50,000 population. The national average was 26 percent and the New England average was 31 percent.

Hard work and low pay characterized many New Hampshire occupations in 1900, thus necessitating multiple wage earners for

TABLE 1.1

Work Force in Selected Occupations and Occupational Categories by Gender and Percentage of Women, 1900

	Men	Women	Total	% Women
Total work force	136,961	41,758	178,719	23.4
Agricultural	37,224	1,558	38,782	4.0
Professional				
Journalists	153	12	165	7.3
Lawyers	466	2	468	.4
Physicians	723	61	784	7.8
Teachers	386	2,821	3,207	88.1
Professors	66	3	69	4.3
Government officials				
National	233	66	299	22.1
State	38	2	40	5.0
County	91	2	93	2.2
City or town	106	7	113	6.2
Domestic/personal service	18,436	12,140	30,576	40.0
Trade/transportation	23,020	2,631	25,651	10.3
Manufacturing	54,033	21,912	75,945	28.0
Boot and shoe	6,368	3,298	9,666	34.1
Cotton	7,694	10,098	17,792	56.8
Woolen	2,164	1,083	3,247	33.4
Owners and officials	1,348	9	1,357	.7
Lumbering/wood products	7,382	385	7,767	5.0

Source: Census Bureau, *Population, 1900,* 2:530–38.

families. Nevertheless the state was not marked by labor unrest. With some exceptions, most workers apparently accepted the limits of their lives. Labor unions tended to be neither large nor militant. In 1902, eighty-five New Hampshire labor unions reported a total membership of 6,446. This represented approximately 5 percent of the nonagricultural, nonprofessional work force in the state. The industrial union strength was minimal. Manchester had seventy-five members in a textile union.[36] In 1900 there was a major granite-workers strike over wages, but the textile industries in the state were as yet unorganized. Strikes in textile mills, when they occurred, tended to be wildcat affairs that stemmed from a specific incident. Generally these were quickly resolved, sometimes with concessions by management but seldom with any appreciable accretion in worker influence or power. The Amoskeag company, for example, turned back a weaver strike in 1886, but company officials followed their victory with an expansion of the traditional paternalistic policies.[37] A common contemporary explanation for labor docility was the high proportion of French Canadians in manufacturing industries. These workers composed nearly 47 percent of the textile mill workers in the state in 1900. Their willingness to work hard for low pay had earned the *canadiens* the description "the Chinese of the Eastern states" in an 1881 Massachusetts Bureau of Labor Statistics report. These workers typically enjoyed a higher standard of living in New England than they had experienced in rural Quebec and the Maritime Provinces, and they often seemed to share anti-union sentiments.[38]

The records are inadequate for verifying such complex reasons for behavior. Probably equally important, and verifiable, was the cultural conflict that mitigated against broad-based cooperation. As the largest and among the most recent of the immigrant groups in New Hampshire, the French Canadians became a convenient symbol for many of the cultural tensions in the state. These tensions were far more complex than simple Yankee versus immigrant or Protestant versus Catholic antagonism.

Perhaps the greatest ongoing conflict was between the Irish-Americans and Franco-Americans in New Hampshire. The Irish began to come to the state before the Civil War to build railroads and to work in quarries and mills, and they had first suffered the antagonism of the Protestant Yankees. By the time significant French-Canadian immigration began in the 1870s, the Irish had established themselves in the mills, in local politics, in unions, and in the church. They had not been fully integrated into New Hampshire life by any means. As late as 1888 the New Hampshire Young Men's Christian Association resolved to support efforts to protect the Republic from "the dangers of Communism, Catholicism, and unrestricted immigration."[39] The Granite State remained Yankee and Protestant in terms of power, influence, and status. But within the non-Yankee substrata, the Irish dominated long after their numbers became less consequential. Of the eighty-five labor organizations in the state, eleven had officers with clearly French surnames. Irish and British names dominated.

Control of the Catholic church proved the most emotional and bitter focus for Irish and Franco antagonism. The diocese of Manchester was controlled by an Irish hierarchy, and most parish priests were Irish, or at least they were not French. Franco-Americans demanded of their church a more traditional liturgy and a greater pageantry than the Irish wanted. Most critically the French-Canadian immigrants insisted upon—indeed in most cases required—French-language sermons and instructions. This battle was a continuing one that flared in public and flamed in the quiet of diocesan reports and correspondence. These disagreements were by no means confined to New Hampshire, nor were Franco and Irish antagonisms the exception to Catholic solidarity. The *New Hampshire Catholic* dismissed Italian workers as "roving stilletto-armed *dagos*" rather than welcome this new immigrant group.[40] The Irish typically were involved in all of these controversies because of their preemptive status among American Catholics and their assimilationist vision of an "American" Catholic church rather than congeries of national churches in the United States. This the Franco-Americans resisted, as an editor in the French-language *L'Impartial* underlined in 1900: "It is known by all that the Irish clergy only work for one end: to make us lose the use of our mother tongue so that they will be able then to confine to the priests of Celtic origin the parishes where we are in the majority."[41] With the loss of language would come the loss of tradition, culture, and solidarity. Children would grow up assimilated in a culture of materialism and religious indifference, as well as "des amusements profanes."[42]

Irish assimilationist impulses were probably less ominous to Franco-Americans and to immigrant groups generally than the homogenizing demands of some of the dominant Yankees. Governor Rollins, in his Rollinsford Old Home Week address, insisted that his townspeople "do everything in your power to assimilate and Americanize the large foreign element which has cast in its futures with this community in later days. This element has brought new responsibilities and difficulties but you must not shirk them. You must meet them in a broad, catholic spirit."[43] If the governor's choice of a final adjective was a curious one, his general sentiments seemed widely shared. Franco-American slogans, such as "I am a French Canadian by origin, and I am proud of it; I am a Catholic and I thank God for it; I am also a citizen of this Republic which I love and respect, and I am happy by it," suggested, at the least, inverted loyalties.[44] New Hampshire Yankees were not anti-immigrant in any uniform sense; nonetheless few would have challenged the assumption that Americanization must take its course.

Obviously *Yankee* is itself an inclusive term that suggests greater cohesion than actually existed. Defined as a Protestant born in New England of New England Protestant stock, *Yankee* is a category of some descriptive value but not one that implies narrowly defined cultural coherence or behavioral uniformity. New Hampshire's population was too diverse for any simple description to have much meaning. The history of the state carried memories of other rifts that still had emotional meaning to some people. In religious terms these old conflicts involved Congregationalists versus Episcopalians, Methodists and Baptists versus these older bodies, and the

sometimes subtle but nonetheless important issues involving Presby-
terians, Freewill Baptists, and Unitarians. Nonreligious differences
might center on native Yankee versus the immigrant Yankee from
Maine, Vermont, or Massachusetts, as well as differences stemming
from occupation or residence. Across the state there were the traditional antagonisms that pitted seacoast against interior, hill country
against valley, Manchester against Concord, and Connecticut Valley
against the central and eastern part of the state.[45] None of this suggests that New Hampshire was in constant conflict. It was not. But
there were differences that had centrifugal effects, and these were
seldom simple or clearly dichotomous. New Hampshire was a plu-
ralist state and from this condition derived strength as well as weakness. The growth and modernization that marked the late nineteenth century both accentuated and attenuated these differences.

The liquor issue was one that regularly inflamed passions in New
Hampshire. In simplest terms this question centered around rural/
urban and Protestant/Catholic dimensions. As we shall see, such interpretations obscure as much as they explain in New Hampshire.
The so-called Maine law, which had prescribed near-total prohibition in New Hampshire since the 1850s, had fallen into patterns of
uneven local enforcement. In Manchester in fact by the 1890s periodic summonses and fines had become a means of providing for an
extralegal licensing system. And the battle over liquor became part
of a broader pattern of cultural and political difference.[46]

In 1906, 45 percent of the total population of the state reportedly
belonged to an organized church.[47] Sermon topics as the new century began included traditional fare such as "The Anchor of Hope"
(Manchester Free Baptist Church) and "The Salt of the Earth"
(Littleton Congregational Church). Some ministers, worried about
modern materialism and secularism, warned Christians not to be
"crippled in your religious life by some bad habit. . . . Crippled by
the theater, maimed by the opera, benumbed by the lodge, lamed
by the euchre party, your spiritual feet slipped on the waxed floor of
the ball room."[48]

Generally the message was of an optimistic, even aggressive,
Christianity that stressed helping as a means to salvation. As the
New Hampshire Good Templars happily agreed, "Some of us are in
this Order, not because we need it, but because we want to do
good." The Rev. Edwin Morrell told his Christian church congregation that "deeds not creeds should be the Christian motto for the
next century. Service for success is the law for a Christian. It is not
so much what I believe as what I do; not my position in society, but
my consecration for my fellows. . . . The old order of caste and blood
must give way to the spirit of unselfish labor." Other topics such as

"The Golden Rule Philosophy of Life" (Lebanon Methodist Church) and "The Model Young Man" (Manchester First Baptist Church) stressed this theme. As Rev. F. S. Bacon told his People's Baptist flock, lay "hold upon opportunities of service" in this new year.[49] Roman Catholic sermons and sermon topics were not published regularly. Those that were underline some differences between Catholicism and the evangelical Protestantism being preached. Creed was at the heart of the Catholic church, and sermons stressed the commandments and church dogma. Nonetheless, deeds and good work had become an institutionalized aspect of the Roman Catholic church by this time. This was primarily directed at caring for their own in orphanages and hospitals. New Hampshire Methodist "missions" to save the state's Franco-Americans presumably did not encourage Roman Catholics to participate fully in this ecumenical gospel, while Catholics generally still had to contend with concern on the part of some Protestants about a "Roman peril."[50]

Efforts to assimilate newcomers meant ultimately efforts to educate. Education in New Hampshire in 1900 was more comprehensive than the formal processes of schoolhouse and lesson. Groups, clubs, churches—virtually all organizations and institutions in the state—performed roles in mass education. In small as well as large communities, citizens on any night gathered to hear lectures or participate in discussions that ranged in subject matter from ornithology to geology. Western culture and history, particularly but not exclusively of the United States, were favored subjects. "The Life and Achievements of Benjamin Franklin" (Manchester Congregational Church YMCA), "The American Artists" (Lebanon Vega Club), "Good Citizenship" (Phillips Exeter Academy lecture series), "Foucault's Experiments" (Manchester Institute), "Cuba" (Claremont lecture course), "Charles Lee, a Soldier of Fortune" (Manchester DAR by historian John Fiske), "Life of Nathaniel Hawthorne" (Goffstown Women's Unity Club), and "The Power of Thought" (Manchester Freethinker's Association) represent some of the many lectures available in January 1900.[51] Visiting dramatic and musical groups seemed to inundate the state.

Obviously those in attendance at such sessions did not represent a cross section of the state's population. This was a system of voluntary, adult education for those who were interested. Education as an acculturating, assimilating process in a complex society cannot depend upon voluntarism. In New Hampshire it did not. By 1901 the state had enacted compulsory school attendance laws, had established high school opportunities for most students, and had provided for citizens, in cities with populations over five thousand, to petition for the establishment of free evening schools.[52] Illiteracy was high in New Hampshire, particularly among the foreign-born in the cities. Certainly educational reformers set a high priority upon dealing with this functional deficiency. Groups saw the public schools as contributors to the solution of other social problems as well. For example, the Grange believed schools should provide for "the scientific teaching of agriculture" and "enhance the pleasures of rural life," while the Woman's Christian Temperance Union saw the schools as transmitters of values of "social purity."[53]

The schools then came to be perceived as having modernizing as well as conserving roles. These influences were not broadly experienced though. Table 1.2 indicates that children of immigrants were less likely to attend school than were children of native-born parents.[54] Particularly this was true in the high school grades, where the new commercial and "practical" courses were taking hold. Also, a sizable number of the children of immigrants attended parochial schools, where the vision of assimilation differed from that of their public counterparts. French Canadians especially were vigorous in establishing French-language schools.[55]

With the exception of the normal school at Plymouth and the land grant New Hampshire College for Agricultural and Mechanical Arts in Durham, there was no public higher education in New Hampshire. The agricultural school had moved to Durham from Hanover in 1893, ending its affiliation with Dartmouth College. The Durham school enrolled about two hundred students, and the Grange aggressively watched that a classical curriculum not interfere with its practical training program. Dartmouth had functioned since its 1769 founding as the equivalent of a state school for New Hampshire students. As late as 1893–94, 40 percent of Dartmouth's students were New Hampshire natives. In that year William Jewett Tucker became Dartmouth's president, and he began a systematic program of expansion. By 1908–9 the school's enrollment had increased by 250 percent, and, while the New Hampshire numbers increased, the state's proportion of total enrollment had been halved. Dartmouth became a more cosmopolitan place; Tucker oversaw the broadening of its curriculum with a corresponding decreased role for classical and religious training.[56]

Insularity and cosmopolitanism were not necessarily mutually exclusive concepts in turn-of-the-century New Hampshire. Among individuals as well as within urban neighborhoods and rural communities, localism and individualism coexisted in a structure that nourished broader relationships. Members of groups as diverse as the Grange, the Christian Endeavor, L'Union Saint-Jean-Baptiste d'Amerique, the state bar association, the Knights of Columbus, the Dairymen, the Granite Cutters Union, the Whist Association, the

TABLE 1.2

School Attendance Showing Percentage of
Various Age Groups in School, by Nativity and Gender, 1900

Gender and age	Native-born of native parents	Native-born of foreign-born parents	Foreign-born
Males: 5–9	66.7	64.6	56.3
Females: 5–9	64.7	62.4	51.3
Males: 10–14	92.3	88.9	67.9
Females: 10–14	92.6	88.3	64.6
Males: 15–19	44.4	24.9	8.8
Females: 15–19	44.8	26.1	7.4

Methodist church, and community baseball clubs, functioned at local, state, regional, and, occasionally, national and international levels. Relatively short distances and a sophisticated railroad network (the Boston and Maine regularly offered "special fares" for meetings, tournaments, and outings) provided opportunities for most New Hampshire citizens to travel and meet like-minded people. The geographical mobility that marked the state's population meant extended family networks that reached throughout New England as well as to Quebec and Europe. Tourists and summer residents gave many communities regular infusions of "outsiders." Telephone exchanges had recently begun to link communities and individuals, and rural delivery of mail was breaking down further the isolation of the country.[57]

For the vast majority of the people in New Hampshire this wider circle of contacts, interests, and information fit into a routine that was fundamentally local and parochial in its orientation. Home, workplace, and, for many, church provided a tripodal focus and foundation for their regular activities. Even in more cosmopolitan cities and circles, New Hampshirites typically worked with, worshipped with, and participated in social affairs with the same people. Their lives largely were bounded by familiar places and acquaintances in their own communities.[58]

Nation and world were intrusive forces in New Hampshire life in 1900, quite apart from the personal involvement of citizens in extra-community activities. The local press gave comprehensive and continuing coverage to the American war against guerillas in the Philippines, the Boer War, the Boxer Rebellion, famine in India, and the nature of world markets.[59] For many these events were little more than curiosities. Much of the newspaper coverage concerned itself with the exotic and the mysterious, and certainly journalism may have seemed to some as little more than a printed version of the midway at local fairs, where "the wonderful novelties of the Orient" coexisted with "the wonderful magic of the East." But for others, such as the Hibernian societies and the Sons of St. George, events such as the Boer War took on deeper emotional meaning.[60] The thirteen hundred New Hampshire men who had marched off to the Spanish-American War in May 1898 never left the United States. They nevertheless served as a reminder of evolving international interests and responsibilities.[61] These never seemed to abate after that "splendid little war." Charitable and missionary work, as well as informational lectures and debates, underlined these concerns.[62]

With the morning newspaper came information about domestic affairs ranging from the curious and the sensational to regular reporting on congressional affairs and President McKinley's activities.[63] Perhaps most would have judged such information as irrelevant at worst and interesting at best. Nevertheless the intrusion of broader concerns was a constant factor, the effect of which probably was a greater sense of national integration. Citizens in places like Gorham, Lempster, and New Durham were regularly reminded of the world outside of their communities.

New Hampshire entered the new century in a spirit of confidence. Certainly there were tensions and uncertainties, new and old as well as individual and social. The tension between modernizing and conserving values and the ambivalence of local orientation in an increasingly cosmopolitan society are conceptually useful in understanding this new century spirit. The Rev. C. J. Staples, in a sermon to his Manchester Unitarian congregation in January 1900, expressed well the spirit of equivocal optimism that was common: "in these latter days . . . the whirl of events, the strong currents of new interests and plans and purposes hurry our old losses and pains behind and into oblivion. The world is getting too crowded, too intent on tomorrow's sensation, tomorrow's chance, or tomorrow's duty." He was confident that "the life of the whole nation, free, vigorous, hearty, advancing, rights the superficial evils by the wiser way."[64] Defining the "wiser way" to deal with the economic and cultural forces that were changing much of the state would prove to have significant political implications.

2

The Politics of Diffusion

IN SEPTEMBER 1900 the *Manchester Union* noted the tardy beginning of the presidential campaign in usually politicized
Portsmouth. "The slow action of both parties has been the cause of
considerable comment." The absence of visible campaigning probably resulted from two factors: the somnolence of a late dry summer
and the implicit recognition by both parties that with that obstreper-
ous Nebraskan William Jennings Bryan again heading the Democratic ticket, it would be no contest in New Hampshire.[1] Despite
these factors, it was uncharacteristically late for the Portsmouth
politicians to be beginning a campaign. For New Hampshire citizens
did seem to enjoy their politics.

Many variables shaped the political culture of New Hampshire;
prominent among these was the simple physical fact that the state
was geographically small and compact. The state capital in Concord
seemed accessible for all but the citizens of the mountainous,
wooded, and sparsely populated north country. More important,
the state was subdivided into some 235 towns and cities, all with
elected officials and significant local responsibilities. Annual town
meetings permitted the adult male citizens not only to choose officials but to participate in policy and budget debates. There seemed
to have been a high sense of involvement and of efficacy.

The failure of the *Union*'s correspondent to find political banners
in Portsmouth should not have led him to conclude that politics was
absent. It was an election campaign that had not begun; politics
never stopped. In a comprehensive sense politics included not only
the process by which New Hampshire selected presidents, governors, and representatives, but as well a range of officials, commissioners, and their associates and assistants. Only a fraction of these
political agents won their position through a public campaign and

election. There were approximately thirty-eight hundred elected officials in New Hampshire in 1900, at town, city, county, and state levels. There were probably an additional five thousand full or part-time public officials ranging from rural "fence viewers" or city firemen to the secretary of state, and not including several hundred postal agents and other federal appointees. All received their positions through a process that was assuredly political if not necessarily partisan or public.[2]

Politics of course is much more than the selection of officials. Public officers continually participated in the formulation and administration of policy, the allocation of resources, the enforcement of established codes of criminal and civil law, the collection and expenditure of public funds, and the mediation of conflict. Some of these matters were deliberated in full public view, such as in meetings of the legislature or the boards of selectmen; occasionally they involved public participation, such as the town meeting each March; nonetheless most decisions probably were made in private, and not necessarily due to a desire for secrecy. It was simply that fences were surveyed, fire departments were organized, corporations were registered, and the scores of other public activities typically were carried out in the absence of continued public interest or controversy.

Governance is the most important dimension of politics, and many citizens in New Hampshire were schooled in both the wider arena and the specific dimension. Given the principles of rotation in some offices and the normal turnover in positions, there may have been some 25,000 citizens in the state in 1900 with some personal experience in positions of public office. For comparison fewer than 93,000 citizens voted in the presidential election in that year.

Experience was but one factor in shaping individual political consciousness. Among others were the participants' personal ambitions and commitments, their values, and their sense of social needs and obligations. The fact that these remain largely unstated and elusive variables does not negate their influence on the public philosophy. There was an ambiguous sense of public interest, but this was seldom conceived of as different from the aggregation and synthesis of private interests. The commonly recommended "civics" textbook in the state suggested that government was the consequence of an implicit contract. Majority sentiments did rule, but government had the additional responsibility of maintaining a protective attitude toward the transcendent, if ambiguous, public good.[3] The bill of rights in the New Hampshire state constitution made this contract explicit. It was all rather formulaic—and often bore little resemblance to the day-to-day processes of government.

Civics book theories, constitutional guidelines, and practical experience converged roughly in an understanding of discrete responsibilities and concentric relationships within the framework of federalism. To say there was basic consensus on many public principles is not to suggest there was agreement on programs or even on the hierarchy of principles. Differences arose about responsibilities, and, while they were often couched in philosophical terms, the latter typically reflected more immediate policy needs or demands. There was little public debate about the constitutional authority of the national government; it carried on foreign affairs, maintained the currency and the postal system, regulated interstate and international commerce, administered national territories, and provided for national defense and "general welfare." These responsibilities were never neatly translated into clear policy options, and the political system in the nineteenth century grappled with them repeatedly at the programmatic level and occasionally in philosophical discussion. Great debates in the last quarter of the century over monetary policy, railroad regulation, the control of "trusts," tariff rates, land policy, federal expenditures on pensions and public projects, and taxes and subsidies had conditioned people to consider the macroeconomic role of the national government.[4]

At the turn of the century the state may have been the least visible level of governmental activity; it remained nonetheless the most important in many regards. For New Hampshire citizens national activities may have appeared more exotic and newsworthy, while town government seemed more immediate because of its visible obligations in the collection and expenditure of taxes, maintenance of schools and roads, and responsibility for sanitation, and police and fire protection. Nevertheless even these important administrative functions were within a framework shaped and monitored in Concord.

The state government of New Hampshire by the end of the nineteenth century regularly touched the lives of all residents of the state. Policy administration commonly rested in the local communities; policy formulation remained with the state government, particularly the state legislature. The state regulated, defined, licensed, prescribed, proscribed, and encouraged a whole range of public and private activities.[5] New Hampshire codes provided for the regulation of retail sales in goods ranging from dairy products to the sale and shipment of lumber and lumber products. Statutes controlled the organization and practices of banks, insurance companies, railroads, and corporations generally, as well as giving cities the option of regulating billiard halls, bowling alleys, restaurants, and groceries and other retail stores. The speed at which one could ride a bicycle or drive an automobile came under state stipulation. Trapping, hunting, fishing, the harvest of ice, the placement of awnings and signs, the use of shade trees, were all within limits defined by the state of New Hampshire. More carefully prescribed was the traffic in poisons, gunpowder, strychnine, drugs, tobacco, and alcohol.

It is possible to learn something about public values and public policy by inquiring into what a state chooses to protect and to discourage. In turn-of-the-century New Hampshire the state protected songbirds and bald eagles, bass and trout, moose and deer, and through the state forestry commission had begun to assess ways to enhance and conserve the state's forest resources. In human terms, the state defined those groups needing special protection to be orphans, the poor, the insane, widows, children, and women workers. And the state considered railroads to be the only private corporations requiring special protection from interference, disruption, and sabotage.

The state of New Hampshire did not like, and set out to proscribe, adulterated foods, especially oleomargarine, obscene literature, blasphemy, cruelty to animals, begging, fornication and adultery, the desecration of state and national flags, Sunday hunting and working, disruption of religious services, usurious interest rates, cursing, swearing, profane songs, and the writing or making of graffiti with obscene words "figure or representation." The state openly declared war on and paid bounties for the destruction of locusts, grasshoppers, and bears.

On the other hand, the state defined certain activities as socially beneficial and sought to further them through tax relief or incentives, through direct state financial assistance, or by permitting towns to offer these forms of encouragement. Through these statutory exceptions, the state defined as "good" public libraries, agriculture, education, public health, good roads, forestry, ornamental trees, town histories, hospitals, temperance, manufacturing and ship building, public worship, and religious societies.

Some activities were of sufficient social consequence, or were particularly susceptible to fraudulent practices, that the state provided for their licensing. State boards, the state executive branch, or towns and cities, under the authority of the state, licensed and controlled plumbers, teachers, junk dealers, hawkers and peddlers, lightning rod salesmen, pharmacists, physicians, traveling shows, attorneys-at-law, dealers in petroleum products, pawnbrokers, and dentists. These controls ranged from a simple license fee to comprehensive examinations and regulation of procedures. The state also required the local licensing of dogs, with New Hampshire beginning to define and check its interests through the charging of differential fees: female dog licenses cost more than male dog licenses due to a growing concern about a burgeoning and free-spirited dog population. When New Hampshire faced a significant movement away from the farm in the late nineteenth century, it seemed perfectly logical for the state government to assume a role in attempting to reverse this trend. The state did, distributing pamphlets to summer dwellers urging them to buy "abandoned farms."[6]

Governmental activities at the turn of the century were not simply intrusive, they were often *visibly* intrusive. Regulation touched birth and burial, marriage and divorce, school and workplace. Social controls aimed at moral behavior and consumption of products such as alcohol, while economic controls dictated railroad consolidation and the weight of a loaf of bread. Fire and sanitation codes had begun to regulate the design and use of private property. Police powers fixed the speed of transportation and the size of wagon wheels. Civil codes intruded into relations between husband and wife, parent and child, employer and employee, and buyer and seller. Gov. Hiram Tuttle told legislators in 1891 that their responsibility included the "moral, mental, and material welfare" of the people of New Hampshire.[7]

This brief survey of the parameters of New Hampshire law cannot reveal how freely legislators and other officials assumed these comprehensive responsibilities; there is little doubt that enforcement of some of these various strictures ranged from uneven to uniformly lax. Spotty enforcement notwithstanding, the authority was there; debate over the role of government had generally passed from the philosophical to the programmatic plane. Questions about desirability rather than those of constitutionality shaped the public dialogue.

For Granite Staters at the turn of the century, *government* was not an abstraction; it may have been an ambiguous term though, in the absence of further clarification. Generally citizens seemed to have an understanding of government that differentiated among national, state, and local responsibilities. In the 1890s political debates over national monetary policy, banking, fiscal, and tariff policies, particularly in the context of the Panic of 1893 which appeared related directly to these policy decisions, reinforced existing images of the relevance of the national government in some significant areas. Foreign policy imbroglios involving the Philippines, Puerto Rico, and the Hawaiian Islands reintroduced old differences about the national government's constitutional role in territories. Debate over the regulation of railroads and trusts and conflicting views on industrial labor policies portended new items on the agenda. New Hampshire individuals and groups seemed to understand these national responsibilities. In petitions, resolutions, and debate they asked for national action in areas of national concern.[8]

These citizens as readily understood the different roles of state and local government, even if they might not all grasp the complexity and nuances of this relationship. Local control and home rule often were more myth than reality in turn-of-the-century New Hampshire. The state established tax procedures and minimum and maximum rates of taxation and expenditure. Roads, schools, police and fire protection, and public health were administered locally, but within a framework that the state government established and monitored. Intensity and significance were often inversely related when a town debated at its annual meeting whether to increase the school budget $100 beyond the mandated minimum.

Local politics generated emotional debate because they were local. The personalities and issues were not distant or abstract, and they fit into the community's collective memory of earlier conflicts. Group identification could play critical roles in intensifying feelings: ethnic, religious, economic, and geographical identities helped inform and provoke political conflict. As a Francestown historian noted, after describing intense conflict there between Unitarians and the established Congregationalists, "Into this joyless rift, all town issues would eventually fall."[9] What outsiders might consider minor issues often took on great local importance. A Benton fight over the location of a road along the Ammonoosuc River in the 1850s illustrated this. The controversy "overshadowed the Compromise act of 1850, its later repeal, the Kansas-Nebraska troubles, the anti-slavery struggle, and dominated not only the political life of Benton but entered into the social, educational and religious life as well."[10]

In the 1870s the legislature removed state elections and most local elections from the annual town meeting day in March to biennial Novembers. This had the apparent effect of making the local town meeting less partisan. It is not so clear that it made it less intense, as debates continued over policy and over the allocation of scarce resources.[11]

Taxation policy and expenditure patterns suggest something of the complex relationship between state and local governments. State law defined all taxation procedures as well as the range of tax rates. The state board of equalization studied and adjusted local taxation plans. The property tax was the dominant source of public money in New Hampshire, and this was collected totally by town government. Towns then contributed a fixed rate to the state government—the total amount ranging from $400,000 to $500,000 per year in this period—and a small proportion to the less consequential county governments. The state government directly collected taxes from railroad and insurance corporations and from savings banks.

The state of New Hampshire was more an administrator than user of public money. State expenses, including debt service, were less than those of the city of Manchester in 1900. The major costs of government were schools, roads, sanitation, and police and fire protection. These were local obligations. The state redistributed most of its pass-through property tax income and corporate tax revenue to the towns. These were proportional transfers, and by a margin of two to one towns had a favorable balance of payment with the state. The only categorical state grants in 1900 were for the purpose of education—the school and literary funds. In addition towns retained approximately 90 percent of the property tax they collected.[12] It was not a totally satisfactory situation. Equalization of tax burdens and public services was difficult. The New Hampshire State Bar was sharply critical of the "notoriously unsatisfactory method of taxation." Rural towns particularly felt burdened by a system that depended upon the property tax; they felt deprived in the delivery of public services.[13]

Citizens certainly retained some significant discretionary authority at the town level. Voters in town meeting determined whether to install sewer systems, to install or franchise water systems, to maintain roads, to light streets, and to expand police and fire departments. In 1903, thirty-four of the eighty-eight water supply systems in the state were publicly owned. Only one of fifty-one electric systems, on the other hand, was public.[14] At school district meetings citizens voted on capital construction, length of school year, and size of teaching staff. None of these were trivial decisions—indeed they were critical qualitative matters—but nevertheless the deliberations and options were always within a framework defined by the state of New Hampshire.

Debate over the respective roles and relationships of the three major units of government tended to be more pragmatic than philosophical. The public philosophy was less shaped by ideological imperatives and proscriptions than it was by imperfect evaluations of the cost and impact of policy options. There were exceptions to this, the prohibition on liquor sales being more complicated by conflicting values and philosophy, but for most issues citizens seemed to disagree more bitterly over marginal costs, local consequences, and administrative efficiency than policy per se. Implicit (and often explicit) in these evaluations was an element of community parochialism and individual self-interest. Policies ranging from the United States tariff schedules to local school districting were calculated in terms of their differential impact. The state superintendent of public instruction had to remind the citizens of New Hampshire that decisions on school location related to educational and community values, not the value of individual real estate holdings.[15] Public interest and private goal were not easily separable concepts. Indeed, the prevailing assumption seemed to be that not only were they mutually supportive, they must be: the former was but the aggregation of the latter.

The complex overlap between public and private concerns colored consideration of many of those matters of public policy that were coming to dominate the political agenda in 1900. One was an old issue, deeply rooted in antebellum New Hampshire (and American) politics: prohibition. In 1855 New Hampshire had passed a so-called Maine law, modeled after the policy of this neighboring New England state. This law provided for a near-total ban on the sale of alcoholic beverages, the exception being sales through liquor agents appointed by the board of selectmen in towns choosing to permit such sale. The town agents had to purchase liquor from state liquor agents, had to maintain careful records, had to sell their alcohol at a price equivalent to cost and overhead, and could sell it only "for medicinal, mechanical, scientific, and sacramental purposes, and for no other use or purpose whatever."[16] In many parts of the state a healthy and not totally clandestine traffic in private liquor sales and saloons had developed in open opposition to the state laws. Occasionally, as under the administration of Republican governor David Goodell (1889–91), the state attempted to stop this trade. Usually however enforcement was left to the discretion of the communities, which resulted in a de facto local-option law.[17]

By the 1890s the prohibition issue had become a matter for continuing public debate. Some religious groups and the temperance organizations advocated rigid and uniform enforcement of the existing law. Others argued for recognition and legalization of the current practices through a local-option law. The latter would permit communities to make their own choice and, not incidentally, provide the mechanism for regulation and taxation of the liquor traffic. This debate largely occurred within a framework of support for the principle of temperance and even prohibition.[18] Certainly public debate did not include a position that held liquor use to be good or beneficial. The state had already mandated public school instruction on "the effects of alcoholic stimulants and of narcotics upon the human system," and required school boards to "see that the studies so prescribed are thoroughly taught in said schools, and that well approved textbooks upon these subjects are forwarded to teachers and scholars."[19] The issue was complicated by a range of moral, philosophical, and partisan considerations, but basically it centered on the right of the state to prescribe behavior in the interest of public health and morals and the conflict of this right with individual choice and freedom.[20]

Another issue with deep antebellum roots in turn-of-the-century New Hampshire dealt with regulation of private economic enterprise. The principle of regulation was well established, but effective administration of this power was becoming more complicated. The growth of massive, foreign (not chartered in New Hampshire) corporations posed particular problems. New Hampshire defined and regulated corporate organization and procedures and required corporations to register with the secretary of state. The most extensive and specific controls apart from railroads dealt with regulation of insurance companies and banks. The legislature permitted towns to vote special ten-year tax exemptions for manufacturing establishments and in the 1880s moved away from its previous anticonsolidation sentiment relative to railroads.[21] The consequence of this latter action had been the aggrandizement of monopolistic control within the state (and northern New England) by the Boston and Maine railroad.

The state had established a railroad commission in 1844 and had gradually expanded its powers. The commission's use of these powers and its overall effectiveness had become a matter of public criticism by the end of the nineteenth century. Paid by the railroads rather than the public treasury, the New Hampshire commission, in the understated words of one scholar, "had few good years."[22] The railroad commission did not challenge rates nor did it perform its role in safety regulation too aggressively. Of the twenty-nine fatal accidents it investigated in 1900, it blamed one railroad official for failing to "exercise reasonable discretion." All other accidents were the fault of the victims, the result of unavoidable equipment malfunction, or simply the consequence of luck (bad).[23] By 1900 there was some public concern focused on the performance of this commission as well as on broader issues such as railroad rates and services and the cooptative "free pass" system by which the Boston and Maine gave passes to ten classes of users, including lawyers, legislators and other public officials, and editors—to anyone, in short, "whose good will is important to the Corporation."[24]

Debates over railroad control focused on efficacy and occasionally on the organization of the state commission. Beyond this there was infrequent debate about the appropriate level of government that might carry this responsibility. In the 1880s New Hampshire had petitioned for national regulation of railroads, and there remained a disposition to look to the Interstate Commerce Commission to control this Massachusetts-chartered railroad.[25]

Economic regulation remained a significant issue of public policy in the new century. While towns and cities had some responsibilities, particularly in regard to retail practices, corporate regulation and taxation was a matter for state or national responsibility. Debate over this issue took place in an environment in which *monopoly* and *trust* became common pejoratives that lacked definition or precision. Unlike prohibition of alcohol, this controversy seemed a step or two removed from the daily concerns of most citizens. As the *Concord Evening Monitor* commented on April 2, 1900, a local brouhaha involving the mayor and the city marshal over the liquor traffic in that city seemed much more consequential than distant fights over economic growth: "The revelations of the business of the Carnegie Company . . . were nothing as compared with this in local importance."

Another matter of some economic significance was the growing concern with deforestation in New Hampshire. This was more than simply an aesthetic issue, and it affected directly industries that depended on water power as well as the summer tourism and the lumber industries. The state forestry commission, a body with few real powers, had increasingly played an advocacy role in urging New Hampshire to conserve its timber resources. By the turn of the century this was an issue of public concern in the state. Gov. Chester Jordan argued in 1901 that restrictions on lumbering would be "a proper function of the state through the exercise of its power of sovereign police."[26] In the New Hampshire address referred to in the previous chapter, Gifford Pinchot of the U.S. Department of Agriculture agreed with vice president–elect Theodore Roosevelt that "ownership of forests, like the ownership of water, entailed public as well as private responsibilities."[27]

Jordan and Pinchot identified the core of this controversy. Restrictions or prohibitions on lumbering represented significant intrusions into traditional practices and property rights. Proposals that government assume ownership and full responsibility for parts of the White Mountain Forest were even more controversial. The debate seldom focused on rights, however; few questioned the right of the state to utilize its power of eminent domain to take private lands for public purposes. The general authority rested in the state constitution. Sewer systems, water and gas lines, schoolhouses, military lands, highways, railroads and street railways, fish culture, and telegraph lines already had explicit statutory authority and procedures that defined them as greater public uses of land. In 1893 the state legislature assigned this right of eminent domain to the forestry commission for the purpose of establishing public parks, except that the forestry commission had to operate with nonpublic money in condemning, purchasing, and establishing these parks.[28]

If the right of the state to assume title to private property was clear, the desirability of such a policy in the case of forest lands was another matter. Complex questions concerning private and public interests, costs, and goals were involved. And many of the pro-conservation forces were not certain that the state government should play a major role in acquiring these lands; it seemed more appropriately a matter for the national government, which, by the turn of the century, had already established parks and forests in the western states.[29]

Related to conservation of forest resources was the good roads movement. Road construction and maintenance were local matters, with labor or equipment accepted in lieu of taxes as late as 1893. By the turn of the century the summer tourist business had given good roads, especially north-south trunk lines, a greater importance. The state assumed the obligation for road maintenance in some of the unorganized or poorer areas that frequently were the most scenic parts of New Hampshire. Gov. Chester Jordan conceded in 1901 that while "we do not believe in a paternal government . . . too frequent exercise of its bounty is weakening and baneful"; nevertheless state-maintained roads in recreation areas represented money well spent.[30]

Rural interests led by the Grange joined with recreation groups to promote a good roads policy in New Hampshire. By the twentieth century there probably was a consensus that the state should take a more active role in this area. Disagreement centered on whether this role should take the form of more stringent standards and engineering advice or whether the state should as well provide money for this enterprise.[31] In 1893 the legislature had terminated all highway and road districts organized at less than the town level. Previously towns had divided into several districts, each responsible for their section of public roads. Legislative discontinuance of this practice had led to some greater centralization of control, although 235 different road authorities still represented a less-than-uniform approach to highway quality. The 1893 law did mandate minimum road taxes, however, as well as abolish the policy of accepting equipment or labor instead of cash for these taxes.[32]

Advocates of a good roads policy in New Hampshire often used reforms in the state school system as a model worth following in its general principles. New Hampshire common-school education after 1805 had been organized along the district system, whereby as few as ten residents of any part of a town might organize an independent school district. These small units were empowered to establish their own schools. It was a system that maximized local control but at some obvious cost in educational quality and administrative efficiency. There was a great variation in school opportunities within the state and even within towns. In 1885 the legislature abolished the district system. Each town was to be a unified school district under the supervision of a single board of education. The number of districts decreased from 1,890 to 275, with 494 small schoolhouses closing immediately.[33]

In response to requests from the state board of education and the state superintendent of education, established in 1867, the New Hampshire legislature imposed statewide standards on schools. By the 1890s these included teachers' examinations and institutes, curricular requirements, minimum school calendars, and free textbooks. In 1899 the legislature carried the town-district plan one step further when it provided that two or more school districts could combine into a single supervisory union and hire a professional superintendent of schools. This aimed at "uniformity of instruction, continuity of work and systematic labor." The state provided one-half of the superintendent's salary for poorer unions; in 1901 the legislature discontinued this controversial test by providing for state reimbursement of one-half the salary of all superintendents.[34]

Equalization of educational opportunity among the towns remained a major issue in the early twentieth century. The state of New Hampshire, in a wide range of policy areas including education, tended to impose requirements and standards on town officials but failed to support these goals through the appropriation of money. In 1899 the state had taken hesitant steps in this direction with the supervisory union act, and further with legislation providing state money for financially disadvantaged school districts. The state treasurer apportioned $18,750 to sixty-two towns under the authority of this statute in the first year. He argued, however, that tests for need and equality were inadequate because some towns received state aid while their tax rate was lower than the state average and their local treasury showed a surplus.[35]

The politics of school reform generated conflict between local and state government. Local control stood in tension with state-articulated concepts such as standardization, equalization, and efficiency. Home rule seemed as much a slogan as a position in this debate, however, as state administrative flexibility and financial support could generally pacify critics.

Public health issues occasionally generated the same local-state tensions as did schools. The state board of health supervised the ac-

tivities of local boards, which state law required in all of the towns
and cities of New Hampshire. Laws providing for the compulsory
vaccination of all schoolchildren and stringent quarantine restrictions upon identification of communicable diseases were cause for
some disagreement over the extent of local autonomy. When the
Bedford selectmen attempted to ignore quarantine requirements,
the secretary of the state board of health pointedly reminded them
that "the people of Bedford have no . . . authority in directing what
your board shall do" except as procedures might be modified at
town meeting. The state law "compels" selectmen to provide financial support for the town board of health.[36] Certainly there was resistance to some of the restrictions and inconvenient effects of the
state public health code, but this seemed minimal in 1900. Few
questioned the need to protect the public from disease. Policy questions centered more on the need to make health codes more effective or less costly, rather than to make them less restrictive.

In 1899 the issue had been underlined when the town of Littleton
as well as other Ammonoosuc Valley communities suffered a typhoid
outbreak due to a contaminated water supply. State laws permitted
the state and local boards of health to consult and advise on such
matters, but gave them limited authority to order action. The state
health board identified the source of raw sewage and other up-
stream contaminants, but could only recommend that the Littleton
Water and Light Company cease to draw its water supply from the
river. As the secretary of the state board of health conceded, the
cause was clear after the outbreak, but "the State Board of Health at
that time had no authority to act and its recommendations proved
valueless because they were not carried out."[37] Following, although
not clearly related to, this incident, the legislature gave the state
board greater police power over water and ice supplies. The controls
remained weak and, in any event, were late for the Ammonoosuc
Valley. In 1902–3 typhoid broke out again in that area, apparently
caused by the same contaminants as earlier. In the later outbreak
there were 139 reported typhoid cases and eleven deaths. In instances like this it was not a question of dominant local authority;
rather it was the absence of any effective authority. Even in 1902–3
the state and the town boards seemed uncertain of their power to
intervene.[38]

The state had granted greater authority to city health boards to
inspect plumbing, drainage, water, and sewer supplies. These urban
officials could force compliance with health codes, but the larger
part of the state lacked such security. Even the state board could
neglect its primary responsibility, as when it dealt with a smallpox
case at an unnamed resort area in 1900. The board "with absolute

secrecy"—and one might then assume potentially less effectively—
handled this so as to prevent "large financial losses."[39]

One final policy area that was assuming greater importance at the
turn of the century related to the problems of industrial labor. New
Hampshire had just begun to face the social and economic consequences of large industrial labor forces. The state had recognized
Labor Day as a holiday since 1891. In 1893 the legislature had established the office of commissioner of labor, but this position had little
responsibility and no authority other than the collection of data and
the publication of annual reports. Policy demands were more substantive and included the fifty-eight-hour work week, an employers'
liability law, more stringent industrial health and safety regulations,
exemption of wages from trustee process (garnishment), and a child
labor law. Some groups pushed for special legislation for New Hampshire's large female work force. The state had provided some protec-
tin for women workers in the form of a sixty-hour work week and the
requirement that manufacturing establishments provide seats for
women workers to use "when they are not necessarily engaged in
the active duties for which they are employed."[40] The Woman's
Christian Temperance Union urged a fundamental economic change
in the form of "equal wages for equal work, irrespective of age or
sex."[41] The absence of effective labor organizations to act as advocates on labor issues, the traditional—if ambiguous—concern about
"class legislation," and the general influence of corporate concerns
mitigated against fully articulating, much less achieving, these goals.
As Governor Jordan noted in 1901, when he asked the legislature to
approve a statute exempting wages from the trustee process, "Capital will usually take care of itself."[42]

In 1901 the legislature approved a child labor/school attendance
law. It prohibited children under the age of twelve from working
in manufacturing establishments, restricted the work of children
under fourteen to those months when the schools were not in session, and prohibited children under sixteen from industrial work in
the months schools were in session unless the school superintendent certified the child as being literate in the English language.
Passage was a partial victory for labor reform advocates, but clearly
the state continued to have a large, unfinished agenda in industrial
relations.[43]

The problems of industrial labor in many regards symbolized the
public policy questions that New Hampshire faced at the dawn of
the twentieth century. In terms of schools, roads, conservation,
prohibition, public health, and economic regulation, as well as industrial labor, the state of New Hampshire was facing, if not addressing,
the consequences of growth and change. The transformation from a

homogeneous, agricultural, rural state to a heterogeneous, industrial, urbanized state was in most cases a gradual process. Gradualism seemed to slow and ease the social disruption accompanying these changes, which also slowed political reaction. There was no sudden and disruptive moment of crisis that demanded political action. For many the problems remained unclear and even abstract. Governor Jordan told the 1901 legislature that the "new century . . . promises beyond what we can think or ask."[44] The New Hampshire political system did not have a tradition of inquiring into and anticipating distant or unarticulated problems.

The diffuse nature of government itself was a problem in identifying public issues and policies. The state's democratic and decentralized political system militated against systematic approaches to new problems. New Hampshire's public tradition was one of shared power, checks and balances, and rotation in office. The governor shared power with what was a colonial legacy, a five-man governor's council representing five councillor districts. The council approved all gubernatorial appointments, approved all nonstatutory expenditures when the legislature was not in session, and "advised" the governor on other matters. Only one person had served more than two years in this position since the 1850s. The governor by tradition never served more than two years.[45]

The New Hampshire state legislature, known as the General Court, consisted of the state senate and the house of representatives. In 1900 voters sent 397 members to the house, one of the largest representative bodies in the world. Approximately 15 percent of these representatives had previous experience in that body. The twenty-four-man senate had similar patterns of rotation, although one second term was not uncommon. Leadership in both bodies by tradition turned over each session.[46] Sessions in the 1890s lasted from sixty-seven to ninety-five calendar days, and as a rule no legislative committee or policy group remained active during the remainder of the biennial terms. The bulk of the state's business was carried on by a small group of officials and clerks in the executive offices and by irregular functional commissions. The large body of noncriminal law was not regularly monitored in Concord. The state tended to define its responsibilities as setting general policies, while in most instances leaving administration of them in local hands.

Local governments generally followed the same pattern of rotation in office. In most communities there were no full-time public officials except police officers. Public administration was the responsibility of part-time commissions, boards, and clerks. City governments often had full-time staffs of public servants and elected officials.[47]

Public administration in New Hampshire then tended to be diffuse and intermittently exercised, with administrative power often in inexperienced hands. In the minds of most citizens in 1900, this situation probably was viewed as desirable; certainly they would not have thought it a problem much less a crisis. Under these circumstances citizen influence in the form of local elections and town meetings, as well as in the brief biennial sessions of the legislature, seemed to have a great symbolic importance; this influence may even have been substantively more consequential than it would have been in a leaner structure. There are no good criteria for measuring this. Certainly there was great rhetorical celebration of New Hampshire democracy; a book published shortly after the turn of the century called the state "An Epitome of Popular Government."[48] Perhaps because of this perceived tradition in the context of the erosion of the traditional homogenous community, there seemed to be a great interest at the turn of the century in defining more precisely the participants in the New Hampshire political system.

A major effort at redefining the New Hampshire electorate, and one that captured some national attention, involved woman suffrage. Women in New Hampshire had voted in school district elections since 1878, and in 1900 there were 170 women serving out of a total of approximately 900 elected school board members in the state. Two women were among the five commissioners on the state board of charities and correction, the extent of women appointees or officeholders in state government.[49] In 1902 a state constitutional convention proposed a constitutional amendment to strike the word *male* from the constitutional clause defining eligibility to vote. The state submitted this item to voters on town meeting day 1903.

The campaign for this amendment was intense. Major themes in this campaign to expand the electorate stressed the equity of such a proposition and the cleansing effect women might have on politics. A second goal that some prosuffrage advocates explicitly addressed concerned the effect of woman suffrage on growing non-native voting strength. As one Concord minister argued, woman suffrage "will decrease the ignorant vote, the vicious, criminal vote and the foreign vote." The latter group became the public target for many suffrage supporters.[50] Antisuffrage forces were organized as well. Their campaign focused less on debating the merits of the reform as a matter of equity and more on predicting the negative effects of such a reform: female suffrage would necessarily degrade women, and it could further politicize prohibition. Further, many speakers, including women, insisted that women did not want the right to vote.[51]

For whatever reason, the suffrage amendment failed—13,089 supported the proposition while 21,788 opposed it—a crushing defeat in the face of the two-thirds endorsement that was needed. Suffrage would recur as an issue, but this would be as close as New Hampshire women would come to the franchise until ratification of the Nineteenth Amendment to the U.S. Constitution in 1920, with New Hampshire among the ratifying states.

If the question of woman suffrage was related in the minds of some to reducing the influence of foreign-born voters, New Hampshire citizens had a more direct opportunity to address this issue. Another constitutional amendment considered in March 1903 provided that citizens who could not speak English would not be permitted to vote. It proved to be a relatively noncontroversial item, as aliens already were denied voting rights and all schools had at least instruction in English. The measure passed overwhelmingly, 28,601 to 8,205.[52]

More controversial was the amendment that proposed to modify article 6 of the bill of rights of the New Hampshire constitution. This article held that government's "greatest security" came from the "evangelical principles" of "morality and piety." Further the article provided that towns might support "Protestant teachers of piety, religion, and morality." This article was mainly symbolic, for the Toleration Act of 1819 had provided that public taxes could not be used to support religion. Nevertheless symbolism was important. In 1876 voters had approved an amendment that removed Protestantism as one of the qualifications for the state chief executive. At the same time voters refused to modify article 6, and repeated that action in 1889. In 1903 voters again considered an amendment that proposed striking "evangelical" and changing "Protestant" to "Christian" in article 6—efforts to expand this article to include citizens who were not Christians failed at the constitutional covention.[53] Despite the comment of one supporter, Edward Niles, son of the Episcopal bishop in Concord, that "no sane person could object" to dropping "Protestant" from the constitution, the amendment failed to get the needed two-thirds support. Indeed, it narrowly received a majority and had a smaller proportion of the vote than the 1876 and 1889 efforts.[54]

If there was a uniform message to these constitutional decisions, it would seem to be that New Hampshire voters sought to reaffirm a restrictive view of citizenship that was native, symbolically Protestant, and male. Certainly this could be inferred, but with caution. A majority of the voters did support striking "evangelical" and "Protestant." But there was far less interrelationship on the popular voting for these amendments than the subject matter might imply. Using the statistical test of correlation, the highest relationship, a positive one, was between support for woman suffrage and for the proposal to strike "Protestant." With a correlation coefficient of

0.41, this was of marginal significance. Further, the vote to strike "Protestant" and the vote to restrict voting, two somewhat contradictory efforts, related positively in their voting support.[55]

This discussion of public policy and governance has dealt with the issues, the structure, and the process of politics. The New Hampshire political system at the turn of the century was shaped by these factors. Yet New Hampshire politics was sharply partisan as well. Discussion of issues and campaigns for office did not take place in either an unstructured, anarchic system or a polite, debate club format. The (Democratic) *Manchester Union* of October 20, 1892, reported one political discussion: "About 10 o'clock last night, just before the close of the Republican caucus and near it, a political discussion between John A. Barbeau, a Republican campaign company officer there, and Joseph Gauthier, Democrat, terminated by the former felling the latter to the sidewalk with a club or slugshot." The bleeding, insensible Gauthier was carried away; Barbeau went to jail; and the caucus continued. Such activities were not distinctly urban nor did either party have a unique claim on victim status. In West Stewartstown up in Coos County, "a good Democrat, being full of rum," lured a young Republican behind a barn where he beat him badly. The (Republican) *Concord Monitor* of November 11, 1890, noted that there was no provocation for these "Southern Methods" except that the victim "voted a Republican ticket."

Violence could be rhetorical as well as physical. The *Monitor* editorialized that "it came as naturally to the average Democrat to kill a negro, stuff a ballot box, and crowd down the wage of labor as to drink a glass of rum." The *Union* linked the GOP with Henry Clay Frick, Andrew Carnegie, and "cut throat Pinkertons," as well as "the crushing trusts that enslave the voters." Each party accused the other regularly of trying to win elections through the use of money, liquor, fraud, and physical coercion.[56]

The two major political parties in New Hampshire were parts of national institutions, and their structure followed that of governmental federalism. National, state, and local organizations and issues fit together in a functional manner, but it was more an implicit coalition than a philosophical monolith. In terms of their position on various issues of public policy or their broader worldview, all national Republicans (or Democrats) were not in total agreement. Nor were all of the common members of either party in New Hampshire. Political affiliation seemed an intense affair, and it certainly was related to public issues, but it also transcended most specific matters of public debate.

Tradition seemed the most important determinant of political affiliation. Family and community environment shaped the nature of political socialization. This tradition was deeply rooted in many parts of New Hampshire. In elections in 1888, 1890, and 1892, over 80 percent of the variation in voting among the New Hampshire towns could be explained by the partisan vote at the previous election.[57] This short-term relationship only hints at the strength of tradition though. Of the twenty-five top Democratic towns in 1890 (all were greater than 68 percent Democratic), nineteen had been Democratic in 1832 by at least a two-to-one margin; three were solidly but less Democratic in the earlier year; two were towns created after 1832 (one of which was simply detached from a town that voted 75 percent Democratic in 1832); and only one of the twenty-five, Holderness, had been less than 50 percent Democratic in this election fifty-eight years earlier.[58]

The presidential election of 1832 is important in assessing traditional Democratic strength. Although the party itself in New Hampshire was still institutionally weak in this year, the 1832 contest nevertheless was a pivotal election in influencing party relationships. In this year Andrew Jackson ran for reelection after having defeated John Quincy Adams in a bitter campaign in 1828. Jackson and his nascent Democratic party, aided considerably in New Hampshire by the able Isaac Hill, and by young supporters like John P. Hale and Franklin Pierce, generated strong—and obviously lasting—feelings.[59] Symbolic of this intensity, in 1829 citizens in the Carroll County town of Adams had changed the town's name to Jackson.

Anti-Jackson sentiment in 1832 was equally intense, but it was also diffuse. The Whig party had not yet been organized, and the beginning of its successor Republican party was over twenty years in the future. Nevertheless, of the twenty-five top Republican towns in 1890 (all with greater than 64.6 percent of the vote), eleven had voted over two-to-one anti-Jackson in 1832, three more had been anti-Jackson by a lesser margin, three were new towns, and the 1832 vote for one is unknown. Seven of the top 1890 Republican towns had supported Jackson in 1832. The conversion of most of these was not recent; three voted Republican at their first opportunity in 1856, and two more swung into the party behind Abraham Lincoln in 1860. Only two of these top 1890 Republican towns, Moultonborough and tiny Waterville, remained Democratic as late as 1864. The former had moved into the Republican column by 1880, after an unexplained increase in the vote, while sparsely populated Waterville remained politically peripatetic through this period.

Looked at another way, of the 84 towns that voted at least two-to-one for Jackson in 1832, 57 remained Democratic in 1890. Of the 26

converted towns, 14 moved into the Republican party in the formative, emotional period 1856–64. Of the 23 towns that voted at least
two-to-one against Jackson in 1832, only one, Temple, was Democratic in 1890. Temple cast its first Democratic presidential vote
in 1868.

No economic, cultural, or demographic variables seem to explain
voting patterns in 1890 better than does the traditional partisanship
of the town; these former variables explain less than 10 percent of
the variation in party voting.[60] Obviously tradition itself is inadequate as an explanation; the switch of nearly one-third of the high
Democratic towns of 1832 suggests dynamism and change as much
as inertia.

Religion has been identified as an important influence on political
behavior in the late nineteenth century.[61] In New Hampshire its
role seemed uneven. Irish Catholic wards were heavily Democratic;
the voting pattern for French-Canadian Catholic wards was much
less uniform although certainly they tended to be Democratic.
Among traditional Protestant religious groups, Baptist towns tended
to be Republican and Methodist towns tended to be Democratic.
But even here, exclusive of the Irish Democratic ties, one begins
immediately to note exceptions.

Table 2.1 suggests the complexity of the relationship between religion and town voting returns in New Hampshire. Congregational
and Freewill Baptist towns were among both the highest and lowest
groups of Republican supporters. Non-Yankee groups tended to be
clearer in their voting, with two urban Irish Catholic wards voting
10.9 percent and 14.3 percent Republican and a French-Canadian
ward voting 38.3 percent Republican. A mixed ethnic ward that was
significantly German Protestant, on the other hand, voted 52.3 percent Republican. Four mixed but dominantly Yankee urban wards
voted 55 percent Republican.[62]

Distinguishing towns on the basis of wealth, economic activity, or
population growth patterns yields the same types of clusters. Partisan strength did not relate significantly to any of these variables.
Ethnoreligious relationships were relatively strongest; but with the
exception of the Irish-Democratic tie, were marginal as predictors
of voting patterns. Ethnic and religious appeals were common in
the campaigns in the early 1890s. Democratic spokesmen reminded
Catholic voters of the Republican "birth in knownothingism." Unfortunately, Yankee Democrats themselves sometimes shared anti-
Catholic sentiments.[63] The Irish were unwavering in their Democratic support; this by itself may have been enough to make the
Franco-Americans cautious. For these citizens the choice between

TABLE 2.1

Percentage Voting Republican in 1890 among Towns Marked by One Church, with Membership Greater than 5 Percent of the Population

	1890 GOP gubernatorial mean vote	1890 GOP gubernatorial vote range
Baptist ($N = 2$)	57.2	56.8–57.7
Congregational ($N = 30$)	47.8	25.7–88.0
Freewill Baptist ($N = 8$)	50.7	26.3–73.2
Methodist ($N = 4$)	35.7	25.4–45.7

Sources: Town religious data are available in the reports of the various churches; Roman Catholic figures are in the archives of the diocese of Manchester.
Notes: Using single-church towns seemed the best way to isolate these influences, although obviously it cannot control for the role of religion in the interactive environment of multireligious communities. There were no single-church Catholic towns. Because of the number of instances of zero value, I did not do correlation analysis on these data.

Yankee Republicans and Irish-influenced Democrats was not a happy one. Variation in Franco-American voting may have depended upon local organizational control as much as anything.[64]

The party system prior to 1894 was competitive even though Republicans managed regularly to control state politics. Democrats continued to challenge, electing 45.5 percent of the members of the lower house in 1888, 48 percent in 1890, and 42 percent in 1892; further, Democrats denied a gubernatorial majority to the Republicans on several occasions in the last quarter of the century. Third parties had been of marginal importance in New Hampshire, except for a Labor Reform party that won over 10 percent of the vote in the 1870 gubernatorial election. Despite the party's name, most of its support had come from farming towns.[65]

The Panic of 1893 initiated a period of Democratic decline in New Hampshire. The Democratic administration of Pres. Grover Cleveland stood responsible, in the public mind, for this economic crisis. New Hampshire Democrats could not escape from the local response to this national burden. The Republican *Granite State Free Press* chortled after the spring 1894 elections that the verdict in most towns was "so decidedly Republican that recounts will be few and far between." The nomination of William Jennings Bryan as Democratic standard-bearer in 1896 exacerbated and completed the process of destruction.[66]

New Hampshire communities with deep Democratic roots, most of which had withstood the strong appeal of the Republican party in New England through the Civil War years, broke ranks in 1896.

TABLE 2.2

Percentage of Total Vote by Democratic and Republican
Candidates, Gubernatorial and Presidential Elections, 1888–1902

	Democratic		Republican	
	Gubernatorial	Presidential	Gubernatorial	Presidential
1888	48.8	47.9	49.4	50.5
1890	49.1		49.3	
1892	47.7	47.1	50.2	51.1
1894	40.9		56.0	
1896	36.0	25.4	61.4	68.7
1898	43.2		54.2	
1900	38.5	38.4	59.3	59.3
1902	42.8		53.2	

Even the negative burden of a Democracy in the 1860s and 1870s, linked pejoratively with secession, did not have the devastating effect of the Bryan fight. Bryan's perceived agrarian radicalism and his inflationist silver theories had little appeal in the Granite State. Many Democratic party leaders and former candidates refused to support the young Nebraskan, a few supporting the hastily formed National Democratic party, others moving fully to support William McKinley's Republicanism. Some would return after 1896; many did not, embracing fully the Grand Old Party. Bryan, as he did elsewhere in the Northeast, devastated the traditional Democratic party in New Hampshire.[67]

Table 2.2 only hints at the devastation suffered by the Democratic party during this realignment period. Democrats sent 27 percent of the members to the General Court in 1894, 18.5 percent in 1896, 30 percent in 1898, 24 percent in 1900, and 34 percent in 1902. Old Democratic grass-roots organizations withered in the 1890s. The vote for supervisors of the checklist suggests the size of this decline. Supervisors were popularly elected local officials who administered voting registration and oversaw the local checklists. This was an important partisan role. In 1889 51.1 percent of the 655 supervisors in New Hampshire towns were Democrats. In 1891 53.6 percent were Democrats. In 1892 voters returned 49.1 percent Democratic supervisors. Then came the decline: 32.2 percent in 1894, 18.3 percent in 1896, 26 percent in 1898, 21.9 percent in 1900, and 26.8 percent in 1902.[68] Democrats became a minority, an endangered political species in parts of New Hampshire. And political minority status had a self-accelerating quality. With fewer friendly supervisors, lacking legislative clout, and with their party organization in shambles, the Democrats were unable to challenge effectively Republican administration of elections and Republican redistricting plans in the legislature.

The shift of voters from the Democratic to the Republican column was more or less uniform among all electoral groups. Seventy-four towns or cities voted Democratic in the 1894 gubernatorial election; the Democrats won thirty-seven towns in 1896. Bryan carried but ten towns and no cities in that year. These ten towns were the hard-core remnant of what had been a vibrant, rural Yankee Democracy in New Hampshire. The surviving towns included Congregationalist, Freewill Baptist, and Methodist religious groups. They all shared Jacksonian roots.[69]

In New Hampshire's cities, the same pattern of loss prevailed, except that the Irish wards remained solidly Democratic. Elsewhere French Canadians, Germans, and urban Yankees joined in the anti-Bryan parade. As table 2.2 implies, not all of these losses were permanent. The Democratic party suffered defeat regularly after 1896—indeed New Hampshire became effectively a one-party state—but nothing quite as devastating as the Bryan debacle. Even the Republicans had difficulty understanding the magnitude and permanence of the realignment. Republican State Committee chairman and U.S. senator Jacob Gallinger warned privately before the 1898 election that he foresaw trouble in the confident attitude with which some members of the party were approaching the election; it was, he believed, "the usual experience after an unusual political victory."[70]

The influence of the Bryan candidacy on New Hampshire politics suggests the complexity of the political culture in the state. Governance was differentiated within the federal structure; partisanship apparently was not. Organizationally parties had clear and distinct local, state, and national bases. But the state and local organizations could not escape from the negative perception of "Cleveland's" Panic or Bryan's "radicalism." Trickle-down seemed to have an empirical basis if a partisan form. To be certain Bryan ran behind his ticket in New Hampshire, but the effect of his candidacy was negative rather than neutral. It did not seem to work the other way. Republicans took Haverhill out of the Democratic column in 1894 in a realignment that affected all offices. In 1897 and 1898 Democrats temporarily seized local control following a fight over roads. This did not negate the growing Republican majorities in gubernatorial and presidential voting in Haverhill in 1898 and 1900.[71]

Much of the research on late nineteenth-century politics suggests that local references had an important formative effect on political attitudes. The New Hampshire political culture seemed largely consistent with this model, except that ethnoreligious values, seemingly of paramount importance elsewhere, had but limited predictive value in assessing political patterns in the Granite State. This uneven pattern however seems to underline the significance of local factors. Indeed, a uniform response from identifiable groups, such as Congregationalists, functioning in different environments, suggests the presence of transcending, nonlocal, cohering forces. The New Hampshire evidence suggests that only the Irish-American voters in the Granite State responded uniformly to partisan appeals.

In 1890 the Democratic gubernatorial candidate received three-to-one support from, among other places, the south-central town of Greenfield, the northwestern town of Landaff, and the northeastern town of Jackson. All were Yankee, largely rural communities. They were not significantly different from other towns in their areas, except for their partisanship in some instances. They were joined in this strong Democratic support by urban areas such as the Irish Catholic Fifth Ward in Manchester. Jackson was a Freewill Baptist town, Greenfield was a Congregational town, and Landaff was a Methodist town. The evidence suggests that these communities were not unrepresentative of the towns that provided continuing Democratic support. The three towns had voted 72 percent and above for Andrew Jackson in 1832; the Fifth Ward had been Democratic since it was organized. The only discernible cohesive element among these voting units was the Democratic party. Party identification itself in the nineteenth century had a powerful impact; in New Hampshire, partisanship was not simply a dependent variable that flowed from other, more important group identifications. Party affiliation may have influenced attitudes toward issues and groups rather than have been simply a product of attitudes shaped by cultural or economic identification.

In 1889 New Hampshire voters considered a constitutional amendment that provided for enactment and enforcement of a statewide prohibition law. Many church groups in New Hampshire, the state Grange, and the Republican party were supportive of prohibition. The Democratic party opposed this measure, arguing instead for a local-option approach to alcohol use.[72] Among the 25 towns that had the highest proportion of Republican support in the gubernatorial election of 1890, 15 supported the amendment while 10 opposed it. Among the 25 top Democratic towns, 3 supported and 22 opposed. The latter group is particularly intriguing, for among the Democratic opponents of prohibition were strong Yankee Methodist, Freewill Baptist, and Congregationalist towns. All of these church groups supported prohibition.

Looked at another way, the 30 dominant Congregational towns in 1890 hint at a complex relationship between partisanship and the prohibition issue. Twenty-nine of the towns have usable returns; of these, Republicans carried the 1888 and 1890 gubernatorial elections in 11, the Democrats carried 12 and 6 towns split the two elections between the parties. Of the 11 Republican towns, 7 supported prohibition in 1889. Of the 12 Democratic towns, 2 supported prohibition. There may be other variables that would better explain these patterns. In their absence, however, one can hypothesize that party played an affective role in shaping attitudes. The two major parties in the Granite State may have been as much guiders as guided in the relationship between voters and issues.

If parties have a formative role in shaping attitudes, as opposed to a more passive function in reflecting attitudes, then the position taken by parties on public issues assumes a greater significance. The two parties' positions tended to be general or ambiguous, however, and were seldom precise and dichotomous. Democrats and Republicans regularly proclaimed their support for government that was fiscally responsible, effective, and efficient. Each affirmed the goodness of progress, liberty, order, labor, and capital. Each accused the other of hypocrisy in its affirmations.[73]

On one level the images projected by the two parties were symbolic; this is not to say they were abstract or distortive. Republican emphasis on the Union and federalism reinforced traditional loyalties; support for the U.S. Constitution and free elections may have been slogans, but they had substantive—if subjective—meaning to those who identified with the Grand Old Party. Symbolism did not mean subtlety either. Republicans affirmed their own traditions through sharp recollections of their opponents' heritage. "There is no difference between the Republican party in 1861 and the Republican party in 1892" was proud boast rather than confessed inertia. Republicans argued that the Democrats in New Hampshire, on the other hand, were guilty of continuity and were condemned to the political inferno of "fire eating Bourbons who followed the fortune of Jeff Davis in seeking to establish a confederacy with human slavery as its corner-stone."[74] These Republican tactics would be judged then and later as "waving the bloody shirt," and in truth it was that. There could be little intent to convert Democrats with those appeals; on the other hand presumably such rhetoric reinforced Republicanism.[75] And Republicanism had a cumulative meaning that took pride in partisan memories.

In 1900 the Republican *Concord Monitor* editorialized that to say "'We are Democrats' repudiates nothing, affirms nothing." Indeed, "For many years the Democratic party has been ashamed of its past and has tried to get out of it." Democrats would have disagreed emphatically with these assertions, though they might privately have conceded some elements of the latter. While the Civil War proved a partisan historical treasure to Republicans in the Granite State, Democrats sought to forget it. The Democracy proclaimed its debt to the "old soldiers" and its loyalty to the union. Beyond this, party leaders sought to emphasize their own sense of history, a remembered past of political battles against privilege and for self-government that antedated Republicanism and rebellion.[76]

Partisan interpretation and affirmation of traditional positions did provide a framework for approaching current policy questions. In simplified form, Republicans tended to be more supportive and Democrats more skeptical of government action. These positions defined a rhetorical framework for issues relating to encouragement of economic growth, supervision of elections, regulation of private institutions, size of government, and taxation and expenditures. Republican and Democratic positions on such dominant issues as the tariff and prohibition were not inconsistent with the rhetoric of their respective perceived traditions.[77]

The amount of debate and dispute over the tariff suggests that it was a substantive issue in New Hampshire politics in this period. Republican support for high tariff rates and Democratic low tariff stands were, however, stated principles rather than universal guides. State and community interests amended these principles: Democrats had to be cautious in discussing tariff rates on specific items such as textiles, which New Hampshire produced; Republicans recognized the disadvantage New Hampshire suffered from high rates on imported commodities such as hides. Tariff debate tended to discuss the divergent principles of the parties at an abstract level we can assume had some meaning to partisan voters. Certainly it is an assumption of this study that political professionals repeat the same slogans only when they have some belief that these are positive and productive.

The tariff was both national and local in its effects. It represented an important mechanism of national macroeconomic policy in the nineteenth century. Its effects were also microeconomic, differentially influencing specific industries, localities, markets, investments, jobs, and prices. The presumed variation may have been greater than the actual variation. Nevertheless this perception remained important in shaping behavior.

Tariff positions and arguments even dominated off-year elections in New Hampshire—less as policy perhaps, but certainly as useful reminders of who and what the parties were. In 1890 the Republicans of New Hampshire called the McKinley tariff bill a good example of their party's tariff policy, "under which our country has made such amazing advances." Democrats associated the same bill as "a deed of conveyance by the Republican party of the enormous power of federal taxation to a combination of manufacturers, and trusts." On the other hand the Republicans in New Hampshire affirmed their support for reciprocity to open further New England markets to Canadian raw materials, while the Democrats avoided "free trade" except for the raw materials that manufacturing required. If the substantive difference was minimal, the symbolic dispute was great.[78]

The liquor/prohibition issue followed the same lines. In point of fact each party supported temperance. Republicans argued that state government should be empowered and entrusted to achieve this public goal; Democrats believed that local option and local enforcement would best achieve this desirable end. Prohibition was the major dispute over state functions in the 1890s, and the difference tended to focus on process rather than goals. Democrats argued that general prohibitory laws encouraged criminality, and should be replaced by "rational, practicable, and reasonable laws" that could be enforced. Republicans countered with support for "wise and wholesome measures which will lessen the evil of intoxicating drink."[79] In the late winter of 1903 the legislature approved a local-option law; in May, after a bitter campaign, communities voted on allowing the sale of alcoholic beverages. In this period party lines were not so clear. Civic and religious groups and other associations carried on the campaign, with the political parties—gratefully, we may assume—staying away from the fray.[80]

Arguments over tariff policy and liquor laws shaped the debate between the two parties in the 1890s. Rhetorical difference and policy convergence marked the partisan positions. Yet it would be a mistake to infer from this a consensual model; rhetorical differences were not necessarily cosmetic. Democratic proclamations that "the people should support the government and not the government the people" ran counter to the Republican pledge to support "all legislation which may tend to advance and promote the interests of our state." Indeed these positions bracketed the decade and suggested differences on several policy questions.[81] In their campaigns among ethnic groups the parties stressed both tariff and prohibition, with the former of greater emphasis at least in the pre-realignment period. The economic consequences of the tariff received top billing in these campaigns, but as well partisans evaluated tariff subtleties as they related to Canadian trade and to Irish-British relations.[82]

Partisan campaign rhetoric in New Hampshire tended to focus primarily on national matters, even in off-year state campaigns. This is perplexing in the face of the local orientation of several policy questions that arose, but in part it was necessitated by localism. National political symbols, rhetoric, and policy positions served to unite rather than divide citizens in different communities with different priorities. National political campaigns called on the collective memory and values of members of the two national parties. They reinforced cosmopolitan concerns in the context of local orientation.[83]

Republican campaigns in the 1890s stressed the wisdom of Benjamin Harrison and William McKinley and the genius of Speaker Thomas Reed. Republicans supported a free ballot, specifically in the South, the "generous recognition" of veterans, a hard-money policy, and "a vigorous and dignified foreign policy." In terms of the latter, New Hampshire Republicans were enthusiastic defenders of the McKinley foreign policy. The Spanish-American War established the American people as "supporters of civilization and humanity and ardent opposers of barbarism and oppression." Rejecting as "absurd" accusations of militarism and imperialism in the Philippines, the Republicans in 1900 reaffirmed their 1856 principle of congressional sovereignty in the territories.[84]

Bryan's nomination in 1896 provided New Hampshire Republicans with an opportunity to expand their support without seriously modifying their principles. The state GOP platform in that year welcomed support "without regard to previous party affiliation." The Democratic party, alas, had been seized by a "revolutionary" group that proposed government "by the mob," that assaulted courts, that engaged in a "seditious" effort "to promote sectional jealousies," that had a "treasonable purpose to incite social war," that sympathized with anarchists, would repudiate debts, and destroy the monetary system.[85]

In terms of state issues, Republicans in the 1890s proclaimed support for "just and constitutional" regulation of railroads and protection against "excessive aggregations of corporate power." Evenhandedly, the GOP assured laborers they would protect them from "unjust exactions," while stopping "the assaults of socialism and anarchy" upon property. The Republican party stood behind good roads, conservation, equalized educational opportunity, and tax reform, while seldom embracing specific propositions to achieve these ends—although by the turn of the century Republicans did accept the concept of state financial aid for education, conservation, and good roads.[86]

New Hampshire Democrats were on the defensive in the 1890s. The Panic of 1893 and the Bryan nomination proved a heavy burden for party officials. In 1888 state Democrats had endorsed statements of support for "tariff reform, broader markets, steady employment, better wages, lower taxation" as traditional Democratic positions, now that "the issues of the war period have passed away." The Harrison administration provided Democrats with targets like the "disunionists," who supported the federal election bill, and the "debasing" monetarists, who supported the Sherman Silver Purchase Act. Democrats stressed the corrupting power of Republicans and worried about national activities spurred by "the Federal Republican party."[87]

Democratic rhetoric tended to be more shrill, more explicitly focused on the powerless, than was that of the Republicans. There were few bounds to this rhetorical concern; Democrats regularly supported Irish home rule in the course of state campaigns. The Bryan nomination caused Democrats in New Hampshire to focus much less on national affairs; they recognized a political liability. Granite State Democrats continued to insist that the tariff should be lowered, that the Republicans nationally were part of a corrupting alliance with "trusts" (Mark Hanna's "imperial plutocracy"), and that soldiers should be honored and rewarded while militarism should be resisted. The latter would provide an issue like the tariff on which Democrats could unequivocally dispute the Republicans. Walking the fine line of supporting the soldiers and affirming patriotism, Democrats lashed out at the Philippine war and expansionism: "as we insist upon the right of self-government for ourselves, we sympathize with every people, aspiring for freedom and worthily struggling therefor, in every land and in the islands of the sea."[88]

In adopting anti-imperialist positions, New Hampshire Democrats followed the lead of national Bryan Democrats. Indeed in 1898 the party expressed "admiration for, and confidence in the wisdom and patriotism of our great national leader, William J. Bryan." Two years earlier, stunned Granite State Democrats had only been officially able to acknowledge "recognizing the action of" the Chicago convention and to pledge "earnest support" for the party ticket before moving to a campaign on state issues. It was not that the state's Democrats came, by 1898, to embrace Bryan; they never did. One young party leader said if the 1900 choice turned out to be between Bryan and McKinley again, as it did, "the Lord help us!"[89]

As a distinct minority party in New Hampshire after 1896, Democrats increasingly stressed state issues. Support for local option "in the interest of temperance and morality" stood foremost among these concerns, but Democrats also struck out at Republican governance in the state. They accused the GOP of subverting home rule by establishing state-appointed public commissions and offices at the state level, and of a "wide departure from the thrift, economy, and simple methods that mark proper legislation."[90]

Democrats advocated reform in state government, including popular election of state executive officers and commissioners. They criticized railroad practices, especially the free pass system, and advocated strict laws to control lobbying. Democrats came to support the fifty-eight hour work week, public ownership of utilities, the initiative and referendum, revision of tax laws so as to force corporations to pay more and to introduce taxes on income. Democrats also applauded equalization of school opportunities and conservation of forests, but they had greater difficulty specifying how to achieve these goals, particularly given their emphasis on reducing the size and the cost of government.[91]

By the early years of the twentieth century the two parties had again settled into patterns of equilibrium. In their election campaigns they attacked one another and attempted to define their own position. The important questions of governance appeared in the campaigns, but seldom enjoyed full exposition and debate. Democrats adapted to their new status as a minority coalition. The most significant change in the party was the loss of substantial parts of its traditional rural Protestant base. Some of these areas maintained Democratic ties, but most moved permanently into the Republican column. Even the town of Jackson, symbolically, was now firmly in the Grand Old Party. The most Democratic parts of the state were urban Irish wards; French-Canadian wards split roughly half and half between the parties. Methodist towns retained marginal Democratic ties; Freewill Baptist, Congregational, and Baptist towns represented increasing levels of Republicanism. The *Monitor* would snicker on May 2, 1900, that old Yankee Stilson Hutchins was "one of the few men of wealth and culture left in the New England Democracy."

On specific items like the constitutional amendments in 1903, there was no real partisan relationship to the voting. Republican voting related positively with votes for woman suffrage, striking the word *Protestant*, and the language requirement and negatively with support for local option. The reverse was true for Democrats, but in all instances the relationship was statistically insignificant.[92] Within communities there was striking unanimity on these issues; these values were apparently not shared along party lines throughout the state. Mitigating this effect was the fact that the parties had not played a role in these elections. Party officials kept their distance from these complicated, emotional issues. Democrats may have supported the concept of local option; they were not prepared to tell voters to permit the sale of alcohol in their home communities. New Hampshire's two major parties seldom took unambiguous positions on dichotomous, local issues.

The relationship between New Hampshire's sharply partisan politics and its public policy is an elusive one. Parties had key roles in recruitment and election or appointment of public officials. The evidence does not suggest, however, that parties played a continual role in shaping electoral successes into policy mandates. Party politics did not translate into party government. Public officials presumably had some sense of loyalty and obligation to their party organizations, and they made policy in an environment influenced by party positions and partisan expedience. But in the absence of clear party positions—and indeed in the absence of the sort of organizational strength needed to pursue these positions, when formulated—it seems credible to speculate that these officials were also influenced by their understanding of the public interest and by their personal values and attitudes.

The state legislature is an institution that should reflect some of the relationships between party and policy. A group profile of the members of the house elected in 1900 reveals some pronounced differences.[93] There were 397 members of the house that met from January 2 to March 22, 1901. Of these, 302 were Republicans and 95 were Democrats. Biographical information on 273 (69 percent; 75 percent of Democrats and 67 percent of Republicans) of these men reveals that Democrats (43 percent) were slightly more likely than Republicans (39 percent) to represent the town where they were born. Republicans (20 percent) were twice as likely as Democrats (10 percent) to have been born in a New England state other than New Hampshire and were slightly more likely (9 percent to 7 percent) to have been born in a foreign country. Democrats were more Catholic (27 percent to 4 percent) and less Congregational (11 percent to 30 percent) than Republicans, with membership in other religious denominations ranging less significantly. Democrats were younger (57 percent were age forty-five or under as compared to 42 percent of the Republicans), more likely to be farmers (40 percent to 28 percent) and less likely to be white-collar employees of a firm (9 percent to 17 percent) or professionals (6 percent to 15 percent). More Democrats had previously held positions in local government (73 percent to 65 percent) and fewer had served previously in the state legislature (16 percent to 22 percent).

Using the 1901 and 1903 sessions of the legislature as representative of one of the most important forums for policy-making, as well as the 1893 session to compare pre-realignment patterns, it is possible to observe partisan conflict. A selection from the available roll calls (see table 2.3) indicates that partisanship in all of these years was greatest when political issues arose.[94] Those listed here include essentially all of the substantive issues on which there were roll calls in these years, excluding those on which there was near unanimity. The index of disagreement is a simple arithmetic measurement calculated by subtracting the percentage voting yes in one party from the percentage voting yes in the other party. The index ranges from zero (each party voting the same percentage yes) to 100 (one party unanimously supporting and the other unanimously opposing).

The 1893 session especially had a significant number of political issues. City charters, police commissions, election disputes, and election processes all had a substantive effect on party fortunes. On such matters members of the respective parties cohered in dichotomous patterns. Matters of public debate that flared in the campaigns, including the liquor issue, regulation of economic activities, and state provision for conservation, welfare, and transportation, were less divisive.

Examining in detail some of the 1901 and 1903 roll calls, rural-urban differences within one or both of the parties exceeded partisan disagreement on the bill to exempt from taxation the property of the Appalachian Mountain Club, the bill to define duties of police commissioners, the bill authorizing the Concord and Maine railroad (a subsidiary of the Boston and Maine) to acquire the Concord Street railway system, the bill establishing a sanitorium, the liquor bill, and the Connecticut River bridge bill. Party may have been the most significant organizing framework within the legislature, but it was not always stronger than other considerations—nor was it obviously always an active force in determining policy questions. Partisan responses to Republican governor Nahum Bachelder's vetoes in 1903 suggest that even on such potentially charged matters, partisanship was mute.

At the local level, partisanship and policy seemed to have an ambiguous relationship. Examining fifteen Democratic and fifteen Republican towns, it is possible to identify their tax and expenditure policies as determined at the annual town meeting.

As table 2.4 indicates, the partisan difference between the two sample groups was minor. Democrats and Republicans at the local level, despite occasionally intense partisanship, followed basically similar patterns on taxation and expenditure. Manchester's Democratic mayor said in 1904 that party counted in local government, but it did not dominate. The political parties had to recognize "the demands of the public, of the citizens who pay the taxes for the harmonious operation and administration of public affairs without reference to partisan considerations."[95]

TABLE 2.3

Party Disagreement Scores for the
New Hampshire State Legislature, 1893, 1901, 1903

Year and issue	Index of disagreement
1893	
Amend Portsmith city charter	100
Amend Concord city charter	99
Establish city of Laconia	97
Establish city of Somersworth	97
Establish board of police commissioners for Concord	98
Establish board of police commissioners for Manchester	99
Determine disputed election	61
Determine disputed election	98
Determine disputed election	90
Prohibit manufacture of liquor	46
Regulate the sale of coal	14
Regulate the militia and examine officers	21
Provide for paupers and indigent insane	14
1901	
Disputed election	82
Amending powers of Manchester street and park commissioners	45
Amending liquor laws	23
Erection of statue of Franklin Pierce	38
Nashua and Fitchburg railroad bill	21
Nashua and Fitchburg railroad bill	2
Suspension of rules to permit committee reports	17
Exempt from taxation property of Appalachian Mountain Club	18
Separate the courts	31
Define duties of police commissioners	2
Provide direct election of U.S. senators	77
1903	
Authorize Concord and Maine railroad to acquire Concord Street railway	21
Resolution on free passes and trusts	69
Amend Laconia city charter	86
Provide for testimony and records from corporate officers	51
Pass over veto bill providing for state sanitorium	10
Amend liquor bill	16
Pass over veto bill providing for free bridges across Connecticut River	0

TABLE 2.4

Average and Range of Valuation, Taxation, and School Expenditures in Democratic and Republican Towns, 1899

	Population	Per capita valuation	Per capita tax	Tax rate	School expenditure per pupil
Democratic average	861	407.21	7.64	1.87	11.92
Republican average	816	453.03	7.52	1.69	13.42
Democratic range	305 to	319.18 to	4.91 to	1.27 to	7.64 to
	2,693	602.04	12.66	2.70	17.41
Republican range	244 to	294.48 to	6.26 to	1.25 to	8.75 to
	1,625	589.56	9.04	2.16	20.57

Source: The tax and expenditure data were calculated from *Report of the State Treasurer, 1900.*

Note: These towns were chosen from the most solid partisan towns, looking to balance the two groups in geography and size.

Looking at the same sample groups, as discussed earlier, in terms of their response to cultural issues, some sharper differences emerge. Table 2.5 summarizes the voting pattern on issues dealing with liquor, woman suffrage, and removing *Protestant* from the state constitution. In these areas the differences between the two groups are more pronounced. On the 1889 constitutional amendment on prohibition, each group tended to support the party position. This pattern was less conclusive in 1903, when the parties avoided official positions. Democratic towns that had in the earlier year tended to oppose statewide prohibition, now had to vote on liquor in their own communities. In this sample group fourteen Democratic towns had opposed statewide prohibition in 1889; only three supported local option in 1903. Eleven Republican towns supported prohibition in 1889; two voted for local option in 1903.

The patterns of New Hampshire politics discussed here, comprehensively viewed as governance, campaigns, and elections, tend to be suggestive rather than conclusive. What these patterns suggest is a political system rooted in each of the 235 towns and cities in the state. Many of these units in turn were composed of geographical and political subdivisions. Each political subdivision in the state had its own variant of political culture, had its own complex interplay of traditions, salient and emotional issues, dominant personalities and institutions, and group identifications.

New Hampshire's political parties, Democratic and Republican, functioned as organizing, cohering institutions. They were not alone in this function; indeed they may have been less important as

TABLE 2.5

Average and Range of Popular Votes on Constitutional
and Local-Option Questions in Democratic and Republican
Towns, 1889 and 1903 (percentage in favor)

	Statewide Prohibition (1899)	Local Option (1903)	Woman Suffrage (1903)	Strike *Protestant* (1903)
Democratic average	34.6	40.8	27.0	38.9
Republican average	57.2	27.7	42.0	44.6
Democratic range	15.4–62.6	14.0–67.3	14.0–50.3	6.0–84.8
Republican range	39.3–76.9	0–56.5	27.6–53.5	14.9–73.5

organizing forces than the institutions, codes, customs, and processes that linked government activity. Parties were to government
what campaigns were to elections, occasionally critical but normally
only one of the elements that informed the choices. Parties played
an important role in bringing the local communities into broader political activities. In this regard political parties offered cosmopolitan
interests, an important counter to the parochial and almost idiosyncratic nature of local politics.

The extent to which this broadening function of parties had implications for governance is debatable. Statewide party organizations relied heavily on the appeal—and inertia—of tradition, on
slogans, and on personalities. Party leaders and candidates used
issues certainly, but in many cases these were issues not constitutionally part of the New Hampshire political agenda. Republicans
could agree or disagree with their party's position on recurrent
issues such as the tariff, monetary policy, or expansion, without
compromising or even affecting their response to local and state
matters of politics and governance. This is not to say that these national matters were irrelevant; they were not, based on the amount
of ink and expressed emotion they generated. It is to say that they
possessed an abstract quality that permitted voters flexibility of interpretation and freedom in responding to immediate and concrete
problems of politics and governance. Even on the dominant state
issues of the period, temperance and prohibition, partisans retained
this freedom and flexibility to respond in terms of personal and community values, not party position. Party influenced; it did not determine. Democrats and Republicans shared primarily their ties to
their parties. Perhaps as important, they shared in antipathy toward
the other party. The ambiguity implicit in this relationship may
have been functional to the parties; it did not necessarily make for

effective governance. Local, state, and national government and local, state, and national parties each functioned in a framework marked by both interdependence and differentiation.

The diffuse framework described here tended to be formidable; if it also appears impersonal, it was not. Strong personalities, enormous egos, and ambitions both broad and narrow fired the political system. In the dominant Republican party these more human forces fought over the control and shape of the political system in the first years of the new century.

3

"Recover the Honor of the State"

O N JANUARY 7, 1903, the biennial session of the New Hampshire General Court convened in Concord. Among the 393
legislators in the house of representatives was the popular novelist
Winston Churchill, Republican from Cornish. A freshman legislator
and a political neophyte, Churchill had a prestigious front-row seat,
and he earnestly and optimistically set about to legislate. He proposed bills to provide for good roads, to maintain free bridges across
the Connecticut River, to protect forest lands, to appropriate money
for a New Hampshire exhibition at the St. Louis fair, and to teach
the principles of the New Hampshire and United States constitu-
tions in the state's public schools.[1]

Representative Churchill saw all of his bills fail. He was not alone
in this regard, of course. The New Hampshire legislature had a de-
served reputation for parsimony and careful scrutiny. The failings
were inconsequential in the long run, for Winston Churchill would
prove tenacious. More important, in a few years he would play a
significant—if often symbolic—role in the New Hampshire reform
movement self-defined as progressivism. If Winston Churchill was
the catalyst, Robert Perkins Bass was to be the agent of this reform.
In 1903, however, Bass was still on his Peterborough estate, managing his substantial investments and looking after his woodlands.
First, in chronology if not consequence, came Churchill.

There is little indication that any of the individuals eventually
involved in the Republican reform movement had a sense of impending insurgency in 1903. Their party dominated Granite State
politics; ambitious and loyal Republicans could generally count on
advancement. The reform spirit already evident in La Follette's Wisconsin and even Roosevelt's Washington had not yet really pene-
trated New Hampshire. The New Hampshire Republican party was
both a political and a governing institution. In the former capacity it

was sufficiently secure that it did not need to raise new issues; in its governing role the party could be responsive to problems but had no demonstrated interest in changing established procedures or in expanding public discourse. The reformers would ultimately do these things. But the initial incentive for their challenge came less from restiveness over policy and more from frustrations over politics. Winston Churchill would assume a key part in this preface to reform politics.

In 1903 Winston Churchill was a prominent and famous citizen of the Granite State. He was a novelist whose books were widely read; *The Celebrity, Richard Carvel, The Crisis,* and *The Crossing,* the latter published in 1903, had earned him financial security. In 1899 he had moved to Cornish, into the Harlakenden House that he and his wife, Mabel Churchill, had built. A lovely, brick mansion, the Churchill estate became a center for Cornish's summer colony. Many former summer visitors, like Churchill, became permanent residents.[2]

Cornish was a picturesque Connecticut River valley town that had recently been discovered by urbanites; it was a stimulating, fascinating place in the early years of the new century. Churchill regularly socialized with other "outsiders" in Cornish, artists such as Augustus Saint-Gaudens, Maxfield Parrish, and Henry Oliver Walker, poets such as Emma Lazarus and Percy Mackaye, writers such as Herbert Croly, and publishers such as Norman Hapgood. Lawyers George Rublee and Learned Hand would join them shortly. Pres. Theodore Roosevelt visited Churchill in 1902. Presumably Churchill and the president discussed politics, history, and letters, their common interests. At the time of Roosevelt's visit Churchill already had placed his candidacy for the state house of representatives before his townsmen.[3]

When Winston Churchill decided to enter politics it represented in some ways a natural expression of some of his interests. He and young Croly had spent many pleasant hours playing tennis on the Harlakenden court and discussing politics. Churchill was thirty-one years old in 1902 and had graduated from the U.S. Naval Academy. He had resigned from the service, determining that letters rather than military life was for him. Yet he had a strong sense of concern for political issues as well as a commitment to serve that at times would intertwine with his own ego. As he would note a few years later, "men who can afford to be disinterested should take a prominent part in politics."[4]

Churchill did not begin as a reformer. Indeed, in 1902 he thought of himself as a practical-minded man of the world. He touched the right bases, visiting local merchant and political "boss" Sylvannus

Bryant to "discuss" a candidacy. With an appropriate retainer, Bryant agreed to manage the Churchill campaign. As one local politico told Churchill: "Keep quiet. . . . Do not say anything. . . . Refuse all *receptions* or *attendance at anything that can be construed in any way as of a political nature* but just keep quiet and let the good work go on. . . . There is a lot going on that you know not of and best you do not." Bryant managed Churchill's nomination through the Republican caucus and apparently secured some Democratic cooperation for the general election.[5] It was easy!

Winston Churchill already had some vague ambitions about serving in the U.S. Congress. His interests and inclinations certainly pointed him in this direction. And as it was practical and logical to consult with Sylvannus Bryant about Cornish politics, Churchill took the next practical and logical step and went down to Boston to discuss his congressional bid with Lucius Tuttle. Tuttle was president of the Boston and Maine railroad.[6] Within a few years Winston Churchill, reformer, would be embarrassed by disclosure of these contacts made by Winston Churchill, political neophyte. For Churchill would join others in concluding that the practical and logical system was also closed, manipulative, and boss-ridden.

It is difficult for historians accurately to assess the extent of manipulative *boss rule* and *corruption* in politics. The terms are debased by regular use and abuse. They have been standard rhetorical parts of political campaigns. The extent to which they have played an actual role in governance is less clear. The legislative and administrative decisions and policies in New Hampshire resulted from a complex set of factors that defy simple explanation. The conflicting forces generated by partisan and personal concerns, philosophical assumptions, and divergent local needs may have seemed frustratingly irrational, but these varied elements might as well have proved a barrier to any real manipulation. Certainly it is hard to conceive of any person or corporation controlling the multiple and democratic institutions in New Hampshire like town meeting or the four hundred citizen-legislators in Concord. Fortunately for the Boston and Maine railroad, there were allegedly more manageable points of influence. The railroad leaders apparently focused their political energies on key nominations for office, selection of important leaders, and critical points in the legislative and administrative process.

The Boston and Maine railroad had necessarily become a politicized corporation in the 1870s and 1880s. This was a period marked by railroad scrambling for lease or other means of control of New Hampshire's many independent railroad lines. These transactions required legislative approval. The B&M then was commonly described as the "Democratic railroad" because it was controlled by

Frank Jones of Portsmouth, a leading state Democrat. With passage of key elements of the Hazen bill in 1887, Jones secured an important victory that gave his railroad a legislative green light to acquire its major competitor, the Concord railroad. The 1887 session of the legislature was marked by allegations of flagrant vote buying. As Jones put it, when asked about bribery by a legislator holding hearings into the circumstances surrounding passage of the Hazen bill, "Men are a good deal like hogs; they don't like to be driven, but you can throw them down a little corn, and you can call them anywhere. That is all there is to it. I supposed such a politician as you are would know that without asking me."[7]

In the course of these politico-economic skirmishes, the Boston and Maine railroad made a powerful enemy: Sen. William Chandler. Born in Concord in 1835 and admitted to the New Hampshire bar in 1855, Chandler had been a Republican since the organization of his party. Chandler had served in a variety of partisan, administrative, and elective posts, including secretary of the Republican National Committee, secretary of the navy under Pres. Chester Arthur, and U.S. senator beginning in 1887. Chandler's Republicanism included continuing support for federal election supervision in the South and, increasingly, nativism and concern about unrestricted immigration. Unusual for a northeastern Republican, Chandler supported bimetallism. He had pronounced antimonopoly views. For both philosophical and partisan reasons, Chandler detested Jones and his railroad. In the course of the 1892 election he publicly charged that "the Democratic party of New Hampshire is controlled by two criminals," identifying Jones and Charles Sinclair, the latter a Portsmouth businessman and railroad official, as well as son-in-law and key party ally of Jones. This was not an isolated example of Chandler's feelings or his style of argument. Chandler used the columns of the *Concord Monitor* (in which he had a significant financial interest), pamphlets, speeches, and letters to castigate the Boston and Maine railroad as well as anyone whom he believed was friendly to the corporation.[8]

In 1892 Jones yielded the presidency of the Boston and Maine to Lucius Tuttle of Boston. No longer was the B&M simply the Democratic railroad; moreover, it was about to become *the* New Hampshire railroad, a process of consolidation essentially completed in 1895. In 1896 Jones and other "railroad Democrats" such as Alvah Sulloway, John Sanborn, Warren Daniell, Irving Drew, and Oliver Branch deserted their old party.[9] The Grand Old Party in New Hampshire found itself possessing the allegiance of not only a reinforced majority, but also many of the corporate interests that had formerly been bipartisan. It would prove a mixed blessing.

Later reform rhetoric to the contrary notwithstanding, the Republican party organization was not synonymous with the railroad. There were several power bases within the GOP. Chandler continued to be a significant force in the party until his death in 1917; his antagonism toward the railroad never abated. Jacob Gallinger, a Canadian-born (1837) physician, had lived in Concord since 1862 and worked from that time for the Republican party. Gallinger joined Chandler in the U.S. Senate in 1891, after making an effort to take the latter's seat from him in 1889. Chandler looked contemptuously upon this "mercenary Republican immigrant" with ties to the Concord railroad, later leased by the Boston and Maine. Gallinger did establish and maintain a good working relationship with the latter, but he also managed to maintain his independence. The *New York Tribune* noted that Gallinger worked with the B&M, but rather than a railroad man, "He is a Gallinger man." [10]

A significant, nonrailroad, base of strength within the Republican party was the prohibition and temperance group. A major spokesman for the prohibitionist Republicans was David Goodell, an Antrim manufacturer who had served as governor from 1889 to 1891. Goodell never had the political instincts—or ambitions—of Chandler and Gallinger. He nonetheless symbolized a group with significant potential strength in the party, and leaders tended to deal with him and his like-minded associates gingerly.

Among important independent political operatives were James Lyford (b. 1853), whose political appointment at the U.S. Custom House in Boston afforded him ample time to work on party affairs, and George Moses (b. 1869), editor of the *Concord Monitor.* Lyford tended to be closely identified with Gallinger, while Moses was linked with Chandler. Moses managed to maintain friendly relations with Gallinger and Lyford with Chandler. Lyford was a political professional, and he sought through compromise and persuasion to maintain Republican dominance. Moses was a more prickly sort, less practical and more impatient than Lyford, and inclined to hold a grudge. Moses tended to be a Moses man who continually sought political appointment so as to give him greater financial security. Moses had an interest in the *Monitor,* along with William D. Chandler, the senator's son. [11]

Always excepting Chandler, the Republican leaders largely managed to get along well with railroad officials. Boston and Maine political activities had apparently not subsided after the railroad had achieved the economic consolidation it had sought. To protect its interests the railroad corporation continued to seek influence in key positions and over critical procedures. If indeed there was outright vote buying in the 1880s, there is little indication that this practice continued. Railroad officials helped shape caucus and convention decisions on gubernatorial and councillor candidates; these latter positions gave them control over appointments, particularly to the sensitive railroad commission. Both parties learned that matters could be expedited by clearing them with Lucius Tuttle. Working especially closely with Republican war-horse James Lyford, Tuttle scrutinized nominations, platforms, and appointments.[12] The railroad even played a role in legislative nominations in some towns through the work of local railroad/party officials such as Sylvannus Bryant.

Because of the tradition of rotation in office, the party generally could offer recognition and advancement to those who were willing to be patient and work with the organization. Even the state's two congressional seats tended to rotate regularly, although Cyrus A. Sulloway of Manchester had held his seat since 1895, a tenure that would continue until interrupted temporarily by the 1912 election, and Frank Currier of Canaan in 1901 commenced holding the Second District seat that would be his until he was defeated in 1912. Congressmen tended to work closely with the organization. The state's U.S. Senate seats had not traditionally rotated, and senators typically had a powerful role in the state party.

The Republican party and the railroad corporation had a mutually beneficial relationship after 1896. Certainly most GOP officials were not disposed to join Chandler in criticizing the corporation, and they helped sustain the railroad's influence. The railroad worked through effective lobbyists in Concord as well as through ties to key house and senate committees. Indeed, some of the latter bodies had come generally to follow railroad leadership. In the house, despite normal patterns of rotation, "Jim" French of Moultonborough assumed a permanent seat as chairman of the railroad committee. The speakership did rotate, but here Tuttle apparently participated in final choices. Sometimes it was necessary to be patient; Lyford had to counsel Tuttle on one occasion that "the selection of a candidate [for speaker] be left open until after the election discloses who are members of the next House."[13]

Overseeing its political interests was the railroad's general counsel, Frank Streeter. Born in Vermont in 1853, Streeter had graduated from Dartmouth and opened a law practice in Concord in the 1870s. He had negotiated on behalf of the Concord railroad in its merger with the Boston and Maine; he then became a key official of the latter. A genial, bright, strong man, Streeter was part of the railroad's Concord phalanx that included chief lobbyist Irving Drew and political strategists Benjamin Kimball and John Sanborn. State officials such as Henry Putney, the irascible railroad commissioner, also worked closely with Tuttle and Streeter.

The railroad lobby's influence over the legislature was built on a complex base. Kimball specialized in legislative strategy; Sanborn kept an eye on General Court nominations; Irving Drew dispensed free passes to legislators, often general passes good on connecting lines and including members of the legislator's family, loosely defined. Influence over legislative nominations, strong ties with the governor, the council, the senate, and the speaker of the house, a sound sense of parliamentary tactics that often befuddled the citizen-legislators, and the good will that came with passes all combined to give the railroad significant influence, and without resorting to such crude tactics as bribes.[14] There were allegations of these, of course, but little supporting evidence after the 1880s. Perhaps much of the direct influence, the tactics, the pressure was unnecessary. On railroad matters there was little disposition to oppose the interest of the Boston and Maine railroad. Its interests and New Hampshire's interests seemed closely entwined.[15]

One politician who was not only disposed but anxious to oppose the railroad was Senator Chandler. Cantankerous, vicious of tongue, if not of spirit, given to partisan moralizing, Chandler rarely let up in his attack on the railroads. In the 1890s, when the Tuttle organization seemed to move into open alliance with his U.S. Senate colleague and political foe Jacob Gallinger, Chandler was enraged. Gallinger assumed control of the Republican State Committee in 1898, which Chandler found an unconscionable violation of the Civil Service Act as well as a foreboding aggrandizement of power.[16] Gallinger and Tuttle were both uneasy with the antirailroad sorties of ex-governor Charles Busiel (1895–97). Busiel threatened to challenge them in 1898 with an antirailroad movement in the GOP. They squelched the challenge with the nomination of accommodating Frank Rollins; following this, antirailroad Republicanism seemed at the least to be muted.[17]

Chandler was another matter. He was an abrasive, powerful opponent. His strength would also be his weakness. Tuttle and Gallinger, uneasy about such a strong opponent, promised neutrality in Chandler's 1901 reelection bid. Gallinger apparently kept his promise; Tuttle apparently did not.[18] In January 1901 the Republican legislative caucus voted overwhelmingly to send the nondescript Henry Burnham to take Chandler's Senate seat. This action shook the foundations of the Granite State GOP. Chandler may have been defeated; he was far from silenced. And the railroad interests in Concord had apparently participated in the senator's defeat, Tuttle's

William E. Chandler (N.H. Historical Society)

personal "neutrality" notwithstanding.[19] "Bill Chandler had been run over by the railroad" would, however, be more interim judgment than obituary. Chandler's 1901 defeat required a public display of power greater than the railroad lobby customarily exercised. Beyond this it appeared an arrogant act that was indefensible as a matter of railroad interests.

Between 1901 and 1905 Boston and Maine hubris created more problems for the railroad. The effective political machine proved too effective; to many it seemed out of control—or at least controlled less for conservative corporate reasons and more for the ambitions of the leaders. Central in the imbroglio was the railroad's chief counsel, Frank Streeter. Intelligent and personable, he was also ambitious and not a little arrogant. He was not content to be an unobtrusive influence, as he was, not content to be one of the most powerful political figures in New Hampshire, which he arguably was, not content at any rate until he could also have equivalent public power. He apparently never understood that his influence was not of a sort to be spent publicly in a state that claimed to take its democratic rhetoric and traditions quite seriously. New Hampshire was not New York or Pennsylvania, Boston or Chicago. Granite Staters may have winked at influence, but not at private power openly used in a democratic forum.

In 1902 Frank Streeter filed as a delegate from his Concord ward to the state constitutional convention. This raised a few eyebrows, but these conventions were officially nonpartisan and Streeter perhaps was only assuming his share of the burden of public service. William Chandler was also a delegate, and he was appalled when Streeter announced his willingness to serve as president of the convention. Willingness was will in this case; in 1902 Frank Streeter's will was sufficient. Despite strong efforts, no proposed changes in fundamental law relative to railroads resulted from the convention.[20] In 1902 Streeter further indicated his willingness to serve as Republican national committeeman from New Hampshire. The potential appointee, Senator Gallinger, was shocked but prepared to withdraw from the fight for the post he insisted he did not particularly desire in any event. Streeter pulled back in the face of criticism, but in 1904 he took the seat from Gallinger.

Streeter's election to the Republican National Committee was a coup really, and one suddenly and ironically executed on the railroad train among the New Hampshire delegates traveling to the Republican National Convention in Chicago. Present and voting for Streeter was Winston Churchill.[21] Henry Burnham's U.S. Senate seat, the term expiring in 1907, seemed clearly the next step for Streeter. If the railroad and the Republican party organization were to continue their mutually supportive relationship, now it apparently would be only on the railroad's terms, as defined by Streeter. Lucius Tuttle was seriously ill at the time of the national committeeman vote, and Gallinger believed, as did Lyford, that the problem was not with the railroad and Tuttle, but with Streeter. Gallinger predicted that if "such tactics continue we will have the Wisconsin situation in New Hampshire with railroad and anti-railroad forces facing each other in every Convention and in the Legislature." Streeter's own motives and ambitions are not clear, except that he was an ambitious man. In making these forceful moves

Jacob Gallinger (N.H. Historical Society)

he alarmed and antagonized not just the Chandlers, but also people like Gallinger and Burnham who were friendly to the railroad. By now Gallinger and Chandler had reconciled many of their personal differences.[22]

The political ambitions of Streeter demonstrated something of the arrogance of power. At that it might have done little more than alarm some political activists and perhaps provide some gossip for the political palaver that dominated the long Concord winters. Probably most people in the state were indifferent to the politics of the national committee post and the constitutional convention presidency. One might assume some greater interest in the deposition of Chandler; there was, but apparently even this was not the sort of contest and resolution that created widespread concerns. Political infighting and jockeying for position were after all not recent or rare activities, and Chandler himself had been a past master of such tactics.

The power of arrogance would prove another matter. Streeter and his railroad lobby associates had developed a well-organized and well-functioning machine. Its purpose had been to protect the interests of the Boston and Maine railroad in New Hampshire. It did this well, apparently acting to block changes in the tax laws, in lobbying regulation, in party nomination procedures, and in the railroad commission. There is no way to determine if the railroad's political tacticians were crucial in stopping all or even any of these. Streeter's success in using his organization for personal goals may have been due to an inept and diffuse opposition more than to his real strength. The fact remained that the lobby had the aura of effective power and clearly could be influential in some matters.

Streeter and his associates erred in the 1903 and 1905 legislative sessions when they used their influence on matters that were not even peripherally connected to railroad interests. Lyford had attempted to counsel Streeter that there was "a wide spread irritation at the prominence in the councils of the party of some men connected with the Boston and Maine Railroad management." The interests of the corporation and the state were close, but "the irritation is over the interference of some of these men in matters political, and oftentimes in very small matters, which can be of no possible interest to the road." [23]

Despite pleas to stay away from such a volatile issue, Streeter supported the local-option bill that passed the legislature in 1903 and that, following voter approval in referendum, repealed the old prohibition law. Local option would significantly open the state liquor traffic. The state's substantial prohibition/temperance movement was appalled. James Lyford warned President Tuttle that those claiming Boston and Maine authority were intervening in the legislature in this matter. "Unless action is taken to discontinue this practice in New Hampshire, there will be a revolt which none of us can check." [24] Some machine loyalists such as Dan Remich of Littleton, an ardent prohibitionist, joined Chandler in voicing opposition to "boss rule." Indeed, Senator Gallinger, already angry with Streeter, was further provoked by this incident because of his own strong temperance sympathy. [25]

This controversy seemed to pass without public division. In fact Streeter had been open in his activity on behalf of local option. The referendum control had represented a compromise that he had worked out with the prohibition forces at the Republican convention in September of 1902. In 1904 Remich even joined Churchill in supporting Streeter for the national committee post. The Republican platform in that year was banal: the document boasted of Republican performance and slammed the Democrats. (That party, its ticket headed by Alton Parker rather than William Jennings Bryan, "asks public confidence solely on the ground that it is no longer insane.") The platform detailed the Grand Old Party's national record and mentioned state affairs briefly and in general terms. There was no mention of local option. The 1904 Republican convention had no unseemly fights, and prohibitionist Republicans were harmonious participants in the conclave. The gubernatorial candidate, manufacturer John McLane, while generally considered independent was certainly acceptable to the organization. He had paid his party dues and had ruffled no leadership or railroad feathers in the process.[26]

In 1905 the legislature passed a seemingly innocuous bill that provided for the incorporation of the New England Breeder's Club. The club sought to improve "the breed of horses and other domestic animals in the state of New Hampshire." The officers were largely out-of-staters with New York City and Saratoga Springs interests. The club was going to construct a racetrack, and, it was noted after the legislative session ended and the bill was signed, the bill's apparently explicit antiwagering provision was in fact a weak palliative compared to the general antigambling law that it replaced in this specific instance. There was outrage in parts of the state when it became apparent that Salem, New Hampshire, would have a racetrack, with wagering likely. The outrage accelerated when it was disclosed that railroad lobbyists Frank Streeter, Irving Drew, and John Brown had played a role in securing passage of this little-noticed bill. Chandler warned Gallinger, "'Reform' seems to be coming."[27]

Antimachine sentiment was crystallized by these disclosures. Temperance Republicans, already concerned by the local-option law, became even more alarmed by the Salem racetrack disclosures. These Republicans, led by David Goodell, had never really been part of the party inner circle; indeed their Republicanism appeared more issue oriented than a statement of organizational loyalty. Now they had something in common with the antirailroad Republicans personified by Chandler. Resentment toward the party organization took on a sharper moral tone.

The last few years had seen changes around the nation in political rhetoric as politicians such as Pres. Theodore Roosevelt insisted on stricter public control of railroads and other corporations. Gov. Robert La Follette in Wisconsin had successfully challenged corporate influence over politics in that state. Both La Follette and Roosevelt were engaged in political battles; they often cast them in fundamentally moral terms. Muckraking journalists discovered and struck out at corruption in public life. There is no indication that New Hampshire political figures consciously modeled themselves after these examples; on the other hand they surely were aware of them. If antimachine politicians in New Hampshire were not emulative, they could at least take some comfort in knowing they were not alone in their battles.[28]

Allegations that the railroad lobbyists had assisted the racetrack interests, after earlier facilitating passage of the local-option bill, elicited some predictable responses from William Chandler and started again the public scoldings from Daniel Remich, Littleton attorney, prohibitionist, and general moral crusader as well as party regular. But now new forces entered the fray: ministers such as Thomas Chalmers, Edward Blake, and M. F. Johnson, and former governor David Goodell, who had earlier made his criticisms largely in private. Perhaps most important, William J. Tucker, the president of Dartmouth College, became publicly involved. An accomplished man of considerable integrity, Tucker, the last of Dartmouth's clergymen-presidents, had presided over the transformation of Dartmouth from a rural, nondescript private school to a modern college. While he had carefully avoided politics, Dartmouth graduates were well represented in public and private affairs in New Hampshire. Frank Streeter was among these, and he was also a powerful force on the Dartmouth board of trustees and an important ally of Tucker's in the president's program of growth and construction. Streeter, Irving Drew, Benjamin Kimball, Ira Colby, William Chase, and Charles Chase were Dartmouth graduates with close ties to the college as well as to the railroad interests. In addition to Streeter, Kimball and William Chase served as Dartmouth trustees. Streeter chaired the trustees' Committee on Buildings and Improvements; Kimball chaired the Finance Committee. These two key railroad politicos then were also critical figures in Tucker's work.[29]

In addition to his personal conviction that the Dartmouth president should not be involved in partisan politics, Tucker then had strong practical reasons for keeping his distance from these matters. The Salem racetrack bill overcame all of the reservations. Tucker became involved with a Committee of Twelve, organized by the New Hampshire Sunday School Association, to investigate and deal with this matter, and as the committee studied the matter Tucker became personally more outraged at what he learned. Some members of this committee began sharply and publicly to criticize Streeter and other railroad lobbyists for their involvement in this affair. In January 1906

Tucker finally spoke out. At a mass rally in Manchester he warned two thousand people that the lobby-racetrack interests had to be challenged: "Their experience, their skill, their resources of every kind have hardly as yet been drawn upon." Tucker admitted that it was "not an agreeable task" to leave his "chosen and urgent work" to take on this obligation. "But unless men are willing to do their duty as citizens, in an emergency, I do not know how the Government can do . . . its duty effectively." Tucker insisted that the law could cope with "new moral situations" only in a "bracing moral atmosphere" which must come from "an aroused public sentiment." The Dartmouth president said New Hampshire had been humiliated: "Let the sense of humiliation remain upon us till we have taken measures sufficient to recover the honor of the state."[30]

Tucker's speech was an inspiring, even courageous, performance. The courage was tangible in private where Tucker lectured Streeter and Kimball and apparently even resisted the pressures of the college's largest benefactor, Edward Tuck. A chastened Streeter admitted privately that his office had some limited role in the passage of the bill, for which he had received a payment. He insisted that the role was quite minor, but he told Tucker that he would resign from the board if the president believed this was necessary. Tucker did not. Tucker personally pushed Gov. John McLane to resolve the gambling question. Secretary of State Edward Pearson told Tucker that McLane was obligated by "ante-election pledges to do what 'the road' wants him to do." There is no evidence confirming this judgment. Under pressure the governor finally asked the New Hampshire Supreme Court for an advisory opinion as to whether the Salem bill superceded the state prohibition on gambling; in March the court determined the older law took precedence. There would be no legal wagering at Salem.[31]

Tucker drew the line at personally engaging in political action; others were not so hesitant. In the spring of 1906 a group of thirteen men formed the Lincoln Republican Club to take up Tucker's plea for "a general fight . . . against the syndicate of bosses and grafters." The group included Daniel Remich (b. 1852), his brother James Remick (b. 1860), a former state supreme court justice and distinguished Concord attorney (they were brothers; Daniel spelled his name differently), Remick's law partners Harry Sargent (b. 1860) and Edward Niles (b. 1865), Niles's father, Episcopal bishop William Niles (b. 1832), Milford newspaperman William Rotch (b. 1859), young Hanover newspaperman Frank Musgrove (b. 1872), Dartmouth professor James Colby (b. 1850), and his medical school colleague John Gile (b. 1864).[32] It was a group impressive in stature but not in political influence. The Lincoln Club organizers included seven attorneys, two journalists, a clergyman, two Dartmouth professors, and a manufacturer. Few had significant political experience, although James Remick had chaired the 1904 Republican State Convention. Their common bond seemed to be a sense of outrage.

The Lincoln Club did not appear threatening to its railroad opponents. Nonetheless Benjamin Kimball apparently raised with President Tucker a concern about Dartmouth faculty involvement in this effort. Tucker was direct in his response as he told Kimball that while he believed the president should not become involved in partisan affairs, any efforts to stifle political activity by Dartmouth faculty had no place in a free institution: "Every one who connects himself with a college or university today properly assumes that freedom of political action is a part of academic freedom as much as freedom of theological opinion [has traditionally been]." The Dartmouth president pointedly suggested to the railroad official that perhaps the most positive step would be for the railroad "to disconnect itself from New Hampshire politics."[33]

By 1906 many of the organization politicians were antagonized by the activities of Streeter; they nonetheless kept their distance from the Lincoln Republicans. Gallinger noted to Moses that Dan Remich had sent him "orders" to participate "in playing the deuce generally in New Hampshire. Dan is a first-class nuisance, and I do not think I will take the trouble to answer his letter."[34] Indeed, the Lincoln Republican Club was the subject of jokes; when on the Fourth of July the group announced that Winston Churchill of Cornish would be their candidate for the Republican gubernatorial nomination, jokes gave way to boisterous laughter.[35]

Churchill was an unusual choice for the self-proclaimed "moral forces" to turn to in 1906. He had not earned a legislative record in 1903 or 1905 to recommend him; he had been rather dilettantish in his Concord activities and had even left midway through one session to vacation in the South. He had supported the local-option bill in 1903, voted for Streeter in the 1904 national committee fight, had taken out a liquor license for a small inn that he proposed to open in Cornish, and had been listed as one of the directors of the New England Breeder's Club. He had generally kept his distance from the antiorganization forces; former governor Frank Rollins later chided him for "a particularly quick shift from your railroad friends, with whom you seemed to be particularly intimate, to the reform party."[36] Churchill explained to Chandler that he had been reluctant to take this step but he was prepared to fight; he had hoped "matters might gradually mend themselves from the inside. You have known better, but young men have to learn by experience. We are going to start at the Canada line and go southward, appealing to the people to . . . throw off the yoke." [37]

The choice of Churchill as leader and symbol of the revolt was more surprising than ridiculous. In fact he would prove to be a good choice and a strong candidate. Churchill was independent professionally and financially. He noted that he could not "be hurt" by this challenge in the way some other reform candidates might have been. He had a statewide reputation, and his political activities the previous four years had erased the newcomer image but were not yet extensive enough to mark him as a jaundiced politico or an ambitious man. His role in the directorate of the Breeder's Club was apparently due to his convivial willingness to lend his name to yet another worthy enterprise. He satisfactorily explained that he had no real role in the plan and was unaware of the gambling potential. He resigned from the board and managed to walk away with the image of victim rather than perpetrator. [38] In this capacity he had plenty of companions. He insisted upon his temperance credentials without embracing the prohibitionist militants. [39] Most important, in 1906 Churchill published his novel *Coniston*.

Coniston never quite proved to be the *Uncle Tom's Cabin* of New Hampshire politics, as some predicted. It was an important book, however, and even an influential political document. The protagonist of *Consiton* was Jethro Bass, modeled loosely after deceased New Hampshire boss Ruel Durkee. The story focused on the political control enjoyed in the rural political fiefdoms of the state in the nineteenth century. Bass controlled votes and voters and became one of the key manipulators in Concord. In many ways a likable figure, he also represented the antithesis of New Hampshire's political ideals. Symbolically, at the end of his career Bass acknowledged the new preeminent power of the railroad organization in New Hampshire. The author had forewarned of this: "After the Boss came along certain Things without souls." President Roosevelt wrote Churchill to say how much he and Mrs. Roosevelt had enjoyed reading the book; the president informed the novelist that *Coniston* dealt "with one of the real and great abuses of this generation." The president's singular reference was unclear for he went on to express abhorrence with both the "wealthy corruptionist" and the "sinister demagogue." [40]

Churchill would call *Coniston* his platform, a revealing observation. *Coniston* articulated no vision, no program. Rather it described and implicitly condemned influence, power, manipulation, and corruption. For the longer-term development of Republican reform, it would prove important that voices combined on these concerns, and they congealed in 1906 behind Churchill. But the

Churchill reform program was defensive and regenerative: to halt the railroad's aggrandizement of power and let democracy again prevail. There was little articulation of a new public agenda among the Lincoln Club group. Churchill campaigned on the theme of permitting citizens "to run their own government," and not to permit the railroad to rule. Government "of the people, for a corporation and by a corporation" must stop. A Mark Sullivan exposé in *Collier's* in August detailed Boston and Maine arrogance.[41] The Lincoln Club's reforms had a purgative tone: to abolish free passes, to establish controls on lobbying, and to open the nomination process. The latter seemed a secondary concern; it would soon take on a much greater significance to the antirailroad forces.

The gubernatorial nominating process in New Hampshire was based upon a caucus-convention system, with the parties having considerable latitude in managing their own affairs. The system had the right combination of certainty and ambiguity, control and chaos, that was generally amenable to the influence of a disciplined organization. Railroad interests had been rather successful in shaping results. Between 1861 and 1900 New Hampshire had twenty different governors. One was the son of a banker–railroad officer; two became railroad officials after leaving office; twelve "had been or were superintendents, treasurers, directors or presidents of railroads."[42]

In 1906 the Republican party faced an election campaign in some disarray. Even before Churchill announced his candidacy, there were several potentially strong gubernatorial candidates. Such public hankering for high office was unusual in the Granite State. Rosecrans Pillsbury, the first to enter the fray, was a Londonderry shoe manufacturer and lawyer who had recently bought the *Manchester Union*. By transferring this important newspaper from Democratic to Republican hands, Pillsbury had immediate influence in the Republican party. He was never fully trusted, however, for he was one of the delegates who voted for Streeter in the national committeeman election in 1904 after apparently commiting himself to Gallinger; he had assisted the Committee of Twelve in the racetrack fight in 1905 and then had pulled back. In March 1906, indicating the depth of his distrust of Pillsbury, Chandler, who had served on the committee, said he would prefer an "out and out railroad man" as governor to Pillsbury. A putative reformer, Pillsbury would prove instead to be simply another ambitious man. In his tiffs with *Manchester Mirror* publisher and railroad commissioner Henry Putney, Pillsbury had expressed reformist outrage. One of Pillsbury's close personal and political friends, however, was the ubiquitous Frank Streeter. In 1906 this relationship proved sufficient to earn Pillsbury the distrust of all Republican factions. Lacking a firm political base and given to malapropisms, the hefty Pillsbury would prove more nuisance than threat. His reformist sallies against "Put" nonetheless piled complication upon confusion.[43]

There were two "good" candidates for governor, in the sense of being good organization men. Charles Floyd, a Manchester businessman and member of the Governor's Council, and Charles Greenleaf, a White Mountain and Boston hotelier and also a member of the Governor's Council, sought the nomination. Each was mainstream Republican. Greenleaf, then sixty-five years old, had no direct or implicit ties to the railroad; Floyd, aged forty-five, was considered more explicitly a railroad candidate. A potentially difficult situation became so when the Republican leaders fragmented among the several candidates. The railroad leadership was particularly equivocal. With the recent death of John Sanborn, many believed this group had lost a wise and cautious voice. Streeter determined to stay out of the open fray, possibly with an eye on the Burnham U.S. Senate seat—although there were indications in the spring that Lucius Tuttle had begun to rein in Streeter. Tuttle, stung by criticism of railroad manipulation, assumed a neutral stance as well.[44] The consequence of these decisions was not neutrality but a confused and competing use of organization resources. Henry Putney led the Floyd forces and Jacob Gallinger assisted in the Greenleaf campaign, although the latter worked privately rather than openly in the early stages.[45]

By 1906 many Republican leaders had come to appreciate the need for their party to keep some public distance from the Boston and Maine railroad. In tactical terms, their judgment was informed by the recognition that the antirailroad forays of the inchoate reform movement could have a negative effect on the party's fortunes. This conclusion explained some of the party leaders' aversion to Floyd, more clearly identified with the railroad. In personal terms, perhaps the more powerful driving force, coolness toward the railroad organization represented the antagonism Gallinger and his allies felt toward Streeter, who was still identified as the railroad man in the state even though this was less clearly the case. None of this disagreement translated into antirailroad sentiment on the part of the party leaders. Lyford and Moses recognized that this sentiment was a real component of the Churchill appeal, and they appreciated the need for the party to make some statement to head it off. They agreed to work on an antipass plank for the party platform. On the other hand Lyford was close to the railroad; he continued to cooperate with Tuttle, working on a retainer for him on a study of the New Hampshire tax situation; Lyford had recently received Benjamin Kimball's assistance on a 1905 bill to bring the budget into balance so as not to cause the party embarrassment in the 1906 election. Gallinger was "not much disturbed over the fulminations of the so-called 'moral forces.'" He considered the Lincoln Club to be part of the prohibition wing of the party, which in fact several of its members were, and believed "mountebanks such as Remick [Remich?] and [Manchester minister and Committee of Twelve member Edgar] Blake will not be able to sweep the sensible and conservative temperance men off their feet."[46]

Churchill campaigned on the railroad issue, insisting that legitimate Boston and Maine interests would be secure but that the corporation had "tried to prostitute the state." Churchill used Theodore Roosevelt as an example; he sought to emulate Roosevelt to the point of telling his own campaign biographer to emphasize that he was "a man of action."[47] William Chandler had confessed as early as 1904 that "in my dreams sometimes I see arise in New Hampshire a conscientious brave strong man like Roosevelt or La Follette to destroy the system. Sometimes he takes your shape." This must have pleased Churchill. But the old war-horse's elliptical postscript was perplexing as well: "and then I awake."[48]

Chandler acted as avuncular advisor to the Lincoln Republicans; he never fully became a part of their group. They needed him as a "practical politician" but also distrusted his strong-willed, often manipulative, ways. He fretted about their stubborness and naïveté. Each exaggerated. Chandler, earlier a lukewarm Greenleaf supporter, was of some help to Churchill, but he saw Churchill as an instrument to break the machine, and nothing more. Chandler's goal was "reform inside the republican party."[49] The Lincoln Republicans' insistence upon avoiding compromise negated some of the influence they might have used. Nevertheless, Churchill and his supporters would prove more sophisticated than anyone might have predicted. There was little indication when they organized their challenge that the insurgents thought they might actually win, but they proved a greater threat than even they might have dreamed.

The details of the campaign for the 1906 Republican gubernatorial nomination need only be sketched. It was a fascinating combination of the dramatic and the comic that might have served as background for one of Winston Churchill's novels, as indeed it ultimately would. Churchill campaigned hard and overcame many initial obstacles of inadequate finances, absence of organization, and spotty support.[50] Only five of seventy-five newspapers supported him; most would not even print his announcement of candidacy. Churchill did not have a strong stump style, but he communicated his convictions and principles well.[51] Pillsbury flirted with the reformers without really alienating the railroad. Indeed he had some contact with Streeter and Tuttle. Putney was Pillsbury's enemy, and the scrap got sufficiently emotional that they physically scuffled and blood spilled, not Putney's.[52]

The aggressive Putney pushed his man Floyd and enjoyed substantial help from many of the regulars. He had another fight with a Greenleaf supporter, and on this occasion the spilled blood was Putney's. Greenleaf did not campaign much but relied on the considerable support and strength of Jacob Gallinger. Frank Streeter as well as Lucius Tuttle ultimately tried to arrest the civil war by seeking a negotiated settlement, without much success.[53]

A high point of the Churchill campaign was the Fourth Ward caucus in Concord. Well-organized insurgents surprised the regulars there and elected a convention slate. It was a significant victory; the Lincoln Republicans in a direct confrontation took convention seats from a regular slate that included Jacob Gallinger, James Lyford, Frank Streeter, and convention chairman–designate Samuel Eastman. These embarrassed officials attended only with proxies. Gallinger was late in recognizing what was happening in the state. In late August he observed, "The losses have been in *railroad* towns and Churchill has been the beneficiary."[54]

The convention that met in Concord in late September was a riotous affair. Chairman Eastman had impaired hearing and a weak voice; he soon gave up on even the pretense of presiding over the contentious gathering. Churchill showed good early strength relative to the leader Greenleaf, and by the eighth ballot the novelist had taken a narrow lead. The hall was chaos, helped along by a Churchill cheering section in the gallery (Gallinger, contemptuous of Churchill since the latter's 1904 vote for Streeter, had earlier warned that Churchill would "blow in with his theatrical aggregation")[55] and by the recognition that several ballots counted more votes than there were delegates. There was little effort at accreditation and control.

Perhaps the greatest fear among many organization Republicans was a Pillsbury victory because of the latter's ties to Streeter. Lyford insisted, "If the choice should come between Pillsbury and Churchill, I am for taking a real reformer rather than a sham one. I will never be dragooned into supporting Pillsbury's candidacy and have Frank S. Streeter boss of New Hampshire politics." By the eighth ballot the machine forces determined to unite behind Floyd. Pillsbury had withdrawn, urging his supporters to rally behind Floyd—eroding the publisher's reform claims and simultaneously having little effect on his delegates. Many went to Churchill. On the ninth ballot, however, Charles Floyd secured a narrow majority to Churchill's surprisingly strong second.[56]

The Churchill challenge was not inconsequential, nor would it prove ephemeral. Chandler had warned the reformers early that they would need staying power for at least a two-campaign fight.[57] It would prove in fact to be a three-campaign fight, but the Churchill supporters left Concord elated and prepared for the longer battle. Importantly, they had secured a reform platform at the convention, part of the machine effort to mollify them as orchestrated by the great compromiser James Lyford. Charles Floyd was an organization man and at least nominally a railroad man, but he incongruously ran on a platform that promised a direct primary system, abolition of free passes, popular election of the railroad commission, regulation and registration of lobbyists, and equalization of taxes. It was a solid platform, one that reflected most of the themes of the Churchill-Lincoln Republican campaign, but one that Floyd kept at some distance in the course of his campaign.[58]

In fact the Democrats could have run on the same basic platform in 1906. While the Republican party in New Hampshire had been inflicted with loud, bitter, disputes, the Democratic party in the Granite State had undergone its own quiet revolution. Relieved of Frank Jones and the railroad Democrats, the New Hampshire Democrats ignored as much as possible the burden of the national Democracy. There was a new generation of party leadership following the disaster of the 1890s. Clarence Carr, a fifty-three-year-old Andover attorney and manufacturer, worked to reenergize his party, focusing his attention on state reform. Carr was an articulate foe of railroad influence, and worked closely with young Concord attorney Henry Hollis (b. 1869), who had served as the party's gubernatorial candidate in the last two elections. Republican regular and railroad commissioner Henry Putney became the focus for Democratic anti-railroad attacks. Carr counseled the 1906 Democratic gubernatorial nominee Nahum Jameson to stress the Floyd-Putney-railroad linkage.[59]

The Democrats were deprived of one potential issue when Frank Streeter resigned his position as railroad counsel in October 1906, under some pressure from Tuttle, the latter by now sensitive to the liability Streeter had become. Streeter shared with president Tucker copies of correspondence between him, Streeter, and Lucius Tuttle. Streeter told Tuttle his resignation was necessitated—there was "no honorable avoidance"—because the two men disagreed on the proper political role of the railroad. Streeter insisted that the railroad had for the last decade manipulated political matters that had no relationship to railroad business. Tuttle retorted that the problem was that Streeter used his railroad connection and power in order to influence nonrailroad matters. Whatever the true story of this powerful relationship gone sour, Streeter's resignation effectively freed the attorney from the now politically negative railroad ties if he chose to initiate his U.S. Senate campaign.[60]

Jameson deprived Floyd of the majority the state constitution required for gubernatorial election. Clearly some Churchill supporters kept their distance from Floyd, with the novelist causing public embarrassment for Republican regulars by taking a publicized "vacation" to Hot Springs, Virginia, until election day.[61] The Republican vote in 1906 suggested some discontinuity with earlier patterns of support.[62] The Lincoln Republicans had not left their party; they had served notice however that they were not to be taken for granted.

Because Floyd had secured only a plurality, it was necessary for the newly elected legislature to name the governor from among the candidates who had run in the fall. As the dominant Republican legislative majority prepared to select Floyd as governor, the Lincolnites made plans to continue their fight. Unfortunately they could not agree on their objectives. William Chandler and Churchill supporter George Leighton held the position that the reformers should put up a candidate to oppose Henry Burnham's reelection to the U.S. Senate. Others followed the argument of Churchill and Lincoln Club president James Remick that to do so would suggest a desire for office rather than a campaign for principle. Remick and Churchill carried the day but did not convince Chandler and Leighton. The former had revenge in mind: the railroad took the seat from him; now he would gain revenge by helping to take it from them. He concluded that the reform movement was "a myth and a humbug," and that Churchill showed "foolish traits."[63] Leighton had equally personal motives: he wanted the seat himself. Frank Streeter made his long-anticipated entry into the race but then pulled out. Burnham had refused to withdraw, and Streeter was a sagacious enough politician to realize that his was a stop-Burnham candidacy with no realistic hope of victory. Perhaps most significant, Chandler and Moses believed that the railroad lobby organized to oppose Streeter.[64]

The Chandler-Leighton and Churchill-Remick wings of the reform club traded charges about their respective political wisdom and personal principles. Nevertheless, Burnham's overwhelming victory in the Republican caucus suggested that no amount of reform cohesion would have been sufficient to deny him reelection.[65] In January 1907 Churchill had his eye on broader concerns than the U.S. Senate seat. He set up in the Concord law office of Sargent, Remick, and Niles the headquarters of a self-defined "People's Lobby." He and his co-workers shared the goal of writing into law

TABLE 3.1

Cohesion and Disagreement Scores, 1907 Legislature

Bill	Percentage in favor			Disagreement	
	Democratic	Republican	Lincoln Republican	Lincoln Republicans v. remaining Republicans	Democratic v. Republican
Postpone free pass bill	66	44	0	46	22
Amend free pass bill	52	15	85	74	37
Amend free pass bill	57	75	8	70	18
Pass amended free pass bill	59	72	0	76	13
Indefinitely postpone free pass bill	63	58	0	62	5
Indefinitely postpone resolution for free pass bill responsive to the spirit of the republican platform	87	47	0	49	40
Indefinitely postpone municipal woman suffrage bill	83	71	64	9	12
Bill to incorporate Spaulding-Jones Power Company	56	58	82	25	2
Substitute minority report on act for regulation of sale of bulk merchandise	68	43	18	27	25
Committee resolution on act for taxation of steam railroads	64	76	36	43	12
Act for armories in Concord and Nashua	61	53	100	50	8
Indefinitely postpone primary election law	50	51	0	54	1
Indefinitely postpone bill to protect sheep	59	47	50	3	12

the principles of the reform campaign. This goal did not appear to be too complicated; after all the Republican party dominated the legislature, and the party had embraced the reform program in their 1906 platform. Churchill now thought of himself as an experienced politician; his willingness to permit Burnham's reelection without opposition and his similar response to the selection of Bertram Ellis as speaker of the house, despite Ellis's railroad ties, suggested his eagerness to believe that now the whole party would pull together for the reform principles. The People's Lobby and their "up-hill fight . . . for decency" would prove another awkward step in the education of Winston Churchill and his Lincoln Club colleagues.[66]

As at the convention in September, the Lincoln Club's main problem in the legislature had to do with numbers. One estimate put the reform group at sixty legislators. This seems exaggerated. In any event, all the Churchill group had achieved was a watered-down antipass bill which some reform advocates believed worsened the situation. The roll calls in the 1907 session were revealing. Defining the Lincoln Club control group as thirteen legislators who formally joined with the Churchill effort, it is clear the GOP was not of one mind on a range of bills (see table 3.1).[67] Lincoln Club legislators and their fellow Republican legislators disagreed more on most issues than did Republicans and Democrats.

This split was true on all of the railroad bills as well as on the primary election law, critical matters on the 1906 reform agenda. Agreement on platform statements and campaign emphases, effected to assure partisan cohesion, did not assure agreement on the specifics of legislation. Politics and governance were related but not synonymous activities. The small group of Lincoln Club activists in the legislature was generally quite cohesive. But even they split over woman suffrage and railroad taxation. These represented significant programmatic disagreements and also reflected a fundamental difference among Lincoln Club officials about the role of reformers. Churchill, on the one hand, believed that those worthy of the reform label should be "with us in all things." Sargent, Niles, and Ed Cook disagreed, arguing that reform meant electing intelligent, independent men who would deal with issues "according to their best judgment." Churchill's approach, they believed, was "entirely at variance" with the reform idea.[68]

The 1907 legislative session symbolized well some of the complexities, the shifting and strange alliances, and the railroad's strength, which marked New Hampshire Republican politics. After Frank Streeter left the Boston and Maine in the fall of 1906, James Lyford predicted that now "he would raise his banner as a reformer and attempt to take charge of the reform forces. He will try now to be a political martyr crucified by the railroad." Lyford was correct, as he often was in his political prophecy. When Gallinger learned that Pillsbury, Streeter, and Churchill were working together during the legislative session, he wryly observed that "the combination . . . seems rather an unnatural one, but . . . 'politics makes strange bedfellows.'" The ultimate combination was larger, and perhaps even stranger: Lyford and Moses, Chandler and, to a lesser extent, Gallinger, worked to enact the basic planks of the 1906 Republican platform. The party officials recognized the need for public independence; they were not prepared to couple this with a private break from the influential railroad corporation. Lyford in fact had negotiated with and received the approval of President Tuttle for the antipass law that the former had composed for the platform. Yet the bill failed, and the participants believed it failed because Tuttle had reneged on his promise to Lyford. The railroad lobby, led by Ben Kimball and apparently facilitated by Bertram Ellis, flexed its muscle. Gallinger had no demonstrated interest in reform; he was worried about the party, however, and insisted that Moses keep "pounding away, demanding that the proper thing shall be done, as it will certainly be a bad situation if we allow these issues to get into the next campaign." [69]

In early summer James Lyford reviewed the situation for Charles Mellen, head of the New York, New Haven, and Hartford railroad and in the process of taking over the Boston and Maine. Lyford insisted that the people of New Hampshire had good feelings toward the railroad but that the imbroglio of 1906 resulted because of "meddling of railroad attorneys and agents in politics and their interference in legislation which did not concern the railroad." He hoped that Mellen would assist in securing strong antipass legislation and that railroad representatives would "keep their hands off of nominations and appointments." Then the Republican party would once again be united and be able to assist "the railroad in all legitimate requests." [70] Gallinger and Lyford saw the problem as fundamentally a political one: the "reformers" had managed to develop their own base of strength in the party, and they were potentially a powerful group; railroad recalcitrance facilitated their effort. Gallinger found the legislative session "disappointing" and feared that it would make the next campaign a difficult one. He and Lyford worried about Streeter and Pillsbury taking advantage of the situation. The latter, Gallinger judged, would "undertake to cheat everybody." [71]

The acquisition of the Boston and Maine by the New Haven railroad never became the issue in New Hampshire that it might have been. Chandler was horrified by this as further consolidation of power and distancing of ownership from the state; he was distressed that the Churchill group did not share his view. In fact they seem not to have even reflected on it very much, in sharp contrast to Massachusetts, where this matter played an important catalytic role in shaping political insurgency.[72]

Churchill had other matters on his mind during the merger fight. After the embarrassing legislative session of 1907, Winston Churchill had again focused his energy on campaign politics. He was convinced that success in legislation could only follow an expanded coalition. Consequently Churchill set out, almost single-handedly and somewhat naïvely, to expand the reform base. He had early on defined the insurgents' problem accurately: the necessity of having a newspaper to represent the reform views and the need for an inclusive rather than an exclusive framework for attracting supporters.[73]

In the late spring of 1907 Churchill negotiated an agreement that would shock and incense many of his supporters when they learned of it. After a series of discussions with Frank Streeter and Rosecrans Pillsbury, all of which were conducted secretly, he formed an alliance with them. The outlines were simple: Pillsbury's *Union* would support the reform effort; Churchill and Streeter would endorse Pillsbury in his 1908 campaign for the Republican gubernatorial nomination; and the three would organize a coalition of Roosevelt/ Taft supporters for the 1908 presidential campaign. It was a bold plan, and one that struck many of Churchill's supporters as a major surrender, both procedurally and substantively, to the old politics against which they had campaigned in 1906. Churchill promised to make himself "personally responsible . . . for Mr. Pillsbury's conduct" now, and if he became governor. Churchill had a signed, secret agreement with Pillsbury that he felt gave him this sort of influence.[74]

Pillsbury's motives in entering into this alliance seemed clear. He wanted to be governor. And if he could accomplish that goal in this manner it would not involve any concession of his principles. Some critics believed that he could achieve his objective in any manner without compromising principles. Streeter's motives were less obvious, although clearly he still harbored political ambitions and perhaps missed already the pivotal role he had earlier commanded in politics. To help make his friend governor and assume a prominent position in a presidential campaign would reaffirm emphatically his importance, most immediately by securing his reelection to the Republican National Committee.

Churchill's thinking is a bit more complicated, but the key to it was Theodore Roosevelt. The president, not standing for reelection himself, had determined that William Howard Taft would be the

Winston Churchill (Dartmouth College)

nominee best able to carry on the Roosevelt policies. The latter included well-publicized efforts to give the federal government greater
visibility in regulating business practices and in conserving natural
resources. As early as 1902 Churchill had argued that federal activity was critical. The novelist held state government in some disdain. In a June 1907 *New York Times* interview Churchill proclaimed, "I am a Federalist," by which he meant a believer in
centralized, national authority. The proposition of state sovereignty
was "absurd": "The advance of this country is retarded to-day be-

cause forty States meddle in affairs which ought to be handled by the Nation alone." Churchill happily allied himself with Alexander Hamilton, "one of the greatest [statesmen] of all ages." [75] As a Roosevelt admirer who could claim a personal friendship with the president dating back to 1901 and as a man who enjoyed some recognition as one of the president's key Granite State political contacts, Churchill was responsive to the Rough Rider's wishes. [76]

Churchill had enjoyed some national recognition as a result of his losing 1906 battle for the gubernatorial nomination. National newspapers and periodicals sympathetic to Roosevelt and reform applauded him as a point man for Republican reform in the Northeast. Churchill was in demand as a speaker, and he advised other nascent reformers, including the Lincoln Republican group in California. [77] Clearly he had come to think of reform as a force more comprehensive than the New Hampshire effort. The *New York Globe* predicted that Churchill would have "missions of political uplift" as part of his obligation as a "national institution." [78]

In an effort to build a broader state base, the Lincoln Republicans decided in September 1907 to disband and become a larger group called the Platform Republicans. It was not simply a cosmetic change—where the Lincoln Republicans had been a dissident group, the Platform Republicans asserted that they were the mainstream. Those who refused to support the 1906 platform were the dissidents. This change in label involved as well a not-so-subtle connection with national politics. The Lincoln Republican decision to disband in favor of "some larger and more efficient organization" was to be "based upon the unanimously declared policy of the Republican party in the state and the policies of President Roosevelt in the nation at large." [79]

Pursuing the Rooseveltian tie, some reformers started a separate organization called the New Hampshire Taft Association, resolving to send a Taft delegation to the 1908 national convention. The strategy was sound: to separate state and national objectives so that potential Taft support would not be restricted to the 1906 insurgents. Related to this was the assumption that activity on behalf of Taft would spill over into a greater base of support for the reformers' state organization. As Churchill argued, "If we win this fight, our prestige will be tremendous for a state fight." The factional fight of 1906 was now warmly remembered as a "movement," and one of which Theodore Roosevelt was the "author." [80] Yet, ironically, with state success a long-term goal, Churchill and some of his colleagues insisted that they did not have "the least intention of undertaking to develop any views upon state matters at the present time." [81] There is little doubt that Churchill considered the national battle more important than the struggle for the New Hampshire Republican party; if the former could help the latter, all the better.

The accretion to the reform ranks that Churchill sought through complex and ambiguous organizational goals eluded him again. In the labyrinth that was New Hampshire politics, personal loyalties, ambitions, and goals intruded into Churchill's plan to bring the state reform movement "into consonance" with "the larger Roosevelt party in the country."[82] Some reformers resisted the intrusion of complicated national politics into the state movement; some favored Charles Evans Hughes or Robert La Follette rather than Taft, an action that did not earn them the antireform label they received from Granite State Taftites.[83] More significant than the reformers' disagreement over Taft, however, was the old guard opposition to him and his New Hampshire supporters.

Jacob Gallinger had plenty of reasons, he believed, to oppose Churchill's operation. Gallinger was a cautious, organization Republican; his major national policy concern was the preservation of high tariff rates. The senior senator from New Hampshire was close to the old guard leadership in the Senate and had never been comfortable with Roosevelt's rhetoric and apparent indifference to high tariff principles. Taft's Roosevelt ties were enough to make Gallinger uncomfortable; Taft's Granite State ties caused Gallinger to experience more than discomfort. The fight became one over control of the state party, its procedures, its direction, and its candidates. Gallinger was not disposed to concede these matters without a fight. The fact that Streeter was involved in the Taft movement and that Gallinger's term in the Senate expired in 1909 gave to these elements a personal dimension and an emotional force. In addition Gallinger insisted that his own influence in Washington and the New Hampshire Republican party's leverage in the national party were enhanced by continuing the tradition of sending an uncommitted delegation to national nominating conventions. Gallinger, Lyford, Moses, and Chandler, and presumably everyone else in the organization, had been shocked when word leaked out of the Streeter-Churchill-Pillsbury agreement. Gallinger was disposed to fight, a disposition that was increased when he learned in the winter of 1907–8 that Churchill was not prepared to compromise on the makeup of the state delegation. Gallinger's series of letters to Lyford and Moses underlined his mood and feisty anticipation. He had had enough of challenges and surprises: "Tell everybody that this is a groundhog case. *We must win*"; "it seems to me plain that we ought to . . . fight it out regardless of consequence"; "we must make a dec-

laration of war, and either win or lose when the battle day arrives";
"I prefer a square out and out fight, so that we may know which
wing of the party is in the ascendency in the State. . . . we can whip
them out of their boots if a contest is made"; "We can do nothing
honorably but fight and I am ready for it"; "Churchill's arrogance is
such that we have got to have a fight in the State sometime with that
fellow and his followers, and I do not care how soon it comes."[84] Gallinger was obviously ready; he relished the scrap. For four years now
the Streeters and Churchills had challenged and embarrassed him.

Lyford, and to a lesser extent Moses, attempted to work more
tactfully and less forcefully with the challenge created by those who
were beginning to be called progressives. The two party loyalists
sought to detach Pillsbury by flattering and encouraging his ambition and more generally to "divide the allies." In the summer of
1907 Lyford conceded that after the recent events and fights, "there
is now no machine," but events would prove that judgment premature.[85] A major concern among all of the old guard was that this
challenge and fight was harmful to the party. Even Gallinger, who
obviously relished the conflict, feared that "if we are to continue to
divide our forces our troubles will multiply instead of diminish."
Party harmony "should outweigh" all other considerations. Gallinger was convinced it was the reform group that had pushed
matters to this unfortunate point.[86]

New York governor Charles Evans Hughes and Vice President
Charles Fairbanks became the favored stalking horses for those who
sought to halt the reformers' move to power. Despite the fact that
Churchill stood on one side and Gallinger and most of the old organization, including several of the Boston and Maine officials, on the
other, the fight was not simply one of philosophical issues or of reform versus regular coalitions. Several prominent old Churchillites
worked against Taft. And the Taft forces had substantial help from
their 1906 foes, notably Streeter, but including Frank Rollins. Officials of the Amoskeag Corporation also supported Taft. The Amoskeag Corporation seldom played a role in—or displayed much interest in—state politics. National politics, and especially tariff policies,
was another matter. The Amoskeag must have been satisfied with
Taft's tariff position; in any event the corporation liked to be on the
winning side. The anti-Taft group sought, apparently with some success, to convince corporate officials to pull back a bit in their Taft
support and promised them one seat on the delegation.[87] William
Chandler, whose support wavered between La Follette and Hughes,
noted the irony of it all: "Rollins and Streeter are singular floor
managers [for Taft];—men who never opened their heads for a

single reform measure and one of them being the best possible example of the class of citizens who created every evil which reform was begun to destroy."[88]

The campaign muddied rather than clarified many issues. And Theodore Roosevelt qua Taft was not a victor in New Hampshire. In Cornish Winston Churchill suffered the ultimate embarrassment when he lost in the caucus selecting local delegates to the district convention.[89] This race previewed the disaster. New Hampshire's Republican convention sent uncommitted or anti-Taft delegates to the Chicago national convention. Frank Streeter lost his national committee seat. James Lyford asked Gallinger, "Does it ever occur to you the retribution that has overtaken several of your colleagues four years ago as delegates to Chicago, Churchill, Remich, . . . Pillsbury and the beneficiary of the conspiracy, Streeter?" Churchill, Remich, and Pillsbury had all voted for Frank Streeter in 1904; presumably the satisfying thought had occurred to Gallinger. He noted of Streeter's machinations and defeat, "What a chump he is!" Taft won the nomination nonetheless, with New Hampshire delegates Gallinger and Moses refusing to make it unanimous. Churchill interpreted Taft's nomination as a Roosevelt victory, which "saved the nation from the greatest evils which have threatened it since the Civil War."[90]

Spring defeat in New Hampshire previewed fall disaster. Pillsbury faltered predictably during the summer, and the reformers found no alternative. Gallinger, now quite satisfied with himself and not a little vindictive, commented that "Pillsbury is as politically dead as the proverbial door nail, but perhaps it is well enough to give him a little punishment after death."[91] An executive "Committee of Twenty," acting for the Platform Republican group, had some success in getting local reform candidates to file for the legislature. But the gubernatorial race was embarrassing to the reformers. Churchill, adhering to his agreement with Pillsbury and by now less personally ambitious, refused to enter the contest. Early in the summer Pillsbury had essentially called the bluff of those reformers who opposed him by offering to withdraw if they could recruit another candidate; they could not.[92] By the time the Republican convention met, there was no unifying reform candidate, although Pillsbury adopted strong antirailroad rhetoric. Reform strength was evident—the platform went beyond that of 1906—but diffuse. Pillsbury ran a surprising second, but the early victor was Henry Quinby of Laconia.[93]

Prior to the convention the reformers had insisted Quinby was the railroad candidate. They were incorrect and had to have known that they were. Quinby was the candidate of Chandler, Lyford, and—presumably but not clearly—Gallinger. Bertram Ellis of Keene was the railroad candidate, and Ben Kimball and Charles Hamblett pushed him hard. Lyford was particularly frustrated. He was attempting, again, to unify the party, and his unity candidate was publicly tarred with the railroad brush while privately the railroad was doing all it could to defeat him. Lyford believed it was necessary for the party organization to accommodate both the reformers and the prohibitionists. He worried that "neither Gallinger nor Moses sense the trend of events, but I may be mistaken." He told Quinby that any candidate had to accept the principles of the 1906 platform.[94]

Quinby was not a clear machine candidate. Following the convention Lyford organized a meeting between Quinby and some of the reform leaders. The latter sought from Quinby more explicit support of their goals, including removal of Henry Putney from the railroad commission. Quinby tacitly accepted their proposal but refused to do so publicly. Negotiations broke down; Lyford gave up, discouraged when Gallinger, learning of this meeting, exploded: "A conference that manifestly was intended to put Quinby in the hands of the Churchillites, ignoring all the rest of us, merits contempt. Please don't have it repeated." Many Platform Republicans refused to endorse the party's candidate; most as well refused to support Clarence Carr, his Democratic opponent. The Taft campaign served to keep them in the party.[95] Carr ran a vigorous campaign on an anti-railroad, proreform platform and was mystified by the absence of Platform Republican supporters. James Remick, former president of the Lincoln Republican club, was the only prominent Republican publicly to support Carr. Quinby defeated Carr while running well behind William Howard Taft.[96]

In November 1908 the reform movement seemed in shambles. Churchill and other mainstays were somewhat discouraged, except that the Taft campaign had become their major concern and they were gratified by what they interpreted to be a national mandate for Roosevelt policies. A national victory was not a state victory for reform, for the Taft/Roosevelt victory ironically buttressed the old guard. The reformers, first to support candidate Taft, became a part of the Republican organization that supported nominee Taft. The discrete identity of reform Republicanism was lost at least temporarily. Dan Remich had warned Churchill early in the fall that he saw "no reason why we should sacrifice our principles and assist the old gang in tightening their hold on the politics of the state, in order to give Taft a big majority." Churchill rejected such advice and insisted that historical and philosophical differences within the state organization should be suppressed for the good of the national reform movement.[97] Remich proved to have a better sense of the situation than Churchill did.

Republican reform had a rocky road from 1906 through 1908. In the earlier year the reformers had benefited from the moral outrage that followed disclosure of the legislative history and intent of the Salem racetrack bill. The Churchill effort was further aided by real divisions in the party leadership as a result of Streeter's use of the railroad's political power. By 1908 these driving forces had begun to dissipate, a situation worsened by inconsistent reform leadership and objectives. The reformers had accomplished little more than to influence platform statements. It remained for them to demonstrate that they had the energy and the capacity to write these into law and to challenge effectively old guard leadership.

In the 1908 election there were a few bright spots for the New Hampshire reformers in legislative victories. In the Fifteenth District, Peterborough reformer Robert Bass won a seat in the state senate despite the opposition of the machine in his own Republican party. Bass told his colleagues not to surrender. "In this work I have tried to get myself into the frame of mind to look on temporary reverses as necessary incidents . . . and I think that the chance of the ultimate success of what we have undertaken depends largely upon our capacity to recuperate and rally from such temporary reverses, for if we do rally I feel very confident that they will be only temporary."[98] Few, least of all Bass, knew that already leadership in the reform movement had shifted and he would lead the process of recuperation and rally.

4

Robert Perkins Bass and the
Reform Victory

IN THE EARLY SPRING of 1910, the time of year called mud season in New Hampshire, the old guard press lashed out at the
reformers when it was reported that the latter had been secretly
making plans to campaign for the Republican gubernatorial nomination in that year. "While all this is being done in the name of reform," one editor fumed, "it is politics just the same and of a kind
just as old as the country. It merely marks the beginning of a new
era in the life of the Republican party in New Hampshire."[1]

The reformers did not engage in politics "just the same" as their
old guard Republican opponents, but neither did they totally challenge the political culture of New Hampshire. Indeed their success
may ultimately have derived from their ability to put the onus on
the old guard, the machine, as the deviant form. The reformers por-
trayed themselves as the real conservators of the state's political heritage. New Hampshire had a strong tradition of paying homage to
principles such as antimonopoly, democratic participation, and political efficacy. The extent to which the old guard Boston and Maine
political leaders may have abused these principles is a secondary
matter; in the period from 1906 to 1910 the reformers succeeded in
convincing citizens that this was the case. The "moral forces" of 1906
had focused on this presumed breach of principle. Their agenda was
essentially remedial. By 1909 this Churchill group had been augmented by others who shared the Lincoln Club's sense of outrage
but who used this outrage as the starting point rather than the universe of their political activity. Insurgency became more programmatic and less moralistic. Rhetorically the progressives still insisted
upon a return to traditional political principles; their activities,

however, symbolized and accelerated some basic changes in the New Hampshire political culture. Recovering the state's honor continued to be the insurgents' cohering theme, their political umbrella, but within this antirailroad coalition reformers sought—and disagreed over—more specific initiatives to meet the new problems of the new century. If, indeed, there was a new era beginning in the spring of 1910 it was one made possible at the outset by one of the few programmatic reforms demanded by the 1906 group: open nominations secured by primary elections. The reformers had played a role in 1909 in securing passage of the new law establishing this procedure; they would be first to understand and to take advantage of it.

The pivotal figure in the reform success was Robert Perkins Bass. In most regards Bass did not fit into the traditional Yankee politician image. Born in 1873, Bass in 1910 was an urbane, intellectually curious, young, wealthy bachelor. Despite the ironic surname coincidence, he was no Jethro Bass. Robert's father Perkins Bass, a Vermont native, had moved to Chicago in the 1850s after graduating from Dartmouth. It was a good time to go to that exploding young metropolis. The senior Bass read law and became involved in Republican politics, heading the Illinois reelection campaign of Abraham Lincoln in 1864. He married another transplanted New Englander, Clara Foster, who counted among her ancestors Jeremiah Smith, who had served as New Hampshire governor in 1809–10. Clara Foster was an intelligent, strong woman. Her father, Dr. John Foster, had amassed a small fortune. Perkins and Clara nurtured their share of it into a greater fortune, primarily in the form of real estate holdings in the vicinity of Chicago's expanding commercial district.[2]

In the 1880s Clara and Perkins left Chicago and moved back to the old Smith family farm which they had purchased. Here, near Peterborough, New Hampshire, in the shadow of Mount Monadnock, they lived a good and active life of semiretirement. Robert Bass was only nine years old when the family returned to New Hampshire. It was a comfortable life for the youngster, and one where he began early learning the responsibilities of managing money and land. Robert Bass attended Harvard College, graduating in 1896. These were exciting years for a philosophy major in the Cambridge school. He studied with James, Santayana, and Royce, participated in debates, joined the Hasty Pudding, the Amphadon, and the Fence Club. He earned his gentleman's B's and C's and apparently had a full social life.[3]

After his Harvard graduation Robert Bass sought a direction for his energies. A year of law school was unsatisfying as was a brief period as manager of family investments in Chicago. When his father died in 1899, Bass moved back to Peterborough. He had apparently already given some thought to a political career. A Harvard classmate and friend encouraged him to pursue it for he was "naturally fitted to influence other people," and while not an intellectual, he had good judgment and "tenacity of character." Further, his friend advised him, he should go to Peterborough for he would find Chicago politics too frustrating.[4]

Bass's interest in politics seemed more motivated by a desire for public service than by simple political ambition. At least there are no indications in his voluminous correspondence of a burning desire for office. He came into politics quite unobtrusively through his interest in forestry. Adopting modern timber management techniques for the several hundred acres of family forest lands in Peterborough, Bass became involved in the New Hampshire forest conservation movement. In 1904 he stood for a Peterborough seat in the state house of representatives and was elected. He was absent for much of the 1905 session, however, as he was convalescing from the effects of a serious attack of appendicitis. In 1906 he was reelected for a second term.[5]

Bass's position during the 1906 Churchill insurgency remains unclear. There is no indication that he supported Churchill or contributed in any way to the campaign. Perhaps his own instincts turned him away from an effort that seemed initially ludicrous; perhaps his own public service interests led him away from an early tarring by the insurgency brush. In the summer of 1906 the secretary of state suggested that Bass stay away from political activity while the latter's appointment to the state forestry commission was pending before the Governor's Council. Certainly Bass wanted this appointment as a logical outlet for his interest in forest conservation and public service.[6] In 1906 his political experiences had been minimal. There was no indication that the Churchill people sought his support—and indeed no reason for them to have done so.

In January 1907 Robert Bass began his second term as a member of the New Hampshire legislature. His concurrent service on the forestry commission was not unusual in New Hampshire. His work on the forestry commission over the next four years would be typically diligent as he and others sought to create the position of state forester, to rationalize conservation efforts, and to encourage national action in the creation of a White Mountain forest reserve.[7] These important—and ultimately successful—activities would eventually be secondary to the broader role he would play in New Hampshire political history. In 1907 House Speaker Bertram Ellis appointed him chairman of the Committee on Retrenchment and Reform. This was an inconsequential assignment; many judged it an

insult. Undoubtedly it was to some, but there is no reason to assume
Ellis's decision was based on any such motive. The thirty-three-
year-old Peterborough legislator had done nothing to earn banish-
ment to this legislative netherworld. And Ellis had also named Bass
to the forestry committee, certainly not suggestive of a punitive attitude on the speaker's part.[8]

The winter of 1907 was an exciting time in Concord. Winston
Churchill's People's Lobby was active in promoting passage of the
antilobby platform pledges of the GOP. Their failure in this session
would be frustrating to many, perhaps most of all to the impatient
Churchill, but one consequence of these activities would be the development of a cadre of young reformers. Robert Bass was one of
them. The Peterborough legislator immediately aligned himself
with the Lincoln Republican group, voted with them on the key
issues, and became a full and respected participant in their strategy
sessions over at the Sargent, Remick, and Niles law office.

Robert Bass's tenacity of purpose became evident that winter in
his Committee on Retrenchment and Reform work. He insisted that
the committee had to fulfill its legislative responsibility and public
obligation to inquire into "administration of public affairs." Further,
the 1906 Republican platform had called upon the next legislature
to inquire into state affairs to make certain there was neither "waste
nor extravagance"; Bass believed this pledge should be fulfilled. He
obtained a small budget and legislative authority to subpoena wit-
nesses. The committee investigated the operation and the budget-
ary controls of state offices, ranging from the secretary of state to
statehouse janitors. The work sometimes intruded into sensitive
areas, touching on public fiefdoms and sinecures. Someone resented
or feared these hearings enough to break into Bass's office and steal
the accumulated material; undaunted, the Peterborough legislator
started again.[9]

The final report recommended several administrative changes.
These included terminating positions, combining functions, insisting on a full day's work from state employees, and introducing a more
systematic accounting of costs and expenditures. The committee
was sharply critical of the end-of-session omnibus bill by which the
legislature appropriated necessary additional money. By custom this
bill included gratuities for state employees and for newspaper report-
ers covering the legislature. The committee pointedly suggested
that "as officials we may not becomingly bestow the people's moneys
as gifts."[10]

The 1907 legislature approved only some of the committee's recommendations. This report would, however, provide a blueprint for
administrative reform over the next several years. And Robert Bass,

who came to Concord unknown in January, left the capital with a solid reputation among the reformers. Allen Hollis, a Lincoln Republican and Concord attorney, wrote Churchill in June that Bass's "quiet determination is most encouraging. I don't know what his personal ambition is—if he has any—but I wish we had more like him. He is the only man in our crowd who really accomplished anything tangible last winter." Bass, observed Hollis, worked hard on "comparatively small things. Such men generally get larger things to manage in due season."[11]

After the 1907 legislative session Bass was fully a part of the reform group. He corresponded regularly with Churchill and others and participated in their discussions in Concord, Boston, and Cornish. He was a member of the Platform Republican group and of the delegation that discussed, unsuccessfully, with Henry Quinby a campaign agreement in 1908. He was also active with the Taft Republicans in 1908.

Bass's relationships with national political leaders were perhaps not as extensive as Churchill's; they were nonetheless significant. To a large extent they stemmed from the contacts of Robert's older brother John (b. 1866). John Foster Bass was an active, intriguing character. Never sharing Robert's interest in being permanently settled, he lived in Chicago from where he participated in a range of national and international activities. The Bass estate was substantial enough for him to have freedom to pursue a variety of interests; he took advantage of this. John Bass was an adventurer; he was a war correspondent who covered most major and minor conflicts in this pre–World War I period, including the Boxer Rebellion and the Russo-Japanese War. Like Robert he was a conservationist; John was active in the national forestry movement, through which he became friends with Gifford Pinchot and Theodore Roosevelt. John Bass also was active in Chicago affairs, including the local reformist Chicago Civic Federation. John then provided Robert with a variety of cosmopolitan connections, supplementing the latter's own ties, primarily those of Harvard.[12]

Robert Bass and Winston Churchill played major roles negotiating with the Taft administration on behalf of the New Hampshire reformers in 1909. The Granite State progressives wanted a federal appointment, one that had both symbolic and substantive importance—the state supervisor for the 1910 census. The symbolism was evident: let the administration acknowledge the reformers' contributions, as opposed to the old guard's resistance, to Taft's quest for the presidency. Substantively the census job had its own significant patronage which could assist the reformers' organizational effort.

The Platform Republicans determined to recommend to Taft, and to insist upon, the appointment of Frank Musgrove of Hanover as state census supervisor. The young Dartmouth graduate had participated in the organization of the Lincoln Club in 1906 and was publisher and editor of the *Hanover Gazette*, a solid reform weekly. Musgrove had done major service for the reformers in the 1907 legislative session and had been active in all of their subsequent activities. The census appointment took on greater importance in April 1909 when Taft named George Moses as ambassador to Greece. Moses had become an important leader in the anti-Churchill, old guard wing of the GOP, had participated energetically in the anti-Taft movement in 1908, and as a delegate to the Republican National Convention had joined with Gallinger in refusing to make the Taft nomination unanimous. In fact, Moses had been angling for this specific appointment for several years and had the assistance of not only Senator Gallinger but of ex-senator Chandler. They had pressed Theodore Roosevelt on this and, through Sen. Henry Cabot Lodge, had raised it with Taft shortly after the election. The president-elect had assured Lodge that there would "be no reprisals" against the New Hampshire party machine. Churchill was shocked at the recognition implicit in the appointment, but Taft privately assured him the move was made to disarm Senator Gallinger and to get Moses as far away as possible. The president reassured Churchill privately that he wanted to see "whether we can divorce the Boston and Maine from the Government." This explanation sufficed but could not remove the public sting of perceived rebuke. Now, the reform group reasoned, administration support for them became even more critical.[13]

Musgrove's nomination proved troublesome. The progressive journalist had been an outspoken foe of the old guard and now Taft, as president, was interested in conciliating all of his differences with Senators Gallinger and Burnham. And Gallinger especially had no disposition to be conciliatory toward the reformers, whom he increasingly thought of as his and his party's enemies. Gallinger had faced no opposition to his 1909 reelection in the state legislature; he was nonetheless uncompromising. He told Lyford that Streeter, Churchill, and their friends were "an unconscionable lot of political pirates. . . . if we cannot beat them, we can, at least, be beaten by them and the issue will have to be drawn sooner or later." If Lyford harbored plans for any more discussions with them, any more compromises, "I want to be counted out of the matter entirely." Burnham was personally opposed to Musgrove because of the latter's sharp criticism of him.[14] In frustration Taft asked Churchill if there "is not some one who has not called Burnham a corruptionist in New Hampshire" whom the reformers would recommend in place of the

feisty Musgrove. There was not, despite Rosecrans Pillsbury's willingness to take the appointment. The reformers stood firm behind
Musgrove; Bass and Manchester attorney Sherman Burroughs visited the president in July. Taft finally conceded the appointment.
Frank Streeter never got the judgeship he was after, however, for
which he privately blamed the Boston and Maine; Gallinger may
have been the more consequential figure in this decision.[15]

The whole Musgrove tempest was not worthy of the time and energy the reformers put into it. And the symbolism of the process was
more consequential in the long run than the symbolism of successful
recognition. Taft as president was more cautious in cozying up to
the reformers than Taft as candidate had been. Now the politics of
the presidency demanded, he believed, a closer relationship with the
old guard politicians who had opposed him in 1908: "It is a good deal
easier to get along smoothly if we can."[16] The distance between the
White House and the New Hampshire reform group would increase
dramatically in the next few years.

By the summer of 1908, Robert Bass had come to play an even
greater leadership role in the reform ranks. Partially this was due to
the vacuum left as Winston Churchill again became fully involved
with his writing and withdrew from most public activity. Churchill
published another novel in 1908, *Mr. Crewe's Career*, dedicated "to
the men who in every state of the union are engaged in the struggle
for purer politics." The novel dealt with the political initiation of a
well-to-do and naïve young reformer who ran up against the Railroad Lobby and the Machine. Mr. Crewe was frustrated at a riotous
convention in his attempt to secure the gubernatorial nomination.
The book ended on a hopeful note, a belief that in flexing their
power too freely the Railroad Forces had spelled their own fate. And
their chief counsel had left the railroad because of his dissatisfaction
with corporate manipulation and his son's distaste for railroad arrogance. Partly autobiographical, partly a composite of actual characters and events, and partly a result of Churchill's fertile imagination, *Mr. Crewe's Career* was another success for the author. It also
was a thinly veiled exposé of New Hampshire politics as Churchill
saw it. The publicity the book generated worked to the advantage of
the reformers. This time they were prepared to capitalize on the
situation.[17]

The 1909 session of the New Hampshire legislature provided the
proving ground and framework for the later reform success. And
here Robert Bass, now a member of the state senate, emerged as a
clear leader among those who increasingly labeled themselves progressives. The reform agenda by 1909 had expanded beyond, while
still including, the defensive antirailroad propositions of 1906. Any

discussion of this process must begin with the recognition that it was political; the reformers articulated and accomplished rather than originated. In fact the reform legislation had been essentially previewed in the 1908 state platforms of the Democratic and Republican parties, clearly due to the growing reform influence within each of these parties but as well due to the realization by party leaders generally that verbal recognition of these demands was politically desirable. After the Churchill effort there was some journalistic focus on the conditions in the state; groups as disparate as the state bar, the Grange, labor organizations, and the Society for the Protection of New Hampshire Forests were pushing for specific policies that the political parties were willing to include in their platforms. Political leaders, including reformers, assumed the role more of policy broker than of creator.[18]

In late 1908 Bass, Allen Hollis, and Edward Niles had begun drafting specific reform legislation. They were determined that in this instance recognition would be more than verbal. Controls on lobbying and greater strictures on the railroad's free passes remained important to the group, as did direct-primary legislation. These issues had been pushed regularly since the organization of the Lincoln Club. The Bass group also supported tax equalization, tougher laws defining corporate and railroad liabilities, reform of the railroad commission, and creation of the position of state forester. In most of these regards they managed to secure at least the nominal support of governor-elect Henry Quinby, who urged passage of these matters in his January address to the new legislature. James Lyford assisted in attempting to deliver on Republican platform promises.[19]

Robert Bass served in the 1909 session as senator from the Fifteenth District. He had campaigned hard on the platform issues and had won despite some old guard efforts to defeat him. Now he and his like-minded colleagues faced the difficult task of legislating. There was a strong group of reformers from each party in the house, sufficient to carry the day on several issues. Clarence Carr and Democratic chairman John Jameson urged the Democrats to support their party's reform promises: "If no action is taken, let the responsibility rest where it belongs."[20] The senate, however, remained the bastion of the old guard. These recalcitrant senators blocked or crippled several key items. Nonetheless the overall legislative record was good. The reformers secured passage, and Quinby signed a direct primary law, antipass legislation, partial tax reform, a law requiring lobbyists to register, and new statutes creating the posts of state auditor and state forester. It was a substantial record and one in which the progressive group took justifiable pride.[21] The railroad lobby was active in this session, but the reform movement and its publicity resulted in the lobby being more cautious—and possibly less powerful. Tax reform was particularly significant to the Boston and Maine railroad. The progressive Louis Wyman of Manchester wrote and submitted legislation that would provide, among other things, for greater railroad taxes. An alternative tax bill also appeared that ostensibly was aimed at the same goals, except it would not raise railroad taxes. Two legislators overheard chief Boston and Maine lobbyist Charles Hamblett in a telephone conversation assure President Tuttle that this specious bill would not harm the railroad and that the "boys" in the legislature were "in line" for the vote. Reporting to the house this conversation, the reformers managed to secure passage of the Wyman bill. It failed in the senate however.[22]

Bass would be proudest of the direct-primary bill, which he drafted and introduced. It provided for a closed (party) primary, for the reformers never challenged the role of political parties as organizing institutions; their goal was to assure that party processes, especially recruitment and nomination, be open. Probably Governor Quinby's support was essential to the passage of the legislation. Even Gallinger had joined Lyford in worrying about the fortunes of their party if the legislature again failed to deliver on platform promises. Lyford feared that railroad lobbying activities and influence were putting the GOP in a difficult position. Gallinger tempered his apprehension about the party record with a distaste for specific reforms such as the primary law: it "will certainly not help to make things in the State harmonious." The new primary law undoubtedly would prove critical to the nomination of a reform candidate for governor.[23]

It is not altogether clear when Robert Bass decided to enter the 1910 gubernatorial race. Certainly by the end of the 1909 legislative session in May he was mentioned as a leading progressive and as gubernatorial material. It is also clear that he did little to kindle this support. In fact he apparently did not want to run, at least at that time. In June a small "reunion" of progressives was held at the Riverside Inn in Hooksett. The group named Bass to an executive committee that included Robert Faulkner of Keene, J. W. Staples of Franklin, Frank Musgrove of Hanover, E. C. Cook of Concord, Clarence Clough of Lebanon, and Sherman Burroughs of Manchester. These were reform veterans, most having participated in the 1906 Churchill campaign. The committee's purpose was to maintain and direct the organization and activities of the progressive Republicans. Certainly many felt this had to include a 1910 gubernatorial campaign. As Clough wrote to Bass, "Abstract principles of political conduct are of little value apart from the men who carry them out. A

Churchill platform and Tuttle Governor have not worked in harmony during the past year." Bass shared the same sentiments with Churchill: "There is beginning to be some slight appreciation of the fact that in addition to passing reform measures in the legislature, we must have officials who will administer the laws in the same spirit in which they are enacted."[24]

Bass played a role in trying to encourage Burroughs or Churchill to run in 1910. The former seemed prepared to do this but surprised the reform group by withdrawing from the discussions in December 1909 when his law partners refused to give him a leave for a political campaign.[25] Churchill was preoccupied with personal and national concerns and showed little inclination to make a real campaign. Churchill felt estranged from his party as well. "Republicanism," he wrote, "is only a name. If Gallinger and Sulloway and Burnham are Republicans, then I am not." Despite William Chandler's energetic effort to get Burroughs back into the race—he believed the latter would be the stronger candidate—almost by default the burden fell on Bass.[26]

Bass's reluctance to run in 1910 stemmed partially from a conviction that any Republican would have difficulty winning in that year. The Republican party nationally seemed to be splintering over Taft's policies, particularly the president's clumsiness in dealing with congressional insurgents, his defenses of and exaggerated support for the Payne-Aldrich tariff, and his handling of the Ballinger-Pinchot affair. When Taft asked for the resignation of Chief Forester Gifford Pinchot because of his conflict with Interior Secretary Richard A. Ballinger, the old Roosevelt group howled. Robert and John Bass, both close to Pinchot, were particularly incensed, although Robert wrote that perhaps it was "just as well," for now the issues would be drawn and new leadership would develop. John Bass went on to make certain that the issues would be drawn as he helped publicize the issue and assist in Pinchot's defense; Louis Brandeis saluted him as the "*causa causams*," and *Collier's* editor Norman Hapgood credited the elder Bass with convincing the magazine to crusade against alleged corruption in Ballinger's Interior Department.[27]

Despite his own misgivings and his brother's conviction that 1910 would see a Democratic sweep in the eastern states, by early 1910 Robert Bass determined to run. The only condition he placed before the other progressives was that they had to generate petitions and offers of support prior to his announcement of candidacy. They did this. The insurgents impressed Bass with the extent of support they elicited for him, including an offer of support from Frank Streeter. By March, Robert Bass was in the race.[28]

Bass and his supporters entered the contest uncertain of how the old guard would respond. Some Bass advisers insisted that the regulars would not challenge Bass who had, after all, regularly affirmed his Republicanism—in distinction to the continued recalcitrance, if not apparent party disloyalties, of James Remick and Winston Churchill. The absence of a challenge was not appealing to Bass. He believed only a victory over their antagonists would consummate the reformers' sense of success. An uncontested nomination would be a hollow victory—and might presage defeat in November before an ominous Democratic challenge.[29] Bass had to insist that he had made no deal whereby the old machine would not challenge him.

The nomination would not come so easily. John Bass found prospects "too bright," and he warned Pinchot that the "machine" would launch "some nefarious scheme."[30] Chandler, only peripherally a part of the Republican inner circle, continued to worry that Bass, of whom he was personally fond, was not electable. Lyford agreed, and he worried about the political sense of "the progressives." Sen. Jacob Gallinger, now the clear leader of the old guard, was not prepared simply to concede the nomination. An early Lyford proposal to have Quinby challenge the single-term precedent failed to elicit either support or enthusiasm. Lyford believed that Benjamin Kimball had sabotaged it; in frustration Lyford exclaimed, "This whole railroad gang deserves to have [Democrat Clarence] Carr for governor." Gallinger met with various Republican—and railroad—officials to discuss possible candidates "of the regulars." He believed Bass was weak and might even withdraw if faced with a challenge. Bass and Gallinger met briefly in Washington, Henry Cabot Lodge handling arrangements, and Gallinger concluded that "Bass always impresses me with the feeling that he is something of a weakling, but perhaps I am mistaken in the man."[31]

As the spring passed Gallinger grew increasingly frustrated at the possibility of losing by default. It occurred to him that most Republicans were indifferent to the power struggle, "the rank and file of the party, especially the conservative end of it, doesn't care a rap what happens."[32] He wondered in May whether the regulars still might "hunt up some bright young man whose name has not yet been mentioned," then "we could sweep the primaries and elect him, but where is the man?" Two months earlier Lyford had anticipated the search and had a pessimistic answer: "We have failed to get hold of the young men for the past fifteen or twenty years." Who, he asked Chandler, could even campaign for a regular candidate in an open primary. Gallinger should not, and "there is nobody left but railroad attorneys, and they would hurt more than they would help." A Concord friend of Chandler's wondered "if the party leaders realize what the popular sentiment really is?"[33] When Benjamin Kimball finally asked Gallinger for help, the latter lashed out: "I have a very vivid recollection of the outcome of the Greenleaf campaign. If the Boston and Maine Railroad, through its agents and attorneys, had stood up in that fight" for Greenleaf, then "a great many of the troubles that are now upon the party would never have developed." He did not understand why the organization could not find a candidate to save the party from "the 'combine' that has been formed . . . to control the politics of the State." While Gallinger was not prepared "to dragoon anybody into the contest," he agreed to meet with Kimball and other interested officials in July when he returned to New Hampshire.[34] In midsummer Bertram Ellis of Keene announced his candidacy. Ellis was clearly in the nonreform wing of the party and was friendly to the Boston and Maine, both of which he demonstrated in 1907 when he served as speaker of the New Hampshire house of representatives. Ellis had an ample campaign fund and many organization Republicans behind him. He insisted that if he were elected he would not be dominated by the railroad "or Winston Churchill or Daniel C. Remich."[35]

Robert Bass's campaign in New Hampshire's first direct primary was a model of superior organization. Orchestrated by Chairman Edmund Cook of Concord, the Bass campaign worked from lists of supporters and potential supporters in each town. Bass traveled the state in an automobile, speaking extensively, and accompanied by a secretary/press agent with a typewriter to issue releases, help prepare speeches, and maintain a massive correspondence. Others were on the stump as well; meetings were well advanced; handbills and buttons were ready—including foreign-language circulars. Pamphlets printed in Yiddish were distributed among the state's relatively small group of Jewish voters. William Jewett Tucker's warm praise for the candidate became the basis for another circular. The young candidate, pulling on some old Smith family roots, confided to a Manchester Irish leader that "I have a bit of Irish blood in my veins." Bass dusted off his shaky Harvard French and gave a few French-language addresses; French-Canadian supporters did the same, presumably more easily. The progressive candidate introduced what the *Union* considered a "novelty" by campaigning at factory gates. John Bass visited the state regularly, offering advice that was not always appreciated by the local campaign workers.[36]

To guard against the election being stolen, John Bass engaged several private detectives to keep an eye on the opposition. Infiltrating political groups in several cities, they sent the candidate's brother daily reports on the Ellis campaign. It is not clear if Robert Bass was aware of this tactic; given the closeness of the two brothers, probably he was.[37] On a different level, however, Robert Bass had been emphatic on several occasions that he would not "buy" an election. All expenditures had to be accounted to him and, despite the insistence of some like Senator Chandler, now a Bass supporter, that buying votes was traditional in some communities and that it was necessary to win before one could reform the system, Bass flatly rejected all such tactics.[38] In 1909 he had attempted unsuccessfully to get a bill passed requiring the disclosure of campaign spending. In the 1910 campaign he determined that he would disclose his expenditures anyway. He would not back away from this promise nor would he countenance hiding any expenditures. He did spend money though. As one associate told him, "When you are out to smash a machine which has outlived its usefulness, it is going to take money every time." In one campaign appearance he was heckled for spending so much money on the campaign; his retort was that at least he was spending his own money and not that of the Boston and Maine, turning the onus back on Ellis and his alleged railroad financing.[39]

Bass did have some burdens in 1910. The opposition depicted him as a young millionaire playboy, and his bachelor status generated rumors about "his conduct with some women." Bass also had to confront the prohibition issue. He drank liquor, a fact about which he was discreet but never dishonest. He told one activist, "I have never professed to be a total abstainer." Bass's legislative record, particularly his support of 1909 legislation to protect nonlicense towns, ultimately earned him the unofficial endorsement of the state Anti-Saloon League.[40] He simply ignored rumors about his personal conduct and weathered the gossip well. On another matter, Bass had opposed woman suffrage in the legislature, a position he shared with some other progressives. By 1910 he had begun to trim on this issue; shortly he would be a warm supporter of the woman suffrage movement.[41]

The Bass campaign stressed the need to defeat the railroad's political influence. The candidate promised reform of taxation, enforcement of existing freight and express laws, establishment of a public utilities commission to replace the railroad commission, conservation of forest and other natural resources, and a workmen's compensation law. His pledge was to put the "people" back in power and to provide a "square deal." The latter Rooseveltian linkage was never far from the surface of his campaign. Bass found himself in the spotlight as a successful eastern Republican reformer. Ray Stannard

Robert P. Bass (Robert P. Bass, Jr.)

Baker published an article in *American Magazine* suggesting that New Hampshire, among eastern states, was "the one nearest political freedom" as Bass, the 1909 legislative leader, now was challenging publicly Lucius Tuttle, whom Baker called "The real Governor." The *Boston Transcript* concluded that Bass had "done most to bring East of the Mississippi the legislative reforms of the West."[42]

Part of Bass's problem in 1910 was the need to educate New Hampshire voters on the operation of the direct primary. He did this by working with the Direct Primary Association, personally purchasing and distributing ten thousand of their pamphlets explaining the new law. This may have had some effect. On September 7, 1910, nearly thirty thousand Republican voters turned out for New Hampshire's first primary, despite a rainstorm, and gave Bass a two-to-one victory over Bertram Ellis. This turnout was approximately equal to two-thirds of the Republican gubernatorial vote in 1908. Excepting the railroad's political figures, there was little surprise or disappointment among most old guard Republican leaders. Gallinger had pretty much washed his hands of the Ellis campaign by August because Ellis seemed uninterested in Gallinger's advice; it was, Gallinger concluded, a "hap-hazard" effort. "I am doing all I can," the senator told Lyford, "but hate to be part of any machine that hasn't any organization. I have never been invited to help organize it."[43] Many considered Ellis more of a railroad man than a party man, an increasingly important distinction. Moses said Ellis's defeat "neither surprises nor disappoints me. I never had any use for Ellis. He has always been such a pet of Ben Kimball's, who made him speaker when nobody else wanted him." If, as seemed the case, the railroad's political operatives were the big losers, there were few mourners.[44]

Bass's immediate concern after the primary was to pull the party together for what appeared to be shaping up as an unusually difficult general election challenge for a New Hampshire Republican. The progressive Clarence Carr again headed the Democratic ticket and had a united party behind him for an election in which the national trend seemed to be toward the Democrats. The Republican State Convention followed the primary by nearly three weeks; in this period Bass and his advisors set out to use this forum to unify their party, but without compromising their goals. Bass was uneasy with Chandler's suggestion for a preconvention meeting of the progressives in a "people's convention" to plan their strategy. Planning went on certainly, but in a private and less provocative manner and with Chandler playing a lesser role. Bass's conciliatory tone was a sign of his confidence: "We are the party and must be a big party," he told one of his close associates.[45]

Robert Bass could afford both conciliation and confidence. The convention was his; the primary law had also provided for direct election of convention delegates, and the progressive organization responded to this new process. Old Lincoln Republican veteran Dr. John Gile of Hanover chaired a convention marked by expressed unanimity. The convention approved without public dissent a platform prepared by a committee named by Bass and chaired by Louis Wyman.[46]

The 1910 Republican state platform was a strong document that asserted the principles of Robert Bass and his fellow progressives, but again without needless provocation. President Taft, increasingly a subject of private scorn, received his due public praise; with a subtle hint at impending difference, the delegates applauded Taft for "carrying out in such a large measure the policies inaugurated by Theodore Roosevelt." The platform encouraged national efforts to gain "more efficient control" over railroads, create a tariff commission, examine the question of employers' liability, enact corporate taxes, and conserve natural resources. Particularly the delegates supported the development of a national forest reserve in the White Mountains. Further the document applauded the insurgent revolt against House Speaker Joseph P. Cannon.

On state matters, the convention congratulated the 1909 legislature for "progressive legislation" by "the party of action." The direct primary, proclaimed those elected by its provisions, was "an unqualified success," which now needed to be extended to include delegates to national party conventions. The platform promised improvements, if needed, in the antilobby law, and enactment of tax equalization, explicitly including greater tax obligations for corporations. The group approved commitments to control effectively railroad rates, establish a vigorous public utilities commission, protect water and forest resources, maintain highways through an automobile tax that increased rates with auto weight, enact employer's liability and workmen's compensation laws, require campaign expense disclosure, pass a corrupt practices act, prohibit corporate political contributions, ratify the federal income tax amendment, and effectively control liquor traffic in nonlicense towns.[47] Frank Streeter drafted and submitted through Chandler a statement insisting that "corporations get out and keep out of politics"; the delegates adopted this language and some other elements of his proposal.[48]

It was a progressive document, and the convention was a heady occasion for the reform majority among the delegates. They proclaimed their party revitalized with its original spirit; traditional Republicanism demands "not only the form but the substance of liberty and . . . insists that governmental action shall be the true expression of the will of the people." Robert Bass spoke to the delegates, affirming his personal commitment to these principles and going beyond the platform by insisting upon the direct election of U.S. senators. The latter was part of the draft platform but was deleted, apparently by Rosecrans Pillsbury, in a spirit of compromise with the old guard that caused some consternation among the progressives. Pillsbury was in a bit of a snit at this time for, as he wrote to Chandler after the primary, "I can hardly understand . . . why all the newspapers in the country give all the credit to Churchill, after I was the originator of the fight, carried it on for months before

Churchill came in, made two campaigns when they couldn't find anybody else to do it, and insisted upon Bass staying in this fight in the
winter." Pillsbury apparently forgot that in May he had recounted
for Chandler his efforts to get Bass to withdraw from the race.[49]

The machine against which the progressives had fought was in
total disarray by the fall of 1910. The railroad had been more cautious in its political activities since 1906, using its influence, which
was still considerable, on matters only of direct consequence for the
railroad. Essentially this meant taxes and the threat of increased tax
obligations through equalization plans. The Boston and Maine and
New Haven railroad merger became the focus of the railroad activity, and New Hampshire was peripheral at best to this fray.[50] In
the fall of 1910 Charles Mellen, president of the New Haven railroad, replaced Lucius Tuttle as president of the Boston and Maine,
effecting and symbolizing the fact of merger. Mellen promised to
stay out of politics.[51] It was a promise heard before in the Granite
State, but at the least it was clear that the railroad had no need to
pick a scrap with Robert Bass or Clarence Carr. Neither had shown
any disposition in the past to be intimidated. Following the primary,
Jack Kelley, Portsmouth lawyer and railroad counsel who had a good
enough mind and quick enough wit that Chandler considered him a
friend despite his connections, wrote Bass that while he did not
agree with the candidate in all regards, "if we have got to have a St.
Louis man for Governor I think I would rather have you than any of
that bunch." Churchill was, of course, from St. Louis; Bass was born
in Chicago. Apparently Kelley considered the Missouri city precise
enough in describing the origins of all of the out-of-state "bunch."[52]

The "machine" and the railroad were really separate entities after
1906, although they had clearly found mutual support to be mutually beneficial. Sen. Jacob Gallinger was the most powerful and significant leader of the old guard (i.e., nonprogressive) wing of the
party. He had cooperated with railroad officials but had not deferred
to them after 1904. He was being too disingenuous when he publicly
suggested before the primary that "we fellows who are candidates
cannot object if perchance men who are supporting us are attorneys
for the railroads." Despite reform overtures for party reconciliation,
Gallinger showed no inclination to compromise his differences with
Robert Bass. These were less personal than his antagonism toward
Churchill; increasingly they were philosophical. By 1910 the conservative Gallinger had come to feel and express a profound contempt
for the reformers' ideas. He asked rhetorically, "How can I participate in a campaign the issues of which will be the heresies of Chandler, Churchill and Roosevelt?" He feared Bass would shift the party

even more in this radical direction, and he presciently worried about "a possibility that Roosevelt may utterly wreck the party and organize a new party, founded on issues even more radical than those which prevail today." Always Gallinger's antagonism toward the progressives revolved around the issue of who would control the Republican party in New Hampshire. His own pride clearly was wounded by insurgent boasts that the progressives had defeated the old guard, of which he explicitly was a part. Gallinger felt insulted by claims that the Bass victory was a victory for "clean politics": "Oh! Lord, Oh! Lord. Wonder if anybody is fool enough to believe that the political situation has been purified by the nomination of Bass." As far as Gallinger was concerned, "It was a rich man's triumph." Despite Lyford's pleas to "put yourself in a proper *party* attitude," Gallinger refused to participate in the 1910 election.[53]

Bass's Democratic opponent, Clarence Carr, bore his scars from antirailroad wars, scars that by 1910 were campaign medals in New Hampshire. Carr was unopposed in the primary, and his party met in convention five days before the Republicans. The spirit and substance of the New Hampshire Democratic conclave were as reformist as the Republican meeting would be. The Democratic platform was a succinct statement of progressive principles and a preview of the Republican document. There was little substantive difference between the two, except the Democrats affirmed their support for local option and condemned "Republican extravagance" in state government. Democrats supported the initiative and referendum, putting them in advance of the mute Republicans on this issue.[54] This reform, of major importance elsewhere, never became an objective of the progressive Republican movement in New Hampshire.

Democrats assaulted Republican "hypocrisy" and "broken pledges"; this was to be a theme of their campaign. Its effectiveness was reduced because it was hard to pin this charge on Robert Bass. Objectively there seemed little difference between the platforms and the candidates. That is not to say voters perceived no difference. Voter images of specific candidates tended to be filtered by their broader perceptions of the history, the constituency, and the leadership of the parties. Here, if there was indeed a reform mood in the electorate, the Republicans may have had an edge. The movement to reform that party over the previous several years had been well publicized. Democratic reformers like Carr, ironically because they had less of a struggle in bending their party, had less of a reform image. And Democrats still projected a cautious approach to government activity as well as an image of ties to saloons and ethnic political leadership, especially Irish, that seemed the antithesis of reformism. Progressive Republicans like Louis Wyman blamed Democrats for the defeat of the tax reform bill of 1909, a theme that Bass, with uncharacteristic partisan distortion, picked up in the campaign.[55]

Bass was embarrassed by some of his own colleagues in his effort to pull together a united party. Recognizing early in 1910 the importance of having reform supporters in the next legislature, Bass had asked Winston Churchill to help recruit and coordinate candidacies, to initiate a "detailed and systematic campaign" to encourage the "right sort of men." The gubernatorial candidate believed that he personally had to stay out of contested local primaries.[56] After the primary there clearly were legislative races where the Democratic nominee was more committed to reform than was his Republican opponent. Some progressive Republicans, led by James Remick of Concord who had publicly supported Carr in 1908, urged Bass to collaborate with Carr in securing the election of progressive representatives, regardless of party. Bass was by nature a strong Republican; he could not be otherwise as candidate. He told Remick that "when great principles and definite policies are specifically adopted by a party and when a majority of that party stands unitedly in support of those principles . . . [then] the best means of securing these ends is through that party."[57] The GOP, he believed, was more principled than the Democratic party. If this conclusion was a practical affirmation of Republicanism in 1910, it also previewed Bass's bolting of his party in 1912 when the assumptions that guided it would be shaken.

Bass kept his party together throughout the campaign, ultimately gaining at least tacit support from key old guard leaders excepting Senator Gallinger. Bass friend Sherman Burroughs, after refusing to run for governor, had finally run against Congressman Sulloway in the primary. Bass stayed out of the fray, which Burroughs lost.

Despite Bass's effort to keep the party organization sound at the grass roots, he would play some role in dividing it at the top. In the spring he had asked Gifford Pinchot about the possibility of Theodore Roosevelt campaigning in New Hampshire if Bass won the nomination. In early July, after Roosevelt's return from abroad, Bass and Churchill met the ex-president at Oyster Bay. Roosevelt was quite willing to campaign for Bass, an offer he eagerly repeated after the latter won the primary.[58] There was a difference of opinion about the Roosevelt visit within the state's progressive ranks. The developing Taft-Roosevelt cleavage seemed to advise against linking the state campaign with the Rough Rider. Bass and Churchill, however, had already chosen sides in this skirmish and rejected advice to keep the state movement separate. Bass insisted that a Roosevelt visit "will gain us more votes in New Hampshire than any other one thing in the campaign." Roosevelt toured the state in October with Bass, warmly endorsing the candidate and lashing out at corporate intervention in politics. The former president insisted that the principles of the progressive movement in New Hampshire were part of a nationwide reform spirit of which Granite Staters were in the vanguard. Roosevelt's *Outlook* repeated these strong endorsements of Bass for putting New Hampshire "well to the front among Republican progressive States."[59]

President Taft attempted to keep his ties open to the Granite State reformers by pressing Gallinger to campaign for Bass. He failed in both the immediate and long-term goals. By 1910 the reformers did not trust the president. In May a Bass friend with Washington ties had warned not to expect "any help or good will from the Taft administration." The president's late gestures were to no avail.[60]

With the aid of Edmund Cook of Concord, his campaign manager who had served Churchill in 1906, and a handful of others, Robert Bass had undertaken an active campaign. He struck out at the railroads and at corporate control of politics, but he also campaigned for the programs of the Republican platform. He believed there was a spirit of reform of which he was but a part, "an insignificant atom." This spirit was "not a movement of a group of men or even of a state. It is nation wide." The question was fundamental: "Are we to be ruled by an oligarchy, or will the people of this country choose to rule themselves, to work out their salvation under the principles of true democracy established by our forefathers?" He believed that the Republic's democratic principles had "been temporarily lost sight of" during the recent period of change and "tremendous development." But now "the virility of our great nation has brought them to the front again" for the citizens to take action. Bass insisted he was not antibusiness: "I am no trustbuster." But he did campaign for "a square deal," for "special interests" to "bear their fair share of the burdens of state," and, using Streeter's language, for business to "get out and keep out of politics." Bass campaigned on his own legislative record and, unlike some of the other Republican campaigners, seldom discussed national matters.[61] He focused largely on state policy and on specific issues, all related to his explicit reform principles; that these principles reflected the personal conviction of Robert Bass there is little doubt. He had repeated them and acted upon them, in private as well as in public, for several years prior to his candidacy. This does not mean necessarily that his election represented a triumph of these principles.

Robert Bass defeated Clarence Carr by some 7,000 votes out of 84,000 cast. It was an important victory; Bass clearly brought with him a house of representatives that was compatible with his views; the senate, where the railroad and its allies had successfully blocked or altered some reforms in 1909, would be another matter. Here there was not a reform majority. Bass's election was both a personal and a philosophical triumph. Certainly the progressive movement, which was marked by some shared views and attitudes, was both broader and older than was Bass's involvement as a reformer. He built upon the Churchill base. Yet Bass was more than a willing point man for the progressives, more than the convenient candidate for an inevitable victory. Churchill played only a minimal role in the Bass campaign. He apparently felt offended by some slight and withdrew temporarily from the campaign. In addition, he was involved with out-of-state speaking, what he called "foreign missions," and campaigned in the fall "for good government" in Illinois and Indiana, in the latter on behalf of Sen. Albert Beveridge.[62]

The electoral support for Bass in 1910 was essentially that of recent Republican candidates. There was no apparent mobilization of new support. Bass had defeated Ellis in the primary by a two-to-one ratio statewide. This margin was repeated in most towns, quite independent of their demographic, economic, or cultural characteristics: poor towns, wealthy towns, farming towns, industrial towns, towns marked by population growth, and towns marked by a declining population. The Bass support was strong in all constituencies. An exception was the greater Ellis support in Freewill Baptist and Baptist towns, particularly the latter group, which he actually carried. Among other religious groups there was no significant deviation from the two-to-one Bass margin.[63] Ironically, given Bass's position as an issue-related candidate, there was no relationship between his or Ellis's support and town voting on constitutional amendments in 1912, including several basic tax items.[64] Bass clearly differed with Ellis, and in some fundamental ways; his voting constituency and that of Ellis did not differ. At the grass-roots, mass political level, Bass's victory was not the product of a coalition marked by any apparent like—or even significantly like-minded—characteristics.

Bass's postprimary effort to bring the Republican party together was either successful or unnecessary. In any event there was no obvious attrition from Ellis support to Carr between September and November. There was some Republican attrition from 1908 to 1910, but this by no means was distinguished by Ellis support in the primary.[65] Bass's support in the general election came largely from traditional Republican towns and wards.

TABLE 4.1
Cohesion and Disagreement Scores, House of Representatives, 1909

Bill	Percentage in favor			Disagreement Scores	
	Democratic	Republican	Bass supporter	Democratic v. Republican	Bass supporters v. remaining Republicans
Establish tax commission	39	21	35	18	27
Reconsider tax commission approval	60	49	76	11	50
Remove tax commission bill from table	35	50	24	15	49
Provide for election of railroad commissioners	95	39	61	56	42
Provide for general corporation law	62	28	45	34	31
Provide permanent improvement of main highways	48	61	48	13	25
Amendment to law providing state aid for main highways	58	74	63	16	20
Provide additional normal school facilities	36	36	35	0	1
Provide municipal suffrage for women	58	60	51	2	17
Refer liquor legislation to next legislature	75	68	49	7	33
Reconsider senate amendment to Liquor Regulation Act	43	30	12	13	34
Resolution approving President Taft's tariff revision plans	9	89	84	80	10
Postpone bill on assessment and collection of poll taxes	48	18	17	30	1

The key to Bass's victory may have been his organization as much as his substantive appeal, although the former clearly related to the latter. The candidate depended on key supporters in all of the towns and cities to mobilize his vote both in the primary and the general election. These supporters, whom Bass's well-used lists defined as "reliable men," give some insight into the ambiguity of the reform victory.[66]

Fully 128 of Bass's reliable men were members of the house of representatives in the 1909 legislature. This is a revealing indicator of accretion in the reform ranks as well as a partial explanation of the success of that legislative session. Yet it is important to note that these legislators were Bass supporters in 1910, but not necessarily supporters of Bass's views. Table 4.1 summarizes the pattern of roll calls on all major issues considered in the 1909 session.[67] The disagreement scores verify what had seemed obvious by this time: Republicans disagreed among themselves as extensively as they disagreed with Democrats on important policy questions. Of the issues summarized here, only on four votes (election of railroad commissioners, a general corporation law, a resolution supporting the Taft tariff policy, and postponement of a change in poll tax assessment and collection) did interparty disagreement exceed Republican intraparty disagreement.

Yet another aspect of the 1909 voting should have been ominous to Robert Bass as he prepared to govern. Only on four of the thirteen issues did his "reliable men" in the legislature exceed two-thirds cohesion. They were less cohesive than the remaining Republicans, and they were only marginally more cohesive than the Democrats. These figures suggest that some of Bass's key support related to factors other than consensus on what were some central issues of the reform program. Like-mindedness on policy questions did not distinguish this group of progressives. Bass was issue oriented; it would be fair to assume that most of his supporters were as well. The evidence suggests that they were not all oriented in the same direction. Reform victory in 1910 related primarily to accumulated grievances against the railroad. The moral outrage of 1906 had never died; now it was fanned by insurgents who had the discipline and the skill to out-organize the party organization. Robert Bass controlled a subset of the Republican party, but a subset not clearly sharing a common attitude on public issues. The 1910 victory was political more than ideological.

Robert Bass prepared to govern, as he did most things, systematically. He did bask momentarily in the attention he received. Progressive Republicanism had an important northeastern victory in this year of Democratic triumph throughout the East. Senator Beveridge wrote Bass that "progressives throughout the country" were inspired to see that "the fires of liberty once more are lighted on New Hampshire's hills." Sen. Jonathan Dolliver of Iowa replied to Beveridge, "Thank God for that; may they burn forever."[68] Bass's problem was more practical though; he had to keep burning the fire of success. As James Remick wrote the governor-elect, the progressives had to "show that we are not mere destructive agitators but *progressive constructionists.*"[69]

5

The Stand at Armageddon

JANUARY 5, 1911, was one of those ambivalent winter days in northern New England. By late morning the temperature in Concord had climbed to twenty-two degrees, and there were intermittent flashes of a bright winter sun reflecting off of the light snowfall of the previous night. Regardless of the weather, presumably the progressives were warm; after nearly five years of struggle, one of their own was governor. Robert Perkins Bass took his oath of office and then spoke to the joint session of the General Court. As befitted his growing reputation, he was direct and he was consistent with his earlier positions. The *Patriot* correspondent noted that Bass's address "should allay the fears of all persons who thought Mr. Bass, once elected, would forget the reform platitudes he sang so well." The *Boston Journal* interpreted this moment more enthusiastically as "the beginning of a new and decidedly encouraging epoch in the history of New Hampshire." The *Monitor* surveyed editorial opinion throughout New England and found a "chorus of commendation." *Monitor* reporter Harlan Pearson wrote William E. Chandler that he found Bass "honest and courageous. They may fool him, but they will not scare him or buy him."[1]

The progressive Republicans would find the next two years marked by success and failure, by excitement and frustration. And more than in the previous period, when Winston Churchill was an intermittent leader if a constant symbol, the history of progressive reform in 1911 and 1912 was linked with the life of one man, Robert Bass. Governor Bass's principles and judgment would lead the reformers to their greatest victories and to their bickering disintegration. He attempted to affix a successful state reform coalition onto a national movement. If his principles were sound and constant, his tactics were not always.

Following his election victory over Clarence Carr, Bass prepared

carefully for his gubernatorial term. Within two weeks of his election he had set up committees of his supporters to draft legislation.
Particularly he wanted bills to deal with automobile regulation and
taxation, employer's liability and workmen's compensation, the establishment of a public utilities commission, a corrupt practices act,
full disclosure of campaign contributions and expenditures, tax reform, improvements in the direct primary law, and an expanded
public advocate role for the state attorney general. As he had done
so often in the campaign, Bass turned to Frank Musgrove of Hanover and asked him to coordinate this effort. The governor-elect personally chose and contacted the individuals to take on these assign-
ments. They included old and familiar names, lawyers primarily,
who had been active in the reform movement, people such as James
Remick, Louis Wyman, Allan Hollis, Ed Niles, and Sherman Burroughs. But the group included influential Democratic progressives
such as Samuel Felker and Raymond Stevens; Bass's friend George
Rublee (b. 1868) had important responsibilities. Rublee was a New
York lawyer and sometime Cornish resident.[2]

Rublee would prove a key individual that winter in negotiations
about New Hampshire railroad policies. In the period immediately
after the election many of these issues remained complicated by recent legal, political, and corporate events. Charles Mellen, the new
president of the Boston and Maine, had reaffirmed his policy of
keeping the railroad out of politics. But this left, he feared, a significant communication gap between the railroad and the state government. Consequently Mellen wrote Bass in early December to describe directly the railroad's position. Mellen suggested that he
should have "the same freedom in communicating with the Executive, in reference to matters affecting" the railroad, that "the head
of any department of State" had. Further, he lectured, the governor
had a responsibility to understand the "needs of these public service corporations" much as he had to be informed about the needs
of state departments. Railroad solicitor Edgar Rich had previewed
this approach when he wrote Churchill that the railroad would like
to communicate directly with the governor-elect regarding legislation since they could not reach the legislature through the "customary means."[3]

There were two complex and related issues that Mellen sought to
negotiate with Bass, each reflecting the demise of railroad political
influence and the effect of several years of reform. In 1909 the state
board of equalization, responding to the criticism of the special 1908
tax commission, increased the valuation, and thus the taxes, of railroad property. Further, in 1908 the attorney general had taken long-

delayed action against the Boston and Maine railroad for excessive rates. State statutes in 1883, 1889, and 1891, designed to accommodate railroad consolidation, had also established maximum rates. As early as 1903 the Boston and Maine had begun exceeding some of these rates.[4]

As Bass prepared to assume office there were two court cases pending that involved the railroad and the state. The Boston and Maine sued the state for what it argued were excessive taxes; the state action against the railroad for exceeding statutory rate limits was still in litigation. Mellen conceded to governor-elect Bass that the railroad desired to compromise these issues and get them out of the courts. A lengthy and expensive legal dispute would drain railroad and state resources and attention while each had other matters to address. Bass was unwilling to accept Mellen's terms for compromise; indeed the governor-elect did not even make a substantive response, a fact that "keenly disappointed" Edgar Rich.[5]

Ironically, by early January James Lyford had begun to express his fear that the reformers were trimming on the railroad issue. He worried that Bass might compromise on either taxes or rates. This concern derived from what he believed to be Musgrove's closeness to Frank Streeter. The latter, the old guard's bête noire for all of these years, proved a veritable political phoenix. Charles Mellen had recently engaged Streeter to do some work for the railroad in Concord—perhaps in response to Edgar Rich's suggestion a year earlier that the New Hampshire situation was "serious" and that Streeter, along with Jack Kelley and John Mitchell, might be useful men for Mellen to meet because of their familiarity with the Granite State situation.[6]

Robert Bass chose his inaugural address as the vehicle to present his position on the railroad dispute. Thus his January 5 address to the legislature took on more than ceremonial importance. In the speech he gave little hint of compromise on the tax dispute: "this [tax] assessment was made by a responsible board acting in good faith and upon honest convictions." Perhaps the state would lose in court, but "principles are involved"; the legislature should appropriate money required for litigation in order to protect "the rights of the State." On the rate case, Bass conceded that railroad rates might need to be higher than the nineteenth-century legislation permitted, but for now the corporation was charging "illegal rates." The legislature should not "oppress" the railroad, but on the other hand "ancient safeguards established for the rights of the people against oppression of monopoly . . . should neither be withdrawn, released nor suspended except for strong reasons clearly demonstrated."

Bass had yet to see this demonstration: "practically all the data involved are in the hands of the party seeking relief. . . . the burden of proof is upon the petitioner."[7]

Bass used these pending matters to advance the reformers' proposition that the interests of the state demanded legislative establishment of a permanent tax commission and a public utilities commission. The latter should regulate the practices and charges of transportation, telephone, telegraph, light, heat, and power corporations "to protect the right and interest of the public." This goal, Bass believed, necessitated a strong commission with authority over the "rates, service and capitalization" of these companies. A tax commission, on the other hand, would insure generally equitable tax assessment, including fixing the tax liabilities of the public service companies which should "bear their fair share of the burden of taxation, no more, no less." Bass repeated his demands that corporations "get out and keep out of politics." Their interests were "selfish" and "injurious to the interests of our citizens." He asked the legislature to prohibit corporate political contributions and to require candidates for office to disclose fully their receipts and expenditures of money.[8]

The newly inaugurated governor called for legislative action in several other areas. He asked for employer's liability and workmen's compensation ("The financial burden of the industrial accident should be frankly recognized as part of the cost of production. It is time that the community at large pay this debt of flesh and blood, which it is in honor bound to take from the shoulders of those least able to bear it, the families of the workingmen"); effective factory inspection and a reorganized Bureau of Labor (that "will be of some real use in advancing and protecting the interests of the working men and women of New Hampshire"); more effective child labor legislation ("The State cannot guard its children too zealously during their period of growth and education"); greater state supervision of dependent minors and regulation of children's boardinghouses (present practices "justly subject us to censure. Humanity and self-respect alike demand that an end be put to these revolting practices"); greater state appropriations for aid to local schools and full support for the normal schools and the State Agricultural College at Durham; state aid for highways, with these moneys partially raised through automobile taxes increasing in proportion to weight and horsepower; extension of the direct-primary law to include selection of delegates to national conventions as well as U.S. senators; ratification of the federal income tax amendment; enlargement of forestry commission responsibilities to include "better" fire protection and management of a state nursery as well as acquisition of

land, particularly Crawford Notch. The *Monitor* reported that the
conclusion of the fifty-five-minute address was marked by "hearty
and long continued" applause.[9]

Governor Bass's speech reflected the growth of the reform movement and its programmatic expansion. The demands he placed before the General Court, most of which were followed with specific
drafts of legislation, would place the state in the vanguard of progressive reform in several policy areas. The political leadership
Robert Bass had assumed in 1909 had given him major responsibilities—and opportunities. The movement that had grown to maturity
in the period from 1906 to 1910 was not always a cohesive force. It
was marked by a general dissatisfaction with corporate and machine
control of the Republican party and, through this organization, influence over the government of the state. Those who defined themselves as progressives shared in this dissatisfaction, and perhaps
they were distinguished from others who felt offended by machine
control in that the progressives believed they could do something
about this problem. They did, but their behavior in forums like the
state legislature suggests they were not a cohesive group. They
shared in the view that corporate control could—indeed, must—be
stopped; they did not share a coherent vision beyond this.

Robert Bass had the opportunity to articulate a vision of the responsibility of the modern state. He began to do this in his campaign, and he continued to develop his ideas while governor. To say
it was his personal vision is not to suggest it was not shared; his legislative success suggests the opposite. Here the key may have been
less shared vision and more shared values, less movement and more
mood, less Bass's creative imagination and more his capacity to assimilate, articulate, and aggressively pursue ideas that others, both
in and outside of New Hampshire, were expressing.

Sometime Cornish resident Herbert Croly would later observe
that successful reform had to move from an insurgency phase,
marked by "just resentment," to a progressive phase marked by "a
thoroughgoing curiosity" that pursued abuses and sought to understand underlying problems. Robert Bass had this curiosity. Prior to
1910 his expressed policy concerns focused on conservation, good
roads, and good government, matters of relevance to a young,
wealthy, gentleman farmer. But as a state senator and as a gubernatorial candidate he began to confront, and to reflect upon, broader sets
of problems. National publications and New Hampshire labor leaders and politicians introduced him to the problems of industrial
labor. He decided that employer's liability was not a sufficient response to work safety problems and campaigned in 1910 as a supporter of workmen's compensation as well. Indeed, from 1910 on

Bass would be increasingly involved in the issues of labor. In another area, Lillian (Mrs. Frank) Streeter and Theodore Roosevelt pushed him on the problems of neglected children and state responsibility for orphans. He listened, studied the situation, and became an articulate spokesman for these and then other social concerns; as governor he advocated state action. In all policy areas Bass cooperated with political figures already working for legislation. He was a political broker, but one who articulated a vision of a modern state that provided a philosophical framework for expanded activity.[10]

Bass's concept of a modern state was in some regards a modification and reassertion of the nineteenth-century view of a responsible state. As such it was marked by inconsistencies and tensions, as are most constructs that flow from experience, values, conflicting demands, and political exigencies. He was a politician and not a philosopher, although it is possible to speculate upon the continuing influence of ideas planted by Bass's Harvard philosophy professors: George Santayana's concept of the virtuous citizen, William James's pragmatism, Josiah Royce's Hegelian idealism. Bass never seemed to reflect upon or identify the connections. His vision of state action was built upon old concepts such as responsible representative government and economy in spending; in addition, newer concepts such as efficiency, organization, and expertise influenced his approach to problems; finally "the general welfare of New Hampshire" meant to him increasingly humanitarian concerns. His call on the legislature for "progressive legislation which will develop the function of the government to meet new economic conditions" expressed his sense of action rather than a careful ideology. Conditions had changed; government must follow; "there can be no progress without movement." He was not frightened of change; he welcomed the "sudden and gigantic growth" his generation enjoyed. He simply believed new conditions required new approaches to retain the "fundamental principles which underlie our form of government."[11]

If Bass, with the help of his brother and close advisers, had formulated a coherent call for legislative action by January 5, the difficult tasks remained. Proposition had to become statute in a process marked by political calculation, conflicting expectations, and cabalistic dispute. Opposition and proposition proved easier than execution. And Robert Bass would falter, at least temporarily, in the use of those skills of organization, anticipation, and political judgment that had served him well in the past few years.

Bass played a role in the selection of Frank Musgrove as speaker of the house. Musgrove's election demonstrated the strength of the reformers within the ranks of legislative Republicans. And Musgrove moved quickly to expand this strength. He named progressive

Democrats to some key committee positions in what was called "unprecedented evidence of impartiality," and he gave the old guard Republicans appointments as well.[12]

The house of representatives, under Musgrove's leadership, responded positively and speedily to Bass's proposals. With the aid of some Democrats the progressive Republicans in the lower house established a solid record. The senate, early predicted as a problem area in the 1911 session, proved to be just that. Senators, both Republican and Democratic, were less committed to progressive legislation. Still, Bass may have accomplished more but for his early unwillingness to function as legislative leader. He became absorbed in the details of appointments and administration, while avoiding a legislative role. In this regard he certainly was consistent with the Granite State political tradition of governors performing largely ceremonial and administrative roles. Nonetheless, for the reform agenda the early results were ominous.

Left to its own devices the house approved much of the governor's program. Roll calls unfortunately were not recorded for many of the substantive reform proposals. It seems clear nonetheless that Musgrove effected a working majority on several key issues. Table 5.1, while not really including the major reform measures advocated by Bass, suggests that party was not a controlling variable except for bills with obvious political implications, as was true for all roll calls examined in this study. The greatest partisan disagreement on these items occurred on legislation that would alter the boundaries of wards in increasingly Democratic Manchester.[13]

Throughout January and February Governor Bass dealt with the legislature in a desultory manner. He was involved in a range of administrative duties, and he seemed to believe that, after his strong inaugural speech, he should not intervene in legislative deliberations. If so it was a strange attitude for someone as politically shrewd as he appeared to have become. Beyond these factors though, he had become involved in speaking about and proselytizing for the reform message. In early February, John Bass gave him a stern warning and practical advice: "It seems to me that from now on to the end of the session you had better cancel and decline all engagements for social entertainments, and confine yourself strictly to the program of achivement [sic] in the Legislature." John conceded that the state constitution separated legislative and executive functions, but he suggested that politics did not allow fine distinctions: "it has become the practice of the people to hold the chief executive responsible for legislative action." Frank Musgrove was more direct: "Can't you help in the Senate in this work?"[14]

Bass did help, and help aggressively once he realized that the

TABLE 5.1

*Party Vote and Disagreement Scores on Selected Roll Calls,
House of Representatives, 1911*

| Bill | Percentage in favor | | Republican-Democratic disagreement scores |
	Democratic	Republican	
Extend municipal suffrage to women, postpone indefinitely	62	53	9
Amend act controlling liquor sales in nonlicense towns	45	77	32
Create board on improvements and conservation, inexpedient	61	39	22
Act for better supervision of public schools	36	45	9
Amend corporation law relating to foreign corporations controlling domestic railroads, indefinitely postpone	27	76	49
Override Bass veto of N.H. college appropriation	53	35	18
Change boundaries of Manchester wards	12	96	84
Revise Nashua charter	87	60	27
Erect armory at Portsmouth, indefinitely postpone	71	60	11
Create new Manchester ward and change existing boundaries	92	30	62

senate was on the verge of killing the reform program. Senate defeat of the bill ratifying the income tax amendment to the U.S. Constitution, despite the governor's special request to approve it as "the most equitable form of taxation," seemed an important catalyst here. Musgrove reported that liquor interests were successful in "steering matters" by keeping bills off of the floor. (Remick blamed "rum and railroad," as did Lyford, while Sherman Burroughs had earlier worried about a combination between textile and lumber interests.) Musgrove told the governor that the Democrats were being helpful on some key reform bills, but the Republicans needed a push: "we are in a precarious situation and the democrats should not be allowed to outgeneral us."[15]

Senate foot-dragging was a complicated matter. Railroad attorney

Jack Kelley told Chandler that the problem with the tax amendment was that the Bass administration "contented itself with a message January 19th, then allowed the proposition to mildew without any further attention." Kelley, generally candid with Chandler, said the railroad played no role in the fight but that some "industrial corporations" did.[16] Lyford had heard rumors that Gallinger had written some senators asking them to oppose the income tax amendment. Lyford would "be sorry" if this turned out to be the case and hoped Gallinger would keep out of other matters and would not be blamed for the defeat of the amendment.[17] Through it all was the specter of Frank Streeter who had, Lyford alleged, convinced Pillsbury to assume the comfortable position of mediator. Certainly Streeter was active, although evidently not on the income tax fight; the most Kelley would concede to Chandler was that "Rich is planning the whole thing. He consults with me much, consults with Streeter some, maybe more than he does with me, maybe not; consults with others." Lyford feared that Bass, perhaps influenced by his brother, had started out too accommodating in his approach to the railroad and that if he did not reverse soon it would be too late for his program.[18]

On March 9 the governor sent a special message to the legislature. It was a forceful, at times blistering, statement. Bass insisted that the people of New Hampshire had spoken clearly in the 1910 elections and that the legislators, regardless of party, had run on platforms unequivocally supportive of the pending legislation. An action like the defeat of the income tax amendment "shakes the faith of believers in representative government." No one opposed the amendment when he stood before the people in the fall; therefore legislators had a contract with the people to fulfill their platform pledges: "If that duty is not fulfilled, I believe it will be a conspicuous failure of representative government and will be so understood by the people of New Hampshire."[19]

The governor conceded that in directly pressuring the legislature in this manner he could be accused of interfering with traditional legislative autonomy. Nevertheless, he reminded the legislators that the state constitution also called for all constitutional offices to function "in one indissolvable bond of union and amity." This was impossible when some legislators reneged on their platforms. The issue was of "great and far-reaching importance," and his own constitutional obligation directed him to demand legislative action. Theodore Roosevelt's *Outlook* applauded Bass as "A Real Governor," one who was "large enough to assume the full responsibility of leadership."[20]

Clearly Robert Bass knew that a message, no matter how artfully constructed and logically persuasive, would be insufficient to break the senate resistance. He also knew that in the senate the railroad was aiding the obstruction because of that corporation's concern with satisfactorily resolving the rate and tax cases. Negotiations between the attorney general and railroad solicitor Rich were slow, although Rich did suggest on one occasion that if they could compromise their differences he would assist in securing passage of the public service commission, the tax commission, and the employer's liability bills—a striking presumption (or admission) of influence on the part of the corporation counsel.[21]

Unofficial negotiations finally were more successful, and the key figure here was George Rublee. Rublee had worked with John Bass on the Ballinger-Pinchot case and was currently a member of a New York law firm that included Joseph Cotton, a close friend and Harvard classmate of Robert Bass. Cotton encouraged Rublee to assist the governor in some manner. Rublee, with Bass's approval, contacted directly President Mellen and arranged a meeting. A key element in these discussions was the recognition on the part of the governor and some key progressive legislators that the rate question was too complicated to be resolved within a hurried legislative calendar. Further there was real possibility that the railroad rates, while illegal, were not too high. Chandler had feared this conclusion all along, and this was the impression gained by a special house committee that employed Louis D. Brandeis as counsel. The latter appointment, made on Bass's suggestion, caused railroad solicitor Rich to demand, "Is it fair to ask Mr. Mellen to submit further to such prosecution?" Pillsbury, serving on the special committee and, in the view of most observers, working very closely with Streeter, fought the Brandeis appointment because he believed it was provocative to Mellen. Brandeis had played an active role in Massachusetts investigations of the Boston and Maine, and he had strongly opposed the merger with the New Haven. The committee finally conceded, as did Brandeis and Bass, that they lacked the information to make a definitive determination of "appropriate" rates for both the railroad and the state. Until this could be done, all current rates should remain fixed—but with the state not conceding its right to claim reimbursement for any charges that may later be found illegal.[22]

The Rublee-Mellen agreement on resolving the problem amounted to near surrender by the railroad. Bass accepted the terms and even Chandler, who had been shrieking about negotiating with the railroad, seemed satisfied. The railroad received a $50,000 rebate on taxes, the amount Attorney General Eastman calculated litigation would cost the state. In return the railroad agreed to drop its tax suits and accept the findings of the tax commission. As for the controversy over rates, the railroad agreed to let the public service commission fix appropriate rates and resolve residual claims. The substantive compromises were less important than the implicit agreement on the arbitrating agencies: Governor Bass had railroad acquiescence in the two commissions he wanted.[23]

Perhaps it was only a coincidence, but when Charles Mellen accepted the progressive reforms, so did the New Hampshire state senate. The *Monitor* noted that "the remarkable discipline of the senate in regard to Mr. Mellen's command is only equalled in history by Caesar's legions." A railroad representative had told Rublee that the corporation "controlled" fourteen senate votes.[24] In the last days of the legislative session the logjam broke and a series of progressive bills came to the governor. Robert Bass signed legislation establishing a tax commission, a public service commission, workmen's compensation and employer's liability laws, a corrupt practices act, a campaign disclosure law, a prohibition on corporate political activity, a factory inspection statute, strict controls on child labor, state acquisition of the scenic Crawford Notch, and automobile licensing and taxation. It was a significant reform record; Bass received nearly all he had demanded, being frustrated only on ratification of the federal income tax amendment and the expansion of the state primary law to include U.S. senators and delegates to national conventions. By May 1911 New Hampshire probably stood as one of the half-dozen states that had achieved comprehensive reform goals. A *Collier's* article that month linked New Hampshire with California, Kansas, Wisconsin, and New Jersey as reform states and saluted Bass as "a New Figure in Our Public Life." *Outlook* compared Bass with reform governors Hiram Johnson of California and Woodrow Wilson of New Jersey. The railroad had effectively and, as it turned out, permanently lost its political influence. The old guard politicians seemed in disarray. As one Bass supporter from Sunapee wrote the governor in reference to their Republican antagonists: "It just makes me laugh to hear the poor sinners squeal when I realize 'we have got them by the tit.'"[25]

Bass and his closest advisers knew the transient nature of both barnyard grips and political success. Immediately after their legislative victories, the progressives confronted political problems of another sort. The governor had to appoint members to the newly created commissions; this required the approval of the Governor's Council, a group that by a margin of three to two was unabashedly conservative and anti-Bass. This conflict was especially evident in the process of naming the three members of the public service commission. The power this latter body would enjoy, particularly over rates, meant that the men who would serve on it would have a major role in defining its effectiveness. Governor Bass insisted that the commissioners should all be progressives. He determined that one of the three should be Democratic representative Raymond Stevens of Landaff. Stevens had helped write the PSC law and had proved a tenacious and intelligent critic of the Boston and Maine. In a May meeting with the council, Governor Bass submitted several possible slates of commissioners. Each contained Stevens; the council voted 3 to 2 against each.[26]

Bass's advisers differed over the extent to which the governor should persist in forcing the Stevens nomination. Pillsbury, by no means a member of the governor's inner circle, was particularly adamant in urging that Stevens's name be dropped. The council gave no sign of yielding on the Democratic nominee, and Bass recognized that the important thing was to have a progressive commission, not necessarily to have Stevens on the commission. Principle was more important than personality. In June the governor asked the council to approve as commissioners John Benton of Keene and Edward Niles of Concord, both Republican reform veterans, and as a Democratic nominee he submitted the name of Dartmouth mathematics professor Thomas Worthen. Worthen was also a veteran of the anti-railroad battle. The council accepted the slate. Each side might claim victory; Bass's was the more substantive claim. At a Bretton Woods meeting he lectured the Electrical Association that "an unregulated monopoly is a public menace." The PSC, he insisted, should be more than a reform in structure. It must insure reform in substance: "we should not have the semblance of regulation, but actual, bona fide regulation of rates, service and capitalization." The governor argued that public service companies ultimately would benefit from the changes because of the stability that would be a consequence of effective regulation.[27]

By the summer of 1911 Bass had an enviable record as governor. The political situation probably demanded that he consolidate his victories and his control over the Republican party in New Hampshire. He did not; he apparently had little sense of conclusion. Rather he viewed reform as a never-ending process. In his inaugural address to the legislature he had warned that "a spasmodic awakening to the importance of the fundamental principles which underlie our form of government is not sufficient to secure and retain control of that government in the hands of the people." The governor did not think reform was or could be an interlude between lengthy periods of inertia and indifference. Nor did he think reformers should be parochially bound in the problems of their own state. By late 1911 he was referring to a progressive movement that was national and even international in its concerns and principles.[28]

Well before he was elected governor Robert Bass was aware of and interested in national reform. National did not mean only or even principally the national government; it meant nationwide. Bass's 1910 election represented an important northeastern reform victory. Certainly Robert Bass was not unique among the reformers—or even among the nonreformers—in having interests and associations outside of New Hampshire. Nonetheless his role as leader of the state reformers gave him a national recognition shared only by Winston Churchill among the Granite State group. Bass's interests led him to become involved in national organizations promoting conservation, child labor laws, the federal income tax, and good roads. He was an advocate of uniform state laws and was active in the National Governor's Conference. He sought new ideas and approaches incessantly. Early in his administration he contacted Frederick Taylor to inquire about developing schemes for the use of scientific management techniques in government administration. In a 1911 Dartmouth commencement address he asked the audience to join in research and activities that would assist policymakers. Government should not be "a matter of politics, but a science." He did not want to bring the university into politics, "but rather that it help take certain functions of government out of politics." The following fall the Amos Tuck School of Business Administration at Dartmouth sponsored a conference on scientific management at which the governor presided over a session titled "The Application of the Scientific Method to the Activities of the State."[29]

There had been some increasing concern among the old guard about Dartmouth's apparent ties to the reformers. In 1907 President Tucker had told the trustees that he wished to retire because of his failing health; he agreed to stay on, at a reduced pace, until his successor could be appointed. In 1909 Ernest Fox Nichols assumed the Dartmouth presidency and apparently Streeter immediately proposed to him that faculty political activity should be reduced. Nichols suggested that the trustees consider issuing a statement that no faculty member "or any other person connected with Dartmouth" use that connection for "any political purpose." Nichols said the college certainly was not a political institution and had "no more right, as a corporation, to try to exert a political influence than a railroad, for example." Streeter replied that he had discussed the matter with Kimball and that they determined it was best not to move too quickly on such a statement. The matter was dropped. Gallinger, when he heard Bass had indicated that Dartmouth supported the reformers, was so distressed he sought out Streeter to tell him "it was about time for Dartmouth College to behave itself." There is no indication that the college had indeed become politicized; what was galling to

Dartmouth College Trustees, 1909–1910. *Front, left to right:* Frank Streeter, Gov. Henry Quinby (ex officio), William Jewett Tucker, William M. Chase, Charles Mathewson, Benjamin A. Kimball. *Rear, left to right:* John R. Eastman, Henry H. Hilton, Samuel L. Powers, Francis Brown, Lewis Parkhurst, Robert M. Wallace (Dartmouth College)

Streeter and Kimball was that some young political activists on the faculty had become close associates of Robert Bass.[30]

It is hard to isolate the impact of Robert Bass on the New Hampshire reform movement. He was the leader and almost certainly the most articulate and informed Granite State spokesman by 1911. He was much in demand as a speaker outside of New Hampshire; a young observer of one of the speeches reported that "he is not an eloquent man. . . . But once in a while in his address he revealed real oratorical power, especially when he was relating his own independence of any corporation or body of men."[31] Bass's growing stature did not necessarily give him more leverage with the New Hampshire progressives; throughout the brief history of this reform movement it is clear that most members had little disposition to be led. Perhaps in the summer of 1911 the group was as coherent as it had ever been. Basking in success, the reformers could be forgiven for feeling optimistic about the future. Most of them clearly had come to respect Governor Bass's judgment. The latter had led them to substantive accomplishment; paradoxically, in the next year Bass's judgment would have a disruptive effect.

The reformers' seizure of control of the Republican party in 1910 and their subsequent legislative success, abetted by a popular governor, never really gave them unchallenged party domination. Governor Bass recognized this. Sen. Jacob Gallinger had become the major open antagonist of the progressives, and he was a man whose antagonism could never be taken lightly. A power in the Republican party in New Hampshire since the 1880s, Gallinger rejected all the suggestions that the old guard make peace with the reformers. The senator had never disguised his contempt for Churchill and his reform faction. Streeter's intermittent appearances among the insurgent ranks did not serve to mitigate this feeling. Robert Bass's success in 1910 was interpreted—somewhat correctly—as a Gallinger defeat. Gallinger was not a gracious loser; in 1911 there were reports, not confirmed, that Gallinger attempted to persuade state senators to scuttle the Bass program.[32]

By the summer of 1911 Bass and Gallinger were sparring openly. The ostensible subject was the role each had played in the state Republican party over the last year. The real issue was who was going to control the party in the future. Each realized the consequences of the outcome of this contest. Gallinger worried that nationally the insurgent Republicans were going to attempt to defeat Taft, perhaps even starting a new party if all else failed. He believed that the old guard should "give a very emphatic set-back to the movement in New Hampshire by nominating a conservative next year and electing him." By late summer Lyford was looking for candidates and doing what he could to encourage quarrels among the progressives.[33] In August 1911 Bass wrote friend and *Collier's* editor Norman Hapgood that "there is every indication that we shall have a very bitter fight to keep control of things up here." He wrote another friend that recent Gallinger-motivated attacks upon the governor involved "the question as to who should control the Republican party in this State." A new campaign was shaping up, and if "it seems to be premature," the issue nonetheless must be joined.[34]

The campaign that concerned Bass was the electoral contest of 1912. He knew, given the continued hostility of Senator Gallinger, that their 1910 victory did not mean the reformers would go unchallenged in 1912. Gallinger had disliked the primary election law, and in 1910 the organization had been unprepared for the fundamental change this meant for the process of recruiting and nominating candidates. Presumably the old guard would not be unprepared again. The governorship would again be the top prize, but some reformers reminded Bass of the importance of recruiting dependable legislative candidates. Behind this lay the recognition that the 1913 legislature would select a U.S. senator. The incumbent Henry Burnham was not of commanding stature; his seat seemed there for the taking. Bass increasingly was mentioned as the next senator, suggestions he neither disavowed nor encouraged. Jacob Gallinger's own security was involved in this shuffling for position. His term expired in 1915, and with the federal amendment to the U.S. Constitution providing for direct Senate elections moving toward apparent ratification, he perhaps would face a popular election campaign.[35]

As governor, Robert Bass learned that the responsibilities of governance had the concomitant of political consequence. Every decision, every appointment, seemed to ruffle feathers. Bass wrote that "every disgruntled politician in the state [is] after my scalp in deadly earnest."[36] In the fall of 1911 the fight for control of the Republican party in New Hampshire was not simply a matter of contending principles and conflicting programs. Differences involved, as they always had, ambition and power and personality. These were not motivating forces that excluded philosophical differences over public policy; indeed they seemed to thrive upon and in turn nurture philosophical conflicts. This is not to suggest that the latter were independent of conviction and sincerity. Robert Bass and Jacob Gallinger, Winston Churchill and Bertram Ellis, William Chandler and Frank Streeter, did stand for different principles and different programs.

If state politics was complicated by various forces and concerns, it was about to become more so. U.S. senator, governor, and the state legislature were not the only offices for which Republican factions were engaged in preliminary skirmish. In 1912 voters would also elect a president of the United States. The 1908 presidential election had provided the reformers in the GOP with an organizational opportunity: the Taft Republican group's campaign had been an important step to their respectability and expanded influence within state politics. As 1912 approached and Taft gave every indication of seeking reelection, 1908's opportunity became a dilemma.

Part of the difficulty stemmed from the fact that in 1908 there had been few "Taft Republicans" in New Hampshire, at least few who professed a genuine personal commitment to William Howard Taft. Rather there were Roosevelt Republicans who followed the president's leadership and supported Taft as designated successor. People like Churchill, Bass, Streeter, and Pillsbury supported Taft for different and often conflicting reasons. Of this quartet of leaders, Bass and Churchill are of greatest interest here. Certainly their Taft support was genuine and even intense; it was never really personal. Taft was the instrument to carry on what the reformers conceived of as Roosevelt policies. They defined these policies as progressive, a concept always susceptible to subjective interpretation. While his presidency resulted in substantive and important accomplishments, like greater railroad regulation, pure food and drug legislation, and some proceedings against "trusts," Roosevelt's reform record may at times have been more rhetorical than substantive. Nonetheless, rhetoric, in the sense of articulating values and voicing the language and concepts that become a part of permissible political debate and the public agenda, is a crucial function of political leadership. For some of the leading New Hampshire reformers Roosevelt, more than any other person, was the symbol and embodiment of progressive principles.[37]

By the fall of 1911 some reformers were looking back wistfully at the Roosevelt presidency. The Oyster Bay politician clearly had his own wistful thoughts. As important as Roosevelt's positive appeal was, President Taft was also guilty of alienating some of the New Hampshire reformers. The Ballinger-Pinchot imbroglio particularly stirred up the group that had been so involved in conservation. Robert Bass was bitter over this, a bitterness fueled by his brother John, who was especially close to Pinchot. John nonetheless recognized the political advantages the Roosevelt supporters might realize from this controversy. He noted as it evolved that the conflict "continues to bear all sorts of unexpected fruit." The Bass brothers and the Pinchot brothers, Gifford and Amos, put up the money to set up an orchard business in Washington State for Louis Glavis, the Interior Department officer who accused Ballinger of improper activities and lost his job even before Pinchot did. The harvest here, however, was not the fruit John Bass had in mind.[38]

Taft's role in the congressional fight over the powers of House Speaker Joseph Cannon and the controversy over the seating of Sen. William Lorimer from Illinois, as well as the president's handling of tariff reform, earned him the suspicion of some of the reformers.[39] Even more important, perhaps, was the manner in which Taft increasingly worked with Senator Gallinger and some other opponents of Bass. The politics of the presidency required some ambivalence, equivocation, and compromise in dealing with warring state organizations. The progressives were never too tolerant of such approaches.

Early in his gubernatorial term Robert Bass had consulted and corresponded with Jonathan Bourne of Oregon and Robert La Follette of Wisconsin about the formation of a Progressive Republican League. Bass was interested but, despite Pinchot's urging that he participate, the governor balked, ostensibly because of state obligations and because he did not want to become involved in an effort that seemed blatantly anti-Taft and pro–La Follette. These were factors certainly; indeed Gallinger publicly criticized Bass as a La Follette man when the governor appeared at a Boston rally with Pinchot late in 1911. Such attacks probably would not have been sufficient reason for the governor to keep his distance; Bass had philosophical reservations as well. Bass was not comfortable with the western progressives who dominated the league, particularly with their emphasis on direct democracy. He had never participated fully in the New Hampshire Direct Legislation League and conceded his preference for representative government. He articulated this in his March special message to the legislature. Bass had written La Follette on January 24, 1911, that his mind was "not clear" on the initiative, referendum, and recall issues the league was supporting. Roosevelt reported to a friend later in the spring that Bass had spent the evening with him and that they discussed these issues. Roosevelt agreed with Bass's view that in the Granite State the town meeting fulfilled the need for citizen participation in decisions. Sharing Bass's uncertainty on the direct legislation issues, Churchill approved of Bass's decision to keep his distance from the Progressive Republican League: "We are likely to get some new developments and new deals before the next presidential campaign."[40]

Winston Churchill had no reservation about opposing Taft. Increasingly Churchill involved himself with national issues, and as he did he found himself criticizing Taft. As early as June 1910 he had declared to a friend that the rotund Taft's "failure is in direct proportion to his avoirdupois." He told Iowa senator Albert Cummins that New Hampshire too had its insurgents and that in the 1910 campaign "we hope the chance may be given us to discuss national issues."[41] Bass and Churchill apparently had a strain in their relationship for much of 1911. The reasons are not clear, although Churchill obviously felt his role in the reform movement had been slighted by the Bass campaign. The always prickly Daniel Remich wrote Churchill that stories applauding Bass were "rank and unjust," for Churchill and Remich worked for reform "before Bass got into the game." Churchill agreed but reminded Remich that their efforts were "not with a view to political reward." Churchill did not attend the Bass inauguration or the governor's January 1912 wedding.[42]

Nevertheless by late 1911 Bass and Churchill seemed to be in accord on the general direction of reform. Bass was increasingly coming to Churchill's view on the national scope of the progressive movement and was talking about the novelist as a candidate for the Republican gubernatorial nomination in 1912. Churchill believed the next campaign would resolve the festering issues—it "should be the cutting of the Gordian knot." In addition, party was less relevant to him. He "never felt less partisan," and sought to be free of the "meshes of party . . . as interpreted by Mr. Taft and his friends."[43]

Robert Bass was more of a partisan, more committed to the Republican party as an institution, than were Churchill and some of the other reformers like James Remick. Bass sought to compromise with the Gallinger forces within the party, but by late 1911 the governor recognized that compromise of this sort meant pulling back from his commitment to reform principles. He balked at this.[44]

In December 1911 Governor Bass spoke at a progressive Republican rally in Boston. Theodore Roosevelt had urged the group to invite Bass as the featured speaker. The governor's future father-in-law, Charles Sumner Bird, was one of the organizers of the Bay Colony's reform group. Bass told the assembly that as government assumed "increased functions," at both state and national levels, the "average man is insisting today that the democracy established and developed by our forefathers, be insured to him not as a mere matter of form but in actual substance and fact." Progressivism in New England was marked by "the insistent demand of the electorate at large, rather than from the independent leadership of individual men." Progressivism was a national movement that must not become sectional for "the same principles are at stake all over the country." These were, Bass argued, principles assuring citizens full and efficacious participation in government. If people agree on principles, men will emerge to lead the fight. But principles were "vastly more important than men." Bass believed the movement had succeeded in New Hampshire because the reformers had "overcome the political inertia which had enthralled the average man under the old system," a system under which most men "didn't know what was going on and . . . didn't care." Now an aroused citizenry in Massachusetts would throw off their inertia. It was, after all, happening everywhere.[45] Bass's concept of national reform still primarily meant reform occurring in different parts of the nation. Shortly he would expand this concept to refer as well to the national government. It was an important shift, and it was one that thrust him—and many other reformers—into a much broader arena.

In January 1912 Robert Bass and Edith Bird were married in East Walpole, Massachusetts. It was a major social event, involving as it did an attractive Massachusetts woman of good family and New Hampshire's handsome young governor. The new Mrs. Bass was familiar with politics. Her father, Charles Sumner Bird, was a successful manufacturer; he was a former Democratic mugwump who had dropped out of politics in 1896 but now was showing a new interest in the reform movement. Edith Bass did not share her husband's activist fascination. The newlyweds left on a honeymoon in the South, deliberately leaving politics behind. Or so it appeared. On February 10, while Bass was still on his wedding trip, a letter was released that was signed by him and six other Republican governors. This letter urged Theodore Roosevelt to run for the Republican presidential nomination. The uproar in New Hampshire startled Bass; certainly not all of his associates in the reform movement were prepared to follow him in his effort.[46]

Bass's Roosevelt appeal immediately started a splintering of the progressive organization in New Hampshire. Part of the problem was that it had always been splintered. New Hampshire Republican progressivism was never a monolith organizationally or philosophically. This fact became readily apparent in the winter of 1912 when Robert Bass discovered that instead of leading a movement he had to reconstitute a coalition. Agreement on some basic principles of state government and politics by no means meant agreement on basic principles of national government and politics. Equally important, challenging an incumbent president had implications for party security and hegemony. Probably by 1911 Robert Bass was in a minority even among the New Hampshire reformers in terms of his positions on issues. There was a conservative dimension to the New Hampshire progressive movement. Stopping abuses by the railroad and modernizing government processes to permit fuller citizen influence was by no means inconsistent with conservative values. Indeed, the antirailroad movement was facilitated by the cooperation and encouragement of many of the old guard politicians. Robert Bass's political agenda only began with the desire to get the Boston and Maine railroad out of politics; the railroad was but part of the problem. In a 1910 primary campaign speech at Wolfeboro he had insisted that "class privilege . . . founded on the money power . . . becomes the greatest influence for corruption there is in the world." The governor's developing views had come to allow the real possibility of government ownership of railroads and utilities; his evolving social concerns, which held that government had a responsibility "to promote, in so far as possible, equal opportunity for all citizens," appeared more radical. By late 1911 he was lashing out at "captains of industry and merchant princes."[47]

Theodore Roosevelt had come to symbolize some of the more radical reform ideas in 1911. Whether Roosevelt was indeed radical is quite secondary in terms of the political implications of this symbolism. Robert Bass's personal and philosophical ties to "Roosevelt Republicanism" made his support for the ex-president natural, if not inevitable. But what was logical for the individual was not necessarily logical for the political leader. The progressive governor gravitated toward this broader movement without seeming to measure all of the implications for the New Hampshire reformers. It was not that he assumed all would follow him; it was more that he never seemed to reflect very much on this crucial political question.

By early 1912 Bass was involved in discussions with Roosevelt about the latter's plans and tactics. Bass urged caution in challenging Taft, and he suggested that Roosevelt be more conciliatory to La Follette, who already was contesting Taft's renomination. Bass believed Roosevelt should not foster accusations that the ex-president was only acting out of personal ambition: "If you do become the candidate of our party, it seems to me absolutely necessary that it be clear to the people of the country that you do so only on their insistent demand."[48]

As Robert Bass prepared to go on his honeymoon, he sent John Bass to confer with several governors. Robert assured Roosevelt, who knew John Bass well, that John was "particularly adapted to this work, being close mouthed, discreet and diplomatic. He is resourceful." The Basses played an important role in getting from the governors the statement Roosevelt desired, the "insistent demand."[49]

Robert Bass did not seek the advice of his New Hampshire reform associates on this delicate matter. One who had been active since the 1906 Lincoln movement, Allen Hollis, wrote that he had read in the newspaper that Bass was going to support a Roosevelt presidential bid. He confessed that Bass's friends were confused. Hollis insisted that "you can easily have their approval of such a step for the asking"—so why not ask for it, at least give the sense of conferring. Lyford claimed that Bass loyalist Frank Musgrove told him that the "Governor made a mistake" by not considering the New Hampshire situation. Another supporter was more negative: "We were all Bass men once, but we are not with you in this deal."[50]

The 1912 version of the Taft Republicans in New Hampshire was an interesting coalition of old machine politicians, many of whom had opposed Taft in 1908, and some reformers as well as Frank Streeter, whom Lyford correctly described as having the confidence of no group. A group of "Taft Progressives" included such names as Willis McDuffee, Thomas Chalmers, Sherman Burroughs, and James Colby, all of whom had unimpeachable reform credentials. Chandler, who found both Taft and Roosevelt unacceptable but went with the former, found Burroughs's behavior particularly curious. After throwing in with Roosevelt, the Manchester attorney turned up in the Taft camp. Chandler insisted that Streeter "took possession of him."[51] The Taft Progressives insisted that the campaign was not "for or against Governor Bass and what he stands for in this state." As progressives whose ties dated to 1906, they argued that "this is in no sense a state campaign and that these progressive issues are not involved." Roosevelt, one progressive Taft supporter argued, and New Hampshire progressivism were not the same. These Taft supporters opposed Roosevelt because they feared his ambition or simply disliked him; they supported Taft because they felt he had been a good president: "safe, sane, honest . . . statesmanship as against petty politics."[52]

Later, upon reflection, Robert Bass would agree that not all the Taft supporters were conservatives. He could not honestly do otherwise. On the other hand he insisted that all of the antireform conservatives were Taft supporters. There may have been exceptions to this; they are not evident. Bass wondered how progressives could help restore "to power the forces that were sent into retirement in 1910." Of course the governor knew as well as anyone that few of the reformers' old antagonists had actually retired.[53]

The Gallinger, anti-Bass forces had been very active before the announcement of Bass's Roosevelt support. Their goal was to regain full control of the state party. They took advantage of the opportunity the governor provided them. Jacob Gallinger, not charitable to his opponents in the best of circumstances, became more vindictive: "let Bass wallow in the mire he has fixed up for himself."[54] The Gallinger Republicans warmly endorsed the president whose nomination they had opposed in 1908. For Senator Gallinger the battle was personal and philosophical as well as political. He disliked Roosevelt as he disliked the insurgents who had been stirring up matters since 1906. As early as 1897 he had characterized Roosevelt as a hypocrite and a man who "clings to office with the tenacity of grim

death." In 1905, after Roosevelt's election to the presidency, Gallinger feared that unless the president was restrained the GOP
would divide into "hostile camps" within the year. Roosevelt was so
impulsive that "the conservative men of our own party are holding
their breath, not knowing what will come next." Gallinger's active
opposition to the Roosevelt-Taft organization in 1908 as well his
record as one of the conservative senate recalcitrants did not thaw
hard feelings. In 1912 Roosevelt in a New Hampshire appearance
verbally abused Gallinger when he said, in response to a concern
about the initiative and referendum fostering impulsive public action, that if true he nonetheless trusted the impulsive judgment
of New Hampshire citizens more than "the deliberate judgment
of Senator Gallinger." Gallinger even worked with old foe Frank
Streeter, at Taft's request, although he confided to the president that
"Mr. Streeter has never yet been known to work harmoniously with
anybody long at a time." He did with Gallinger on this occasion, and
Chandler found it "quite a sight."[55]

It was a vicious political season, that late winter and spring, as
intraparty strife, pitting friend against friend, has the capacity to become. And the Republican reformers, who had largely controlled
their party, lost it. The Republican State Committee, dominated by
the reformers since the 1910 primary, voted for a Gallinger rather
than a Bass proposal for selecting delegates to the national convention. It was a casual procedure, approved hurriedly, that provided
for local caucuses to vote for delegates committed to candidates.
Senator Gallinger's uncommitted delegation principle of 1908 had
been discarded in the intervening four years. Gallinger had fought
successfully against a state law providing a mechanism for delegate
selection. So this plan was a partial concession on his part, one of
the few he would make. The old street-fight language reappeared:
"we have got that crowd beaten to a frazzle if we stand up in our
boots and fight . . . stand up like men and fight to win." The senator
was not prepared to go too far to accommodate the progressives, even
those who were with Taft in this contest. An exasperated Lyford,
doing most of the organizing work, lectured the senator that "you
fail to realize what a dead organization we had to galvanize into life
and that the men who were doing work ten years ago either can not
or will not" help out now. "We have been through Hell in getting
the organization that we have," Lyford exclaimed, and pointed out
that if the Taft group had not "broken into the Bass organization . . .
we would have been licked to a standstill."[56]

Gallinger and Lyford finally agreed that their delegate slate would
include only men who were both pro-Taft and anti-Roosevelt. Even
if the president faltered then, New Hampshire would not go for the

Rough Rider. Gallinger ignored Streeter's complaint to the president that the Taft progressives were not being treated fairly. Gallinger asked only that if Taft won the results be described as an
endorsement of the senator; he confessed to "trembling at the possibility of our losing the State."[57] He did not have to worry; the jug-
gernaut rolled on. The Roosevelt campaign was marked by more
emotion than organization. Bass warned Gifford Pinchot that it was
"a great fight" but that "all the old organization, the whole press and
the Congressional delegation are against us, also the leading business men." Amidst charges of fraud and vote buying, the Taft delegates won in the April caucuses.[58]

Robert Bass was shaken but not surprised by the defeat. He insisted that the Roosevelt vote was "a fair expression of the voter,
whereas the Taft balloting was a series of outrageous tricks, yet we
came out pretty close."[59] Challenging an incumbent president, even
with a popular ex-president, was not an easy task. And Roosevelt
was not, despite his popularity, always a good candidate. His Columbus, Ohio, speech in February, in which he supported popular
recall of judicial decisions, alarmed many who were already disposed
to fear Roosevelt as a radical. Louis Wyman described the doctrine as
"political and governmental heresy." Gallinger told Lyford it was
"incredible" anyone would support Roosevelt after that speech.
Bass confided to his father-in-law, active in the Massachusetts Roosevelt effort, that Roosevelt "has made it very difficult to conduct a
campaign in his interests."[60]

The easy Taft victory at the New Hampshire caucuses brought
Bass, Churchill, and other Roosevelt progressives to a real juncture.
They felt that caucus processes and procedures had worked to de-
prive Roosevelt of the victory that should have been his. There was
a residue of bitterness and of uncertainty. What had appeared a few
months ago as a probable Roosevelt nomination now seemed much
less likely. Bass assured the Taft progressives, as well as his own
Roosevelt group, that now they would unify again. Everyone "interested in clean, progressive politics" would work once more for New
Hampshire reform.[61] Such a condition was easier to propose than to
create. It would have essentially meant starting over again. The old
guard was in control of the Republican party. Gallinger made clear
his view that the party must not "be delivered by compromise into
the hands of the Bass crowd again." He suggested people stop talking about "progressives" and simply refer to Republicans. His theme
was constant: to unite the party. His mode of achieving unity was to
disregard "the agitators" and to avoid the "mongrel" posture of including all of the groups in the leadership.[62] It might have been possible for the old reformers to reunite and redirect their attention on

the state; it is not clear that anyone's mind and energy focused sufficiently on this considerable task. Presidential politics continued to dominate the attention of New Hampshire politicians.

In January 1912 some of the Republican progressives, encouraged by Governor Bass, had begun to lay plans for the state primary election in September. Bass had earlier been involved in discussions about the gubernatorial candidacy of Frank Worcester. Worcester had some progressive ties and impulses, but he clearly was the Lyford candidate for governor. Lyford had been working to identify a candidate acceptable to both Gallinger and the reformers. Worcester conceivably could have been such a person. The progressives at that time had neither the need nor the desire to compromise so fully. And Gallinger had no disposition to do so. He dismissed Worcester as "timid," and Gallinger had contempt for such instincts. He sarcastically suggested that a Worcester letter must have been written by "Brother John" Bass; it was the "worst kind of twaddle that I have ever read." As far as Gallinger was concerned, if Worcester "is not willing to become a candidate without putting himself absolutely in the hands of the Churchill-Bass crowd then he must get along as best he can without any help from some of us who do not believe in that sort of thing."[63] Progressives like Remich were equally unyielding in their refusal to participate in a Worcester unity campaign. A January survey of some progressives indicated that Bass, Churchill, and Musgrove were the most acceptable candidates, with some believing that Bass had the strength to overcome the single-term tradition.[64] There is no indication Bass had ever seriously considered such an effort.

The old guard continued its efforts immediately after the spring presidential caucuses. Lyford wanted to take advantage of the reform split, for "if time is allowed to intervene, this feeling may cool off and new adjustments take place."[65] There was, however, no reform-wing counterpart of Lyford to attempt to facilitate the needed adjustments. By June of 1912 nothing more had been done to organize a progressive primary campaign. By June 1910 the Bass effort was already well along. Recovery of lost time was not out of the question, but no one even tried. In June 1912 the presidency dominated.

Robert Bass attended the Republican National Convention in Chicago in late June, but as observer rather than as delegate. The Taft Republicans in New Hampshire took full advantage of their caucus victory and controlled the delegation. The first-ballot Taft nomination at Chicago and the Roosevelt bolt placed many reform Republicans in a difficult spot. Bass hurried back to New Hampshire to confer with other Roosevelt Republicans.[66] He advised caution; Robert Bass was not yet prepared to leave his party. Winston Churchill was. He told Bass he "could no longer conscientiously work" in the GOP. At a July meeting in Manchester the progressives decided to send delegates to the National Progressive Convention in Chicago in early August. That conclave's revivalistic tone and inevitable nomination of Theodore Roosevelt meant bolt in New Hampshire. For the true believers, Roosevelt's peroration was as a clarion call: "We stand at Armageddon, and we battle for the Lord."[67]

Robert Bass's health was poor in July and August. The governor was hesitant to join in a third-party effort. He did not attend the Progressive Convention. George Rublee later recalled that he had convinced a reluctant Bass to join the Progressive party. This claim is probably inflated. Certainly the pressure was on Bass to participate with his brother, his father-in-law, and Churchill and other close New Hampshire allies, in supporting Roosevelt. Bass did attend a crucial conference of progressives at Manchester on August 9. This meeting took an equivocal but major step toward a third party. The participants agreed to endorse a Bass proposal to support "progressives" of either party in the September 3 primary and then to file independent candidates for those races in which there was no general election candidate who was progressive. The governor had come to concede that there were "Taft progressives" with whom the Roosevelt forces must work in New Hampshire.[68]

Given the time available, it was a legitimate strategy but one that required fine judgments of candidate credentials as well as a superb organizational framework. It is not clear that the progressives ever had the capacity for the former; they had not had the latter at least since the Roosevelt split in February. The progressives did essentially agree at this August meeting that they should nominate a gubernatorial candidate and that this candidate should be Bass, Churchill, or Musgrove. These three were empowered to determine among themselves which of them would head the third-party ticket.[69]

On September 6 Governor Bass announced the formation of the Progressive party of New Hampshire. He insisted that the new party represented "a genuine effort to lessen in some measure the tremendous difference in the opportunity and well-being which exists between those who are struggling for the very necessities of life and those possessed of great wealth." It was a far cry, this "work for humanity," from the slogans of 1906. The Boston and Maine was no longer the issue. And Winston Churchill agreed to run for governor. If the circle was complete, it was not at the starting point.[70]

The Progressive party of New Hampshire met in convention at Concord on September 26 and nominated Winston Churchill for governor. Robert Bass addressed the delegates and spoke eloquently

Robert P. Bass addressing 1912 election rally in Concord, speaking at length due to delay in Theodore Roosevelt's arrival (Perkins Bass)

Theodore Roosevelt addressing same crowd, with an exhausted-looking Robert Bass to his left (Robert P. Bass, Jr.)

about the need for a new party that would bring together the best of
the two old parties: there were no substantive differences between
the Democratic and Republican parties. "Except in the election of
United States Senators, there has been practically no division in our
legislature strictly along party lines for several years." Indeed, "the
cause which gave birth to these parties have [sic] disappeared, the
old issues which divided them have ripened off and are now dead."
The Progressive party would change the political agenda: Bass promised to deal with new conditions, to "make it possible for the men
and women of this country to earn a reasonable living wage without
endangering their health or their lives. . . . we want to see the children under sixteen years of age spend their time not in the mills but
at school. We intend to prevent the night employment of women,
and to limit their employment to such reasonable hours as will en-
able them to bear healthy children who will be a credit to this country." Better-educated, more intelligent, and more secure voters will
assure "real popular government."

Bass addressed as well older progressive concerns about business
regulation. He believed tariff and trust regulation would stabilize
business and create greater opportunities for all business. But he
made clear that business prosperity must be a social benefit: "prosperity shall be shared equitably and equally by great and small, by
the rich and by the poor." "Our cause," Bass concluded, "is the
cause of suffering humanity."[71]

The Progressive platform picked up the same themes: "the welfare of the American people, the future of the American republic
call for the democratizing of American government and the human-
izing of American industry." Only a new party could accomplish this
task. Specifically the Progressive party called for greater cooperation between the government and higher education, particularly
better ties, in the Wisconsin manner, with Dartmouth. The platform
supported new proposals such as the initiative, the referendum,
and woman suffrage, as well as publication of committee proceedings and "the abolition of every secret point of access to legislation."
The New Hampshire Progressives explicitly endorsed the national
platform call for greater industrial safety regulation, abolition of
child labor, minimum wage for women, a six-day work week, and an
eight-hour day in twenty-four-hour industries. The Progressive
delegates pledged to work to reduce the liquor traffic. They advocated greater state support for agricultural education, for highway
improvement and maintenance, and for preservation of water and
other natural resources as "the heritage of the people . . . developed
under state control." They sought to change the state constitution in
order to enlarge the senate, change property tax laws, institute an in-

heritance tax and an income tax on public service corporations, eliminate the words *evangelical* and *Protestant* from the state bill of rights, provide for plurality elections, elect senators and councillors from districts determined by population rather than property, and to give the governor power to veto separate appropriation items.[72]

The platform was the most comprehensive and substantive one developed by any New Hampshire party in this period. It reflected the growth of reform concerns as well as what Bass called "our declaration of independence" from compromise and "the insidious influence" of "reactionary" delegates and candidates. Support for initiative, referendum, and woman suffrage, as well as greater emphasis on social issues, represented the greatest expansion of the reform agenda. As recently as January 1912 Bass was still hedging on woman suffrage, still insisting that it was necessary to "ascertain that a reasonable percentage of them want it." In contrast Winston Churchill, after opposing suffrage in 1903, had strongly supported this issue for several years. Mary Chase of Andover had been tirelessly organizing and pushing woman suffrage for over a decade. She and her co-workers elicited support from people as divergent as Clarence Carr, Jacob Gallinger, James Lyford, Henry Quinby, and Churchill. George Moses opposed suffrage actively. Bass did not, but his equivocal position on this matter was curiously inconsistent with his general stand on reform matters. In his speech to the State Progressive Convention, Bass applauded Jane Addams and called for "support of all that is best in American manhood and womanhood."[73]

The convention was the high point of the Progressive campaign. Poorly organized and short of funds, the new party faced a difficult fight. Roosevelt and "impulsive" politics became the issue, and all three parties focused on presidential politics. Bass helped respond to an old problem when he arranged financial support for a new newspaper, *The Leader*, and assisted in arranging to bring Frank Knox into Manchester as publisher. Knox was a Michigan newspaperman who had played a key role in the winter effort to draft Roosevelt.[74]

The Republicans nominated Frank Worcester for governor and attempted to conciliate some progressive voters, but not the progressive leaders. The major Republican concern in the campaign was more than the possibility of a Democratic plurality. A plurality was symbolically important but not commanding. The constitution provided that in the absence of a majority the gubernatorial choice would be left to the house. The GOP could not risk alienating Progressives who might provide the margin of victory in the new house. Lyford worried about the "Bass people" getting the balance of power. But he rejected Chandler's request that the party be more conciliatory toward these wayward Republicans. As far as Lyford was concerned they had controlled the party and accomplished nearly all they wanted in terms of legislation. When they couldn't "deliver it" to Roosevelt, they petulantly set out "determined to destroy" the GOP. Gallinger basically agreed with the position Taft took in a meeting the two had after the convention: even if they lost the election, Roosevelt was defeated and "the organization will still exist." Gallinger reprimanded Chandler for his continued admiration of the reformer's accomplishments, asking, "isn't it about time to stop talking about the wonderful progress New Hampshire made under the leadership" of the progressives.[75]

William Chandler stood with his party. Poor health had prevented Chandler from playing a role in the spring primaries and still restricted his activities. But Chandler, more than any of the old Republican leaders, sympathized with the Progressives. He had told Moses in the spring that the Roosevelt challenge represented something more than "a crazy candidate and a crazy constituency." He had pushed Gallinger after the primaries to be more conciliatory to Bass, to permit the governor as well as Chandler to join the new ruling "trio" of Lyford, Gallinger, and—Gallinger must have flinched—Streeter.[76] Even after Bass and Churchill bolted, Chandler called them "two friends whom I have been so glad to know and labor with." Despite his reform instincts and his gadfly nature, Chandler primarily was a Republican; this was the final determinant. As he wrote Charles Eliot in 1910, "Do you not think that I was fortunate because born a hater of slavery and a Unitarian . . . I have had nothing in politics or religion to unlearn?" For Chandler the party was not simply an organization, it was an institution. In the fall of 1912 he was worried, reaching back to hallowed rhetoric to express his concern and outrage: "A house divided against itself cannot stand: Roosevelt has done a very wicked thing." Chandler continued to insist that Roosevelt did not embody *his* progressive principles: "My fight against monopoly in the concrete and specifically was against the U.S. Steel and the B&M. Roosevelt betrayed me on both."[77]

In the midst of all the Republican scuffling and feuding, New Hampshire Democrats quietly organized for a victorious campaign. Woodrow Wilson at the head of their ticket provided them with a popular figure with reform credentials, a condition they had not enjoyed since Cleveland's 1892 campaign. For four elections they had been burdened by the frightening Bryan or the colorless Alton Parker. The Democrats nominated Samuel Felker of Rochester for governor. Felker was a strong reform Democrat who had helped draft legislation for Bass in late 1910 and had worked to secure its passage. It was hard for the Progressives to justify slating their own candidate for governor with Felker in the field. The Progressive party did endorse the Democratic congressional candidate in the Second District, Raymond Stevens. It would have been difficult to do otherwise given all of Stevens's work for progressive legislation in 1911 and Bass's well-publicized fight to appoint him to the PSC.[78]

Robert Bass was too intelligent and seasoned a politician not to know that the Progressives were at an insuperable disadvantage. In a letter marked by untypical desperation he begged his brother to join in the Granite State effort: "Need you now. Can you come [?]" John could not. This time Robert Bass engaged the Burns Detective Agency to infiltrate and monitor the opposition.[79]

The Progressives, with limited out-of-state help, campaigned hard, brought out large crowds, and lost badly. As a Manchester Progressive noted to Bass, "I guess *all* our men come out to the rallies." Since 1906 Progressives had too often confused enthusiasm with organization and power.[80] Wilson and Felker carried their predicted pluralities, with Roosevelt and Churchill a distant third in the state. Democrats carried both congressional seats, three of five council seats, and fourteen of twenty-four senate races. Republicans nominally controlled the house. The progressives apparently would have a small balance of power in the house.

Bass, Churchill, and other reformers were not surprised nor even deeply distressed by the election results. The campaign had, they felt, served as an important first step toward a more rational—meaning clearly ideological—party system. Bass and Churchill waxed in Roosevelt's praise that they were "the two pioneers in this fight in the East, . . . no more valiant soldiers ever waged the battle for civic decency."[81] The battle was not over, not for any of the principals, but as they faced the last six weeks of the Bass governorship and the unpredictable 1913 legislative session, the old reform political organization was shattered. As the veteran William Chandler noted to a friend, "Reformers do have a hard time of it."[82]

6

"The Last Act of the Drama"

O N THURSDAY, JANUARY 2, 1913, the New Hampshire General Court was engaged in organizing itself and in sorting out the inconclusive returns from the last election. There were several contested races, mainly from contests in which no candidate secured the constitutionally required majority. Early in the afternoon members of the two houses met in joint session to hear Gov. Robert Perkins Bass deliver his farewell message. Winston Churchill had advised Bass to "appeal to the enlightened conscience of the state" and to provide "a final commentary on an administration which started so many valuable reforms" in New Hampshire. The governor did; his comments reflected a pride of accomplishment as well as a challenge to the new legislature. Bass concluded:

Today New Hampshire stands as one of the leaders in establishing more liberal and humane practices of government. The legislature of 1911 did its full share towards that end. The future rests in your hands, and as my parting message upon retiring from office, let me urge you to keep New Hampshire where she now stands, in the vanguard of progress, as a leader among the states of the Union which are striving to create better social, industrial and political conditions under a government directly controlled by its citizens and administered solely in their interests.[1]

Bass left the statehouse and the capital city. The 1913 session of the legislature continued, and the legislators returned to their own agenda which was headed, as so often had been the case in the new century, by a struggle for office. In this instance the prizes the representatives had to bestow were more significant, the contests were of greater public interest, and the process more complicated than in past legislative squabbles. Party lines, the traditional guide in such political matters, confused as much as they clarified the situation for many of the citizen-legislators.

The Republican majority returned to the house of representatives in the 1912 election was a nominal one. The Progressive party leaders had organized too late to slate members under their own ticket for legislative races. Progressives had managed, however, to secure nomination and victory in several instances on the Republican slate. Of the 208 Republicans who won in the general election, at least 14 explicitly associated with the new Progressive party; they had run on the Republican ticket out of necessity rather than affinity. This gave numerical advantage to the 197 Democrats, if they could work with the Progressives. The legislators needed to resolve their own election disputes and select the house and senate leadership; then they had to elect a governor and a U.S. senator to assume the seat currently held by Henry Burnham. Burnham was not seeking reelection.

George Moses, recently returned to Concord from his diplomatic assignment in Greece, attempted to conciliate the Republicans and the Progressives. Moses had resigned his ambassadorship when it became evident he would be replaced by the incoming Wilson administration. He discovered in Concord a mood of suspicion and vindictiveness. The Republican loyalist attempted to orchestrate a complicated plan whereby the Republicans would support a Progressive, William Britton, as speaker; this move presumably would provide Progressive support for the Republican gubernatorial candidate. The Bull Moose candidate in the fall, Winston Churchill, was ineligible for legislative election since only the two candidates with the most votes in November could be considered. Moses's plan collapsed when Charles Floyd, former governor and a man the frustrated Moses described as one "in whom the truth never was," insisted on another candidate for speaker. The Progressives then struck a deal with the Democrats.[2]

This new coalition elected William Britton as speaker of the house and chose a Democrat as president of the state senate. The Democratic nominee, Samuel Felker, was elected governor. Felker (b. 1859) was the first Democrat to serve as governor of the Granite State since James Weston in 1874. Felker was clearly in the dominant reform wing of his party. The Progressive Republicans went on to combine with the Democrats to give all contested races to the Democratic candidate. The result was that Democrats controlled the governorship, all five seats on the Governor's Council, and the state senate, the latter by a margin of 14 to 10.[3]

The U.S. Senate seat was another matter. Many Progressives believed this seat should be theirs. Despite Rosecrans Pillsbury's expression of interest and availability, their nominee was Robert Bass. Although he had encouragement from political leaders as different as William Chandler and Theodore Roosevelt, and support from a hard core of Progressive legislators, Bass never seriously pursued the race. He went to Chicago in the early stages of the voting and then left for an extended stay in Europe as the voting continued. Mrs. Bass was in ill health and her husband explained to Roosevelt that "it seems essential that I take her away for a time."[4] While his absence frustrated some supporters, Bass had warned the Progressives of his plan to take this trip when they asked him to be their candidate. By 1913 the governor was an experienced politician; certainly he could count. It was highly unlikely Robert Bass could secure the legislative support he would need to win the race. Few, if any, old guard Republicans would consider supporting him. Moses believed many would prefer a Democrat to Bass because the latter tried to "smash the party" when he could not command its "blind following" of him.[5] The Democrats, on the other hand, were determined to send a member of their party to the Senate. Gallinger worried that the Democrats ultimately would support Bass "with the view of further demoralizing the Republican party in our State. Heaven save us from such a calamity."[6]

Bass never requested that his name be withdrawn, despite his inactivity as a candidate. James Remick insisted that the Progressives move to another candidate; few did. Rosecrans Pillsbury offered to broker the affair and break the deadlock; few were interested in his offer—some saw the shadow of Frank Streeter in his ploy—and Moses dismissed the publisher as "an ass." Moses offered himself as a compromise candidate and sought to generate support and pressure to move matters in this direction. The Amoskeag interests monitored the situation with much greater attention than they normally devoted to state affairs. Moses joked that they "would cheerfully commit burglary, arson and murder" to halt the election of low-tariff Democrat Henry Hollis![7]

Chandler urged Bass to remain in the race so as to prevent a Democratic victory. Beyond this, he insisted that Bass was his choice for the position. Chandler, and to a lesser extent Moses, believed that Republican resurgence depended on the successful reassimilation of the 1912 bolters. Bass's objectives remained somewhat unclear. Before leaving New Hampshire he had reaffirmed his willingness to continue as the candidate as long as the Progressives wanted him, but no longer. His only admonition to his supporters was that they stay firm on their principles: no deals. It could be that Bass decided to remain in the contest in order to secure a secondary goal, the defeat of the old guard Republican candidates, without formally allying with Democrats. Bass may have agreed with Roosevelt's advice that "no Republican who supported Mr. Taft and the Republi-

can Party at the last election has any claim to be considered a progressive at all." Roosevelt concluded that if "worst came to the
worst" it was better to send a progressive Democrat to Washington.
On the other hand Bass may have agreed with Chandler that the
principles he had been stating for the last several months compelled
him to remain as a nominal candidate rather than making a deal with
anyone.[8]

After two months and forty-three ballots, the New Hampshire
legislature voted to send Henry Hollis of Concord to the U.S. Senate. Hollis, the brother of Republican and now Progressive reform
activist Allen Hollis, was the first Granite State Democrat to serve
in that body since the Know-Nothing sweep of 1855. Hollis won
with constant Democratic support in the face of Republican divisions, abetted by consistent Bass voting from a dozen Progressives.
Hollis was definitely in the progressive wing of his party, a location
he would continue to occupy in Woodrow Wilson's Washington. The
senior senator, Jacob Gallinger, did not like it at all. He found an
early Hollis speech "rabid," marking the junior senator as a "radical
of radicals, in favor of labor unions, declaring that men should spe-
cially protect their wives," the latter apparently a reference to Hollis's support for greater regulation of the working conditions of women
in industry. Gallinger also was distressed by the Hollis claim that
corporations in the Granite State had kept Democrats out of the
U.S. Senate. Gallinger, still struggling with the new century, found
it "an absurd speech, such as no New Hampshire man ought to
make." Hollis and Democratic congressman Raymond Stevens, as
well as Progressive George Rublee, would play roles in writing and
enacting reform legislation, especially that establishing the Federal
Trade Commission.[9]

The 1913 session of the New Hampshire state legislature was the
object of criticism for its length, its wrangling over office, its ineffi-
ciencies, and its partisanship. Perhaps the same charges could have
been levied against most of the sessions that preceded it; the difference this time was that Democrats were in control.[10] Governor Felker proposed to the legislature a reform agenda; he achieved much
of what he requested. Felker, Hollis, and Stevens represented a new
and more activist type of Democrat. They were the type of younger
party official and candidate nurtured and encouraged by Clarence
Carr after the Bryan debacle of 1896. These younger Democrats had
no explicit fear of governmental action, and they had a commitment
to stopping business abuse and improving industrial conditions. The
latter, along with their sensitivity to traditional Democratic opposition to state prohibition laws, gave them the support of old-line
Democrats.

Among other things, the 1913 legislature approved legislation empowering the public service commission to fix railroad rates; it enacted more restrictive limits on working hours for women and expanded the child labor law; it established a commission to deal with destitute and delinquent children; it established a board of conciliation and arbitration; it provided for assistance to the blind, to mothers with dependent children, and to families of prisoners; it required the reporting of occupational diseases; it fixed penalties for the desertion of a family; it modified the direct-primary laws, including the important addition of popular election of delegates to national political conventions; it established a legislative reference bureau and ratified the Sixteenth (income tax) and Seventeenth (direct election of senators) amendments to the United States Constitution. These were matters of some substance and were consistent with the social welfare concerns that had been a part of the recent reform movement in the state Democratic party as well as central to the Progressive campaign in 1912. In addition the legislature, under Democratic leadership, redistricted senate and council districts in ways that many felt unfairly favored Democratic candidates, and they "reorganized" many state boards and commissions that provided opportunities for wholesale new appointments.[11]

Although the Progressive Republicans supported much of this social and economic legislation, their role seldom seemed crucial. An analysis of the voting behavior of the twelve legislators who supported Bass's U.S. Senate candidacy down to the final vote suggests that only on an amendment to the state liquor law, which they unanimously opposed, did their voting strength hold the balance of power. On other votes they were not consequential; indeed, on few did they repeat unanimity. As has been true on other occasions analyzed in this study, cooperation on political matters did not necessarily translate into, or derive from, group coherence on public policy questions. Defining coherence arbitrarily as agreement among at least three-quarters of those voting, the twelve Progressives agreed on the liquor law amendment, procedures for fixing maximum railroad rates, and the reorganization of the state tax, license, and liquor boards, as well as political reorganizations for Dover, Manchester, and Portsmouth and for new state senate districts. They disagreed over the establishment of a minimum wage commission, restriction on injunctions, and limits on the definition of "conspiracy," authorizing woman suffrage, amendments to the public service commission law, and reorganization of the state bank board, among other bills considered and voted by roll call.[12]

The Progressives in the 1913 legislature were nominally Republican. Elected by necessity as members of the GOP, they nevertheless thought of themselves as the first wave of a new party. Yet by the end of the 1913 session the Progressive party was already a diminished entity. Bass, Churchill, and Roosevelt had all agreed following the 1912 election that they must now build a grass-roots organization with an eye to becoming the majority party of reform.[13] None of these principals apparently had the time or energy, or perhaps even the interest, that such an enterprise demanded. By the summer of 1913, the Progessive party state chairman, George Wicker, a Dartmouth economist, wrote Bass that he was "wretchedly discouraged" at the state of affairs. His attitude was not so much due to pessimism about the party's "prospects," but "at the thought that everyone expects things to be done while no one expects to do anything." Wicker hoped Bass could rally the reformers.[14]

Bass may have had some ambivalence about party building, some concern about political parties developing electoral rather than policy goals. In a July speech at Newport, Rhode Island, he insisted that the reformers' "single purpose is to accomplish those reforms which we know to be necessary," and "not to get certain men out of office and ourselves in." He continued to provide financial support for the party and participated in its deliberations, but he was interested in the party as a means, not an end. By the spring of 1914 Wicker had had enough; at a meeting at Frank Knox's Manchester home, Wicker resigned. On the eve of another election, the party was in shambles.[15]

Much of the Progressives' organizational chaos probably stemmed from their strategic confusion: it was clear they had little idea of how to approach the 1914 elections. There continued to be attrition from the ranks as reformers returned to the GOP. Frank Knox proved a major disappointment to many who had encouraged and supported his move to New Hampshire in 1912. His newspaper was successful; by April 1913 he wrote Bass that he did not "have the least trace of doubt on the success of The Leader." He had broken a brief boycott among advertisers; indeed, the enterprise was so successful that in 1913 Knox bought Rosecrans Pillsbury's *Union*. Suddenly he was the dominant journalist in the state; but, as Robert Bass observed, in this larger enterprise the reformers who brought Knox in from Michigan and provided some of the initial capital for the progressive *Leader* were now "a very small minority of creditors." Rosecrans Pillsbury, whom they had sought to counter with the *Leader*, now was a larger shareholder than they in the new *Union-Leader* corporation. Knox, who had described Progressivism as "the greatest political and moral awakening since the Civil War," set out to affect a reconciliation among the reformers and the old guard. This was to be accomplished in the Republican party.[16]

Early in 1914, Knox predicted to Churchill that that year's election might be "the last campaign in which the republican party appeared as an important factor."[17] In September of that year, Robert Manning, a Manchester progressive who had helped Knox establish the new reform newspaper in 1912, reported to Bass that Knox had been observed on primary day; the publisher "took a pink ticket, thereby registering as a Repub. Wouldn't that make a chap weary?" The next spring Allen Hollis wryly observed that Knox "seems to be making a success out of his newspaper venture, though on lines somewhat different from those which we had in mind when he originally came to New Hampshire. The atmosphere of the Granite State appears to have a steadying effect on his political notions."[18] By "notions" Hollis was referring to regular Republicanism, and whether or not the condition related to atmospheric factors, it proved contagious among most of the 1912 dissidents.

As far as many of the Progressives were concerned, the key race in the 1914 election was the U.S. Senate contest. Ratification of the Seventeenth Amendment to the U.S. Constitution meant that, for the first time, there would be popular voting for this position. The term of Jacob Gallinger, the Progressive nemesis, was expiring. Gallinger would have to stand for a statewide, popular election, his first. Symbolically and substantively, this should have been important enough to the Progressives for them to have organized and waged a major challenge for this seat. The challenge never really got off the ground. Progressives had a fundamental disagreement over their priorities. Some attached the highest importance to the defeat of Gallinger; others wanted only to maintain the independence and integrity of their new party. In the best of circumstances it may have been impossible to achieve both goals; some third-party stalwarts found their way back to the GOP, rejecting each of the goals.

In January, Churchill, writing from Aiken, South Carolina, where he was wintering, asserted that he "would rather be shot than amalgamated" back into the Republican party. His "instinct" was that the third party would simply "have to hold on tight" and wait for a "crystallization" that he believed was taking place within the national Democratic party. Here were many "natural allies" for the Progressives. If the latter remained "fired with the same zeal that we showed in 1912, we ought to win to us a considerable number of recruits from the Republican Party, or rather from their Progressive elements." Churchill was impressed with Democratic congressman Stevens with whom he met in February. Stevens was going to "drop state's rights . . . and make a speech on federalism. Out of all this we are distilling men like Stevens." Stevens was going to challenge Gallinger for the Senate seat. Given the circumstances, Churchill believed that support for Stevens would be sensible. The problem was that many remaining Progressives were of the "no compromise stripe, the never-say-die Progressive who's 'got religion.'" It would be a mistake to reject these diehards, Churchill concluded, for they could be critical in the "emergency of 1916."[19]

Churchill summarized well the Progressive problem. Moreover, in his concern about a potential "emergency" in 1916, he underlined the difficulty of finding solutions. The Progressives' coherence in 1912 came largely from their concerns about national affairs and their support for Theodore Roosevelt. This had helped splinter the reform energies in New Hampshire. Now, in 1914, looking beyond the state elections and calculating possible scenarios for 1916 that could result in a Roosevelt victory, the Bull Moose loyalists still could not systematically confront the problems—and opportunities—of state politics.

Progressives approached the 1914 elections in a state of some confusion. Everyone had become a strategist. Some felt that cooperation with the Democrats was the best approach: this could have the desirable effect of replacing Gallinger with Stevens. Others argued that the Republican party had learned its lesson in 1912 and that the regulars would be accommodating to the returning Bull Moosers; if some of the diehards were not, the reformers would have to take over the party. After all, they had done it before. Finally, some Progressives were convinced that their party was a viable and growing institution. It would inevitably replace one or both of the old parties, so the reformers should patiently hunker down, take their lumps, and wait for everything to fall into place. By all means, this third group insisted, the Progressives had to maintain their integrity as a political organization. In the absence of a clearly articulated party strategy, and in the presence of independent individuals with great confidence in their own judgment, each of these strategies was followed.

In the summer of 1914, party leaders searched for a direction—and for candidates. Churchill correctly predicted that the Progressives would have "a deuce of a time" successfully finding the latter. Robert Bass, under some pressure to enter the Senate race against Gallinger, refused to run. George Rublee argued that the third party should endorse Congressman Stevens for the U.S. Senate race: "I don't know of anything more important to be done in politics this year than the replacement in the Senate of a reactionary like Gallinger by a progressive with Stevens' ability and character." Bass agreed with the sentiments; he considered Gallinger's record the "most consistently uncompromisingly reactionary of any man now in the Senate." Bass said that while he personally would support endorsement of Stevens, he predicted the party would not. He was correct. The Progressive party filed its own candidate, Benjamin Greer, as well as a gubernatorial candidate, Henry Allison, and candidates for Congress and for some local seats. Most of the races proved symbolic at best. The candidates were not strong, nor were their races. Bass asked Rublee to prepare remarks for Allison to deliver at the state Progressive convention. Bass feared that Allison, a member of the legislature in 1913, "will doubtless prepare a discussion of certain State issues himself, but I feel that an intelligent statement of the present position of the Progressive party is a little beyond him." The observation was ironic if not cruel. It was not clear that anyone could have prepared such a statement in the fall of 1914.[20]

At their fall convention, the Progressives "rejoice[d] in our deliverance from the old parties and repudiate[d] any suggestion of amalgamation or alliance with either of them." The Republican party and its candidates "give the lie to any claim or pretence that the party is other than the same old organization prating of progress in platform and repudiating performance by the types of candidates nominated. The heart and fibre of the Republican party has not changed." The Progressives criticized the Republican platform for taking credit for the enactment of progressive legislation: "such legislation was enacted in spite of the present leaders of the Republican party, rather than because of them, and Republican candidates for high office before the electorate this year conspicuously opposed such progressive legislation." Nor do the Democrats, factional and ambivalent, "offer any hope to him who seeks political association with a party united, free, and vibrant with a great and lofty purpose."

The party platform reaffirmed the principles of 1912 and expanded them to include demands for a national presidential primary, support for "old age pensions," and a promise to support "effective legislation to prevent industrial accidents, occupational diseases, overwork and involuntary unemployment." The Progressives demanded the abolition of the Governor's Council and an expansion of the governor's powers. And the delegates voted a plank supporting "national prohibition of the liquor traffic." They pledged their "earnest and persistent efforts" to elect their party's candidates. They concluded, "Proud of our party and confident of the ultimate triumph of our principles, we joyously face the future."[21]

Among the delegates were Robert Bass, George Rublee, and Winston Churchill. They set out to work for Raymond Stevens. Rublee even gave a speech praising Stevens at the Progressive convention, causing at least one delegate to threaten to walk out. "We are a party" insisted O. L. Frisbee of Portsmouth. His was an increasingly isolated voice. Rublee was working with Stevens in Washington in the early fall, bringing their Federal Trade Commission legislation to successful conclusion. He became an important supporter of Stevens in New Hampshire. Robert Bass, who insisted that the Progressive principles would be better served if the party proved its integrity rather than its electability, provided Stevens with material on Gallinger's voting record and gave him campaign advice.[22]

One of the major Progressive disappointments that fall was the attrition from their ranks into the Republican party. The Republican platform, apparently largely written by Frank Knox, recognized and encouraged this process: the present is "preeminently a time for toleration and cordial good feeling toward those who, for what seemed to them good reasons, left the party in 1912. We hold that there is not and cannot be permanent grounds for disunion of these two elements. In fundamentals they think alike." As part of this effort toward reconciliation, Republicans nominated for governor Rolland Spaulding. Spaulding had been part of the old Republican reform group, but had been a "Taft Republican" in 1912. Bass insisted such efforts to make the Republican party appear progressive were "not only ridiculous but pathetic." He considered Spaulding to be weak: "I have no sympathy with those men who compromise their principles in order to get into office."[23]

Progressives were disheartened to see old companions like Sherman Burroughs and James Remick embrace the GOP, "actually advertising" the fact, Clarence Clough noted. Bass had warned that "any expectation or delusion that the Republican Party is going to be Progressive must fade from the mind of any sane man." Gallinger controlled the party. Frank Knox, still learning about New Hampshire politics, discovered in the fall that Gallinger was a tough fighter in party meetings. Knox sought, on behalf of the returning progressives, some greater influence than Gallinger was prepared to concede. As far as Gallinger was concerned, the "so-called Regulars" outnumbered the "so-called Progressives" by six or eight to one. The former might make "liberal concessions" to the latter, but did not care to have it "rubbed in." Nonetheless, all Gallinger wanted was "peace and happiness in the Republican family." Knox struggled and criticized some unnamed GOP members for being "as blindly and dully reactionary as ever," but insisted that the only way Democrats could win would be for the Republican leaders to be "sufficiently stupid" and Progressive leaders to be "sufficiently selfish" to permit such a thing.[24] Desite Knox's fulminations, the campaign continued with little further reconciliation.

In the fall Bass provided money for the Progressives to print and distribute circulars. He suggested to Frank Musgrove that these campaign documents describe the 1909 legislative record of Republican congressional candidate Edward Wason, particularly his opposition to measures then supported by Burroughs and Remick and "other so-called progressive Republicans." Bass wanted Burroughs mentioned by name and advised that it "might be well to make reference" to the "fact" that Remick's "change of heart dates approximately from the time of his employment as Attorney for the Grand Trunk Railroad."[25]

Bass's health continued to trouble him. He apparently believed he had contracted tuberculosis. This, along with his wife's continuing ill health, left him unable to participate regularly in Granite State political activities; he left New Hampshire in October for the drier climate of Arizona. He told Progressive gubernatorial candidate Allison that his "hope lies with the Progressive party." The former governor kept in touch with the campaign, particularly with Rublee's effort to elect Stevens. Churchill stayed on the sideline in Cornish due to the demands of his writing, but affirmed his support for the Progressive ticket and for progressive principles.[26]

For the Progressives and the Democrats, the 1914 elections were a disaster. The Republican party swept back into power in New Hampshire. Spaulding and Gallinger secured majorities, as did Republican congressional candidates Cyrus Sulloway and Edward Wason. All five of the Republican candidates for the Governor's Council were victorious. The GOP had overwhelming majorities in both houses of the General Court. The Democratic interlude was over. The voting returns indicated that the Progressive appeal had significantly deteriorated as well:

	Republican	Democratic	Progressive
Gubernatorial	46,413	33,674	2,572
U.S. Senate	42,113	36,382	1,938
U.S. Congress (1st District)	20,657	19,140	971
U.S. Congress (2d District)	21,793	16,101	1,409

There was little popular support for the Progressive candidates. Even their pivotal balance-of-power position had evaporated in the face of the rejuvenated Republican organization. If Progressives took some satisfaction from Gallinger running behind Spaulding, it was small satisfaction. Congressman Stevens was coming home. Jacob Gallinger was returning to a fifth term in the U.S. Senate, unprecedented in Granite State history; election reforms had not apparently affected his power. Theodore Roosevelt saw in the returns from New Hampshire and several other states that the GOP "had returned to the very worst of its old leaders" like Gallinger. Most of the reformers were once again regular Republicans. Tensions remained; Knox feared that the old guard, "our reactionary friends," would misinterpret the results and "return to something of their old arrogance," believing that they "can again nominate anybody and get away with it." Frank Streeter determined that he would be peacemaker, setting up a postelection dinner with some party activists, including Senator Gallinger. Streeter believed that the "common purpose" was to cooperate on party matters, and he was critical of the Bass administration for not encouraging such cooperation.[27]

Gallinger found magnanimity and cooperation difficult; he privately was embarrassed and angry that he ran behind the ticket in his first statewide race. He insisted in a letter to Moses in the spring that it was "ancient history"; he surely was "not seeking political revenge" because of this incident. He was not "troubling myself about such matters." There was one thing Moses could do though: the senator had learned that John Benton, the Bass progressive and member of the public service commission, had written a letter critical of Gallinger. Benton had to be removed: *We cannot afford to keep in office a man who betrays the party to the extent that Benton has done.*"[28]

After the election, Robert Manning of Manchester wrote Bass, insisting that he was "still full of fight." The Progressive party had, after all, received enough votes to be assured a place on the ballot in 1916. Manning was distressed about the ease with which some of the old reformers had gone back to the GOP: "some of our former men say they are just as much Progressives as ever they were (guess that is true, by gosh, tho not as they mean it)." Resignation quickly replaced bitterness among the reformers.[29]

A small core, centered about Robert Bass, refused to make the move back to the Republican party but came largely to accept the new party's inconsequential role in New Hampshire. Redemption, if it would come at all, would have to result from events outside the Granite State. The presidential election of 1916, which Bass predicted would be "the last act of the drama," might provide the necessary catalyst.[30] But even here the reformers were thinking less of regaining control in the state than they were of Theodore Roosevelt regaining the presidency.

The First World War, beginning in August 1914, introduced an entirely new range of issues to politics. Preparedness, the national policy of developing military plans, equipment, and forces to cope with any eventuality, came to dominate among these in terms of domestic politics. Some Progressives, led by Theodore Roosevelt, were sharply critical of Wilsonian policies, which they believed inadequate to defend national interests. Robert Bass, influenced by his brother John who had visited the western front as a correspondent, largely shared Roosevelt's views even if he shied away from the former president's more militaristic and romantic instincts. Robert and John spent a night with Roosevelt at Oyster Bay in the summer of 1915 to discuss the European situation. In the fall John prepared to go back to Europe, and Robert was repeating to associates that "from what he [John] has seen over there he thinks it is high time that we put ourselves in condition to protect this country in case of emergency."[31] Through the winter, John attempted to persuade Roosevelt to make a trip to Europe to see the situation for himself. In the summer of 1916 Roosevelt ultimately rejected the idea: "I have never been among those whose one idea in life is to survey what other people are doing at a momentous time. If I went to Europe at the present time, I would wish to go with arms in my hands, or else as the representative of an armed and resolute nation."[32]

Roosevelt was convinced that Wilson had failed to provide the necessary national resolve. This concern increasingly dominated the Rough Rider's political calculations. He wrote Churchill that he was fed up with a "lamentable" pacifism among some progressives like "poor foolish Jane Addams," and was generally suspicious of labor leaders, muckrakers, and "the doctrinaire reformer." By the time Roosevelt rejected the European trip he had also rejected the Progressive party presidential nomination for 1916. Theodore Roosevelt, determining that the defeat of Woodrow Wilson must be the first priority, had decided to support Republican nominee Charles Evans Hughes. Hughes had progressive credentials and pledged himself to preparedness. Perhaps even more important, he had served as justice on the U.S. Supreme Court and thus had not taken part in the internecine Republican warfare that flared in 1912. Roosevelt assumed most of his Progressive party supporters would follow him in this last twist. Many did; the Progressive National Committee endorsed Hughes. Churchill wrote an article for *Collier's* in which he described himself as "a witness to and an actor in the tragedy." As far as the third party was concerned, the last act of the drama played to an empty house.[33]

Roosevelt's actions caught many of his supporters unprepared. Robert Bass had been consistent in his loyalty to Roosevelt; he also had been consistent in his argument that the Republican party was "hopelessly reactionary."[34] In this denouement to reform, Robert Bass would be, as he had always been, independent, even if this meant breaking with his mentor and friend. Bass had trouble with Hughes's campaign as it developed; more important, he had continuing problems with the Republican party of New Hampshire, dominated by Jacob Gallinger. Gallinger was fighting off Frank Knox for this control. The senator wrote of Knox that "the gentleman has a plan in his alleged brain to take possession of the party in our State, and he will need watching." Gallinger refused to answer Knox's letters. The outcome of their battle was of no real interest to Bass.[35]

The former governor was particularly chagrined at Gallinger's successful use of senatorial privilege to block approval of Wilson's nomination of George Rublee to the Federal Trade Commission. Lyford had encouraged the senator to take this position. There is no evidence that any encouragement was necessary. Gallinger, angry at Henry Hollis for his support of the appointment of "Mavericks" rather than "real Republicans," had his revenge for Rublee's role in the 1914 Stevens campaign. Gallinger, who had privately dismissed Churchill as a "scab," had little disposition to welcome back any of the Roosevelt rebels; he had absolutely no disposition to work with anyone who had opposed his own 1914 reelection.[36]

In September 1916 Bass wrote Norman Hapgood that he was "in every sense an Independent." In New Hampshire, the Democrats were not "a particularly attractive alternative," and the GOP continued to be headed largely by "reactionaries." He did not feel like a member of any party. On the national level he confessed to liking Wilson's "large measure of Progressive and constructive legislation"; while he had "a high regard for Mr. Hughes's character," Bass continued to be "much disappointed to date with his speeches and his lack of constructive program." The former governor symbolized the frustration and ambivalence of many of the old Progressives. He took no part in the 1916 presidential campaign. Frank Musgrove found it hard to be enthusiastic about Wilson, perhaps largely because "my instincts have always been Republican," but Musgrove admitted that "common justice" was leading him to a Wilson vote "because no logical reason has been advanced yet why somebody else should take his place." Churchill, on the other hand, whose Cornish home President Wilson had used as a summer White House, announced for Hughes and considered accepting a Lyford request that he take the stump for the party. The old Progressives did agree on one thing: they would support the Democrat Raymond Stevens in his campaign to regain the congressional seat he gave up in 1914. Bass, Churchill, and Musgrove joined fifteen other old Progressives in signing a circular letter "To The Progressive Voters Of The Second

District," drafted by Churchill and Rublee, urging the election of Stevens "as a matter of real public interest." Lyford decided it would be best if Churchill not be featured at Republican rallies.[37]

The Progressives had lost their discrete identity ten years after the first act of political rebellion, the Churchill campaign of 1906. There was, however, to be one more surprise for the old guard politicians in New Hampshire, the old guard whose hubris had set them up for many surprises over this decade. Despite an ostensibly united party, one whose strength seemed so secure and predictable they could snub some of the returning progressives, the Republicans lost New Hampshire to Woodrow Wilson in 1916. By the narrow margin of fifty-six votes Wilson defeated Hughes in the Granite State on his way to a stunning reelection victory. Most of the Bull Moosers were back in the GOP, yet approximately ten thousand of Taft's 1908 supporters did not support Hughes, and Wilson's 1916 vote was approximately ten thousand votes greater than Bryan's in 1908 and his own in 1912. The total vote was quite consistent in all three of these presidential elections. Some of the old Bull Moosers, perhaps half of them, may have voted for Wilson in 1916. In October Gallinger had decided not to play an active role in the campaign because he was piqued at Knox, and in any event the senator predicted that the Hughes ticket "cannot fail" to win New Hampshire by ten thousand votes. Stevens did lose his race, and the Republicans repeated their 1914 successes in the state; this was inadequate balm for the sharp slap of losing a national election.[38]

In the postelection period there was little elation among the reformers. The ominous European war would have reduced contentment in the best of circumstances. But these were not even the best of circumstances. The GOP had lost a national election. The reformers had lost much more: they no longer had a political identity either as a discrete organization or as a coherent group within the Republican party. Individuals often continued their activities, but the heady sense of sharing in a profoundly important movement was gone.

The breakdown seemed complete. George Perkins, executive committee chairman of the Progressive National Committee, wrote Churchill shortly after the election, insisting that the reformers were "as deeply interested in and committed" to their principles as ever. It was just that now no one seemed to know what they should do, Perkins concluded, in order to achieve their goals "in a practical and efficient way."[39] The reformers had often prided themselves on their practicality and efficiency, characteristics, they felt, of their modern world. Now they had so lost their direction that they apparently did not know how to be either practical or efficient. The Great

War and the loss of confidence in popular support for reform shook Churchill. He had had one more private battle with the Boston and Maine railroad. In 1910 President Tuttle of the railroad had initiated a study for an extension of track in Cornish; President Mellen later reported that Tuttle had hoped to "get as near" Churchill's house as he could. Churchill spent several years and a significant amount of money fighting this plan.[40]

In the war years Winston Churchill withdrew and became philosophical, even mystical, and less activist. He told Robert Bass in 1917 that "between ourselves I think they [the Wilson administration] would be glad to have me endorse the administration, and back up their conduct of the war. I am not prepared to do this, nor am I prepared to oppose it. I feel that I must keep myself free." In his novel *Dwelling Place of Light*, published in 1917, there was less hope and optimism than in the earlier writings.[41] The novel was Winston Churchill's last. In 1930 he asserted, "Life goes according to fashions and fads. I am not deploring it. I think everything in life has its place, and one can hardly say that life progresses. . . . It is all temporary."[42]

Robert Bass had never shared Winston Churchill's ego or his dilettantish interests. Now he did not share his pessimism. Bass continued to be active in a variety of ways, despite his complaints about health problems. He and Edith built a new home at Peterborough and by war's end were enjoying it with their children Edith, Perkins, and Joanne. Bass continued to be active in forestry and had an interest in agricultural experiments and innovations. He worked with Herbert Croly and Walter Lippmann on a few projects for the *New Republic;* he engaged in some studies on international trade with George Rublee and Frank Taussig; he was active with organizations promoting conservation, equal suffrage, preparedness, and postwar peace; he participated in lobbying for approval of the Federal Trade Commission, the Rublee appointment to that body, and the appointment of Louis Brandeis to the U.S. Supreme Court. He became deeply interested and involved in labor problems, particularly in mediation of disputes. During the war he served the federal government as vice chairman of the shipping board and chairman of the National Adjustment Commission.[43] Robert Bass quietly rejoined the Republican party in 1917.

The curtain call was brief. If the stage was a little different and some old faces were missing, there was enough of the old cast around:[44] The United States entered the Great War in April 1917. In November William Chandler died at the age of eighty-one. Cyrus Sulloway died in that same year, and Sherman Burroughs replaced him in Congress. In 1918 Jacob Gallinger died, and, in a special election coinciding with the November general election, George Moses, who shared Gallinger's distaste for the reformers, narrowly won the U.S. Senate seat. Henry Hollis decided not to be a candidate for reelection in that year; his seat was taken by the Republican candidate Henry Keyes. Republicans won both congressional races. John Bartlett, who had been one of the regular Republican candidates for the U.S. Senate seat in the contest that had tied up the state legislature in 1913, was elected governor. In that same month, November 1918, the Great War ended. Six hundred and ninety-seven Granite Staters had lost their lives in that struggle.

Sen. George Moses participated in the successful fight to block Woodrow Wilson's peace treaty and in the unsuccessful fight to defeat the constitutional amendment giving suffrage to women. In his reelection bid in 1920 Moses's Democratic opponent was Raymond Stevens. In 1920 New Hampshire gave the Republicans large majorities in all statewide races, including over 60 percent for presidential nominee Warren Harding. The 1916 embarrassment had been redeemed. Moses's conservative positions seemed vindicated. Frank Knox enjoyed journalistic domination in New Hampshire and was more successful than his *Union* predecessor, Rosecrans Pillsbury, in influencing Republican party affairs. In 1920, running now as a Democrat, Pillsbury lost his bid for a congressional seat.

After consultation with some members of his old progressive network, former governor Robert Bass ran in the 1922 election as a candidate for the New Hampshire General Court. Bass won and in January 1923 quietly took a seat as a Republican representative from Peterborough.

7

The Progressive Yankees

O N FEBRUARY 14, 1920, Robert Bass spoke to the City Club of Chicago. It was a tense time in the United States. Sharp labor-management conflict had marked the postwar years. Bitter and violent racism exploded in many cities, including Chicago. Anti-immigrant sentiments openly flared. The attorney general of the United States, A. Mitchell Palmer, had recently initiated a series of raids to ferret out the "radicals" many citizens were convinced were behind the labor unrest. Some believed the Republic was under siege. A conservative reaction to the war, to internationalism, to reformist experiments, to alien ideas, was abroad in the land, a mood that would contribute in November to the election of Warren G. Harding and his promise of a return to "normalcy."

These events provided the subject for Bass's address. In the comfortable setting of the City Club, the former New Hampshire governor was direct, as was his style. Bass was not only dealing with distant problems. A series of raids in New Hampshire on January 2 had netted a number of alleged radicals. Some 140 of these had been taken to the Deer Island jail in Boston harbor. Despite the flimsy evidence and the disdain for civil liberties that the procedures represented, the action had been almost uniformly applauded in New Hampshire, but not by Robert Bass. Bass told the City Club audience that the climate of opinion in the United States concerned him. There was, he observed, "a surprisingly bigotted [*sic*] and hostile intolerance toward all those who hold political and economic beliefs fundamentally at variance with the views of the majority." The United States faced no danger except from the current policy of intolerance. Americans were loyal to their country during the war; now "Americanism is much more difficult to define." Unfortunately some seemed to believe that repression, along with a crusade for "Americanization and loyalty in our schools and among our immigrants," would dispose of all threatening ideas. But, Bass warned, "we can neither imprison [n]or defeat ideas."

The governor feared that domestic policies in the United States were falling too far behind those of European nations; other industrial countries were providing old-age pensions and medical and unemployment insurance. They were working on improving industrial relations and working conditions. "The time has almost arrived when we shall be asked, not by a little handful of radicals, but by the American people, what we have done, or propose to do, to meet these and other similar issues." The answers to these questions and "not any policy of political repression" will determine the ultimate conclusion to the current unrest. The speaker challenged his audience to turn their attention to solving "many urgent industrial, educational and social problems. These are the issues which I should hope might replace lurid accounts of raids[,] plots, and deportations in the headlines of our newspapers." The task will be difficult, but it could be done: "when finally accomplished, we may all feel assured that the safety of the Republic no longer requires that the American wage earner be completely isolated from the violent agitator."[1]

In 1920 James Remick, chair of the old Lincoln Republicans, Bull Mooser, and object of scorn from Bass and others when he campaigned for Jacob Gallinger in 1914, announced that he was supporting the Democrat James Cox in his presidential campaign against Senator Harding. The politically peripatetic Remick said, "I believe in progressivism, and I believe in the 'normal'; but the truly normal is always progressive. I have learned to my sorrow that voting for candidates who are the incarnation of political Bourbonism and reaction is not the way to promote the Progressive cause.

"To turn away from a concrete opportunity to defeat the forces of reaction, to promote the Progressive cause, and to secure a League of Nations to enforce peace, for no other reason than that the opportunity comes from a Democratic source, while at the same time writing and speaking in favor of political independence, would be worse than impractical idealism—it would be the rankest hypocrisy."[2]

These positions of Bass and Remick, the withdrawal from public affairs of Churchill, the increasing conservatism of Frank Knox— who now worked closely with Moses and whose newspaper applauded the mass arrests in New Hampshire—all attest to the difficulty of developing generalizations about the reform movement in New Hampshire. During the progressive period in New Hampshire, there was never a definable, intellectually coherent, politically cohesive, and continuing movement that was composed of members with shared views on the range of policy questions that the state faced. But the reformers' primary focus, as well as their only common concern, was politics. American political history does not include many examples of movements or organizations, or even of political parties, that have these characteristics *and* are viable in electoral politics. Any generalizations about progressivism in New Hampshire must begin by recognizing its fundamental political context.[3]

The Lincoln Republicans of 1906 were a distinct group with a shared purpose—and a brief existence and a rather narrow focus. They were the first of several progressive organizations: the Platform Republicans, the Taft Republicans, the legislative reform coalition of 1909, the Bass supporters of 1910, the Bass supporters in the legislature in 1911, the Roosevelt Republicans, the Bull Moose Progressives of 1912, the Progressive "Republican" coalition in the legislative session of 1913, the Bull Moose Progressives of 1914, the Bull Moosers for Stevens, the Independents of 1916. All were ephemeral as constituted groups. There was an ad hoc quality to each; each shared only their articulated purpose: to nominate a candidate, to elect a candidate, to secure passage of legislation.

Despite their differential and transient nature, these various reform organizations were not quite discrete groups. Many of the same people were involved in each.[4] Bass and Churchill had significant involvement in nearly all of them. They, along with several other activists, had important roles in several of the committees or organizations and provided a sense of continuity and experience to the Republican/Progressive reform effort. Most of these other key individuals may have broken with the Bass-Churchill leadership at one time or another, and of course Bass and Churchill were not together in either 1906 or 1916, but this does not mitigate the existence of a reform nucleus that functioned in several organizational forms. The loyalty tests the reformers occasionally imposed on each other should not provide the basis for historical analysis.

The Carr-Felker-Hollis-Stevens Democrats probably provided a more coherent and continuing example of a reform organization. They were essentially conterminous with the Democratic party during this period. Elements of the old rural, Jacksonian Democracy remained, but the new Democracy was more urban and cosmopolitan. The *Monitor* observed that this party had broken away from its Granite State moorings and, representative of this shift, the new Democracy did not even make much of Andrew Jackson's birthday. Symbolically, on March 23, 1909, James McGregor died in Newport at the age of 109. McGregor had seen two new centuries, and he claimed to have voted on three occasions each for Andrew Jackson, Grover Cleveland, and William Jennings Bryan, a feat of longevity and of partisan persistence that likely had no equal.[5] The party at

the time of McGregor's death had more of an urban-labor orientation than the party represented by these three candidates. The reform Democrats were in control. They had a solid, if minority, institutional base. The Republican reformers never really enjoyed
such a base; they were but a part of the majority party. Even during
the Bass governorship the GOP may have been as much Gallinger's
as it was Bass's. Control of the party, which probably best describes
the goal of the Churchill insurgents of 1906, always eluded the Republican reformers, despite their successes in electing candidates
and in enacting legislation.

The Republican party that had emerged from the realignment of
the 1890s dominated New Hampshire politics in the early twentieth
century. New Hampshire was essentially a one-party state. With the
demise of the Democratic party as a viable statewide institution, the
Republican party had become the major forum for defining and
the political instrument for accomplishing public policy goals. In
this dominant position Republican party officials and officeholders
often resisted change and innovation. For many this was likely less a
philosophical response than it was a self-protective impulse. The old
guard was aided in its defense by the inertia that seemed to accom-
pany one-party supremacy. Party strategist James Lyford warned
Frank Streeter in 1902 that the "present abnormal majority" ironically portended weakness: "Party ties do not bind as closely."[6]

Institutional inertia may have had its counterpart in electoral apa-
thy. In 1890 an estimated 73 percent of the age-eligible voters cast
ballots in the gubernatorial election; in 1902 the figure was 60 percent and in 1910 it was 62 percent. Presidential races elicited more
interest; in 1892 an estimated 76 percent of the age-eligible voters
went to the polls for the Cleveland-Harrison contest. In the second
McKinley-Bryan race of 1900 the figure was 71 percent; the Taft-
Bryan election of 1908 drew an estimated 66 percent. Examining
presidential elections in the period from 1888 to 1916, more total
votes were cast in 1888 than in any of the races that followed, excepting only the one in 1900, despite an increase of approximately
20 percent in the eligible electorate.[7]

The reformers could score an occasional victory but they lacked
the organizational strength—and probably the energy—to carry on
the fight for control of the party after elections or after legislative
sessions. The Bass Republicans demonstrated their appeal in the
1910 primary; they may have had the strength and the momentum
to follow this success by securing control of the party. Louis Wyman
had insisted before the primary that the reformers had to build and
maintain their own version of a machine: "A machine is a necessity
and yet we deprecate the existence of one which does not give equal

opportunity to every citizen to be heard with respect to the passage and the execution of the laws."[8] It is by no means unlikely that Bass could have led a victorious fight against the old guard in the legislature in 1913 and taken Burnham's U.S. Senate seat, but this would have required a major effort in 1911 and 1912, an effort to build a "reform machine." Bass had neither the ambition nor the interest that such a campaign would have required. While the reformers were hesitating, Jacob Gallinger, through the efforts primarily of James Lyford, was working to rebuild an organization. Lyford particularly believed that the old party leadership had to accommodate the reformers and some of their accomplishments. Following Bass's nomination this meant adapting to the new primary law. "Our old organization has gone to pieces," Lyford observed. He repeatedly insisted that it was necessary to reach out and engage the "young voters."[9]

At its core, New Hampshire progressivism was marked by a continuing struggle for control of the Republican party. This was the continuity and cohesion that marked the reform effort from 1906 to 1912, and it explains the alarm that some reformers expressed when Bass and others determined to walk with Theodore Roosevelt and the Bull Moosers. Louis Wyman told Bass that the Republican reformers had achieved many of their goals and "were on the threshold of attaining our ideal in party management." Many, like Wyman, refused to join Bass in the bolt; of those who did join him, the majority were back in the GOP by 1914. In political terms they were not comfortable with an independent movement, at least not one independent of their party. The reasons for this response were individual and complicated; the relapse to Republicanism represented more than innate conservatism or irrational ties to the party as an institution, although the reform ranks had its share of these feelings. More important, many progressive Republicans argued that starting a new party was not simply inconsistent with their original purposes: it was antithetical to these purposes in that it necessarily left the GOP in the hands of the old guard, the "revival of antedeluvian [sic] leadership," in Wyman's view. By 1912 the Bull Moosers had concluded that the reform priority was writing into law a reform agenda, indeed an expanding reform agenda. In accepting the Bull Moose nomination for governor in 1912, Winston Churchill stressed the themes of social justice, public conscience, and Christian values. He insisted, "No longer do the citizens of our republic regard with complacency a system in which men and women and even little children are exploited in mills and mines and factories like cattle." This statement represented a broader set of concerns than those Churchill had articulated in 1906.[10] Party, the Bull Moosers insisted, was only a means to these broader concerns, and the Republican party proved an inadequate means. Those reformers who resisted bolting, on the other hand, claimed that only through control of their party could they hope to see the reform agenda enacted. The argument focused on means, but it would be a mistake to infer that there was consensus on the ends.

The Republican progressives never fully agreed on the contents of the reform agenda. In 1905 and 1906 there was an inchoate frustration and concern with what many conceived to be the corrupting and arrogant influence of the Boston and Maine railroad in New Hampshire politics. From the Churchill-led Lincoln Republican insurgency in 1906 through the Bass election in 1910, the railroad's influence was their primary driving and cohering force. The recognition that "business corrupts politics," as Richard L. McCormick has argued, occurred in many states in 1905–6 as a series of allegations, investigations, and disclosures swept the country.[11]

Although the reformers took the rhetorical high ground in their antirailroad campaign, they were not alone in this effort. The progressives never acknowledged the support they received from some old guard leaders in their fight against Boston and Maine arrogance. The old guard were concerned less with the institution and the system than they were with the opportunistic Streeter, and they sought to reduce railroad influence quietly, not altering the parameters of public rhetoric or of policy. Chandler was an exception; he was incapable of doing things quietly, and he defined the corporation as the enemy. Chandler, however, was never quite a member of the old guard after Gallinger's rise to power in the 1890s. Chandler was the party's gadfly. In any event Streeter's defeat of Gallinger in the 1904 national committeeman vote may have started the demise of the railroad's political influence as much as the Salem racetrack disclosures did. For much of the antirailroad old guard, a quiet Greenleaf victory in 1906 would have sufficed. The Lincoln Republicans needed a public campaign for Churchill to have any hope of winning. Their rhetoric and early goals reflected their concern with cleansing politics and government: abolishing free passes, controlling lobbying activities, and freeing the nomination process from manipulation. In the 1907 legislative session these matters represented the limits of Lincoln Republican cohesion. Chandler had insisted this should continue as the focus; particularly if the New Haven/Boston and Maine merger were effected, he warned, all politicians would "live by the breath of the nostrils of the magnates of the monster railroad corporation."[12]

In the successful 1909 legislative session and 1910 campaign, Chandler's warning notwithstanding, the reform agenda had expanded, largely due to the influence of Robert Bass, and included a wider range of political reforms, greater economic regulation, conservation activities, and some social and labor demands. Nonetheless, the continuing antirailroad, antiboss rhetoric probably provided the only cohering themes for the reformers. The absence of policy agreement on broader issues among the Bass supporters in the 1909 legislative session and the undifferentiated response of the 1910 Bass voters to the constitutional amendments suggest this was the case.

As governor, Robert Bass articulated a comprehensive vision of reform. His aims were broader than removing the Boston and Maine from politics, defeating the old guard, and opening up the processes of the GOP. He continued to pursue these goals, but only as necessary first steps. Jacob Gallinger may have conceded the first goal— removal of the railroad's political influence—but he was not prepared to go beyond this. With the help, and prodding, of Frank Musgrove and others, Governor Bass managed to secure significant legislative victories in 1911 that were much broader than the original reform goals. In this he had the cooperation and support of progressives in both the Republican and Democratic parties. This support rested on his personal influence or on shared views on specific matters of public policy; it did not derive necessarily from a common ideology. The coalition that produced reform legislation continually shifted.

When Bass and some other reformers took the steps toward partisan independence in 1912, they found themselves in a minority. The old 1910 electoral coalition disaggregated. Presumably the Bull Moosers shared agreement on the state reform agenda; limited evidence suggests this was not even the case. There was no statistical relationship between the Progressive vote in 1912 and voting for the several constitutional amendments that went to the New Hampshire electorate in this period.[13]

One study of the New Hampshire Progressives has concluded that they were relatively young, middle class, Protestant, and Yankee; they were marginally distinguished from their old guard adversaries by being younger, somewhat better educated, and more likely to be in business or education. In this regard the New Hampshire progressives were not unlike those who joined reform efforts in other states, nor were they significantly unlike the reform opponents. *Yankee* may be a useful description of the New Hampshire Republican progressive movement; it was not a differentiating label.[14]

Their personal characteristics may provide some insights into the reformers' attitudes and style; they coincide with the image left in the correspondence of several of the leaders: young, curious, intelligent, and cosmopolitan. *Modern-minded* and *broad-minded* were terms people like Bass would have used as synonyms for *progressive:* citizens of the new century. But despite the fact that they liked to think of themselves as unique from their antagonists in this regard, the difference may have been little more than minimal. The term *progressivism* itself had—and has—some descriptive usefulness, but it was conceptually flabby. Occasional reformer Montgomery Rollins said the movement appealed to those "who are sincerely interested in political and national progress, and in righteous upbuilding; in other words, those who are definitely committed to the Progressive cause."[15] In other words, presumably everyone. Except that the "cause" part of his definition imposed real limits. The reformers early on took and maintained the rhetorical high ground, no small advantage in politics. They had a heady sense of participating in a cause; this notion rather than a coherent and substantive new program shaped the progressive group. At the level of belief in abstractions like progress and righteousness, the reformers may have been little different from most of their opponents. Belief in a progressive cause may have never defined the reformers. It helped to describe them.

The progressives had to contend with the complex, pluralistic, symbolic, and at times evanescent, nature of the American political system. Local, state, and national politics may have been part of a whole, but surely not an undifferentiated whole. The Republican progressives focused in the first instance on state politics; they sought to capture their party and through this instrument to reform state politics. The Republican party of New Hampshire, however, like its Democratic counterpart, was not an independent or monolithic entity. The state party depended on local organizations and support; these had some independence and, more important, were responsive to idiosyncratic local needs, alliances, and antagonisms. The GOP had a half century of experience of adapting to these by 1906, of recruiting and developing local leaders through the distribution of patronage and influence, of establishing voter loyalty through appeals as symbolic and emotional as they were substantive. The two old parties were deeply rooted in the political topsoil of New Hampshire; they did not have to remake their organization and voting coalition for each new political season. Their partisanship may have been all that some of these local organizations shared; this was by no means an inconsequential thing to share.

The emotion and symbolism that were critical factors in the strength of the New Hampshire parties emanated largely from outside of the state. The New Hampshire GOP may have recited the lines, but the national Republican party furnished the script and the cues. State parties were critically dependent on national developments, but their national counterparts faced many of the same organizational problems with which the state parties had to cope. The national parties had to maintain a semblance of institutional integrity and political rationality in the face of conflicting local and state needs and demands. Fortunately they only had to do this under close public scrutiny every four years.

Although they had some significant organizational independence, local and state parties could not escape from the actions, or perceived responsibility, of their national political leaders. New Hampshire Republicans were convinced that a major factor in their loss of the state to the Democrats in 1874 was the national economic problems at that time and the allegations of corruption in the Grant administration.[16] During the Panic of 1893, Republican governor Charles Busiel conceded that "the primary causes are beyond our control."[17] Despite this fact, the Democratic party in New Hampshire suffered directly from the voters' perceptions that Grover Cleveland was responsible for the Panic of 1893. The Bryan nomination in 1896 effectively destroyed the old Democratic party in New Hampshire; the opposition of most New Hampshire Democratic leaders to Bryan proved irrelevant to the voters.

New Hampshire politicians had continually to juggle the interplay between local and national politics. Sometimes this meant emphasizing national appeals, such as the Republicans did with the tariff; on other occasions it meant trying to keep distance from the national context, such as the Democrats with Bryan in 1896. As a general proposition, these examples were consistent with the voting patterns throughout this period. Republican presidential candidates ran stronger than that party's gubernatorial candidates in New Hampshire; the Democratic vote tended toward the opposite pattern. One might infer from this that the Republicans were strengthened by national candidates and campaigns more than their opponents were. The Democrats could typically run stronger gubernatorial races in the off-year elections than they could in presidential election years.[18]

New Hampshire politicians were always alert to the national issue they might profitably introduce into—or avoid in—the state campaigns. In 1904 Clarence Carr and Henry Hollis attempted to convince New Hampshire voters that the acquisition of the Panama Canal Zone was an issue in the state. Apparently it did not catch on. In 1908 Carr regretted not campaigning on the tariff and "the full dinner pail."[19] Others, in contrast, attributed his loss in the gubernatorial race in the latter year to the intrusion of national issues.[20] Among "local" issues, probably only that of liquor had the potential to cut a wide electoral swath: the Republican *Monitor* insisted in 1900 that the Anti-Saloon League effort to influence the selection of delegates to the national convention was misplaced; the convention would deal with issues that "are entirely national in character"; the later state meeting would "deal with state affairs and state issues. There, and there alone, belong questions relating to local affairs."[21]

The Republican progressives, in their later Bull Moose form, attempted to rationalize this loose federal structure of American politics. In 1913 Robert Bass complained to his father-in-law, Charles Sumner Bird, that Republicanism had little meaning, that there were greater differences between the state Republican platforms of Rhode Island and Oklahoma than there were between the national Democratic and Republican platforms. It was "absurd," Bass wrote, to think of a single party that was represented by people as different as Jacob Gallinger and Boies Penrose, on the one hand, and reformers like Robert La Follette and Albert Cummins, on the other. The Progressive party, in contrast, was consistent in all its organizational forms: "It is really the only party of which this can be said."[22]

The Republican progressives were not above the strategic introduction of national issues and personalities into their campaigns. Reformer support for Taft's effort to secure the nomination in 1908 was partially due to such calculations. Progressive Allen Hollis, following the frustrations of 1906 and 1907, chortled over the prospect of linking the cause with President Roosevelt and Taft: "The progressive Republicans in New Hampshire can afford to make their fight on those lines. If there are divisions in our camp as to who should hold New Hampshire office, they are likely to become obliterated in a good fight on the National ticket." He told Churchill that the impending struggle over the nomination "gives us a chance to organize on impersonal lines—impersonal, at least, as regards New Hampshire men."[23] Churchill's thinking partially coincided with Hollis's strategic concept; the former had put together the complicated plan involving Frank Streeter and Rosecrans Pillsbury in order to expand reform strength in New Hampshire. The novelist/politician may have erred when he agreed with Republican regular James Lyford not to form Taft clubs for the fall campaign because there already were Republican organizations in place and they had the same goals.[24] For Churchill in any event strategy was secondary; Churchill had already made clear in a variety of ways, including his "I am a Federalist" statement, that national issues were of primary concern to him. Churchill and Bass, in their contacts and their interests, were political cosmopolitans. This was not necessarily a distinguishing aspect of the reform movement—not all reformers shared

cosmopolitan views nor was the old guard exclusively led by paro-
chial-minded politicians.[25]

Among the reformers Bass and Churchill represented an aggrega-
tive concept of political issues. The issues of national politics were
as important and relevant to them as were the issues of state politics.[26] By 1912 they were certainly more important to Churchill and
probably were to Bass. These two progressive leaders were less political strategists than they were issue-oriented political activists.
Their approach to politics held that issues made coalitions; the older
political practice tended toward the opposite approach. The 1905–6
allegations in New Hampshire as well as President Roosevelt's sharp
rhetoric had altered the political climate. Lyford said as much in
1908 when he noted that people were asking harder questions about
positions and candidates and were persuaded that "multi million-
aires" were trying to control politics: "They are not the rabble but
just the average Republican voter."[27] The reform movement helped
create this new mood; more important, it was sustained by it. In
retrospect, given the tone of New Hampshire politics for the previous four years, it is hard to imagine Bertram Ellis defeating Robert
Bass in the 1910 primary. Ultimately the reformers' political vulner-
ability—and perhaps much of their strength—related to their refusal to search for the issues that composed the common denomina-
tors among their supporters, and potentially among the voters.
There were no brokers, counterparts of James Lyford, in the reform
ranks. Many of the reformers, certainly Bass and Churchill, seemed
genuinely to believe that candidates were secondary and that winning votes was only a means to accomplish more fundamental goals.
The latter were their focus. This baffled the old guard. Moses said
the reformers were "fools" who persisted "in preaching the gospel of
gush, insisting on fighting for abstractions rather than centering
their fight for principle around some person."[28]

The Taft-Roosevelt primary battle in the spring of 1912 provided
anti-Bass Republicans with a tactical opportunity. Bass later reflected that all of the old guard "united in this campaign to get a
crack at me."[29] It would seem that they did, but not all the Taft supporters were anti-Bass. Many echoed the insistence of one who said
that while he supported Taft, he believed Bass was an "ideal governor, and the fittest man in sight"; he would stand by Bass "in state
matters—fully, and as firmly as ever."[30] In September, when some
reformers were breaking from the GOP to follow the call of Roosevelt's Bull Moose, such divergent loyalties became more difficult to
reconcile. Some of the reformers never quite shared—or perhaps
never understood—the strength of party ties. Allen Hollis warned

that a new party was a strategic mistake: "these third party enthusiasts should pay some heed to the local situation in New Hampshire, in this campaign at least."[31] Hollis was consistent with his earlier suggestion to seize the Taft opportunity to build a state organization; the Roosevelt exodus represented an opportunity lost. Churchill, Bass, and the other Bull Moosers were consistent as well with their earlier position that issues guided their political decisions. National politics had given the reform effort a boost in 1908; in 1912 the Roosevelt insurgency destroyed the progressive political movement.

State tactical considerations had little influence on national strategies. Bass implored Roosevelt to assist in New Hampshire in the March primary effort by visiting the state. The former president replied, "You are the one man in this fight for whom I would do anything he asked." And then the Rough Rider put the appearance into its proper context: "Is it too late to speak in Portland?"[32] Roosevelt's campaign arena was necessarily larger; the universe of the New Hampshire state reformers was but a small part—indeed, an expendable part—of the national campaign. Former governor John McLane, sympathetic to the Republican reformers, found it "unfortunate that developments in the national political situation have brought it about that the satisfactory state of affairs which has prevailed in this State for the last two years can not continue indefinitely." McLane agreed nonetheless that "it is necessary to take a stand on national issues," and he agreed to identify with the new movement.[33] Frank Musgrove considered a plan to preserve the Republican reform identity by supporting the third party at the national level and maintaining his Republican affiliation in the state. Daniel Remich warned that Musgrove would "make a fatal mistake, in my judgment, if he tries to ride two horses at the same time."[34] Musgrove shortly recognized the difficulty of these political acrobatics and resigned as chairman of the Republican State Committee and joined the Progressive party. He agreed with the other third-party supporters that great national issues were restructuring politics. In 1914 he counseled a supporter not to return to the GOP because the reformers shared no views with the Republican party as shaped by people like Gallinger, except the tariff which was of "secondary importance." For too many voters, as it turned out, weaned on Republicanism and tariff rhetoric, the latter may have seemed primary; in any event their party was much more than a policy instrument continually to be reevaluated.[35] Gallinger won in 1914 because he was a Republican; the reformers never seemed to fully understand the partisan motive forces of politics.

In 1908 one of Churchill's friends and supporters reminded him of the importance of local caucuses and of local issues such as liquor

licenses. He noted that "while I have great interest in state &
nation we must not forget the foundation which is the town."[36]
The Progressive Republicans largely remembered this warning in
1910; there was some forgetfulness in the Burroughs congressional
primary campaign in that year. Churchill had insisted that the
Burroughs effort would be successful because "the people of New
Hampshire are beginning to think seriously about national issues,
high tariff and conservation."[37] Burroughs ran on "Cannonism" and
on the White Mountain Forest Reserve bill and he lost. As one observer noted, "I do not want to question his methods but to be successful one must have living issues vitally important to the people
whose suffrage he asks."[38] In 1912 the Bull Moosers forgot this
lesson or neglected its implications. The old guard once more controlled the Republican party.

This outcome would seem to conclude failure for the Republican
reformers. Except it is failure defined narrowly in terms of their
effort to capture the Republican party. If this was their major cohering and continuing theme from 1906 to 1910, it was not their singular purpose. The progressives articulated an expanding view of
reform; their successes would indicate that others shared this vision. In the early years of the twentieth century, the state of New
Hampshire was marked by legislation that significantly changed the
nature of politics and government. The various groups and coalitions that accomplished these alterations in the law and its protection, in political institutions and their processes, and in government
and its functions, may have been too vague, too shifting, and even
contradictory in their purposes and their composition, to accommodate sharp definition and analysis. This does not negate their
accomplishment.

From the dawn of the new century to the beginning of the Great
War in August 1914, much of the basic law of New Hampshire was
rewritten and new law was written. The Lincoln Republicans were
vindicated by antipass laws, regulation of lobbying activities, and
direct-primary legislation. These, along with the establishment of
the public service commission, effectively reduced the political and
economic influence of the Boston and Maine railroad. The reform
impetus, however, had expanded beyond this. The legislature in
1909 wrote a whole new body of law on business and commerce, describing rights and liabilities. In 1907, 1909, and 1913, the legislature stiffened state insurance regulations, and in 1911 approved detailed banking regulation; in 1909 the legislature outlawed "bucket
shops."[39]

In an industrial economy, traditional commercial regulation did
not suffice. Some of the significant innovations of this period came

in public health and welfare and in employment and labor relations. The 1907 legislature established separate court procedures for juvenile offenders and forbade the incarceration of juveniles with adults. In 1909 the legislature defined and proscribed unhealthy tenements and established fire regulations for public buildings; established procedures and supervision for adopting children born in state institutions; passed new laws regulating the adulteration of food and drugs and restricted to controlled pharmacists, upon the prescription of a physician, the sale of cocaine and its derivatives; authorized the state board of health to employ sanitary inspectors; and forbade county almshouses to house individuals judged to be mentally incapacitated, transferring responsibility for these persons to the state hospital. The 1911 legislature defined further and proscribed unsanitary practices and brought under state licensing and regulation all hospitals and boardinghouses for infants. In 1913 the legislature and Governor Felker approved laws requiring physicians to report suspected occupational diseases, requiring counties to provide an income supplement for single mothers with dependent children, and establishing state support for locating employment or developing industries for the blind. Throughout this period the several legislatures sharpened the rights and protection of minors and gave courts new responsibilities and powers in cases of marital separation and desertion. The 1911 legislature expanded older criminal codes on prostitution to include procurement and pandering.

In 1911 the Bureau of Labor received greatly enlarged powers, including arbitration and mediation. In that same year the legislature established employer liability and workmen's compensation laws and greatly restricted and regulated child labor; legislators made illegal the practice of employers compelling workers to accept goods or merchandise in lieu of wages. In 1913 the legislature forbade employers from restricting worker union membership, regulated the hiring of new employees during a strike or lockout, and approved maximum-hours legislation for women workers.

Conservation of natural resources was a major interest of many of the reformers. In 1909 the legislature approved a comprehensive forest protection law; this was augmented in 1911 and 1913. The 1911 legislature sharpened fire protection in the state's woodlands. Throughout this period the state expanded significantly its fish and game protection laws and its regulation of fishing and hunting. Of great importance to the New Hampshire conservationists was passage of the Weeks bill in the U.S. Congress in 1911, providing for the White Mountain Forest Reserve. Many of the New Hampshire reformers, including notably Robert Bass, participated actively in the effort to secure passage of this legislation. In 1911 the state legislature also passed legislation enabling the state to purchase and establish a forest reserve at Crawford Notch.[40]

Reform in education was more halting, marked by continual modification of the state's expectations and responsibilities. One student of education in New Hampshire wrote of the period 1885–1919 that "it was one in which the state, through more insistent and stringent legislation, ever-increasing state appropriations for the assistance of economically unfortunate communities, and the spending of these funds for better equipment, professionally trained teachers, and a system of professional school administration and supervision," dealt with the problems of nineteenth-century organization and with economic changes. Through these changes "the ancient tradition of the right of the local community to decide all school policy and practice was ignored": the state, in matters of "school funds, child labor and school attendance, high schools, illiteracy, teacher certification and training, school health and sanitation, and supervision of educational efforts and administration of school work," began to oversee and regulate local standards. This culminated in 1919 in a major educational reform law in New Hampshire that resulted from the recognition during the war years that the state's educational system was lagging behind those of other states.[41]

In the progressive period perhaps the most significant contribution to education was the 1909 revision of the equalization formula to provide greater state support for the poorer school districts. Governor Bass, who continually stressed the importance of a strong system of public education, including the statement that "it is the duty of the state to give every one of its boys and girls" the opportunity to prepare for and go to college, ironically had difficulty with the New Hampshire College for Agricultural and Mechanical Arts at Durham. Because of budget considerations he vetoed a special capital appropriation bill that included money for a new engineering building at the school. The senior class unanimously disinvited him from speaking at their commencement in 1911. He did not attend. Nonetheless, during the progressive years support for the state agricultural college expanded; in 1911 a reorganization established a division of liberal arts, an important step toward the school becoming a comprehensive university in 1923.[42]

In 1905 the legislature provided for the establishment of a state highway system. Town responsibilities and expenditures were mandated, with the state sharing in the cost. In 1911 the state began registering and licensing automobiles and their operators. State law required safety devices, prohibited speeding and racing, and forbade the operation of automobiles by intoxicated drivers. Bass took great interest in the engineering questions the highway department faced, and he continually sought to discover other states' experiences with new processes and materials.[43]

The reformers increasingly posited the state government as the locus of authority in New Hampshire. The state could mediate among the various local authorities, could equalize, and could regulate. Efficiency was a watchword for this generation, and the assumption was that centralized control facilitated professional and efficient operation. A prerequisite for effective public administration was uncorrupted and open political processes. In this prewar era the state legislature initiated the direct primary, controls on lobbying, and requirements for disclosure of campaign receipts and expenditures; they forbade corporate campaign contributions, provided controls on political advertising, and tightened definitions of and penalties for bribery. New laws regulated ballots, their size, and the methods of policing and counting them. In 1913 these regulations were extended to voting machines. The reform impulse included streamlining and clarifying the legislators' own practices and modifying the appropriation process to exclude standing appropriations. After 1909 the state was forbidden to spend any funds without specific authorization and appropriation. All state departments and agencies had to prepare and submit budgets to the house appropriation committee. The state tax commission, established in 1911, equalized and regulated the collection of local taxes and collected all state taxes from railroads and other corporations. In the same year the legislature significantly expanded the attorney general's responsibilities to include appearances "to protect the interests of the state or of the people" whenever instructed by the governor and council.[44] Governor Jordan had recommended this change a decade earlier, referring specifically to legislative hearings, where "great interests are represented by great lawyers."[45] In 1913 the legislature established a legislative reference bureau in the state library in order to supply information to legislators and members of the executive departments.

In 1914, when the Gallinger-led old guard regained control of New Hampshire politics, the state government was quantitatively and qualitatively different from that of the nineteenth century. The number of state officers, board members, agents, and commissioners, exclusive of the judiciary department, increased from 138 to 198 between 1901 and 1913. Such counts can be difficult, if not misleading, because of the variation in importance among the various appointments. The types of positions perhaps reveal more: in 1913 New Hampshire had new state positions such as the superintendent of highways, state auditor, state forestor, state medical referees, and a state agent to suppress gypsy and brown-tail moths. Expanded responsibilities often meant new institutions and new boards: the school for feebleminded children, the state sanatorium, the license commission and its state liquor agents. There was a new normal school at Keene, joining the older school at Plymouth. The New Hampshire Asylum for the Insane became the state hospital. New boards existed for examination and registration in optometry, nursing, and veterinary medicine. The public service commission, tax commission, and public printing commission replaced older, allegedly ineffectual commissions. Many of these reforms were replicated in other states, and not simply by accident. New Hampshire had a Commission for the Promotion of Uniformity of Legislation in the United States.[46]

Specific and detailed studies of these various policy areas would be necessary in order to determine the legislators' intent and the substantive impact of the legislation. What is clear is that the nature of state government, its scope, and its explicit responsibilities, changed during this period. State expenditures, shown in table 7.1, illustrate this change.

These figures reflect a qualitative and quantitative difference in the functions assumed by the state in this prewar period. Annual state disbursements of funds, including direct expenditures, transfers to towns, and debt service, increased from $1,170,744 in 1900 to $2,514,054 in 1912, an increase of 115 percent. The revenue side of the ledger is complicated by state receipts from and disbursements to the various towns. State receipts from the towns, the state share of the property tax, increased in this period, but transfers to the towns increased more (net state payments to towns increased from $163,386 to $215,999); the bulk of the expanded state activity was supported by increased corporate tax liability. Railroad taxes increased from $358,878 to $724,903; bank taxes increased from $348,907 to $533,687; insurance company taxes increased from $32,285 to $97,229; telephone company taxes increased from $5,506 to $41,048. Licensing and other fees collected by the insurance department and the secretary of state increased from $17,384 to $143,004. The legacy and succession tax, passed in 1905 and revised in the following years, provided $171,639 of revenue in the fiscal year ending in 1912.[47]

State fiscal influence expanded apace with new state responsibilities in regulation and control. Town taxes, net of the state tax collected locally, increased 49 percent in this period. The state share of revenues collected at all levels in New Hampshire increased from 31 percent to 37 percent in these twelve years.[48] Perhaps equally important were the greater influence of state standards and control

TABLE 7.1

State Expenditures in Specific Areas for Fiscal
Years Ending May 31, 1900, and August 31, 1912 (in dollars)

	1900	1912
Department of Public Instruction	5,537	11,565
Asylum for insane/state hospital	40,072	181,143
Education of deaf, dumb, blind	7,448	15,975
Railroad commission/PSC	8,389	26,938
State industrial school	15,400	59,338
N.H. college	10,769	20,955
Normal school(s)	17,902	39,900
Fish and Game Department	9,626	17,068
Soldier's home	18,030	26,215
State prison	5,608	36,112
Board of health	4,250	12,857
Forestry commission/department	1,191	18,542
Labor bureau	2,730	3,324
Suppression of gypsy moth	—	12,500
School fund (disbursed to towns)	18,750	94,026
Literary fund (to schools)	36,627	41,403
Roads and highways	6,938	187,589
Board of Charities and Corrections	317	21,591
School for feebleminded	—	48,711
State sanitorium	—	52,833

over expenditures in the two major areas of local expense—schools and roads. Through a variety of changes, many subtle and incremental, there was a new state for the new century.

Among the reforms that failed, woman suffrage perhaps would be the most significant. Generally the progressives supported this reform; although Bass's own conversion was late, Churchill's was early. Woman suffrage was not simply or narrowly a progressive measure. In 1912 Jacob Gallinger suggested that perhaps another constitutional amendment could be submitted for popular ratification, even though he was convinced "the chances are a thousand to one the people would defeat it" in the vote. James Lyford worked with Mabel Churchill (Mrs. Winston) on the issue.[49] In 1912–13 an estimated 27 percent of the school board members in the state were women; some 20 percent of the boards had a majority of women. Of the top nine progressive towns in the 1910–14 period, 43 percent of the board members were women; four had women in the majority.[50] It was not until 1920 that woman suffrage was ratified. Bass's own growth on this matter revealed his changing concept of reform. By the end of his governorship he was not simply supportive, he had become an activist in the movement. In 1915 he was the featured speaker at the annual banquet of the Massachusetts Woman Suffrage Association in Boston, and his comments revealed his own process of conversion and his own understanding of reform.

The ex-governor told the Bay State group that while "confession" might be politically "bad form and inexpedient," he wanted to share with them his slow response to the issue. His original indifference to suffrage resulted from a sense that it would come when enough women wanted it, and "I was not particularly interested in bringing this result about." He came around when he realized there was a significant prosuffrage sentiment and, perhaps more important, when he realized the "great work" that was required from all citizens to accomplish reform. Ten years earlier, as a political neophyte, he admitted he had thought all that was required was to bring into politics those men who had "held aloof" from it and establish with them a "more efficient, more honest, and above all, a more adequately democratic form of government." He felt that the progressives had made "considerable progress" in this regard, but he had come to recognize that to accomplish anything of consequence the women as well as the men would need to become involved in politics: "we need your help."

In this address Bass explicitly rejected the antisuffrage argument that women should not become sullied in politics. In 1905, he said, some men kept away from politics because they had this same fear of "contamination," a fear he believed both wrong and harmful. "That it should be degrading to help make and administer the laws under which the American people live, seems to me ridiculous." Women must join men "to take all suggestions of disrepute from the business of government." Bass said that the reformers needed the assistance of women in dealing with "domestic problems," under which he included child labor, housing problems, and pure food, as well as liquor. But, he went on, "fundamental economic problems" were equally pressing. His detailed example was workmen's compensation, focusing on the problems of the wives of incapacitated workmen. Women's interests were greater than this, however, for the governor reminded his audience that 7 million of them were employed, and "their claim for a voice in controlling the conditions under which they work would certainly seem in this Twentieth Century to be beyond argument." He reminded the women that while they needed the vote for "self-protection, . . . we need to give you the vote for the well-being of the men and children as much as for your own." For finally, "Our welfare is unalterably interwoven with yours."[51]

Robert Bass had increasingly become concerned about the social and economic conditions labor faced. Near the end of his governorship he had to confront directly some of these issues. In February 1912, while Bass was on his wedding trip, workers had organized a Manchester rally to generate support for the Industrial Workers of the World strike at Lawrence, Massachusetts. Manchester police chief Michael Healy broke up the meeting. Bass investigated the matter and in hearings in the fall attacked Healy's assumption of authority and his assault on free assembly. As a lawyer, Louis Wyman agreed with Bass; as a citizen of Manchester he worried about the potential for labor unrest and crime, given Manchester's "mixed population."[52] Bass spent several years studying the labor question and even did some consulting work in industrial relations. He slowly worked out his own political positions on these matters. Bass ordered and presumably read Herbert Croly's *Promise of American Life* and Elihu Root's *The Citizen's Part in Government*, with their different civic prescriptions. It is not obvious that either helped him shape a comprehensive ideology, although he clearly came to share many of Croly's attitudes. In 1913 he wrote to former Dartmouth president William J. Tucker that he believed *laissez-faire* concepts had little relevance in their world. Government needed to help lessen inequalities and to mediate between labor and capital, for the issues would not be resolved by the "benevolent and somewhat paternal attitude" assumed by some capitalists. If labor and capital reached an accommodation, the government would need to protect the "unorganized consumer."[53] By 1915 Bass would be calling the attitudes he articulated *liberal*, a term with the same definitional problems as *progressive*. In drafts of speeches he prepared for the Massachusetts campaign, Bass argued that the source of insurgency could be found in the recent control of the GOP by "men and interests fundamentally reactionary and thoroughly selfish," leaders who "represented capital often at the expense of labor." Leading Republicans were "naturally and fundamentally conservative," and they represented "the moneyed interest and what I would call the ruling class." Bass insisted that any similarities between Progressives and Republicans on ideas like efficiency and economy in government represented only superficial agreement, for the reformers went beyond such matters and also sought to provide governmental protection to wage earners; "in some cases this can be accomplished only at some expense to the people that pay the wages." (Robert Bass kept in his speech file a quote from the Italian Giuseppe Mazzini, enjoining "a constant disposition to ameliorate the material conditions of the classes least favored by fortune.") These matters, Bass insisted, would have to be faced at the conclusion of the war, and the Republican party offered little ground for optimism. Regardless of party, Bass insisted, government must "be in the hands of men of liberal convictions and sympathies."[54]

Even though Bass's views sharpened, it may be impossible to extrapolate from the overall progressive reform efforts and accomplishments a guiding philosophy of government. Too many people, with too many reform agendas, identified with the progressives at one time or another. The changes and reforms described earlier in this chapter occurred over a period of years as a result of the activities of various individuals and coalitions. Legislators enacted some reforms prior to the organization of the Lincoln Republicans in 1906; most of this activity occurred in the 1909–13 period. In general terms the laws and platforms they wrote and the speeches they delivered suggest that the progressives emphasized a reduction of corporate influence, open processes of government and politics, equity in taxation, efficiency of governmental operation, and an expanded, albeit limited, state responsibility to the citizens who were most vulnerable and deprived.

The Yankee reform mentality tended to be political and economic at the outset; it expanded by 1911 to include the goal of countering some negative workplace consequences of industrialism and providing better public support for the disadvantaged. These categories are broadly defined and represent a comprehensive set of reforms ranging from the regulation of automobiles to child labor laws. Yankee progressivism at times preached about moral force and character, but with the notable exception of prohibition, where the progressives never did enough as far as the temperance forces were concerned, the reformers never included in their vision of the active state an expansion of the state's laws regulating personal behavior. Proscriptions on individual conduct were the product of the nineteenth century; the reformers focused more on proscribing corporate conduct.

The progressive vision, on the other hand, had little room for cultural diversity. The progressive Yankees tended to think of a single, homogeneous, culture. The Irish Catholics would have kept their distance from the Republican reformers in any case simply because they were Republican. French Canadians were another matter. They continued to be ambivalent toward the two major parties down through the progressive period. Table 7.2 indicates the voting returns in three Manchester wards for several elections from 1908 to 1916.

While the Ninth Ward Republicans participating in the 1910 primary were strongly for Bass, the total electorate in the ward remained inconsistent in these years. Partially this reflected some

TABLE 7.2

*Votes Cast for Statewide Candidates in
Selected Manchester Wards, 1908–16*

	Ward 2 (Yankee)	Ward 5 (Irish)	Ward 9 (French)
1908 Taft	983	232	682
1908 Bryan	307	875	551
1910 Bass primary	620	80	356
1910 Ellis primary	274	23	150
1910 Bass	923	107	598
1910 Carr	430	918	687
1912 TR	350	92	165
1912 Wilson	393	669	555
1912 Taft	694	134	607
1916 Hughes	539	160	336
1916 Wilson	341	718	343

anger at the GOP for its approach to French candidates and issues. Some Franco-American community leaders were particularly distressed at the 1910 Republican primary defeat of Aimé Boisvert in his quest for the Hillsborough County solicitor nomination. Boisvert defeated Harry Spaulding 518 to 66 in the Ninth Ward and lost to him by 645 to 232 in the Second Ward. *L'Avenir National* commented that these results demonstrated that Republicans "vote for the Yankee."[55] In November many Ninth Ward voters split their tickets, giving Republican candidate Bass 598 votes and Republican candidate Spaulding 383 votes—and 866 votes to Spaulding's Democratic opponent, Patrick Sullivan. The Republicans slated all Franco-Americans for their General Court nominees from the Ninth Ward; Democrats carried five of the seats to the two won by Republicans. The victorious Republicans were Odilon Demers and Oscar Moreau, who defeated Democrats Patrick O'Connell and Daniel Sullivan. After the returns were in, *L'Avenir National* predicted greater recognition now for party leaders shrewd enough to recognize that it would be suicidal to continue "*leur mouvement antifrançais.*"[56]

To salve the Boisvert defeat, Franco-Americans looked to Concord for some recognition after the 1910 election. By late 1911 even Senator Gallinger asked Chandler to intercede with Bass on this problem in order to still the dissatisfaction of French Republicans.[57] Robert Bass's appointment policies infuriated many Franco-Americans. *L'Avenir National* editorialized that all of the potential candidates for Burnham's U.S. Senate seat, Bass included, "have benefited from our support in their political careers. Never, by contrast have they recognized us."[58] Bass's problems may partially have resulted from the attitudes of Robert Manning, Bass's progressive friend from Manchester and advisor on appointments. Manning wrote to Bass after a meeting of Manchester progressives called to discuss Franco-American demands for an appointment: "there is *no* Frenchman here, who can stand up and make a fight for *right* as men of your type (and mine, I pray) see the *right.*" Nonetheless Manning conceded it was "*legitimate* policy" to make a Franco-American appointment. He joked that Catholics were entitled to a post on the board of the state industrial school (a school for juvenile offenders): "for the reason that they are well represented on the *inside* of the School." A Manning associate consulted with a Father Davignon from the Ninth Ward on possible appointees.[59] Bass ultimately made several Franco-American appointments to state offices, boards, commissions, and state-appointed local positions. Catholic bishop Albert Guertin wrote the governor directly on appointments; the governor responded positively to at least one of the bishop's requests, a Democratic reappointment to the state license commission. This was a difficult decision for Bass as it ran counter to pressure from temperance Republicans, headed by Dan Remich, to replace this person.[60]

The reformers focused more on policy than they did on politics. The new urban immigrants had few policy demands as immigrants, other than to be left alone culturally. As workers they had a more comprehensive set of economic demands; here the reformers' record was better even if Bass's increasingly comprehensive views on these matters developed after his governorship. Politically the immigrants sought recognition and participation, but reforms like the direct-primary laws seemed to reduce their leverage. No longer could political leaders simply slate a balanced ticket. In open elections beyond ward boundaries the Boisverts were likely to be less strong than the Spauldings. There is little doubt that this new state of affairs was the intent of some of the reformers, not against ethnic candidates *per se*, but against the old "vote-buying" system that they generously defined and about which they constantly complained.[61]

Given some of their political errors, it is even more remarkable that the reformers implemented so much public policy. The record indicates that they had some success in meeting their goals. And perhaps this is the best level at which to evaluate them. As Clarence Carr observed in summarizing the reforms passed in the 1909 legislative session, "They may be . . . defective . . . but many of them at least are in the right direction, and the road will be travelled until the journey ends in good and equitable laws honestly enforced."[62] The process did not end in 1913. Philip Ayres, Bass's friend and colleague in the forestry fight and official of the Society for the Protection of New Hampshire Forests, wrote Bass in 1917 that the legislature had approved a $52,000 forestry budget and an additional $28,000 to fight white pine blister rust: "I did not expect to see the day when the New Hampshire Legislature would appropriate $80,000 at one time for forestry. The leaven appears to be working."[63]

The leaven took other forms. On Christmas 1913 Robert Bass sent over the hill to Temple a gift—a pig—to a young man, Charles W. Tobey. Tobey had enlisted in the progressive cause and had recently indicated that he wished he had a pig. Bass hoped to encourage and support Tobey; in 1915 Bass concluded that Representative Tobey was "the one Progressive in the last House" and a "bully good fellow" besides. At the same time that the Bass-Tobey friendship was developing, in 1914 Winston Churchill asked Bass to meet with John Winant, a young instructor at St. Paul's School whom Churchill had met. Churchill gushed that "it is possible I have found the young man" the Progressive leaders had been looking for to do some work for the party. Winant had told Churchill he was "most anxious to help in the Progressive cause, and to do anything this summer."[64] Bass and Winant began a long political relationship.

The failure of the Bull Moose party disillusioned many reformers; the Great War rechanneled their energies. The postwar years were marked by a climate, as noted at the beginning of this chapter, that was less auspicious for reform. If many of the old progressives never returned to reform activities, their earlier accomplishments were not negated. In any event, some did return; some never truly left.[65] When Robert Bass spoke to the City Club of Chicago in February 1920 and eloquently insisted upon reform rather than reaction, it was a statement consistent with his activities elsewhere.

In 1921 Robert Bass organized the New Hampshire Civic Association as a forum for the discussion of public issues and began organizing some of the old progressives into a political network. He won a seat in the legislature in the 1922 election, and in the 1923 legislative session he led the fight for a forty-eight-hour work week, a measure that failed in the senate after house approval. In 1924 he helped organize and guide the Republican gubernatorial primary campaign of young John Winant. It was an audacious challenge to the leadership of Sen. George Moses and to the gubernatorial candidacy of Frank Knox. Bass was accustomed to audacious challenges. So was Moses. When Bass announced that he hoped to commit the New Hampshire delegation to the 1924 Republican National Convention to Pres. Calvin Coolidge, Moses resisted and insisted upon an "uncommitted" slate. There was a *déjà vu* tint to the scuffling. Moses wrote James Lyford, "The whole thing reminds me greatly of

1908 when Bass and his crowd, with Streeter, undertook to start a movement which, hiding behind the ample skirts of Taft's frock coat, meant really a movement to get Gallinger out of the Senate. We know what happened then and I think we can foresee what is going to happen now. Nevertheless, I do not think we should lie down on the job and I do not intend to." Coolidge won and Lyford worried about its effect on the Knox candidacy and more generally was concerned with Moses's lack of "political sagacity": "He acts first and thinks afterwards." Winant defeated Knox and went on to win the general election despite Knox's sabotage efforts. Bass's support for the conservative Coolidge added more than a tinge of irony to the scuffle. The former's position seemed genuine enough, but his focus was Moses: to isolate him and to tar him as being much more reactionary than the president. Bass believed Coolidge's strong appeal in the Granite State could work to the reform Republicans' advantage.[66]

Bass and his young personal secretary, Styles Bridges, worked to organize the new legislature for Winant. They managed to get reformers elected to leadership positions in both houses, including Charles Tobey as president of the senate. The reformers lost two major battles, over the forty-eight-hour week and ratification of the child labor amendment to the U.S. Constitution. They did beat back a Knox-Moses campaign to repeal the state's direct-primary law, and they accomplished banking reforms, expanded highway construction, passed a cooperative marketing law, arranged for state purchase of the Old Man of the Mountains, and expanded state support for the University of New Hampshire. The Moses group secured the governorship in 1926, but Bass helped Tobey win the position in 1928, played a role in Winant's election again in 1930 and his 1932 reelection, and assisted Tobey's successful campaign for the U.S. Senate. These two men continued largely to reflect the tradition of Republican progressivism; Styles Bridges did not, and as his political career and style evolved, his relationship with Bass soured. As Winant's biographer commented, "Bass never turned his back on the maturing progressive ideology of the twentieth century, and displayed unique talents as kingmaker and strategist who, with Winant would keep progressivism homegrown and Republican in the rolling hills of the Granite State."[67]

Bass made one more electoral effort himself. In 1926 he challenged incumbent U.S. senator George Moses in the Republican primary. Bass had begun methodically planning for this race in 1923, but his effort was delayed because his young friend and protégé, Governor Winant, had Senate ambitions himself and refused to leave the field to Bass. When Winant finally determined not to run it was too late to organize the sort of campaign it would have taken to defeat a powerful politician like Moses. Bass campaigned on support for U.S. participation in the World Court and on the need for legislation that would provide for the conscription of property as well as men during war: "Not only will this effectually block the profiteer, but it will be a strong deterrent against future wars." He was critical of Moses for his successful effort to exclude Japanese immigration; this was "racial discrimination" and a "needless affront to a great nation." Bass insisted that it was "high time that steps should be taken by Congress to protect the public from periodic exploitation by the coal industry." He noted the growth of the electric power industry and called for regulation to benefit the consumer of this power; where state regulation was inadequate, national efforts were necessary, with their goal regulation "as far-reaching in its authority as the monopolies with which it must deal." Bass also applauded the Coolidge administration for its "introduction of efficiency and economy in the affairs of our national government," and was critical of Moses for his late support of Coolidge in 1924.[68] Robert Bass was once more a regular Republican—although he would identify himself as an "Independent Republican"—and he was still in the reform wing of his party.

Robert Bass lost to Senator Moses by a two-to-one margin. James Remick also ran, but his campaign and vote were of little consequence. Bass's list of supporters included many familiar names from 1910; the old "reliable men" had their ranks augmented by younger men and by women. They may have been personally reliable; this time they could not help to deliver the votes. The old progressive carried but forty-two towns and three wards. Of the twenty-four towns Bass had carried by a nine-to-one margin in his 1910 campaign against Ellis, he could only secure a majority in eight in 1926.

The activities of Robert Bass cannot represent the entire progressive "movement" of which he was a part. He was an integral part, however, and the key leader of the reform coalitions for many years. At the least his experiences symbolize the difficulty of generalizing too broadly or, in contrast, concluding that nothing was there. Bass stayed with his party, even through the New Deal years, despite his sympathy with many New Deal innovations. He never stopped trying to shift his party. In 1936 he reminded Republican presidential candidate Alf Landon, whose running mate ironically was Frank Knox, that the GOP had its tradition of humanitarian reform. He told Bridges, "If we are to escape class alignments in this country, the permanent minority party must present a sufficiently liberal constructive program to meet the needs of the average citizen in the light of present day conditions."[69] Bass chaired the board of the Brookings Institution in the 1940s and in the 1950s stood with those Republicans who were opposed to the McCarthyites. This pitted him against the sons of two of his old progressive colleagues, William Loeb and Louis Wyman. Robert Bass lived until 1960, always a force pushing his party toward internationalism and domestic reform. On the occasion of his death the historian Bernard Bellush, who knew Bass personally and was completing his own study of the Winant years, wrote, "history . . . must record that it was Robert Perkins Bass who laid the foundations for twentieth century progress in this State. It was Bass who was instrumental in converting the Granite State from a reactionary, political and social unit to one of progress and enlightenment."[70]

By the time of Bass's death the new century was well into middle age. It had already proved a time of greater progress and of more profound change—and of far greater frustration, suffering, and tragedy—than the most speculative of country editors or politicians could conceivably have dreamed when it began. Robert Bass and his Progressive Yankees had helped their state come into the twentieth century. If some of their reforms were inconsequential, others were not; if some of their actions were ill advised and some of their attitudes self-serving, others were not. They had revitalized their political system, no small accomplishment for any generation.

Notes

Preface

1. Benjamin P. Dewitt, *The Progressive Movement: A Non-partisan, Comprehensive Discussion of Current Tendencies in American Politics* (New York, 1915), pp. 3, 4–5.

2. Although its interpretive power has been significantly blunted over the years, the seminal work in the postwar historiography of progressivism is Richard Hofstadter, *The Age of Reform: From Bryan to F.D.R.* (New York, 1955). For discussions of this historiography see John D. Buenker, "The Progressive Era: A Search for a Synthesis," *Mid-America* 51 (1969), pp. 175–93; David P. Thelen, "Social Tensions and the Origins of Progressivism," *Journal of American History* 56 (1969), pp. 323–41; Peter Filene, "An Obituary for 'The Progressive Movement,'" *American Quarterly* 22 (1970), pp. 20–34; Robert Wiebe, "The Progressive Years, 1900–1917," in William H. Cartwright and Richard L. Watson, Jr., eds., *The Reinterpretation of American History and Culture* (Washington, D.C., 1973), pp. 425–42; David M. Kennedy, "Overview: The Progressive Era," *Historian* 37 (1975), pp. 453–68; Richard L. McCormick, "The Discovery That Business Corrupts Politics: A Reappraisal of the Origins of Progressivism," *American Historical Review* 86 (1981), pp. 247–74; Dewey W. Grantham, "The Contours of Southern Progressivism," *American Historical Review* 86 (1981), pp. 1035–59; Daniel T. Rodgers, "In Search of Progressivism," *Reviews in American History* (1982), pp. 113–32. See as well the essays in Lewis L. Gould, *The Progressive Era* (Syracuse, 1974) and in John D. Buenker, John C. Burnham, and Robert M. Crunden, *Progressivism* (Cambridge, Mass., 1977). This preface does not intend to replicate these articles and essays nor to survey the rich—and voluminous—literature on progressivism. A good bibliographical source is William M. Leary, Jr., and Arthur S. Link, comps., *The Progressive Era and the Great War, 1896–1920*, 2d ed. (Arlington Heights, Ill., 1978). See also, Arthur S. Link and Richard L. McCormick, *Progressivism* (Arlington Heights, Ill., 1983).

3. For California, George Mowry, *The California Progressives* (Berkeley, 1951); Spencer C. Olin, *California's Prodigal Sons: Hiram Johnson and the Progressives, 1911–1917* (Berkeley, 1968); and Mansel G. Blackford, *The Politics of Business in California, 1890–1920* (Columbus, Ohio, 1977); for Wisconsin, Robert S. Maxwell, *La Follette and the Rise of the Progressives*

in Wisconsin (Madison, 1956); Herbert F. Margulies, *The Decline of the Progressive Movement in Wisconsin, 1890–1920* (Madison, 1968); Stanley P. Caine, *The Myth of a Progressive Reform: Railroad Regulation in Wisconsin, 1903–1910* (Madison, 1970); and David P. Thelen, *The New Citizenship: Origins of Progressivism in Wisconsin, 1885–1900* (Columbia, Mo., 1973); for New York, Robert F. Wesser, *Charles Evans Hughes: Politics and Reform in New York, 1905–1910* (Ithaca, 1967); and Richard L. McCormick, *From Realignment to Reform: Political Change in New York State, 1893–1910* (Ithaca, 1981). For urban reform, Melvin G. Holli, *Reform in Detroit: Hazen S. Pingree and Urban Politics* (New York, 1969); and idem, "Urban Reform in the Progressive Era," in Gould, *Progressive Era*, pp. 133–51; see also Michael H. Ebner and Eugene M. Tobin, eds., *The Age of Urban Reform: New Perspectives on the Progressive Era* (Port Washington, N.Y., 1977). With one exception—Russel B. Nye, *Midwestern Progressive Politics: A Historical Study of Its Origins and Development, 1870–1950* (East Lansing, Mich., 1951)—the only regional studies are several that look at the progressive experience in the South: Arthur S. Link, "The Progressive Movement in the South, 1870–1914," *North Carolina Historical Review* 23 (1946), pp. 172–95; C. Vann Woodward, *Origins of the New South, 1877–1913* (Baton Rouge, La., 1951); Jack Temple Kirby, *Darkness at the Dawning: Race and Reform in the Progressive South* (Philadelphia, 1972); and Dewey W. Grantham, *Southern Progressivism: The Reconciliation of Progress and Tradition* (Knoxville, Tenn., 1983), as well as idem, "Contours of Southern Progressivism." Important books on progressivism in New England are Winston Allen Flint, *The Progressive Movement in Vermont* (Washington, D.C., 1941); and Richard Abrams, *Conservatism in the Progressive Era: Massachusetts Politics, 1900–1912* (Cambridge, Mass., 1964). My focus and interests in this book are similar to those of Robert S. La Forte, *Leaders of Reform: Progressive Republicans in Kansas, 1900–1916* (Lawrence, Kans., 1974).

4. See Wiebe, "Progressive Years," for a discussion of modernization; also Wiebe, in *The Search for Order, 1877–1920* (New York, 1967), stresses the rise of organized groups articulating values of professionalism, the scientific method, and bureaucratization. See as well the seminal work of Samuel P. Hays, *The Response to Industrialism, 1885–1914* (Chicago, 1957); Hays has several important essays, conveniently available in his *American Political History as Social Analysis* (Knoxville, Tenn., 1980). See also, Louis Galambos, "The Emerging Organizational Synthesis in Modern American History," *Business History Review* 44 (1970), pp. 279–90; and Wayne K. Hobson, "Professionals, Progressives and Bureaucratization: A Reassessment," *Historian* 39 (1977), pp. 639–58.

5. Jerome Beatty, "The Rescue of New Hampshire and the Rise of a New Figure in Our Public Life," *Collier's*, May 6, 1911; *The Outlook*, October 22, 1910.

6. Scholarly articles that focus on the New Hampshire progressive movement are Jewel Bellush, "Reform in New Hampshire: Robert Bass Wins the Primary," *New England Quarterly* 35 (1962), pp. 469–88; Geoffrey Blod-

gett, "Winston Churchill: The Novelist as Reformer," *New England Quarterly* 47 (1974), pp. 495–517; Thomas Agan, "The New Hampshire Progressives: Who and What Were They?" *Historical New Hampshire* 34 (1979), pp. 32–53. The latter is derived from Agan's doctoral dissertation, "The New Hampshire Progressive Movement," State University of New York at Albany, 1975.

7. Agan's "New Hampshire Progressives" includes a group profile of the progressive Republicans and their old guard opponents. It is my *impression* that the same characteristics describe the Democrats; certainly their statewide leaders were old stock. For a review of this approach to progressivism, see Jerome M. Clubb and Howard W. Allen, "Collective Biography and the Progressive Movement: The 'Status Revolution' Revisited," *Social Science History* 1 (1977), pp. 518–34.

8. With the critical assistance of Jo Ellen Roodman, Ronald Cima, Peter Marsden, and Peter Fowler, I identified and coded a range of variables for the 235 towns in New Hampshire. These included all elections from 1888 to 1916, economic data from tax reports, religious data from church reports, and organizational data from various group reports. We also did extensive sampling from manuscript census returns for 1880 and 1900.

All of these data were coded, variables were constructed, and analyses completed on Dartmouth College's IMPRESS software system. There were in excess of three hundred raw and constructed variables. Comprehensive regression analysis was complicated by data distribution patterns (most towns did not have a Baptist church, for example), or by data availability (we did not do place-of-birth tabulations from the manuscript census for all of the towns). To compensate for these factors as well as to complement the regression analyses that I did, I also grouped towns by variable, using a program written by Peter Marsden, and generated descriptive statistics for these subsets.

9. Hale to Bass, July 29, 1911, in Robert Perkins Bass papers, Special Collections, Baker Library, Dartmouth College. The Bass papers are currently being reorganized so it is impossible to give box and file references. When completed the manuscript letters will be organized chronologically, with further divisions into incoming and outgoing and in alphabetical order. Thus this letter would be in July 1911 correspondence, incoming, with the *H* letters.

10. A very important exception to this generalization continues to be V. O. Key, Jr., *American State Politics: An Introduction* (New York, 1956). See as well the essays in Alan Rosenthal and Maureen Moakley, eds., *The Political Life of the American States* (New York, 1984), especially Rosenthal's "On Analyzing States," pp. 1–29.

1. New Hampshire and the New Century

1. *Granite State Free Press*, January 5, 1900; *Manchester Union*, January 1, 1900.

2. *Manchester Union*, January 1, 1900. Chester Jordan message in "Mes-

sage of His Excellency Chester B. Jordan, Governor of New Hampshire to the Two Branches of the Legislature, January Session, 1901" (Concord, 1901), p. 4.

3. *Manchester Union*, January 1, 1900. Rollins's speech at Woodstock, August 15, 1900, in *Old Home Week Addresses by Governor Frank Rollins, 1900* (Concord, n.d.), pp. 31–44; newspapers stressed the prosperity and progress theme, e.g., *Manchester Union*, January 22 and March 5, 1900.

4. Newspapers regularly described disease incidence or epidemics in 1900; see, for example, *Manchester Union*, January 15 and March 26, 1900, and *Concord Evening Monitor*, June 5, 1900.

5. E.g., *Manchester Union*, January 1, 8, 15, 22, and 29, and March 5, 1900.

6. Census Bureau, Twelfth Census, 1900, *Vital Statistics*, (Washington, D.C., 1902), pt. 1, pp. 561, 566–67; pt. 2, p. 92; and *Population*, pt. 2, p. 66.

7. *Concord Evening Monitor*, January 3, 1900; *Manchester Union*, January 1, 8, and 15, and *Granite State Free Press*, January 5, 1900; for fires, *Report of New Hampshire Insurance Commissioner, 1900*, pp. lxx–lxxvii; also *Manchester Union*, January 1, 8, 15, and 29.

8. See annual report of the New Hampshire State Board of Health; Census Bureau, *Special Reports, Central Electric Light and Power Stations, 1902* (Washington, D.C., 1905) pp. 13, 106–7; for an example of expanding services in one community, see A. N. Somers, *History of Lancaster, N.H.* (Concord, 1899), pp. 157–59, 162–64; see examples in *Manchester Union*, e.g. January 15 and September 17, 1900.

9. *Report of the New Hampshire Board of Agriculture, 1898–1901* (Manchester, 1901), p. 218; for full summary of activities, see pp. viii and 195–284. See Ronald Jager and Grace Jager, *Portrait of a Hill Town: A History of Washington, New Hampshire, 1876–1976* (Concord, 1977), pp. 182–87, for Old Home Day in one community. This book is a fine local history that describes in one community many of the themes summarized in this chapter.

10. *Third Biennial Report of the Bureau of Labor of the State of New Hampshire* (Manchester, 1900), p. 8. See Frank W. Rollins, "New Hampshire's Opportunity," *New England Magazine* 16 (July 1897), pp. 534–42, for a plea to capitalize on New Hampshire's appeal to tourists.

11. *Old Home Week Addresses*, Woodstock, pp. 31–44; see also Salem speech, pp. 26–27; *Report of New Hampshire Board of Agriculture, 1900*, pp. 95–101; Bureau of Labor, "Special Report on Summer Business, 1900," p. vii; and *Sixteenth Report of the State Board of Health of the State of New Hampshire, 1900* (Manchester, 1901), pp. 156–57.

12. See Census Bureau, *Population*, Twelfth Census, 1900, vol. 1, pt. 1, pp. lxxxi–lxxxviii, and cxxxvi; also *Population*, Thirteenth Census, 1910, pp. 56–57, for different definition of *urban*. In 1900, using the definition "greater than 4,000" as an indicator of *urban*, the New Hampshire proportion was 46.7 percent; in 1910 2,500 became the conventional measurement; this measurement indicated a 1900 urban percentage of 55 percent.

13. Harold D. Wilson, *The Hill Country of Northern New England, Its Social and Economic History, 1790–1930* (New York, 1936), pp. 52–53.

Census Bureau, *Population, 1900*, vol. 1, p. xc. Using 2,500 as an index of *urban*, in 1880 New Hampshire was 39 percent urban, and in 1910 it was 59 percent urban; Census Bureau, *Population, 1910*, pp. 56–57.

14. At Rollinsford, *Old Home Week Addresses*, p. 8; also at Woodstock, pp. 42–43.

15. Census Bureau, *Population, 1900*, vol. 1, pp. cxxvi, cliii; also *Supplementary Analysis*, pp. 288–89.

16. Census Bureau, *Supplementary Analysis*, pp. 312–14.

17. Census Bureau, *Population, 1900*, vol. 1, pp. ccix, ccxxi, clxxiii, clxxxii. A good study of French-Canadian migration patterns is Ralph D. Vicero, "Immigration of French Canadians to New England, 1840–1900: A Geographical Analysis," Ph.D. dissertation, University of Wisconsin, 1969.

18. Census Bureau, *Population, 1900*, vol. 1, p. cvii; *Supplementary Analysis*, p. 302; *Special Reports*, pp. 628–31.

19. H. H. Metcalf, "A Prosperous Industry and Its Manager," *Granite Monthly* 28 (1900), pp. 308–14.

20. May 31, 1883, quoted in Edward C. Kirkland, *Men, Cities, and Transportation: A Study in New England History, 1820–1900* (Cambridge, Mass., 1948), vol. 1, p. 464.

21. Wilson, *Hill Country of Northern New England*, and Howard S. Russell, *A Long, Deep Furrow: Three Centuries of Farming in New England* (Hanover, N.H., 1976), *passim*. See also Rexford B. Sherman, "One Year on a New Hampshire Farm, 1888," *Historical New Hampshire* 32 (1977), pp. 1–17; and Paul W. Gates, "Two Hundred Years of Farming in Gilsum," *Historical New Hampshire* 33 (1978), pp. 1–24.

22. Paul G. Munyon, "A Reassessment of New England Agriculture in the Last Thirty Years of the Nineteenth Century: New Hampshire, a Case Study," Ph.D. dissertation, Harvard University, 1975, *passim*, for a revisionist view of economic difficulties in New Hampshire agriculture. See also William L. Taylor, "The Nineteenth Century Hill Town: Images and Reality," *Historical New Hampshire* 37 (1982), pp. 283–309.

23. Harry N. Scheiber, "Coach, Wagon, and Motor-Truck Manufacturer, 1813–1928: The Abbot-Downing Company of Concord," *Historical New Hampshire* 20 (1965), pp. 3–25.

24. Two recent studies have significantly aided our understanding of the Amoskeag: James Hanlan, *The Working Population of Manchester, New Hampshire, 1840–1886* (Ann Arbor, 1981); Tamara K. Hareven, *Family Time and Industrial Time: The Relationship between the Family and Work in a New England Industrial Community* (Cambridge, England, 1982). See as well Daniel Creamer and Charles W. Coulter, *Labor and the Shut-Down at the Amoskeag Textile Mills*, Works Progress Administration, National Research Project (Philadelphia, 1939); Tamara Hareven and Randolph Langenbach, *Amoskeag: Life and Work in an American Factory City* (New York, 1978); Grace Blood, *Manchester on the Merrimack: The Story of a City* (Manchester, 1948), chaps. 8–15; James D. Squires, *The Granite State of the United States* (New York, 1956), vol. 1, chap. 13, and vol. 2, chaps. 19 and 20; Hobart Pillsbury, *New Hampshire: Resources, Attractions, and Its People, A History* (New York, 1927), vol. 3, pp. 637–45; William P. Straw,

"Amoskeag in New Hampshire—An Epic in American Industry," New-comen Society Address (Princeton, 1948).

25. Robert G. LeBlanc, *Location of Manufacturing in New England in the 19th Century*, Geography Publications at Dartmouth, no. 7 (Hanover, N.H., 1969).

26. George P. Baker, *The Formation of the New England Railroad Systems: A Study of Railroad Combination in the Nineteenth Century* (Cambridge, Mass., 1937), chaps. 5–7; Kirkland, *Men, Cities, and Transportation*, vol. 2, chap. 16; Barry A. Macey, "Charles Sanger Mellen: Architect of Transportation Monopoly," *Historical New Hampshire* 26 (1971), pp. 3–29; James Hokans, "Railroad Combination in New Hampshire, 1835–1900," honors thesis, Dartmouth College, Department of History, 1974.

27. LeBlanc, *Location of Manufacturing in New England in the 19th Century*, pp. 86–96. Jager and Jager, *Portrait of a Hill Town*, chap. 1.

28. Squires, *Granite State*, vol. 2, p. 454.

29. William R. Brown, *Our Forest Heritage: A History of Forestry and Recreation in New Hampshire* (Concord, 1958), chaps. 1–3; also *Manchester Union*, January 15 and 22, March 5 and 12, 1900.

30. *Report of the New Hampshire Board of Agriculture*, 1900, p. 27.

31. Brown, *Our Forest Heritage*, pp. 29–30; Nicholas Theodorou, "Conservation in New Hampshire: A Bald Grab for Power?" honors thesis, Dartmouth College, Department of History, 1979, pp. 9–13.

32. Commissioner of Bureau of Labor, "Special Report of Summer Boarding Business and Resorts in N.H., 1899" (Manchester, 1900), pp. ix–x.

33. James D. Squires, *Mirror to America: A History of New London, New Hampshire, 1900–1950* (Concord, 1952), pp. 14, 15–16; Jager and Jager, *Portrait of a Hill Town*, pp. 187–204; William H. Child, *History of the Town of Cornish, New Hampshire with Genealogical Record* (Concord, n.d.), vol. 1, chap. 17 (by Homer St. Gaudens); Hugh Mason Wade, *A Brief History of Cornish, 1763–1974* (Hanover, N.H., 1976), chaps. 3 and 4; George A. Morison, *History of Peterborough, New Hampshire* (Rindge, N.H., 1974), chap. 19; Thomas F. Anderson, "Our New England Alps as a National Health Resort," *New England Magazine* 38 (1908), pp. 313–27; *Manchester Union*, March 5, September 3 and 10, 1900; *Concord Evening Monitor*, July 13, 1900.

34. "Special Report of Summer Boarding Business, 1899" pp. ix–x.

35. Census Bureau, *Supplementary Analysis*, 1900, p. 466. For a revealing study of family organization and work patterns, see Hareven, *Family Time and Industrial Time*, especially chaps. 7 and 8 for 1900 analyses.

36. Compiled from New Hampshire Bureau of Labor, *Fourth Biennial Report*, 1902, pp. 233–47.

37. Ibid., pp. 209–17; Hanlan, *Working Population of Manchester, New Hampshire*, pp. 164–67; *Manchester Union*, March 19, 1900. French Strother, "A City without Strikes," *World's Work* 15 (Nov. 1907), pp. 9534–37.

38. George F. Theriault, "The Franco-Americans in a New England Community: An Experiment in Survival," Ph.D. dissertation, Harvard University, 1951, p. 4; see also chap. 4; Vicero, "Immigration of French Canadians," pp. 214–24, 350–56; estimates of proportion of textile work

force, ibid., p. 345. Tamara Hareven notes that the French Canadians played an active role in the 1922 Amoskeag strike, in *Family Time and Industrial Time*, p. 330.

39. New Hampshire Young Men's Christian Association, *Annual Convention* (n.p., 1888); see also Theriault, "Franco-Americans in a New England Community," p. 5; other indications of prejudice are in *Manchester Union*, July 20, 1893, January 15, March 5, 1900, January 3, 1903: a U.S. senator from New Hampshire affirmatively answered his own question in William E. Chandler, "Shall Immigration Be Suspended?" *North American Review* 156 (1893), pp. 1–8.

40. Quoted in *Manchester Union*, July 24, 1893; for Irish/French-Canadian conflict see Theriault, "Franco-Americans in a New England Community," p. 195; Hareven and Langenbach, *Amoskeag*, p. 45; examples of French-Canadian insistence upon their own priests are in Theriault, "Franco-Americans," pp. 142–43, *Manchester Union*, March 26, 1900, *L'Impartial*, September 18, 27, and October 16, 1900, and October 31, 1905; these tensions are implicit in the annual census reports in the Manchester diocesan archives.

41. *L'Impartial*, December 15, 1900. For the growth of national churches in Nashua, see Theriault, "Franco-Americans in a New England Community," pp. 155–56.

42. *L'Impartial*, November 24, 1900; the November 28, 1905, issue of this newspaper implored French-Canadian parents to speak proper French at home so the children would not become corrupted. A good discussion is Mason Wade, "The French Parish and *Survivance* in Nineteenth-Century New England," *Catholic Historical Review* 36 (1950), pp. 163–89; see also Vicero, "Immigration of French Canadians," pp. 360–64.

43. *Old Home Week Addresses*, p. 16.

44. *L'Impartial*, April 28, 1900; in January Father P. J. Scott told his congregation that Christian unity was fine, but only on the Roman Catholic church's terms. The latter "cannot yield one jot or tittle of principle." *Manchester Union*, January 22, 1900.

45. Charles B. Kinney, Jr., *Church and State: The Struggle for Separation in New Hampshire, 1630–1900* (New York, 1955), *passim;* one example of Protestant tensions is John Schott, *Frances' Town* (Francestown, N.H., 1972), chap. 5; for general discussion of geographical and other differences, see Jere R. Daniell, *Experiment in Republicanism: New Hampshire Politics and the American Revolution, 1741–1794* (Cambridge, Mass., 1970); Lynn Turner, *William Plumer of New Hampshire, 1759–1850* (Chapel Hill, N.C., 1962); Donald B. Cole, *Jacksonian Democracy in New Hampshire, 1800–1851* (Cambridge, Mass., 1970).

46. Squires, *Granite State of the United States*, vol. 1, pp. 309–11; Blood, *Manchester on the Merrimack*, p. 285; newspapers in 1900 had regular stories about prohibition enforcement and temperance agitation, e.g., *Granite State Free Press*, January 5; *Manchester Union*, January 1, March 5 and 12.

47. Census Bureau, *Special Reports, Religious Bodies: 1906*, pt. 1 (Washington, D.C., 1910), pp. 58, 232–33.

48. *Manchester Union,* January 15, 1900; other sermons, ibid., January 22 and 29.

49. "Journal of Proceedings of Grand Lodge of New Hampshire, 1896," Resolutions, p. 1004. *Manchester Union,* January 1 and 8, 1900. *Granite State Free Press,* January 5, 1900.

50. *Manchester Union,* January 8, 15, 29, and March 5, 1900. For a discussion of service, educational, and charitable activities in one parish, see Theriault, "Franco-Americans in a New England Community," pp. 333–37. Annual Conference of the New Hampshire Methodist Episcopal Church, *Official Journal* (1896), p. 30; see also *Manchester Union,* January 3, 1903.

51. *Manchester Union,* January 1, 15, 22, and 29, 1900.

52. Eugene A. Bishop, *Development of a State School System: New Hampshire,* Contributions to Education, no. 391, Teachers College, Columbia University (New York, 1930), pp. 83, 86–87, 90.

53. New Hampshire State Grange, *Journal of Proceedings* (1894), p. 132; New Hampshire Woman's Christian Temperance Union, *Minutes of the Annual Meeting* (1894), p. 16; Census Bureau, *Supplementary Analysis, 1900,* pp. 372–73; idem, *Population, 1900,* vol. 1, p. ccv.

54. Compiled from Census Bureau, *Population, 1900,* vol. 2, pp. 66–67, 362–74.

55. For an example of parochial school development, Theriault, "Franco-Americans in a New England Community," pp. 333–37; see also Kinney, *Church and State,* pp. 156–74.

56. Leon Burr Richardson, *History of Dartmouth College* (Hanover, N.H., 1932), vol. 2, chap. 12; University of New Hampshire, *History of the University of New Hampshire, 1866–1941,* (Durham, 1941), chaps. 3–5.

57. News of organizations convening at larger geographical meetings, as well as regular individual travel and socializing, is covered throughout the contemporary newspapers; see as well Vicero, "Immigration of French Canadians," p. 361. Rural mail delivery was expanding rapidly in 1900 (see, for example, *Manchester Union,* January 8, for Pembroke, March 19 for Lebanon); new telephone systems were reaching into the smaller towns (see, for example, March 5 *Manchester Union* for discussion of fifty new telephones in Pittsfield).

58. The neighborhood or community "surprise" party where friends would gather and provide gifts to the honored one, in celebration of some event, in support of a difficult time, or simply to show affection, was apparently a common event. E.g., see Dover and Manchester descriptions in January 15, 1900, issue of *Manchester Union.* For a good summary of community activities, Jager and Jager, *Portrait of a Hill Town,* pp. 32–34.

59. These events dominated in 1900 in the *Manchester Union* and *Concord Evening Monitor.* See also Squires, *Mirror to America,* pp. 22–23, for discussion of turn-of-the-century New London's fascination with these diplomatic and military activities.

60. Discussion of events at Nashua fair, *Manchester Union,* September 3, January 15 and 29, 1900.

61. A discussion of emotions generated by troops marching to war in 1898 is in James O. Lyford, ed., *History of Concord, New Hampshire from*

the Original Grant in Seventeen Hundred and Twenty-Five to the Opening of the Twentieth Century (Concord, 1903), pp. 592–97; see *Manchester Union,* January 1, 1900, and *Granite State Free Press,* January 5, 1900.

62. See, for example, sermon topics summarized in *Manchester Union,* January 8, September 3; see other examples, such as Tilton Seminary debate on British claims in South Africa (Jan. 29), East Rockingham and Rye Granges discussing Puerto Rican tariff (Mar. 12), missionary programs described at Rockingham County Home Missionary Union (Sept. 3), Concord High School Lyceum debate on withdrawal of American troops from China (Sept. 17), Littleton Christian Endeavor Society's decision to send contributions to India, to Talladega College, and to Hampton Institute (Sept. 24). All dates refer to *Manchester Union* description.

63. These domestic items received regular front-page coverage in the newspapers, although international events dominated for much of 1900. On January 29 the *Concord Evening Monitor* reminded readers that "the Southern question is very far from being rightly settled," in a discussion of black voting rights.

64. *Manchester Union,* January 15, 1900.

2. The Politics of Diffusion

1. September 3, 1900. See similar comment in *L'Impartial,* August 7, 1900: "la politique est une drole de chose."

2. Calculations on elected and appointed officials from biennial *New Hampshire Manual for the General Court, State Treasurer's Reports,* and various town and city reports.

3. Charles F. Dole, *The American Citizen* (Boston, 1892). Dole likens government to the rules of family, playground, and school: "The more honorably liberty is used, the more liberty must be given; but the authority must rest with the teacher to forbid whatever would injure the school, since the teacher is responsible for the welfare of all" (p. 10).

4. The press gave these issues extensive coverage in the 1890s. For a summary of congressional interests and accomplishments, see *Concord Monitor,* June 7, 1900.

5. This and the following discussion are based on an analysis of William M. Chase and Arthur H. Chase, comps., *The Public Statutes of the State of New Hampshire and General Laws in Force, January 1, 1901* (Concord, 1900). What is not clear from the statutes, of course, is the efficacy of these controls, and the extent to which public officials followed them.

6. See *Manchester Union,* January 7, 1890; *Annual Report of the New Hampshire State Board of Agriculture, 1900,* p. IX.

7. "Message of His Excellency, Hiram A. Tuttle, Governor of New Hampshire. To the Two Branches of the Legislature, January Session, 1891" (Concord, 1891), p. 31.

8. The New Hampshire Grange was particularly discriminating in its resolutions, directing some to Congress and some to the New Hampshire state legislature. See "Resolutions" for 1888, 1890, 1892, and 1898 for examples. The Grange looked to Congress for action on railroads and trusts, pure food

legislation, rural mail delivery, and postal savings banks. They turned to Concord for trust regulation as well, and asked state legislators for anti-margarine legislation and protection of lands from trespassing sportsmen. After success with a state anti-oleo law, the Grange sought national enforcement assistance (*Concord Monitor*, May 7, 1900). For a discussion of the state Grange and its lack of real influence, see Rexford Sherman, "The New Hampshire Grange, 1873–1883," *Historical New Hampshire* 26 (1971), pp. 3–25. State dairymen sought state help in developing cooperatives (in 1900 *Report of the N.H. Board of Agriculture*, p. 299.) The Freewill Baptists sought to protect the family through more stringent state divorce laws (1890 "Annual Resolutions"), while the Baptists looked to a national movement for uniform state marriage and divorce laws (1898 Convention, "Resolutions.") The Woman's Christian Temperance Union sought a state curfew law "to protect the character and reputation" of citizens and the state (1898 "Resolutions"). Generally groups looked to the national government for regulation of economic organizations like railroads and trusts, looked to state government for economic and moral regulation, and looked to local government for material amenities such as street lighting. See *Manchester Union*, January 29, and March 12, 1900.

9. Schott, *Frances' Town*, p. 127.

10. William Whitcher, *Some Things about Coventry-Benton, New Hampshire* (Woodsville, 1905), pp. 200–201.

11. It is difficult to recover systematic town meeting information. Town histories and newspapers provide uneven coverage. See A. N. Somers, *History of Lancaster* (Concord, 1899), p. 246; Whitcher, *Some Things about Coventry-Benton*, pp. 196–97; idem, *History of the Town of Haverhill, New Hampshire* (n.p., 1919), pp. 201–2, 206–9; John Armstrong, *Factory under the Elms*, (Cambridge, Mass., 1969) pp. 166; *Manchester Union*, January 8, March 12, March 26, 1900.

12. State Board of Equalization, "Valuation and Taxation of the State of New Hampshire for the Year 1900" (Manchester, 1901); "Report of the State Treasurer of the State of New Hampshire for the Year Ending May 31, 1900" (Manchester, 1900); "Fifty-Fifth Annual Report of the Receipts and Expenditures of the City of Manchester, New Hampshire, for the Fiscal Year Ending December 31, 1900" (Manchester, 1901); "Report of the New Hampshire Tax Commission of 1908" (Concord, 1908); Maurice Robinson, *A History of Taxation in New Hampshire*, Publication of the American Economic Association, 3d series, vol. 3, no. 3 (New York, 1902).

13. Bar Association of the State of New Hampshire, *Proceedings*, 1902, p. 718.

14. New Hampshire State Board of Health, "Biennial Report, 1901–02"; Census Bureau, *Special Reports, Central Electric Light and Power Stations, 1902* (Washington, D.C., 1905), p. 13. See also James O. Lyford, ed., *History of Concord, N.H. from the Original Grant in Seventeen Hundred and Twenty-five to the Opening of the Twentieth Century* (Concord, 1903), vol. 1, pp. 528–30; "Annual Report of Selectmen and Other Town Officers of Canaan, N.H. for the Year Ending February 15, 1897" (Canaan, 1896 [*sic*]); Martha Frizzell, *Second History of Charlestown, N.H.: The Old*

Number Four (Charlestown, 1955), p. 149. "Annual Report of Selectmen and Other Town Officers, 1901" (Claremont, n.d.); see also "Report" for 1902, 1903, 1904. *Manchester Union*, January 29, March 19, 1900.

15. *Annual Report of State Superintendent of Public Instruction, 1900*, p. 272.

16. Chase and Chase, *Public Statutes*, p. 349.

17. *Manchester Union*, January 9, March 1, April 12, 1890.

18. For Goodell-Democratic debate, ibid., January 25, 1890.

19. Chase and Chase, *Public Statutes*, p. 299.

20. Protemperance sentiment was not distinctly a fundamentalist Protestant concern. See Episcopalian support in *Concord Monitor*, November 12, 1890; Universalists in 1892 "Resolutions"; and Grange in 1890 "Resolutions."

21. Kirkland, *Men, Cities, and Transportation*, vol. 2, p. 256, believed that New Hampshire was the most provincial (anticonsolidation) of all New England states until 1883; see also p. 313. Chase and Chase, *Public Statutes*, p. 204.

22. Kirkland, *Men, Cities, and Transportation*, vol. 2, p. 266.

23. See "Fifty-Sixth Annual Report, Railroad Commissioners of the State of New Hampshire, 1900" (Manchester, 1901), pp. 179–209.

24. Kirkland, *Men, Cities, and Transportation*, vol. 2, p. 300.

25. Ibid., pp. 263–64.

26. "Message of Governor Jordan," pp. 11–12.

27. "Report of Board of Agriculture, 1900," p. 35; see also *Concord Monitor*, November 11, 1890, and September 15, 1892; and "Report of State Forestry Commission, 1900," p. 8.

28. Chase and Chase, *Public Statutes*, p. 881. "Report of State Forestry Commission, 1900," pp. 4–5; Governor Rollins address at Concord, *Old Home Week Addresses*, pp. 76–77.

29. Theodorou, "Conservation in New Hampshire"; see, e.g., State Grange, "Resolutions," 1902.

30. "Message of Governor Jordan," pp. 13–14.

31. Grange, "Resolutions," 1898; "Message of His Excellency Nahum J. Bachelder, Governor of New Hampshire, to the Two Branches of the Legislature, January Session, 1903" (Manchester, 1903), pp. 10–11.

32. Robinson, *History of Taxation in New Hampshire*, pp. 209–12; "Message of His Excellency John B. Smith, Governor of New Hampshire, to the Two Branches of the Legislature, January Session, 1893" (Concord, 1893), pp. 21–22.

33. Bishop, *Development of a State School System*, pp. 83, 86–87, 90. Bush, *History of Education in New Hampshire*, pp. 34–36. For a discussion of the effect of this change at the local level, see William Child, *History of the Town of Cornish, New Hampshire, 1763–1910* (Concord, n.d.), vol. 1, pp. 143–46; and Jager and Jager, *Portrait of a Hill Town*, chap. 5.

34. Bishop, *Development of a State School System*, pp. 67, 79–81; *Concord Monitor*, February 21, 1900; *Manchester Union*, January 8, March 12, and March 19, 1900.

35. "State Treasurer's Report, 1900," p. 15; *Manchester Union*, January 1, 1900.

36. Bishop, *Development of a State School System*, p. 90; Armstrong, *Factory under the Elms*, p. 159; *Manchester Union*, September 3, 1900; "Annual Report of State Board of Health, 1900," pp. v, 75–77, 81.

37. "Report of the Board of Health, 1900," pp. 12–36; Chase and Chase, *Public Statutes*, pp. 339–40.

38. "Report of the Board of Health, 1903–04," pp. 91–108.

39. See Lyford, *History of Concord*, vol. 1, pp. 547–49; "Annual Report of the Board of Health, 1900," pp. ix, xiv, vi–vii.

40. Chase and Chase, *Public Statutes*, p. 606.

41. WCTU, "Resolutions," 1898.

42. "Message of Governor Jordan," p. 39.

43. Bishop, *Development of a State School System*, p. 87.

44. "Message of Governor Jordan," p. 4.

45. *The New Hampshire Manual for the General Court with Complete Official Succession, 1680–1891* (Concord, 1891), pp. 124–25.

46. H. B. Brown, comp., "Biographical Sketches of the Governor, Councilors, and Members of the Senate and House of Representatives of the New Hampshire Legislature for 1901–02" (Concord, 1901). When the senate re-elected John McLane (Milford) as president in 1893, it was the first time this had happened in over fifty years. Pillsbury, *New Hampshire*, vol. 3, p. 706. Of the 413 delegates sent to the 1902 constitutional convention, only 23 had been at the 1876 or 1889 conclaves. Ibid., p. 694. For argument on behalf of a large legislature because it is "better" and "nearer . . . to the people," see *Granite State Free Press*, January 5, 1900.

47. For Manchester office holding, see "Annual Report." Other cities had fewer officials of course. See, e.g., "Sixth Annual Report of the Municipal Government of the city of Franklin for the Financial Year, 1900" (Franklin, n.d.).

48. Frank B. Sanborn, *New Hampshire: An Epitome of Popular Government* (Boston, 1904).

49. State of New Hampshire, *Manual for the General Court, 1901* (Manchester, 1901), pp. 1–14. *Manchester Union*, March 19, 1890, reported that "the number of women elected to serve on school boards is steadily increasing from year to year." Figures for 1900 calculated from "Report" of the superintendent of public instruction in that year.

50. WCTU, "Resolutions," 1902; the *Manchester Union* supported woman suffrage, and its columns in January, February, and March 1903 covered extensively the prosuffrage position; e.g., January 7, 10, 19, 31, February 2, 7, 12, 26, March 5, 9, 10. Quote is in last cited item.

51. The *Concord Monitor* was a major antisuffrage forum. See, e.g., January 28, February 5, 10, 16, and 24. See also "Woman Suffrage in New Hampshire," *Outlook*, February 21, 1903, p. 481.

52. The growth of foreign-born population was becoming a matter of increasing concern in New Hampshire. Allyn A. Young, "The Birth-Rate in New Hampshire," *Quarterly Publications of the American Statistical Association* 9 (Sept. 1905), pp. 263–91. See *Portsmouth Times* editorial in *Concord Monitor*, February 21, 1903.

53. Kinney, *Church and State*, pp. 133–41.

54. *Manchester Union,* March 2, 1903; Kinney, *Church and State,* pp. 140–41.

55. Pearsonian correlation, the technique used here, measures the relationship between two variables, with values ranging from + 1.00 to − 1.00. These data are only statistical indexes that relate to voting units (cities and towns in this case) and reveal nothing about individual behavior. The correlation coefficients are: Strike *Protestant* and Woman Suffrage = 0.43, Strike *Protestant* and Language Requirement = 0.23; Woman Suffrage and Language Requirement = 0.29. The square of these values (called coefficient of determination) reveals the percentage of variation in one explained by the other. Thus with an r^2 of 0.17 the Suffrage and *Protestant* relationship is not very strong.

56. *Concord Monitor,* November 4, 1890; *Manchester Union,* July 7 and 29, and November 2, 1892. See as well, *Concord Monitor,* November 6, 1890, October 31, November 1, 8, 9, 1892. In 1892 New Hampshire Republicans attempted unsuccessfully to get federal marshals to monitor the polls in Portsmouth. But see Democratic charges in *Manchester Union,* April 8, 1890, October 28 and 31, 1892.

57. These are coefficients of determination; see n. 55. The Democratic gubernatorial vote in 1890 correlated with that of 1888 at 0.90; the gubernatorial vote of 1892 correlated with 1890 at the same value. The respective Republican coefficients were 0.91 and 0.89.

58. The 1832 manuscript returns are available at the New Hampshire State Archives.

59. See Cole, *Jacksonian Democracy in New Hampshire, passim,* but especially chap. 6; see also Richard H. Sewell, *John P. Hale and the Politics of Abolition* (Cambridge, Mass., 1965), pp. 10–12; Roy F. Nichols, *Franklin Pierce: Young Hickory of the Granite Hills,* rev. ed. (Philadelphia, 1958), pp. 28–59; Sue Taishoff, "New Hampshire State Politics and the Concept of a Party System, 1800–1840," *Historical New Hampshire* 31 (1976), pp. 17–43.

60. A comprehensive study of New Hampshire voting in the 1890s is Robert K. Sholl, "Critical Elections and Political Paradigms: A New Hampshire Case Study," Senior Fellow project, Dartmouth College, 1977.

61. See Richard Jensen, *The Winning of the Midwest: Social and Political Conflict, 1888–1896* (Chicago, 1971); Paul Kleppner, *The Cross of Culture: A Social Analysis of Midwestern Politics, 1850–1900* (New York, 1970); and idem, *The Third Electoral System, 1853–1892: Parties, Voters, and Political Cultures* (Chapel Hill, N.C., 1979). Chap. 9 of the latter includes a discussion of the literature on this subject and a defense of the research against critics, including James Wright, "The Ethnocultural Model of Voting: A Behavioral and Historical Critique," *American Behavioral Scientist* 16 (1973), pp. 35–36, for "misreading" the material.

62. Ward data were developed from an analysis of the 1900 manuscript census, at the National Archives. Wards used here: Irish (Dover Fifth and Manchester Fifth), French-Canadian (Nashua Third), mixed (Manchester Eighth), Yankee (Concord First and Fourth, Nashua First, and Portsmouth Fourth). French Canadians are particularly difficult to work with because so

many were aliens and participation was lower. I have allowed for these factors in my characterization of wards.

63. *Manchester Union,* October 6, 19, and 24, 1892. The Democratic *Union* found "food for solid reflection" in the allegation that the pope had "more power in the States than in any Catholic country in the old world." March 7, 1890; see also September 9, 1890. For Republican countercharges of Democratic nativism and anti-Catholicism, see *Concord Monitor,* September 27, October 2, November 1 and 12, 1890; October 10, 1892.

64. For similar conclusions, see Abrams, *Conservatism in the Progressive Era,* pp. 50–51.

65. Gordon B. McKinney, "The Politics of Protest: The Labor Reform and Greenback Parties in New Hampshire," *Historical New Hampshire* 36 (1981), pp. 149–70.

66. *Granite State Free Press,* March 16, 1894; for discussion of the reaction to the Panic of 1893, see, e.g., ibid., July 18, 21, and 28, August 18, 19, and 25, 1893; Manchester was particularly hard hit when the Amoskeag mills closed in early August. The Democratic *Union* had a difficult time treating the impact of this event: July 18, August 1, 4, 12, and 24. By early August the newspaper conceded that French Canadians particularly were leaving the city, returning to Quebec; by later in the month "hoodlums" and "tramps" were a cause of concern. For news of similar patterns elsewhere, see ibid., July 28 (Keene) and August 5 (Laconia and Pittsfield).

67. V. O. Key, Jr., "A Theory of Critical Elections," *Journal of Politics* 17 (1955), pp. 3–18; and idem, "Secular Realignment and the Party System," *Journal of Politics* 21 (1959), pp. 198–210. Samuel T. McSeveney, *The Politics of Depression: Political Behavior in the Northeast, 1893–1896* (New York, 1972). David Hammond, "New Hampshire Gold Democrats," seminar paper, Dartmouth College, Department of History, 1975.

68. Calculated from supervisor returns in biennial *Manual for the General Court.*

69. For an extensive analysis of the realignment pattern in New Hampshire, see Sholl, "Critical Elections," especially pp. 253–332. The towns that gave Bryan a majority in 1896 were Albany, Eaton, Freedom, Wentworth's Location, Easton, Ellsworth, Wentworth, Deering, Sharon, and Newington.

70. Gallinger to Charles Marseilles, September 26, 1898, in Marseilles File, Box 2, Jacob Gallinger papers, New Hampshire Historical Society.

71. William F. Whitcher, *History of the Town of Haverhill, New Hampshire* (n.p., 1919), p. 208.

72. General Association of Congregational and Presbyterian Churches, "Resolutions," 1888, pp. 15–16; WCTU "Resolutions," 1888; State Baptist Convention, "Resolutions," 1888; Freewill Baptists, "Resolutions," 1888.

73. This and following discussion based on reading of party platforms, speeches, and the partisan press. I cannot validate the veracity of partisan argument, nor do I try, and I cannot argue that either the sources or audiences for these positions believed them. On the other hand, repeated slogans, positions, and themes do suggest something of the *nature* of party appeal—without getting into more complicated questions about the rela-

tionship of appeals to behavior. There are no ways of determining whether these appeals generated new support or even maintained old support. On the other hand one might infer—from repeated use and from general voting in the early 1890s—that they did not lose support.

74. *Concord Monitor*, October 22, 1892; September 1, 1890.

75. E.g., ibid., September 8, 17, October 29, 1890, October 12, 1892.

76. Ibid., February 1, 1900. Also see ibid., September 6, 1890; *Manchester Union*, September 7, 1892.

77. See the 1892 party platforms in *Concord Monitor*, September 6 and 8.

78. *Concord Monitor*, September 2 and 17, 1890; see also ibid., September 15, 1892, and *Manchester Union*, March 25, November 1, 1890, October 6, 29, 31, and November 4, 1892.

79. *Concord Monitor*, September 6, 8, and 19, 1892, September 5, and 6, 1894. The Prohibition party declared that the Democrats were hopeless and the Republicans were hypocrites on this issue. *Concord Monitor*, September 9, 1890; *Manchester Union*, September 10, 1890. The post-realignment Democrats continued their position that local control was preferable to state control; see Clarence Carr to Henry Hollis, March 16, 1903, in Box 10, "Correspondence, 1902–03," in Clarence Carr papers, Dartmouth College Library Special Collections.

80. This campaign was covered extensively from January to May. E.g., *Manchester Union*, January 12, 22, February 16, 19, March 9, 19, April 24, 27, 29, May 4, 7, 8, 9, 11, 12, 18, 1903. The organizational work was carried on by Protestant churches of all denominations, uniformly opposing license, by various ad hoc groups, led by the Anti-Saloon League, and by some ethnic groups and craft unions. French Canadians, Irish, and Germans seemed to take the most active prolicense position, with some French Catholic priests supporting this view. The political parties were notably absent, although individual leaders from both parties were active on each side of the controversy.

81. *Concord Monitor*, September 2, 1890, September 11, 1900.

82. The 1892 campaign was particularly marked by ethnic appeals focusing on the tariff and prohibition. See, e.g., *Concord Monitor*, October 3, 17, and 22; *Manchester Union*, September 21, October 24, 27, 29, 31, and November 4.

83. For example, in the off-year election of 1890 both parties addressed repeatedly the McKinley tariff, the Lodge bill, and the Sherman Silver Purchase Act as issues, almost to the total exclusion of state issues. See *Concord Monitor*, August 20, October 25 and 29, and *Manchester Union*, September 3. Prohibition was the major state issue discussed in this campaign.

84. *Concord Monitor*, September 17, 1890, September 6, 1892, September 5, 1894, September 3, 1896, and September 13, 1898; September 11, 1900.

85. Ibid., September 3, 1896. The stage earlier had been set for this Republican appeal when each party attempted to portray the other as controlled by free-silver advocates. See *Concord Monitor*, December 11, 1890, and September 22, 1892; *Manchester Union*, April 26, 1890, July 19, 1892. Partisans from both parties blamed the Panic of 1893 largely on the Sher-

man Silver Purchase Bill. *Granite State Free Press*, July 7 and 14, and August 11 and 18, 1893; *Manchester Union*, June 21 and 23, July 6, and August 30, 1893.

86. See platforms cited in n. 84.

87. *Concord Monitor*, September 6, 1888; September 2, 1890, September 8, 1892.

88. Ibid., September 2, 1890; August 1, 1900.

89. Clarence Carr to Edwin Mead, September 21, 1899, in Box 10, "1892–99 Correspondence," in Clarence Carr papers, Dartmouth College Library Special Collections. See quoted party responses in *Concord Monitor*, August 31, 1898, and September 2, 1896. Early in 1900 Bryan briefly visited Concord and even the antagonistic *Monitor* conceded that "never was a political leader anywhere given a more enthusiastic reception by his friends (Feb. 2, 1900).

90. Platforms in *Concord Monitor*, September 2, 1896, August 31, 1898, August 1, 1900, and September 10, 1902.

91. Ibid.

92. The following correlation coefficients measure the relationship between local option and 1903 constitutional amendments and the 1902 gubernatorial vote:

	Democratic	Republican
Woman suffrage	−.07	.08
Strike *Protestant*	−.18	.16
English language	−.22	.27
Local option	.10	−.08

93. Tabulated from Brown, "Biographical Sketches"; the return rate from legislators, from which Brown compiled the directory, was lower for both parties among urban legislators. An examination of the names that are missing suggests that his tabulation may significantly understate Irish and French-Canadian Democrats. Among missing Republicans are French, Irish, and German surnames, but the great majority are of older English stock.

94. The New Hampshire legislature did not regularly record roll call votes.

95. *Manchester Union*, January 13, 1904.

3. "Recover the Honor of the State"

1. Ronald P. Cima, "The Emergence of Winston Churchill, New Hampshire Author of Progressivism," honors thesis, Dartmouth College, Department of History, 1975, pp. 60–62.

2. Ibid., p. 58; "Winston Churchill," *Harper's Weekly* 43 (Aug. 26, 1899), p. 836; William Wallace Whitelock, "Mr. Winston Churchill," *Critic* 40 (Feb. 1902), pp. 135–41; Hugh Mason Wade, *A Brief History of Cornish, 1763–1974* (Hanover, N.H., 1976), pp. 57–60.

3. Mason, *Brief History of Cornish*, chap. 3; Geoffrey Blodgett, "Winston Churchill: The Novelist as Reformer," *New England Quarterly* 47 (1974), pp. 495–517; Christine Ermenc, "Economic Give-and-Take: Farmers and Aesthetes in Cornish and Plainfield, New Hampshire, 1885–1910," *Historical New Hampshire* 39 (1984), pp. 105–21; David W. Levy, *Herbert Croly of the New Republic: The Life and Thought of an American Progressive* (Princeton, 1985), *passim*, but see pp. 79–80; *Boston Journal*, August 31, 1902, in Winston Churchill scrapbooks, Winston Churchill Collection, Dartmouth College Library Special Collections.

4. Churchill to Amos Tuck French, July 9, 1906, in Churchill Collection. The Churchill manuscripts have recently been reorganized, following the bulk of my research into these materials, so my box and file references to these materials are no longer appropriate. The new organization is by major subject category (all of these references are to the political collection unless otherwise noted) to year or other time period, and to correspondent. This French letter then would be in the political category, 1906 F carbons.

5. Cima, "Emergence of Winston Churchill," pp. 58–60; W. H. Sisson to Churchill, October 15, 1902, in Churchill Collection.

6. *New York Herald*, August 10, 1902, in Churchill scrapbooks; Churchill to E. B. Hoskins, September 24, 1906, in Churchill papers; Churchill to George Moses, April 28, 1903, in Box 1, File 10, George Moses papers, New Hampshire Historical Society.

7. Quoted in Kirkland, *Men, Cities, and Transportation*, vol. 2, p. 21. Kirkland concluded that in the 1880s the railroads in New Hampshire "got all they asked for [from the legislature]. They asked for all they expected to ever need." Ibid., p. 24. See also Gordon McKinney, "The Hazen Bill of 1887 and the Ascendancy of the Boston and Maine," *Historical New Hampshire* 38 (1983), pp. 209–28. For a sketch of Jones by a Republican official, see James Lyford, *Life of Edward H. Rollins: A Political Biography* (Boston, 1906), pp. 326–27.

8. Chandler allegation in *Concord Monitor*, September 24, 1892; see also reference to the Democratic ticket as "the B&M railroad slate" on September 20, 1892, and attack on Jones for his goal to use his "enormous wealth" to "own his native state and to make it Democratic and to become the uncontrolled dictator and ruler of its politics," on October 13, 1890. Of Chandler, Kirkland concluded, "there was about his case more instinct than consistency or logic." *Men, Cities, and Transportation*, vol. 1, p. 449. See Richardson, *William E. Chandler*, chap. 27 and *passim*. Chandler published several anti-Boston and Maine pamphlets. See, e.g., "The Growth of the Use of Money in Politics and of Railroad Power in New Hampshire" (Concord, 1899). See also Chandler articles, "National Control of Elections," *Forum*, August 1890, pp. 705–18; "Methods of Restricting Immigration," *Forum*, March 1892, pp. 128–42; "Shall Immigration Be Suspended," *North American Review*, January 1893, pp. 1–8 (Chandler's answer to this question was yes).

9. Richardson, *William E. Chandler*, p. 523; see *Concord Monitor*, September 22, 1890, for a prediction that "factions based upon railroad questions are dying out," followed by concession that they have not yet faded. In

1904 a supporter of Sen. Jacob Gallinger complained that the old Democrats who bolted to the GOP in 1896 "took full control" of the latter. John Crawford to Gallinger, July 12, 1904, File 1, Box 2, Gallinger papers, New Hampshire Historical Society. Probably the biggest flap—and example of the influence of the converts—came when Frank Jones was "sent" as a delegate to the 1900 Republican National Convention.

10. *Concord Monitor*, September 19, 1892; Richardson, *William E. Chandler*, pp. 384–407, 607–14. *Tribune*, quoted in *Concord Monitor*, December 5, 1890.

11. These characterizations based on reading of the correspondence in the James Lyford Collection and the George Moses Collection at the New Hampshire Historical Society. See Merrill A. Symonds, "George Higgins Moses of New Hampshire—The Man and the Era," Ph.D. dissertation, Clark University, (1955), chap. 1.

12. In 1894 Democratic leader Clarence Carr learned that his choice for an appointment had been vetoed by Boston and Maine officials. J. W. Fellows to Carr, April 2, 1894, in Box 10, Correspondence 1892–99, Clarence Carr papers, Dartmouth College Library Special Collections; in 1896 Boston and Maine official Charles Hamblett negotiated the Republican State Convention chairman with Gallinger, Hamblett to Gallinger, August 4, 1896, File 5, Box 1, Gallinger papers; in 1898 Republican officials discussed their platform and the gubernatorial nominee with Lucius Tuttle; James Lyford acted as intermediary and informed his colleagues that Tuttle "has put a veto upon" the Chester Jordan candidacy but has approved the platform draft: Lyford to Gallinger, August 21, 1898, File 7, Box 1, Gallinger papers. Chandler noted the irony of this in that the railroad now ignored the Democrats so the latter were moving to a position critical of the railroad; he feared the Republicans could end up in a politically untenable position but could only hope "our masters" have "acted with discretion and good faith": to Lyford, September 2, 1898, File 2, Box 1, James Lyford papers, New Hampshire Historical Society. (See also Lyford to Chandler, August 16, 1898, ibid.) In 1899 there was some resentment over railroad involvement in the appointment of a new secretary of state, Moses to Chandler, March 10 and 14, 1899, File 3, Box 1, Moses papers. In the earlier letter Moses wrote that "there are a great many Republicans who, while they take their railroad views from Mr. Sanborn [railroad official John Sanborn], do not follow him when a Republican contest is the only thing in hand." In 1902 Lyford told railroad official Frank Streeter that he, Lyford, had no direct debt to Streeter for his help in getting Lyford a patronage plum in the naval officer post at the Boston Custom House: "Your service at that time was in fulfillment of a promise made by Mr. Tuttle to me in consideration of what I had done for the road and did do for the road thereafter." Lyford to Streeter, March 6, 1902, File 4, Box 1, Lyford papers. In 1903 Lyford told Chandler he had to check with Tuttle "in regard to the calling together of the Constitutional Convention," July 20, 1903, in File 5, Box 1, Lyford papers.

13. Lyford to Gallinger, June 6, 1904, Lyford papers; the "throne room" was the center for machine planning and discussions when the legislature was in session. Entrance was through the Eagle Hotel across from the state

capitol. On the second floor of the hotel was an enclosed walkway that passed over an alley directly to the throne room in an adjacent bank building. The walkway was called the Bridge of Sighs. See, e.g., *Boston American*, February 17, 1907, in Churchill scrapbooks. See also John Garland to Churchill, August 7, 1906, ibid.

14. A humorous but apparently accurate account of machine influence, written by a legislative veteran, is A. J. Lucier, *The Machine: A Political Satire* (Boston, 1908); see also M. C. Lamphrey to Churchill, July 7, 1906, Walter Creamer to Churchill, August 13, 1906, and Conrad Crooker to Churchill, September 10, 1906, all in Churchill papers.

15. Harry Torrey of Portsmouth wrote Robert Bass on February 12, 1910, that "in Rockingham County most of the prominent men are R.R. from honest belief and many of the others because they have known nothing ever different." In Bass papers.

16. Chandler to Lyford, December 22, 1898, File 2, Box 1, Lyford papers; *Manchester Union*, January 1, 1900; Richardson, *William E. Chandler*, pp. 586–89, 607–15.

17. Lyford to Gallinger, August 21, 1898, File 7, Box 1, Gallinger papers; Richardson, *William E. Chandler*, pp. 534–36, 585–86.

18. Richardson, *William E. Chandler*, pp. 631–40; Gallinger's role was not altogether clear. See Louis Hoyt to Gallinger, September 6, 1900, in File 9, Box 1, Gallinger papers. File 4 through 6 of Box 1 of the Moses papers report on Moses's efforts to monitor the situation for Chandler; he did find Boston and Maine pressure on legislators to oppose Chandler.

19. Richardson, *William E. Chandler*, pp. 631–40; Lyford had warned a friend that this may happen because of the senator's caustic manner, to J. V. Hanscom, December 21, 1900, Box 3, File 1, Lyford papers.

20. James Lyford, loyal to Gallinger and upset over Streeter's effort to get the national committee seat eyed by Gallinger, worked with Chandler in attempting to block Streeter. See Chandler to Lyford, November 19, 1902, and Lyford to Chandler, November 20, 1902, in File 4, Box 1, Lyford papers. Lyford insisted that Streeter was not the railroad's candidate but rather was his own candidate. See also Lyford to Chandler, November 26, 1902, in File 5, Box 1, Lyford papers, and Lyford to Gallinger, November 5, 1902, in File 4, Box 1, Lyford papers. Moses told Chandler that the railroad was not clearly in this fight for Streeter, and "so long as the railroad does not help Streeter, he cannot win." November 21, 1902, Box 1, File 7, Moses papers.

21. Streeter and Gallinger had apparently always been uneasy allies. See Streeter to Gallinger, June 19, 1894, in File 3, Box 1, Gallinger papers. For the maneuvering over the national committee post, replacing the late Charles Means, Streeter to Mark Hanna, copy to Gallinger, February 3, 1902, File 11, Box 1, Gallinger papers; Gallinger to Lyford, February 5, 1902, Box 1, File 4, Lyford papers; Hanna to Gallinger, March 11, 1903, File 12, Box 1, Gallinger papers; Lyford to Chandler, March 16, 1903, File 5, Box 1, Lyford papers; Chandler to Lyford, January 15, 1904, and Lyford to Chandler, January 16, 1904, File 6, Lyford to Chandler, September 22, 1904, File 7, in Box 1, Lyford papers; Chandler to Gallinger, July 8, 1904,

File 1, Box 2, Gallinger papers. John Walker to Gallinger, September 28, 1904, File 3, Box 2, Gallinger papers; for press coverage of the 1904 vote, see Churchill scrapbooks.

22. Streeter to Lyford, January 30, 1902, and Lyford to Streeter, January 31, 1902, in File 4, Box 1, Lyford papers; Harry Sargent to Lyford, January 12, 1904, Chandler to Sargent, January 13, 1904, Gallinger to Lyford, January 15, 1904, and Lyford to Chandler, January 28, 1904, in File 6, Box 1, Gallinger to Lyford, June 20, 1904, and Lyford to Chandler, June 23, 1904, in File 7, Box 1, ibid.; Frank Churchill to Gallinger, July 17, 1904, File 1; Chandler to Gallinger, September 1, 1904, and Frank Shapleigh to Gallinger, September 2, 1904, File 3; all in Box 2, Gallinger papers. In 1907 Streeter shared with Winston Churchill his version of the affair: Tuttle had decided that Gallinger should stay because of the controversy, but Streeter did not halt the process he had set in motion. Streeter to Churchill, October 21, 1907, in Churchill papers.

23. Lyford to Streeter, January 31, 1902, in Box 1, File 4, Lyford papers.

24. Lyford to Oliver Branch, March 25, 1903; Branch wrote Lyford on March 23 that Streeter had occupied a desk next to House Speaker Cheney during the local-option debate, File 5, Box 1, Lyford papers; Lyford to Tuttle, March 3, and to Chandler, March 16, 1903, in ibid.; in 1902 Lyford believed he had agreement from Streeter and Tuttle that the railroad lobby would stay clear of this issue, "looming up ahead of us fraught with trouble." Lyford to Streeter, January 31, 1902, in Box 1, File 4, ibid.

25. Remich to Lyford, January 31, 1902, File 4, Box 1, Lyford papers; Gallinger was active with temperance and prohibition groups; see e.g., J. H. Davenport to Gallinger, July 16, 1904, File 1, Box 2; J. H. Robbins (director of New Hampshire Anti-Saloon League) to Gallinger, September 9, 1904, File 3, Box 2; Ellen Richardson (president of New Hampshire Woman's Christian Temperance Union) to Gallinger, September 22, 1904, ibid.; E. M. Sweet (of the Indian Territory Church Federation for Prohibition Statehood) to Gallinger, File 5, Box 2; and Gallinger speeches and statements in "Temperance" File, Box 4, all in Gallinger papers. One discussion of growing resentment toward the railroad among party regulars is Calvin Page to Lyford, September 14, 1903, in File 5, Box 1, Lyford papers.

26. Platform in *Manual for the General Court, 1905* (Concord, 1905), pp. 59–64; see Pillsbury, *New Hampshire*, vol. 3, pp. 705–6. The 1902 and 1904 conventions are described in *Concord Monitor*, September 15–18, 1902, and September 20 and 21, 1904.

27. Chandler to Gallinger, July 31, 1905, in Box 2, File 4, Gallinger papers; Cima, "Emergence of Winston Churchill," pp. 79–85.

28. A good survey of this nationwide mood is McCormick, "Discovery That Business Corrupts Politics"; see also Louis Filler, *The Muckrakers* (University Park, Pa., 1976).

29. The William Jewett Tucker papers in Presidential Papers, Dartmouth College Archives, include records of trustee activity and correspondence between Tucker and individual members of the board.

30. The Tucker speech is reprinted in William Jewett Tucker, *Public*

Mindedness: An Aspect of Citizenship Considered in Various Addresses Given While President of Dartmouth College (Concord, 1910), pp. 177–88; see also Cima, "Emergence of Winston Churchill," pp. 85–86.

31. File 96 of the Tucker papers has many letters on the Committee of Twelve and the racetrack controversy; materials referred to here include Pearson to Tucker, December 18, 1905, Streeter to Tucker, December 25, 1905, Tucker to McLane, January 23, 1906, Kimball to Tucker, February 13, 1906; the latter is in File 20 of the Tucker papers. For the court decision, see *Manchester Union*, March 14, 1906.

32. Cima, "Emergence of Winston Churchill," pp. 92–93, has brief biographical information on the original Lincoln Club members. See Remick to Churchill, June 28, 1906, Churchill papers, and *Manchester Union*, July 21, 1906.

33. Tucker to Kimball, August 24, 1906, in File 20, Tucker papers.

34. Gallinger to Moses, December 17, 1905, in Box 1, File 10, Moses papers.

35. See *Manchester Mirror*, August 12, 1906, for satire on Lincoln Club being exclusively for college graduates who use "ayether" and "neighther." In Churchill scrapbooks. The *Laconia Democrat* said the effort was "novel" but "largely a joke; something hatched out during the silly season in politics." July 14, 1906, ibid. One participant observed that Churchill had support from the women and "the young fellows," but had trouble in many towns getting someone to introduce him: "The first ones who supported him openly here generally had some grievance to satisfy, and were regarded as fanatics." Harry Torrey (Portsmouth) to Robert Bass, April 8, 1910, in Bass papers.

36. Rollins to Churchill, September 5, 1907, in Churchill papers; as early as November 1905 Daniel Remich had set out to "try to induce" Churchill "to cast his lot with us." Remich to Chandler, November 10, 1905, in Box 42, File 1, Chandler papers. See *Manchester Union*, January 13, 1903, *Newport Champion*, January 15, 1903, *Portsmouth Times*, February 9, 1903, and *Boston Globe*, February 17, 1906, all in Churchill scrapbooks, for references to Churchill's social activities in Concord.

37. Churchill to Chandler, July 6, 1906, in Box 42, File 4, Chandler papers.

38. Churchill to Henry Hollis, July 13, 1906, Gilbert Colby, July 15, 1906, and E. B. Hoskins, September 24, 1906, Churchill papers.

39. Rev. D. C. Babcock of Newmarket wrote Churchill on July 28, 1906, asking him to "confess like a man" any errors he may have made, for "the moral forces are taking an unusual interest in politics." Churchill explained his position to Babcock on August 4, 1906. On September 7, Rev. J. H. Robbins, the superintendent of the New Hampshire Anti-Saloon League, wrote Churchill, "while you have not been making a campaign on a temperance issue you have put yourself where the temperance people could not object to you and could consistently support you." See also Churchill to Rev. George Furness, July 23, 1906, and to Harry Cheney, October 4, 1906, all in Churchill papers.

40. Winston Churchill, *Coniston* (New York, 1906), p. 1. Theodore Roose-

velt to Churchill, August 18, 1906, in Elting E. Morison and John M. Blum, eds. *The Letters of Theodore Roosevelt* (Cambridge, Mass., 1951–54), vol. 5, p. 378. William Chandler led the public criticism of what he believed to be a slander of Ruel Durkee, in "Jethro Bass Unreal" (Concord, 1906). For agreement with Churchill's characterization and amusement over the defense of Durkee, see Clarence Carr to Frank Rollins, December 15, 1906, and Rollins to Carr, December 18, 1906, in "Correspondence, 1906," Box 10, Clarence Carr papers, Dartmouth College Library.

41. "Political Speeches, 1906," in Churchill papers. Mark Sullivan, "The Way of a Railroad," *Collier's*, August 11, 1906. See also Churchill to Ames Judson Bailey, July 10, 1906, and to Col. F. E. Kaley, July 6, 1906, in Churchill papers. On *Coniston* as platform, see, e.g., Churchill to editor Barton of the Newport *Argus and Spectator*, July 21, 1906, ibid. Chandler had insisted that "we could not carry on the movement with CONISTON as a platform." Chandler note on his comments at a July 10 meeting with the Churchill group, Box 42, File 4, Chandler papers; Chandler provided Sullivan with information for the *Collier's* article, e.g., Sullivan to Chandler, July 26, 1906, ibid.

42. Kirkland, *Men, Cities, and Transportation*, vol. 2, pp. 473–74.

43. Chandler to Thomas Chalmers, December 2, 1905, Box 42, File 1, and June 11, 1906, Box 42, File 3, Chandler papers; Lyford to Chandler, November 21, 1905, Box 1, File 8, and Lyford to Gallinger, June 14, 1906, Box 1, File 10, Lyford papers; Chandler to Moses, March 18, 1906, Box 1, File 9, Moses papers; Cima, "Emergence of Winston Churchill," pp. 88–90.

44. Jack Kelley to Chandler, April 13, 1906, Box 42, File 3, Chandler papers; Gallinger to Moses, May 15, 1906, Box 1, File 10, Moses papers; Thomas Agan, "New Hampshire Progressive Movement," p. 53.

45. Gallinger kept his distance from the campaign, at least in public, but George Moses asked the senator "just how troublesome you would like me to be" at an important state committee meeting. Moses to Gallinger, August 2, 1906, in File 6, Box 2, Gallinger papers. See also Cima, "Emergence of Winston Churchill," pp. 88–90, and Agan, "New Hampshire Progressive Movement," pp. 51–53.

46. Gallinger to Moses, May 15, 1906, in Box 1, File 10, and Moses to Chandler, July 18, 1906, in Box 1, File 9, Moses papers; Tuttle to Lyford, December 29, 1905, Box 1, File 8, and Lyford to Tuttle, January 2, 1906, Box 1, File 10, Lyford to Benjamin Kimball, March 3, 1905, Box 1, File 8, and February 16, 1906, Box 1, File 10, Lyford papers.

47. Churchill to M. C. Lamprey, July 10, 1906, and Churchill to Joseph Smith, n.d. (July 1906), in Churchill papers. James Remick wrote an article, published in *Outlook*, that made the same Roosevelt linkage: September 1, 1906, pp. 19–22.

48. Chandler to Churchill, November 7, 1904, in Churchill papers; ironically in 1906, when E. C. Niles sent Chandler a note asking to meet with him for a few minutes, at which time Niles informed Chandler of the impending Churchill candidacy, Chandler penned on the bottom of the note, "Never dreamed of the Churchill movement until I saw Mr. Niles and Mr.

Cook at Concord about 11 in answer to this." Niles to Chandler, July 6, 1906, Box 42, File 4, Chandler papers.

49. Chandler to Moses, July 17, 1906, Box 1, File 9, Moses papers; Remich to Chandler, July 10, 1906, in Box 42, File 4, Chandler papers; Richardson, *William E. Chandler*, p. 683. Chandler urged conciliation with the Pillsbury group, which caused the reformers to be suspicious of him. See Churchill to Norman Hapgood, July 31, 1906, in Churchill papers.

50. The campaign cost $4,915.59, of which Churchill personally contributed $4,358.00; see the Edmund Cook account in 1906 campaign materials, Churchill papers.

51. Churchill to Justin McGrath (editor of *New York American*), June 29, and July 10, 1906; Churchill later admitted to a hesitant speaking style, but wrote to one journalist critic asking him to "give me credit for improving in speaking a litle bit." Churchill to Stanley Johnson, September 21, 1908, in Churchill papers.

52. Fred Hale to Churchill, September 12, 1906, in Churchill papers; Cima, "Emergence of Winston Churchill," p. 89.

53. *Boston American*, September 2, 1906, Churchill scrapbooks.

54. Gallinger to Moses, August 29, 1906, Box 1, File 10, Moses papers; for the Concord caucus, *Manchester Union*, September 7, 1906. This was a satisfying victory and form of revenge for Churchill and his supporters who felt they had been deprived of many caucus votes because of old guard control and use of unannounced caucuses, fake ballots, and ringers. See James Joyce to Churchill, August 30, 1906, Frank Sawyer to Churchill, September 6, 1906, G. S. Adams to Churchill, September 12, 1906, and Willis MacDuffie to Churchill, October 10, 1906, all in Churchill papers.

55. Gallinger to Moses, August 3, 1906, in Box 1, File 10, Moses papers.

56. Lyford to Frank Currier, September 10, 1906, in Box 1, File 10, Lyford papers. Pillsbury embittered many by his action. One Greenleaf supporter noted that "Rosecrans W. Pillsbury mounted the platform, turned his back upon the delegates, and took down his pants." In Robert Jackson, "Recollections of Winston Churchill's Campaign for the Republican Nomination for Governor of New Hampshire in 1906," typescript, Dartmouth College Special Collections, p. 45; see Winston Churchill to W. C. Clapp, September 22 and 25, 1906, in Churchill papers; *Boston American*, September 19, 1906; *Manchester Union*, September 19 and 21, 1906; and Cima, "Emergence of Winston Churchill," pp. 107–9. Chandler was furious at the Churchill forces for never having attempted to work with Pillsbury. Because of the way they had treated Pillsbury, the former senator insisted that the Churchill group should not have expected the publisher to have behaved differently. Chandler was also enraged that James Remick, on behalf of the Churchill group, had moved to make Floyd's nomination unanimous. Chandler to Remick September 19, 1906, and to E. C. Niles, September 19 and 27, 1906, Remick to Chandler, September 20, 1906, all in Box 42, File 5, Chandler papers. Hildreth Allison, "Hassle for the Top Spot: The Republican Gubernatorial Convention of 1906," *Historical New Hampshire* 36 (1981), pp. 73–84.

57. Chandler to Churchill, July 7, 1906, in Churchill papers: "It will be harder than travelling over Truro Pass or along Coniston waters." Churchill agreed it would take two campaigns, to Chandler, July 8, 1906, in Box 42, File 4, Chandler papers.

58. Churchill in fact claimed he was "elated" over the accomplishments, to Gen. Frank Battles, September 20, 1906, in Churchill papers; Agan, "New Hampshire Progressive Movement," pp. 55–59.

59. See speeches and correspondence in Box 10, "Democratic Platform, 1906" File, Clarence Carr papers, Dartmouth College Special Collections. The Democrats attempted to capitalize on the antirailroad, antimachine themes of the Churchill campaign.

60. Streeter to Tuttle, October 29, 1906, Tuttle to Streeter, October 31, 1906, and Streeter to Tuttle, November 12, 1906, copies in File 21, Tucker papers.

61. Cornish friend Norman Hapgood urged Churchill to run as an independent: "with Floyd the nominee the platform becomes nothing but air, and that, however distasteful to you, the situation forces you to continue your fight until the Election." Most New Hampshire allies, however, urged Churchill to be a good Republican, with an eye to the future. Churchill's absence from the state seemed to lend credence to the "carpetbagger" label. Hapgood to Churchill, September 19, 1906, and Harry Sargent to Churchill, October 26, 1906, in Churchill papers.

62. Republican voting patterns had shown some discontinuity since the 1894–96 realignment period. The 1906 election extended this trend. The simple correlation coefficients in the accompanying table show the relationship of 1902, 1904, and 1906 Republican gubernatorial voting in New Hampshire towns with earlier elections (N=234).

Table for Note 62

	1902	1904	1906
1888	.631	.602	.425
1890	.616	.670	.462
1892	.697	.700	.516
1894	.648	.670	.446
1896	.716	.659	.467
1898	.748	.706	.595
1900	.773	.780	.619
1902	—	.801	.717
1904	—	—	.682

63. Chandler to Henry Robinson, December 21, 1906, in Box 42, File 7, Chandler papers; in the same file there are a number of increasingly acerbic exchanges between Chandler and James Remick. Unsigned letter (obviously from James Remick) to Churchill, December 22, 1906, in Churchill papers, reviewed the conflict with Chandler. Chandler had written Churchill in October that to not contest the seat "would be a practical abandonment of your movement as a *continuous reform*." The old warrior urged the reformers to "contest everything, and take defeat when it comes." To Chur-

chill, October 2, 1906, in Churchill papers. The Lincoln reformers were convinced that a contest for this seat would indicate that office rather than principle motivated them. See Churchill exchanges with Daniel Remich and James Remick in November–December 1906, ibid. For public confusion over the club's posture, see, e.g, *Boston Herald*, November 29, 1906, and *Concord Monitor*, December 6, 1906, in Churchill scrapbooks.

64. Chandler to Moses, January 12, 1907, summarizing Moses's reports on the caucuses: "It was railroad power which after all stopped Streeter and Drew [railroad lawyer Irving Drew who had indicated some interest in the seat himself]." Box 2, File 2, Moses papers.

65. Churchill to John Dame, December 7, 1906, in Churchill papers; Richardson, *William E. Chandler*, pp. 686–89; *Manchester Union*, January 4, 7, 9, and 19, 1907.

66. Churchill considered this effort part of "an up-hill fight here for decency." To Henry Daniels, February 15, 1907; see also Churchill secretary Josephine Keefe to Robert Bass, January 18, 1907, and Churchill to Bass February 9, 1907, all in Churchill papers; Chandler had tried to stop Ellis because of his closeness to the railroad. He instructed Moses: "He should be beaten but his throat should be cut with a feather if you can do it." Chandler to Moses, December 3, 1906, Box 1, File 9, Moses papers. Also Chandler to Leighton, January 12, 1907, in Box 42, File 8, Chandler papers; Lyford had warned Floyd after the election that the railroad must not seem to "force Ellis upon the House as its speaker." November 17, 1906, Box 10, File 1, Lyford papers. Agan, "New Hampshire Progressive Movement," pp. 65–91.

67. The Lincoln Club legislators were Elisha Wright, Allen Hollis, Robert Manning, Fred Wadleigh, George Worcester, Harry Greeley, Robert Bass, Wilbur Webster, John Benton, Robert Merrill, John Dame, Frank Musgrove, and Oliver Toothaker.

68. Harry Sargent to Churchill, October 26, 1906; Dan Remich, after a vote on a pass bill, complained to Churchill that he was "surprised to see how many of the men, supposed to be heartily in sympathy with the Lincoln Club, voted on the different questions relating to the passage." February 15, 1907, Churchill papers.

69. Gallinger to Moses, January 21, 1907, in Box 2, File 1, Lyford to Moses, January 22, 1907, in Box 2, File 1, Moses to Chandler, December 31, 1906, Box 1, File 9, all in Moses papers. Henry Robinson to Chandler, January 2, 1907, Box 42, File 8, Chandler papers. Lyford to Churchill, January 21, 1907, and to Frank Currier, November 14, 1906, Box 1, File 10; to Stilson Hutchins, February 19, 1907, and to Governor Floyd on the same date, Box 1, File 11, Lyford papers.

70. Lyford to Charles Mellen, June 13, 1907, Box 1, File 11, Lyford papers.

71. Gallinger to Moses, April 9, 1907, Box 2, File 1, Moses papers. Lyford to Gallinger, June 20, 1907, on heading off Streeter who seemed to be trying to bring in Leighton; Lyford proposed bringing the latter into "the machine" as a counter to this. Box 2, File 8, Gallinger papers.

72. See, for example, Chandler, "Merger Will Destroy Competition,"

New England Magazine, May 1908, pp. 276–78; a good description of the
merger battle is Abrams, *Conservatism in a Progressive Era,* chap. 8.

73. Churchill to James Colby, January 12, 1907, and to James Lyford,
January 23, 1907; also Lyford to Churchill, January 21 and 24, 1907, on
hope of getting cooperation from George Moses and the *Concord Monitor,*
Churchill papers.

74. This negotiation was conducted in great secrecy; apparently Churchill did not consult with or confide in his supporters. Wadleigh wrote
Churchill on May 8 that Pillsbury had made overtures for a "congenial" arrangement; Churchill responded to Wadleigh on May 10 that this "interested and amused me a great deal." Yet on May 10 Churchill was responding
as well to a direct May 7 overture from Pillsbury, albeit with some coolness. Pillsbury to Churchill, May 7, and Churchill to Pillsbury, May 10. On
May 27 Churchill and Pillsbury met in White River Junction, Vermont,
where they signed a preliminary agreement. In Churchill papers, File
"1907 P–Q." In June Churchill sent his attorney a final document for safe-
keeping. (I did not locate this among the Churchill papers.) Guy Murchie to
Churchill, June 18, 1907. By August Churchill was discreetly informing
friends of the arrangement: e.g., he wrote Cong. Theodore Burton of Ohio
on August 23 that "my organization" had united with Pillsbury's. He assumed the personal responsibility quoted in the text in a letter to Robert
Bakeman on August 29. On September 3, he informed some friends of the
agreement in a "Dear Sir" mailing. The reaction from some was strongly
negative. See especially several September letters from Daniel Remich and
James Remick. All of this correspondence in Churchill papers. The canny
James Lyford had sensed some such arrangement in the summer. He wrote
Senator Gallinger on July 18 that he had warned Moses that it was a "mistake" to be "continually belittling Churchill and that his [Moses's] course
had led to a better feeling, if not an understanding, between the Churchillites and Pillsbury." In File 8, Box 2, Gallinger papers. Also *Manchester
Union,* September 3, 1907.

75. *New York Times,* June 9, 1907, in Churchill scrapbooks. See also
Blodgett, "Winston Churchill, The Novelist as Reformer," for early Churchill views on federal authority. Churchill's ideas bear some resemblance to
those of his Cornish friend Herbert Croly.

76. See, for example, Roosevelt to Churchill, July 20, 1901 (vol. 3,
p. 126), and February 13, 1907 (vol. 5, pp. 586–87), and to William Dudley
Foulke, January 19, 1908 (vol. 6, pp. 914–15), all in Morison, *Letters of
Theodore Roosevelt.* See also Churchill to Roosevelt, October 14, November 9, and December 8, 1907, in Churchill papers.

77. Hugh White Adams to Churchill, May 2, 1907, Churchill papers;
Churchill to Robert Bass, October 26 and November 13, 1909, Bass papers.
For continuing national interest in Churchill, see *Outlook,* September 29,
1906, p. 243, and September 19, 1908, pp. 93–94; also "Winston Churchill," *Arena,* October 1906, pp. 410–14; and Stanley Johnson, "A Novelist
and His Novels in Politics," *World's Work,* December 1908, pp. 11,016–20.

78. *Globe,* September 14, 1907, Churchill scrapbooks. Finley Peter
Dunne ("Mr. Dooley") wrote Churchill that "as an amateur politican of

some experience, I can tell you that your campaign, whether successful or not, has already given you a position in national politics that is bound to be advantageous to you in the future." September 10, 1906, in Churchill papers.

79. Resolution approved at Lincoln Republican meeting, Edmund Cook to Robert Bass, September 15, 1907, in Bass papers; see also Churchill to Sherman Burroughs, November 12, 1907, in Churchill papers.

80. Churchill to John Benton, September 14, 1907, and James Remick to Edmund Cook, May 1, 1907; see also Churchill to Bass, April 16, 1907; "If we can amalgamate our forces as the Roosevelt wing . . . it seems to me that we shall gain strength for the State campaign." Churchill papers.

81. Churchill to Allen Hollis, March 6, 1908; the implicit contradictions were clear in a Churchill letter to Roosevelt: "all factions, however they may have quarreled about state progressive matters last year, are lined up to make an unequivocal fight for 'Roosevelt policy' delegates." November 22, 1907, Churchill papers.

82. Churchill to John Benton, March 21, 1907, Churchill papers; Churchill to Robert Bass, April 16, 1907, Bass papers.

83. For expressions of concern about linking the state group with Taft, see, e.g., W. H. Beasom to Churchill, November 21, 1907, and James Colby to Churchill, January 22, 1908, Churchill papers.

84. Gallinger to Moses, January 6, 1908, February 14, 1908, February 28, 1908, all in Box 2, File 3, Moses papers; to Lyford, February 26, 1908, February 28, 1908, April 10, 1908, all in Box 2, File 1, Lyford papers. Also Gallinger to Robert Merrill, April 11, 1908, copy to Moses, in Box 2, File 3, Moses papers. For Gallinger, the tariff, and Roosevelt, see Morison, *Letters of Theodore Roosevelt*, vol. 3, p. 296n.

85. Lyford to Gallinger, July 23, 1907; also July 18 and September 24, 1907, all in Box 2, File 8, Gallinger papers; Lyford to Chandler, January 31 and March 19, 1908, and to Frank Currier, February 13 and 17, 1908, all in Box 2, File 1, Lyford papers; Currier to Moses, February 1, and 22, 1908, Box 2, File 3, and Moses to Chandler, Box 2, File 4, Moses papers.

86. Gallinger to Frank Rollins, January 3, 1908, Box 2, File 9, Gallinger papers; to George Moses, n.d. (early in 1908), Box 2, File 3, Moses papers.

87. Moses to Chandler, January 3, 14, and 24, 1908, in Box 2, File 4, Moses papers; Lyford to Frank Currier, February 10, 1908, in Box 2, File 1, Lyford papers. Just as the Taft support represented largely pro-Roosevelt sentiment, so the anti-Taft coalition tended to oppose the president. Senator Gallinger had earlier become disenchanted with Roosevelt's treatment of New Hampshire in patronage matters. See Elihu Root to Gallinger, March 26, 1906. Gallinger friend George Moses referred to the president as "Theodore the Sudden." Moses to Gallinger, March 30, 1906, in File 6, Box 2, Gallinger papers; Gallinger refused to meet Taft when the latter visited New Hampshire in January 1908; he felt the state party was only being further divided by such campaigning. Gallinger to Frank Rollins, January 3, 1908, in File 9, Box 2, Gallinger papers. Vice President Charles Fairbanks solicited Gallinger's support actively. See Fairbanks to Gallinger, May 26, 1908, ibid. Much of the old guard's opposition to Taft came from Streeter's

involvement in his campaign: see Moses to Gallinger, September 15, 1907, in File 8, Box 2, Gallinger papers. A newspaper publisher friend of Churchill's perceptively noted that part of the anti-Taft activity stemmed from a need on the part of the old guard to demonstrate that they had not been "entirely knocked out" of control. W. B. Rotch (*Milford Cabinet*) to Churchill, March 20, 1908. Richardson, *William E. Chandler*, pp. 700–701.

88. Chandler to Chester Jordan, March 24, 1908, in Box 43, File 4, Chandler papers. Chandler and Roosevelt had a rocky relationship; the former senator had worked with the president in order to secure passage of the Hepburn bill in 1906. But they had fought over naval matters when Roosevelt was assistant secretary of the navy; in 1907 Chandler had resigned as president of the Spanish Treaty Claims Commission in a pique at Roosevelt over an appointment. Perhaps most important, Chandler did not feel Roosevelt was tough enough with corporations, and he especially was angry when Roosevelt did not join him in trying to halt the New Haven–Boston and Maine merger. See, in Morison, *Letters of Theodore Roosevelt*, TR to Chandler, October 26, 1897 (vol. 1, pp. 700–701), November 2, 1901 (vol. 3, p. 186); TR to Henry Cabot Lodge, May 19, 1906 (vol. 5, pp. 273–75), and September 21, 1907 (vol. 5, pp. 803–4). Richardson, *William E. Chandler*, describes this stormy relationship, *passim*, but see especially pp. 656–74.

89. Churchill insisted that his defeat came from Bryant's use of the "liquor element" as well as "aliens and democrats" in the caucus. To Daniel Remich, April 16, 1908, Churchill papers; also Churchill to Cong. Theodore Burton, April 24, 1908, ibid; on general manipulation in caucuses—including spurious "Taft" slates—see Robert Merill to Bass, April 4, 1908, Bass papers. *New York Times*, April 22, 1908.

90. Churchill to Roosevelt, June 24, 1908, Churchill papers; Lyford to Gallinger, May 6, 1908, Box 2, File 1, Lyford papers; Gallinger to Moses, June 24, 1908, Box 2, File 3, Moses papers.

91. Gallinger to Chandler, July 21, 1908, in Box 43, File 5, Chandler papers.

92. Churchill to John Henry, May 27, 1908, and to Rosecrans Pillsbury, June 3, 1908. The only real alternative seemed to be Harry Sargent of Concord. Sargent said he would agree only if Gallinger would support him. Gallinger refused. Churchill to Robert Bass et al., June 12, 1908, in Bass papers. Churchill and many of his friends as well as Frank Streeter then stumped hard for Pillsbury. *Boston Herald*, August 27, 1908, in Churchill scrapbooks; Streeter to Churchill, August 8 and 25, 1908, Churchill papers.

93. Tuttle and the railroad were on the defensive as the convention met. In August Tuttle insisted that the Boston and Maine no longer intervened in New Hampshire politics, and he apologized for and attempted to explain his 1902–4 efforts in the national committeeman fight. In 1904 especially, Tuttle argued, his goal was to keep railroad counsel Streeter off of the committee. *Manchester Union*, August 11, 1908, and *Concord Monitor*, August 12, 1908.

94. Lyford to Quinby, June 12 and September 24, 1908, to Willis McDuffie, July 2, 1908, to Alvah Sulloway, August 24, 1908, Box 2, File 2, Lyford papers; Henry Robinson to Chandler, January 3, 1908, Box 43, File 3,

Chandler papers; Moses to Chandler, July 13, 1908, Box 2, File 4, Moses papers.

95. Gallinger to Lyford, October 3, 1908, and Lyford to Gallinger, October 5, 1908, a hurt and angry reply, Box 2, File 2, Lyford papers. Churchill played a critical role in these discussions; Robert Bass of Peterborough came to be the major negotiator for the reformers. Lyford to Churchill, September 28, 1908, and Churchill to Lyford, September 29, 1908; Churchill to Remich, October 8, 1908, "Original Quinby Paper and Memorandum"; when Bass met Quinby to finalize the agreement, Quinby backed off, saying it "would do him more harm than good." Churchill to Remich, October 13, 1908. All following Gallinger-Lyford exchange in Churchill papers. Bass to Moses, October 13, 1908, Box 2, File 3, Moses papers. Chandler happened into the meeting and kept notes on it; "Memorandum of Conference," October 2, 1908, Box 43, File 6, Chandler papers. *The Outlook*, on October 3, 1908, suggested that Quinby's earlier railroad ties were broken and said he would live up to the platform: "the railroad influence in politics is practically eliminated."

96. For Carr campaign: "Campaign Speeches, 1908," in Box 10, Carr papers, Dartmouth College Library; see *Manchester Union*, October 30, 1908. Carr was a reluctant candidate who early believed he had little chance to win; by early November he had become more optimistic and believed the race would be his if the Republican reformers had "not attempted to play politics." To his son Proctor Carr, November 3, 1908, in "Correspondence 1908," Box 10, Carr papers; Carr to Proctor Carr, October 19, 1908, ibid. He had limited support from Frank Musgrove and James Colby, but they refused to stump for him. Musgrove to Carr, November 3, 1908, and Carr to Musgrove, November 3, 1908, and Remich to Carr, October 3, 1908, all in Box 10, Carr papers. See also Remick to Edward Niles, September 5, 1910, copy in Churchill papers. On November 2, 1908, Churchill wrote Daniel Remich: "haven't the Democrats made a splendid fight upon our principles?" Churchill papers. Carr was perplexed by Churchill's refusal to support him, for Churchill had always held that principles were more important than party. Carr wrote a friend several days after the election: "it does not seem to me to be greatly to the credit of Mr. Churchill and men who follow him to fail to take a situation when it arises, but they either did not see it, or didn't want to, or were afraid." To Rev. Samuel Beane, Lawrence, Massachusetts, November 9, 1908, in Box 10, Carr papers.

97. Remich to Churchill, September 28, 1908, Churchill to J. W. Staples, September 11, 1908, Churchill papers. Clarence Carr had observed after the spring primary that Churchill's work for Taft "has done much to disorganize and disrupt the Lincoln Club, has driven away its former president and left it in this state wholly discredited." Carr exaggerated somewhat but he keenly noted that the Taft club was "in part at least antagonistic to the former position of the Lincoln Club." Carr to H. D. Sharpe, June 18, 1908, in Box 10, Carr papers.

98. Bass to James Tufts, November 28, 1908, in Bass papers.

4. Robert Perkins Bass and the Reform Victory

1. *Portsmouth Times*, quoted in Agan, "New Hampshire Progressive Movement," p. 163.
2. "Governor Robert P. Bass," *Granite Monthly* 43 (Feb.–Mar. 1911), pp. 35–37.
3. Robert P. Bass file and Class of 1896 "Reports," in Harvard University Archives.
4. Ned Burling to Bass, December 5, 1899, Bass papers.
5. See "Forestry" and "Business" files in Bass papers.
6. Edward Pearson to Bass, August 24, 1906, in Bass papers.
7. Nicholas Theodorou, "Conservation in New Hampshire: A Bald Grab for Power?" honors thesis, Dartmouth College, Department of History, 1979.
8. Agan, "New Hampshire Progressive Movement," pp. 84–85.
9. Ibid., p. 85.
10. "Report to the House of the Committee on Retrenchment and Reform" (Concord, n.d.), p. 42.
11. Hollis to Churchill, June 3, 1907, in Churchill papers.
12. The John Bass papers, which document much of this adventurous life, are in the possession of John Bass III of Englewood, Florida. Mr. Bass has agreed to deposit the papers in the Dartmouth College Library and has permitted me to examine them fully. Robert Bass was fascinated by his brother's activities and wrote a biography of him which was never published. A copy is currently in my possession, provided by the children of Robert Bass. I will place this with the John Bass papers. The "business" correspondence of Robert Bass has many letters between the brothers. For John Bass conservation activities, see as well John Bass to Thomas Shipp (U.S. Forestry Department), April 24, 1909, and Gifford Pinchot to John Bass, April 30, 1909, in Series 4, Box 199, Pinchot papers, Manuscript Division, Library of Congress. The latter wrote urging Bass to meet with him and James Garfield: "there is a big lot of work for you to do if you come to undertake it, as I most sincerely hope you will."
13. Taft penned on the bottom of the quoted letter to Churchill, "I am going to send Moses to a place as [*sic*] from home as possible." Taft to Churchill, March 30, 1909. He said he agreed to Gallinger's request on this appointment because it "gives me in certain respects a leverage" in New Hampshire. To Churchill, April 8, 1909. Both letters are in the Churchill papers. For the pressure for the appointment, Moses to Chandler, February 25, 1905, Box 1, File 8; Gallinger to Moses, December 10, 1908, Box 2, File 3, and March 17, 1909, Box 2, File 5; Moses papers.
14. Gallinger to Lyford, May 29, 1909, and June 28, 1909. In Box 2, File 3, Lyford papers.
15. Taft to Churchill, July 17, 1909. See also Taft to Churchill, April 21, 1909; James Colby to Churchill, June 3, 1909, and Churchill to Colby, June 4, 1909; Edmund Cook to Churchill, July 22, 1909, and Churchill to Cook, August 6, 1909, all in Churchill papers. On the Streeter appointment, railroad attorney Jack Kelley wrote Chandler on January 3, 1910, inquiring

what had happened, because Streeter claimed the railroad beat him and Kelley knew nothing of this; indeed Kelley stated he would be pleased to see the appointment. Chandler replied from Washington on January 15 that he did not know what had happened; Chandler was willing to see him appointed and believed that Gallinger, while "hardly willing," was reconciled. In Box 44, File 1, Chandler papers.

16. Taft to Churchill, July 17, 1909, in Churchill papers.

17. Winston Churchill, *Mr. Crewe's Career* (New York, 1908). Clarence Carr provided a friend with a good analysis of the book, relating it to actual events and characters. Carr to H. D. Sharpe, June 18, 1908, in "Winston Churchill, Correspondence Concerning, 1908," Box 10, Carr papers.

18. For some of the publicity that created the climate for this expanded agenda, see Frank Putnam, "What's the matter with New England? New Hampshire: A Study in Industrial Vassalage, Political Medievalism, and the Aristocratic Ideal in Public Education," *New England Magazine* 36 (Aug. 1907), pp. 643–69. Philip Ayres published a series of articles on forest conservation under the general title "Is New England's Wealth in Danger?" *New England Magazine* 38 (Mar.–June 1908), pp. 35–48, 145–60, 291–308, and 435–49.

19. "Message of His Excellency Henry B. Quinby, Governor of New Hampshire to the Two Branches of the Legislature, January Session, 1909" (Concord, n.d.). Daniel Remich to Lyford, January 30, 1909. Box 2, File 3, Lyford papers.

20. Open letter, March 26, 1909, in "Correspondence 1909," Box 10, Carr papers.

21. Headline story and summary: "How New Hampshire Platform Republicans Defeated the Machine," *Boston Herald*, May 3, 1909.

22. Ibid.; Agan, "New Hampshire Progressive Movement," pp. 129–31.

23. Gallinger to Moses, March 19, 1909, Box 2, File 5, Moses papers. Bass wrote to Churchill that he thought Governor Quinby was "using his influence to a considerable extent to urge the enactment of the various planks of the platform." March 14, 1909, in Bass papers. Lyford wrote Governor Quinby, March 12, 1909, to hold fast on the pledges, in Box 2, File 3, Lyford papers.

24. Clough to Bass, January 9, 1910, and Bass to Churchill, February 25, 1910, in Bass papers. For an account of the Hooksett meeting, see Bass to Leason Martin, June 23, 1909; Bass to F. H. Foster, May 20, 1909, and Foster to Bass, May 25, 1909, involve planning this conclave. All in Bass papers.

25. Bass to Robert Faulkner, November 1, 1909; James Remick to Bass, December 10, 1909 (both in Bass papers); and Daniel Remich to Churchill, November 27, 1909, and Robert Faulkner to Remich, November 29, 1909 (both in Churchill papers), show some of the scuffling about for a candidate in the late fall. Burroughs emerged as the likely one, and his withdrawal caught the progressives unprepared. James Remick had alerted Churchill that some Boston and Maine officials had met to discuss ways of pressuring Burroughs not to run (Remick to Churchill, December 23, 1909, in Churchill papers); Burroughs telephoned Bass on December 27 to inform him that his

partners had refused to let him run (Burroughs to Robert Bass, December 29, 1909, in Bass papers). Bass had been an active supporter of Burroughs—see, for example, Bass to Churchill, December 4, 1909, in Bass papers.

26. Churchill to Bass, November 26, 1909. There had been pressure on Bass in the early fall, e.g., Edmund Cook to Bass, September 28, 1909. Bass remained reluctant to offer his candidacy throughout the winter. See Bass to Clarence Clough, February 10, 1910, to Churchill, February 25, 1910, to James Colby, March 25, 1910. All in Bass papers. Chandler's correspondence suggests a great deal of activity on behalf of Burroughs, with little response or assistance. E.g., Chandler to Burroughs, February 26 and 28, 1910, to Henry Robinson, March 14, 1910, to Daniel Remich, April 1, 1910; David Taggart to Chandler, March 17, 1910, Frank Currier to Chandler, March 20, 1910, Sherman Burroughs to Chandler, March 24, 1910; all in Box 44, File 1, Chandler papers; Chandler used the *Monitor* for his campaign, e.g., letter published April 2; Chandler to Moses, March 4, 1910, Box 2, File 8, Moses papers.

27. Robert to John Bass, January 9, 1910, Bass papers; Robert wrote John on September 30, 1909, that the best policy might be one of "diplomatic negotiations with the administration." In John Bass papers. Brandeis to John Bass, July 13, 1910, in Melvin I. Urofsky and David W. Levy, eds., *Letters of Louis D. Brandeis* (Albany, N.Y., 1972), vol. 2, p. 347. Norman Hapgood, *The Changing Years* (New York, 1930), p. 182. Nearly fifty years later Pinchot remembered John Bass's friendship, support, and wise advice that helped him through this difficult period, in Gifford Pinchot, *Breaking New Ground* (New York, 1947), pp. 460, 473.

28 Bass to Churchill, November 1, 1909, and Churchill to Bass, November 2, 1909, Churchill papers; Bass to Edmund Cook, January 9, to Clough, January 12, to John Bass, February 5, and to Gifford Pinchot, April 5, 1910; Frank Streeter to Bass, February 28, 1910, all in Bass papers.

29. Bass to Daniel Remich, June 17, 1910, and Edmund Cook to Bass, June 20, 1910, Bass papers. The Bass correspondence in the spring of 1910 was marked by the assumption that there would be no challenge.

30. John Bass to Gifford Pinchot, June 29, 1910, in Series 4, Box 132, Pinchot papers.

31. Gallinger to Lyford, February 23, 1910; also January 12 and February 19, 1910, Box 2, File 4, Lyford papers. Lyford to Gallinger, March 7, 1910, and to Chandler, April 13, 1910, ibid.

32. Gallinger to Lyford, March 3, 1910, ibid.

33. Robinson to Chandler, May 7, 1910, in Box 44, File 2, Chandler papers; Gallinger to Lyford, May 6, 1910, Box 2, File 5, Gallinger papers; Lyford to Chandler, March 2, 1910, in Box 2, File 4, Lyford papers.

34. Gallinger to Kimball, June 22, 1910, copy to Lyford on June 23, with a note: "He wrote me saying they were waiting for me to get home to take hold and straighten out matters." Box 2, File 5, Lyford papers.

35. Ellis to Frank Musgrove, August 30, 1910, in Frank Musgrove papers, Dartmouth College Library. Also in *Manchester Union*, September 1, 1910. In the 1890s Gallinger and Ellis had feuded briefly, but Gallinger felt

Ellis's attitudes were still basically correct. Gallinger to Charles Marseilles, March 19, 1896, "Marseilles" File, Box 1, Gallinger papers. A good study of the subject is Jewel Bellush, "Reform in New Hampshire: Robert Bass Wins the Primary," *New England Quarterly* 35 (Dec. 1962), pp. 469–88.

36. Bass to M. E. Ahern, March 25, 1910; see Cook to John Bass, August 15, Cook to Robert Bass, August 15 and 25, 1910, Bass papers. John to Robert Bass, March 14, 1910, John Bass papers. *Manchester Union*, August 19, 1910. Bellush, "Reform in New Hampshire."

37. The reports and the bills came directly to John Bass; the former are often fascinating and seldom conclusive. See, e.g., Portsmouth reports that the Elk's Club members there opposed Bass and the allegation that votes were available elsewhere for "a pint of beer or a cigar." "WHR" reports, September 1 and 3, 1910, "Boston Investigators" File, Bass papers. The Burns Detective Agency billed John Bass; the bill is in the John Bass papers. There seemed no systematic effort to defeat Bass or to "buy" the election; see W. H. Russell to Frank Musgrove, September 5, 1910, Musgrove papers.

38. Chandler proposed a committee to make expenditures "that should not be made public." Bass made clear to his associates that he was "unalterably opposed" to any plan that would conceal expenditures. Bass to E. C. Niles (to whom Chandler made the proposal) August 7, 1910; Bass wrote to one of his Manchester organizers that if it would take vote buying to win, "I prefer rather to be defeated." To William Savacool, August 30, 1910. Supporters in some towns insisted, especially for the general election, that vote buying was essential: Harry Beckford of Belmont to Bass, November 1, 1910, and William Marston of Center Sandwich to Peterboro Bass Club, October 5, 1910, all in Bass papers. Bass antagonist Calvin Page of Portsmouth insisted that John Bass helped buy the election there: "with a 'knowing wink' a man would smile and say simply 'Brother John.'" Page to Bass, November 9, 1910; Bass offered to help prosecute vote fraud and personally engaged James Remick to assist in the action. Bass to Page, November 14, 1910. Nothing came of this. All in Bass papers.

39. Allen Hollis to Bass, November 23, 1910. During discussion of the 1909 campaign spending bill, Bass had opposed a stricture on candidates spending their own money on newspaper advertising: "Should not a candidate have the privilege of stating his position in the press and the measures he advocates, even if he has to pay for the insertion?" To John Benton, January 19, 1909, all in Bass papers. Bellush, "Reform in New Hampshire," p. 477. Bass clearly was involved in the management of his investments, although family financial manager H. C. Edmonds in Chicago had considerable latitude. In 1910 Bass even linked his political and economic calculations. He wrote to John that Taft's policies presaged political and economic backlash, perhaps even a financial panic. It was necessary to protect investments and even "make a little money if we are ready to take advantage of it." Bass to John Bass, March 6, 1910, Bass papers. In 1913, according to his income tax returns, Bass had personal gross income of $45,000, of which $35,000 was from stock, dividends, rents, and interest. Box 12, Bass papers.

40. During the winter former governor and prohibition activist David

Goodell interrogated Bass privately about the issue. Goodell to Bass, February 18, 1910, and Bass to Goodell, February 25, 1910, Bass papers. Goodell reported to Daniel Remich that Bass was good on the issues, but he (Goodell) understood that the young senator had, on occasion, been "manifestly under the influence." March 7, 1910, copy in Bass papers. In the midst of these winter discussions, Allen Hollis wrote to his friend Bass, advising him that the barrel had been delivered: "as soon as the juice gets settled . . . we [will] have a nice time." March 3, 1910, Bass papers. One of John Bass's detectives reported the comment of a Manchester bartender and Bass political opponent, Mike Ahearn: "Bass is a fine fellow to preach temperance . . . he goes on a drunk for two or three weeks at a time and talks too much." D. J. K. report, September 1, 1910, in Bass papers. There is no corroborating evidence for such allegations. Bass's role in the 1909 legislative session in securing passage of the Preston amendment, protecting non-license towns, ultimately served him well. Rev. J. H. Robbins, superintendent of the New Hampshire Anti-Saloon League, wrote Bass that in response to "inquiries from our temperance voters . . . I give you the highest possible commendation for the service you did." March 3, 1910, Bass papers. See also Arthur Dickey, an executive committeeman for the Good Templars to Bass, August 6, 1910. The Anti-Saloon League and the reform movement had been in an alliance of sorts since 1906. In 1907 Robbins wrote Churchill: "You must regulate the railroad. We must destroy the saloon. We join hands in the fight" (June 3, 1907). In 1910 Robbins had to caution Churchill that it was better for the progressives if they and the league did not "*appear* to be working together" on the primary campaign (July 8, 1910, in reply to Churchill letter of July 2, 1910). Churchill-Robbins letters in Churchill papers. In 1909, at the time of the critical vote, James Colby had suggested to Bass that progressive support for the Preston amendment would serve well the effort to enlarge the coaltion. March 6, 1909, Bass papers.

41. Daniel Remich, always a careful monitor and critic of personal behavior, wrote Winston Churchill in late 1909 that he had "investigated" charges about Bass's "moral character." Remich was "extremely sorry to say that they are founded upon facts. He has been indiscreet and foolish." December 1, 1909, Churchill papers. Harlan Pearson, of the *Monitor*, on the other hand, reported to Chandler that "stories as to his [Bass's] personal character are afloat. I know people who have investigated them fully. They say that so far as they relate to women they are entirely untrue. As to liquor Mr. Bass is not a total abstainer, but I have never seen him drunk. N.d., obviously the spring of 1910, in Box 44, File 4, Chandler papers. Allegations about Bass's conduct with women never seemed to go beyond whispered innuendo, perhaps because the only substance seemed to be that Robert Bass was a young bachelor who seemed to enjoy the company of women. On woman suffrage, Agan, "New Hampshire Progressive Movement," p. 150, and Bass to Mary Chase, December 14, 1908, Bass papers.

42. Ray Stannard Baker, "Is the East Also Insurgent? Signs of Revolt in Republican Strongholds," *American Magazine* 69 (Mar. 1910), pp. 579–87; *Boston Transcript*, July 20, 1910. In addition to extensive descriptions of

the campaign in Bass papers, see Bellush, "Reform in New Hampshire," and *Manchester Union*, September 2 and 5, 1910, and *Granite State Free Press*, August 5, 1910.

43. Gallinger to Lyford, September 1, 1910, also August 27 and 28, 1910, in Box 2, File 5, Lyford papers. Gallinger did appear with Ellis at a Concord rally on September 2 at which he warmly endorsed the candidate but spent much of his time defending his record and criticizing the divisve nature of the Bass campaign; in *Manchester Union*, September 3, 1910.

44. Moses to Chandler, October 9, 1910, in Box 2, File 8, Moses papers.

45. Agan, "New Hampshire Progressive Movement," pp. 178–82. Chandler had come back to the state during the summer planning to play a role in the campaign. But, as he wrote Sen. Frank Briggs, "I hope to pursue the malefactors somewhat during the coming canvas. It is very difficult, however, for me to do this because I love so many of them so dearly." June 7, 1910, vol. 160, p. 20,728, Chandler papers, Library of Congress. See Chandler to Bass, September 8, 1910, in Box 44, File 3, Chandler papers, and Chandler, Cook, and Musgrove invitation to a caucus "for the purpose of making some preliminary arrangements for the organization of the Convention." Ibid. Chandler telegrams to Bass on September 7 and 8, 1910, Bass papers; also Bass to Edmund Cook, September 15, 1910, ibid.

46. Agan, "New Hampshire Progressive Movement," pp. 181–82.

47. *New Hampshire Manual for the General Court, 1911*, pp. 59–63, reprints the 1910 platform. *Concord Evening Monitor*, September 27, 1910.

48. Streeter to Chandler, September 22, 1910, in Box 44, File 3, Chandler papers. Streeter unsuccessfully argued that there was no place in this platform for Roosevelt; the "plain duty" was to "stand strongly" beside Taft.

49. Pillsbury to Chandler, September 9 and 30 (File 3), and May 18 (File 2), 1910, Box 44, Chandler papers. See Chandler to Bass, September 28, 1910, Bass papers; Agan suggests it was Wyman who deleted the section in order to avoid a floor fight, in "New Hampshire Progressive Movement," p. 184. In his September 30 letter Pillsbury said, "we struck the paragraph . . . for the sake of harmony."

50. Richardson, *William E. Chandler*, p. 710.

51. Agan, "New Hampshire Progressive Movement," pp. 187–89.

52. Kelley to Bass, September 7, 1910, copy in Box 44, File 3, Chandler papers.

53. Lyford to Gallinger, September 8 and 21, 1910, and Gallinger to Lyford, September 11 and 28, 1910, Box 2, File 5, Lyford papers; Gallinger to Edmund Cook, November 5, 1910, Bass papers. Bellush, "Reform in New Hampshire," p. 481. Others from the old guard, such as Ellis and Cong. Cyrus Sulloway, immediately offered their support to the nominee. See telegrams from each to Bass on September 7, 1910, Bass papers.

54. See platform in *New Hampshire Manual for the General Court, 1911*, pp. 71–72.

55. Agan, "New Hampshire Progressive Movement," pp. 191–92. Frank Musgrove, a key Bass supporter, wrote Carr after the 1909 legislative session that the fight was largely successful: "In this the democrats were as conspicuous as the reform republicans." May 8, 1909, "N.H. Gen. Ct. Corr."

1909–1910," Box 10, Carr papers. Also Clarence Clough to Carr, May 10, 1909, ibid.

56. Bass to Churchill, May 11, 1910, Bass papers; see, e.g., Churchill to W. Dubois Pulver, June 3, 1910, to J. H. Robbins, July 1, 1910, and to Daniel Remich, July 4, 1910, Churchill papers.

57. Bass to Remick, October 18, 1910, Bass papers.

58. Bass to Pinchot, April 5, 1910; Bass later urged Pinchot to campaign for him before the primaries. Pinchot "keenly" regretted previous commitments. Bass telegram to Pinchot (n.d.) and Pinchot response to Bass, August 21, 1910. Series 4, Box 132, Gifford Pinchot papers, Library of Congress. Bass to Theodore Roosevelt, June 17, 1910, August 1, 1910, Bass papers. John Bass to Robert Bass, March 14, 1910, File E, John F. Bass papers.

59. Edmund Cook to Bass, September 13, 1910, and Bass to Cook, September 15, 1910, Bass papers; James Colby to Churchill, September 24, 1910, Churchill papers. *Manchester Union*, October 24, 1910; *Outlook*, September 17 and October 22, 1910; Agan, "New Hampshire Progressive Movement," pp. 195–97.

60. Winston Churchill (referring to a George Rublee statement) to Bass, May 23, 1910, Churchill papers. Taft apparently attempted to obtain Gallinger support for Bass, telegrams from presidential secretary Charles Norton to John Bass, November 4 and 5, 1910, Bass papers. Chandler also pleaded unsuccessfully with Gallinger to participate: "We will have some fun, it will be an agreeable affair and will do us good and everybody else, and the party we love." To Gallinger, October 27, 1910, Box 44, File 3, Chandler papers.

61. See "Speeches" and "Literature referring to the Campaign," Robert Bass's 1910 File, Bass papers; the *Union* provided good coverage of the Bass effort and continued to give play to Roosevelt's activities; see, e.g., October 31, November 2, 3, 4, 5, and 7.

62. Cook wrote Robert Bass on August 4, 1910, informing him that Churchill had asked to have his name removed from the speaking itinerary: "I hope that nothing has been said to Mr. Churchill to hurt his feelings or to make him think that his help is not wanted." If this was the case, it is not clear what caused it. Cook to Churchill, August 4, 1910; Musgrove wrote, "rest assured that you are appreciated and needed," to Churchill on August 6, 1910; also Clough to Churchill, August 6, 1910. John Bass arranged Churchill's Illinois tour; see Harold Ickes to Churchill, June 16, 1910; Albert Beveridge to Churchill, November 16, 1910; for "foreign missions" reference, Churchill to Daniel Remich, July 1, 1910. All in Churchill papers.

63. Towns at the extreme end of the distribution had the pattern shown in Table 1. Correlation coefficient values for those variables for which there is a good distribution are shown in Table 2.

64. The correlation coefficients shown in Table 1 relate local-option votes and constitutional amendment votes, 1903–12, with Bass primary vote, 1910. Another way of looking at these relationships is to examine the top Bass towns (>75 percent) and the top Ellis towns (>50 percent) and their mean vote on the 1910 and 1912 referenda. This is done in Table 2 (p. 224).

Table 1 for Note 63

Variables	Bass mean percentage
Wealthy farming ($N=26$)	63.4
Poor farming ($N=13$)	67.7
Wealthy industrial ($N=17$)	72.7
Poor industrial ($N=7$)	62.9
Declining agriculture, increasing population ($N=10$)	68.8
Declining agriculture, decreasing population ($N=18$)	65.2
Increasing population ($N=48$)	68.4
Declining population ($N=55$)	63.9
Single church towns	
Congregational ($N=24$)	68.5
Baptist ($N=24$)	41.9
Freewill Baptist ($N=10$)	59.7
Methodist ($N=18$)	64.5
Roman Catholic ($N=1$)	64.7

Table 2 for Note 63

Variables	Correlation with Bass primary vote
Change in proportion of farms to total population, 1880–1920	−0.1
Mills and machines as percentage of 1911 assessed valuation	.06
Per capita assessed valuation, 1911	− .04
Population change, 1900–1910	.0
Manufacturing workers as percentage of 1910 population	.05

Note: None of these values are of statistical significance.

Table 1 for Note 64

Issue	Correlation with Bass primary vote
Yes on antimonopoly, 1903	.14
Yes on inheritance tax, 1903	.14
Yes on English for voting, 1903	.19
Yes on liquor license, 1903	.02
Yes to strike *Protestant* from constitution, 1903	.10
Yes on woman suffrage, 1903	.08
Yes on liquor license, 1906	.04
Yes on liquor license, 1910	−.09
Yes on corporation tax, 1912	−.07
Yes on inheritance tax, 1912	.07
Yes to strike *Protestant* from constitution, 1912	−.01
Yes on basic tax	.05

Note: None of these values are of statistical significance.

Table 2 for Note 64

Issue	Mean percentage of issue vote	
	Bass towns	Ellis towns
Yes on liquor license, 1910	31.2	29.6
Yes on inheritance tax	60.6	59.5
Yes on strike *Protestant*, 1912	42.5	41.6
Yes on basic tax, 1912	59.2	59.1
Yes on corporation tax, 1912	61.2	62.3

65. Bass's top primary towns, as defined earlier, had a mean Carr general election vote of 40.2 percent; Ellis's top towns had a Carr general election vote of 41.5 percent. The *Lancaster Gazette* and the *Concord Monitor* agreed that Bass's victory had to be credited partially to the near unanimity with which the Ellis supporters rallied to their party in November. *Concord Monitor,* November 18, 1910.

66. The "List of Reliable Men" as well as a drawer of three-by-five cards with local campaign contacts are in the Bass papers, 1910 Campaign Material. There were no Concord names on the list, probably because the campaign headquarters was there.

67. The table represents an analysis of voting on roll calls in the 1909 house using four groups: Democrats, All Republicans, Bass Republicans (defined as those Republican legislators who were listed as Bass supporters in the source described in n. 66), and the remaining Republican legislators (presumably, but not necessarily, non-Bass supporters). Because Concord names were not on the Bass list, Concord legislators were excluded from this analysis.

68. Beveridge to Bass, November 21, 1910, and Beveridge 1912 New Hampshire speech, "Speech" File, both in Bass papers.

69. Remick to Bass, November 18, 1910, Bass papers.

5. The Stand at Armageddon

1. January 11, 1911, in Box 44, File 5, Chandler papers. *Monitor,* January 5, 10, 11, and 17, 1911; also *L'Avenir National,* January 5, 1911.

2. Bass to Musgrove, November 17, 1910, and Sherman Burroughs to Bass, November 18, 1910, Bass papers; Wyman to Bass, December 17, 1910, copy in John Bass papers, 1910–11 File Book.

3. Rich to Churchill, November 25, 1910, Churchill papers. Mellen to Bass, December 6, 1910, and Bass to Mellen, December 19, 1910, Bass papers; see Chandler letters to *Monitor* in early December, e.g., December 3, 1910.

4. Mellen to Bass, December 6, 1910, Bass papers.

5. Rich to Bass, December 23, 1910, Bass papers.

6. Rich to Mellen, November 22, 1909, Box 4, File 1, Charles S. Mellen papers, New Hampshire Historical Society. Lyford to Chandler, January 4,

1911, and to Gallinger, January 6, 1911 [the latter is dated 1910 but the text clearly indicates it was written in 1911 and it is so filed], Box 2, File 6, Lyford papers. Chandler to Mellen, October 29, 1910, reviews the problems with the railroad and challenges Mellen to keep his promise to stay out of politics. Box 44, File 3, Chandler papers. Chandler and others worried that the railroad was overcapitalizing its stock, and he and Clarence Carr were fighting this. Chandler to Kelley, November 17, 1910, and Kelley to Chandler, November 30, 1910 ("The Railroad being out of politics—absolutely, cleanly, entirely out—is it to be the more cuffed, kicked and sandbagged because of the declaration that it will not lift a finger?"), Carr to Chandler, December 7, 1910, with copy of a letter the former sent to Edgar Rich on the same day. Ibid., File 4.

7. "Message of His Excellency Robert P. Bass, Governor of New Hampshire, to the Two Branches of the Legislature, January Session, 1911" (Concord, n.d.), pp. 8, 9, 13.

8. Ibid., *passim.*

9. *Monitor,* January 6, 1911; "Message of His Excellency Robert P. Bass, January Session, 1911," *passim.*

10. Herbert Croly, *Progressive Democracy* (New York, 1914), p. 7. Bass's correspondence includes examples of pressures to include matters in his inaugural address and his legislative program. For example, Bass included the Crawford Notch proposal under pressure from Frank Rollins, see Rollins to Bass, December 21 and 27, 1910, Bass papers. The dependent children issue was successfully lobbied by Lillian (Mrs. Frank) Streeter, chairman of the state board of charities and corrections. Bass apparently ignored an earlier inquiry of hers, but press reports on "baby farms" in New Hampshire and a strong letter from Theodore Roosevelt (with whom Mrs. Streeter had been in contact), brought Bass into the fray. Lillian Streeter to Bass, December 28 and 31, 1910; Roosevelt to Mrs. Streeter and to Bass, December 23, and Bass to Roosevelt, December 26, 1910; Mary Boyle O'Reilly to Bass, January 6 and 9, 1911, all in Bass papers. O'Reilly had published a two-part article that influenced Roosevelt and the debate: "The Daughters of Herod, A Plea for Child-Saving Legislation in New Hampshire," *New England Magazine* 43 (Oct. 1910 and Nov.–Dec. 1910), pp. 137–48 and 277–90.

11. "Message of His Excellency Robert P. Bass, January Session, 1911," *passim.*

12. *Monitor,* January 6, 1911.

13. Roll call data from *Journal of the House of Representatives, January Session, 1911* (Concord, 1911).

14. Musgrove to Bass, February 5, 1911, Bass papers; John Bass to Bass, February 10, 1911, in John Bass papers, File E. On February 16 Bass declined a Gifford Pinchot request to assist in the Lorimer case before the U.S. Senate. The governor noted "the complicated legislative situation" in New Hampshire and concluded that he could best serve the reform movement by getting his program approved. Pinchot to Bass, February 6, 1911, and Bass to Pinchot, February 16, 1911, in Pinchot papers, Series 4, Box

142. On the day he wrote Pinchot the governor also wrote Clarence Clough that "the lobby is beginning to make its appearance." February 16, 1911, Bass papers.

15. Musgrove to Bass, March 4, 1911, and "Income tax file" (1911) in Bass papers; Remick to Chandler, February 8, 1911, and Burroughs to Chandler, January 6, 1911, Box 44, File 5, Chandler papers; Lyford to Chandler, March 10, 1911, Box 2, File 5, Lyford papers.

16. Kelley to Chandler, March 3, 1911, Box 44, File 6, Chandler papers.

17. Lyford to Chandler, February 20, 1911, Box 2, File 6, Lyford papers.

18. Ibid., also Lyford to Chandler, February 26 and March 10 and 13, 1911, in the same file; Kelley to Chandler, February 13, 1911, and Chandler to Remick, January 29, 1911, Box 44, File 5, Chandler papers.

19. *Journal of the House of Representatives, 1911*, pp. 594–601.

20. Message, ibid. *Outlook*, March 25, 1911.

21. Rich to Bass, March 24, 1911, Bass papers.

22. Rich to Bass, January 30, 1911, and "Letters—Rate Case Settlement," Bass papers; Remick to Chandler, February 4, 1911, Henry Robinson to Chandler on the same date, Harlan Pearson to Chandler, February 14, 1911, Lyford to Chandler, March 20, 1911, all in Box 44, File 5, Chandler papers; "The Reminiscences of George Rublee," Columbia University Oral History Research Office. Agan, "New Hampshire Progressive Movement," pp. 219–22.

23. Agan, "New Hampshire Progressive Movement," pp. 223–25; Richardson, *William E. Chandler*, pp. 712–13. Rublee to Bass, March 20, 1911, and to Edmund Cook, April 12, 1911, Bass papers. For criticism of Rublee and Bass see James Remick to Bass, April 18, 1911, ibid. John Bass, in his usual independent manner, was discussing with Oregon reformer Joseph Teal the New Hampshire problem. Robert refused to invite Teal to the state as a consultant because he was sensitive to the "outsider" charge at this delicate time. See Teal to John Bass, April 4, 1911, and John Bass to Teal, April 27, 1911, John Bass papers.

24. Rublee to Bass, March 20, 1911, Bass papers. Railroad attorney Jack Kelley made this claim. *Monitor*, April 11, 1911.

25. A. D. Felch to Bass, September 10, 1911, Bass papers. Jerome G. Beatty, "The Rescue of New Hampshire and the Rise of a New Figure in Our Public Life," *Collier's*, May 6, 1911. *Outlook*, May 13, 1911. Agan, "New Hampshire Progressive Movement," pp. 224–29.

26. Robert to John Bass, June 2, 1911, John Bass papers, 1910–11 File Box.

27. September 28, 1911, address to the Electrical Association, "Speeches," Bass papers; Remick led the chorus of those who insisted Bass should stand by Stevens, pointedly noting that Stevens had refused to meet with Mellen during the debate. Remick to Bass, May 18, 1911, Bass papers. The May 1911 correspondence in the latter is filled with the appointment fight, e.g., George Phinney to Bass: "Stand by your guns. Make them come to you. You were elected governor not your council. Stick and you are bound to win" (May 24, 1911). Robert Jackson to Chandler, June 9, 1911,

Box 44, File 6, Chandler papers; Agan, "New Hampshire Progressive Movement," pp. 230–34.

28. See Boston speech, December 16, 1911, "Speeches," Bass papers. For example of meeting to discuss "new matters," see Bass to Churchill, October 19, 1911, ibid.

29. Dartmouth address, June 28, 1911, "Speeches," Bass papers. Bass to Frederick Taylor, January 24, 1911, and Taylor to Bass, January 30 and February 6, 1911; H. G. Pearson to Bass, March 30, 1911; ibid.

30. Nichols to Streeter, February 11, 1910, and Streeter to Nichols, February 21, 1910, File 9, Ernest Fox Nichols papers, Dartmouth College Archives. Gallinger reported that Streeter "said he had had a talk with President Nichols, who deprecated what Bass said, but I did not understand that anything was to be done to stop the propaganda." Gallinger to Lyford, January 15, 1912, Box 2, File 7, Lyford papers.

31. John Whitley to Scott Sloane, February 27, 1912, on a speech at Harvard, copy in Bass papers; he received many invitations in late 1911, typical of these was one from the New York Young Republican Club asking him to speak on a program with President Taft. Arthur Ludington to Bass, December 6 and 18, 1911, Bass papers. The governor declined.

32. In addition to the Lyford allegation regarding the income tax amendment, Harlan Pearson to Chandler, February 14, 1911, Box 44, File 5, Chandler papers. The Gallinger papers, spotty in any event, have no correspondence that would seem to confirm this.

33. Gallinger to Lyford, May 2, 1911, in Box 2, File 6, Lyford papers; Lyford to Gallinger, September 20, 1911, in Box 3, File 5, Gallinger papers. See Bass to James Colby, December 28, 1911, and to Robert Faulkner, December 29, 1911; also Bass general letter to editors of newspapers, n.d. (Dec. 1911), Bass papers.

34. Bass to F. C. Shattuck, August 14, 1911, and to Norman Hapgood, August 16, 1911, Bass papers. The *Manchester Daily Mirror and American* published a series of articles headlined "Progressives' Lust for Power," on August 31.

35. Gallinger had challenged Bass on election law changes immediately after the governor's inaugural; Gallinger letter to the editor in *Concord Monitor,* January 12, 1911. Also *Manchester Union,* August 13, 1910, for Gallinger criticism of the law and the state committee's tardiness in recruiting local candidates.

36. To Robert Valentine, August 5, 1911, Bass papers.

37. The Roosevelt literature is, of course, very large. Particularly useful are John Morton Blum, *The Republican Roosevelt* (Cambridge, Mass., 1954); George Mowry, *The Era of Theodore Roosevelt, 1900–1912* (New York, 1958); and William H. Harbaugh, *Power and Responsibility: The Life and Times of Theodore Roosevelt* (New York, 1961). A good survey is Lewis L. Gould, *Reform and Regulation: American Politics, 1900–1916* (New York, 1978). A provocative and imaginative look at Roosevelt is in John Milton Cooper, Jr., *The Warrior and the Priest: Woodrow Wilson and Theodore Roosevelt* (Cambridge, Mass., 1983).

38. John Bass to George H. Myers, December 12, 1910, John Bass papers; John Bass to Gifford Pinchot, June 29, 1910, and Pinchot to John Bass, July 4, 1910, Series 4, Box 132, Pinchot papers. In the former, John wrote that buying stock in the "Glavis orchard" will "be helping along the cause of justice, at the same time getting a good return." By late 1911 Glavis was out but the investors continued development of the orchard, the White Salmon Fruit Company. John Bass to Pinchot, November 2 and 18, 1911; to "Stockholders," November 3, 1911; Pinchot to John Bass, November 22, 1911, Series 4, Box 142, Pinchot papers.

39. For Taft problems see James Holt, *Congressional Insurgents and the Party System, 1909–1916* (Cambridge, Mass., 1967), chaps. 1–3; Donald F. Anderson, *William Howard Taft: A Conservative's Conception of the Presidency* (Ithaca, 1973), especially chap. 4; Paolo E. Coletta, *The Presidency of William Howard Taft* (Lawrence, Kans., 1973), chaps. 3–6.

40. Roosevelt to Charles Dwight Willard, April 28, 1911, in Morison, *Letters of Theodore Roosevelt*, vol. 7, pp. 253–54. Churchill to Bass, January 23, 1911, Churchill papers; La Follette to Bass, December 28, 1910, and January 10, 1911, Bass to La Follette, n.d. (early January 1911), and January 24, 1911, Pinchot telegram to Bass, January 16, 1911, Bass to Senator Joseph Bristow (Kans.), January 24, 1911, all in Bass papers. In the latter, Bass said he would like to discuss with Bristow "the relation between the East and the West in regard to Progressive politics. . . . It has a direct bearing on my relation to the league and may be typical of the situation in some other eastern states." Bass had provided some financial support for the New Hampshire Direct Legislation League, and despite pleas from the director that he involve himself more fully, Bass hedged. George Duncan to Bass, January 9, 1912, and Bass to Duncan, January 16, 1912, ibid. Churchill made a small contribution to the New Hampshire group, but confessed he was "particularly shaky" on the issues. Churchill to George Duncan, February 17, 1911, Churchill papers. *Nashua Telegraph*, December 27, 1911 (Bass scrapbooks) for Gallinger criticism.

41. Churchill to Robert Faulkner, June 4, 1910, and to Sen. Albert Cummins, July 14, 1910, in Churchill papers. Cummins replied on July 18 that he applauded and hoped for the success of the New Hampshire effort so that "under your leadership the East will join the ranks of the 'insurgents.'" Ibid.

42. Remich to Churchill, April 9, 1911, and Churchill to Remich, April 15, 1911; F. Wadleigh to Churchill, January 12, 1911, on inauguration; Churchill to Bass, January 23, 1912, said he did not go to the wedding because "I was in such a situation with my work." On February 24, 1912, Churchill declined an invitation to meet with Bass and Theodore Roosevelt in Boston. All in Churchill papers.

43. Churchill to Remich, November 28, 1911, ibid.

44. Ibid.

45. December 16, 1911, in "Speeches," Bass papers.

46. For Charles Sumner Bird characterization see Abrams, *Conservatism in a Progressive Era*, p. 284. Bass had told Roosevelt that he would "make no public statement of my position until I return from my wedding

trip, which will be about February 10." Bass to Roosevelt, January 15, 1912, Bass papers. The letter is available in Morison, *Letters of Theodore Roosevelt*, vol. 7, p. 511, n. 2. The other signatories were William Glasscock (W. Va.), Chester Aldrich (Neb.), Joseph Carey (Wyo.), Chase Osborn (Mich.), William Stubbs (Kans.), and Herbert Hadley (Mo.).

47. Speech at Clinton, Massachusetts, November 3, 1911, in "Speeches," Bass to Overland Syndicate, April 29, 1911, Bass papers; Wolfeboro speech in *Manchester Union*, August 17, 1910; Agan, "New Hampshire Progressive Movement," p. 237.

48. Bass to Roosevelt, January 15, 1912; Roosevelt replied on January 18 that he might "*have* to speak openly soon." The former president was "indignant at the attitude of the administration" in attacking Roosevelt on the steel issue and was distressed at the La Follette manager in Ohio for a "particularly impertinent and foolish letter." In November 1911 Roosevelt wrote his son that Robert Bass was down to go over a Roosevelt statement on the trusts: "he represents the large class of progressives who very earnestly wish to go forward and yet do not want to get embarked on some wild crusade against business as a whole." To Theodore Roosevelt, Jr., November 13, 1911, in Morison, *Letters of Theodore Roosevelt*, vol. 7, pp. 434–35.

49. Bass to Roosevelt, January 15, 1912, Bass papers; John Bass's papers indicate great Roosevelt activity on his part early in 1912; he worked closely with Frank Knox on this. In late January Robert wired John to meet him in Palm Beach; earlier he had given John letters of introduction to Governors Osborn (Mich.), Stubbs (Kans.), Glasscock (W. Va.), and McGovern (Wis.) as well as Judge Lindsey of Colorado. These letters said, "it is for the purpose of advancing those principles in which we believe that my brother is seeking your counsel." All in John Bass papers. Roosevelt to John Bass, March 21, 1912, in Morison, *Letters of Theodore Roosevelt*, vol. 7, p. 530.

50. V. L. Parker to Bass, February 29, 1912, and Hollis to Bass, February 10, 1912; the only letters I discovered in the Bass papers in which Robert Bass alerted his New Hampshire supporters were letters to Clarence Clough and, somewhat surprisingly, William Chandler, on January 30, 1912, Bass papers. On Musgrove, Lyford to Gallinger, February 14, 1912, Box 2, File 7, Lyford papers. For criticism, *Littleton Courier*, February 15, 1912, *Concord Patriot*, February 16, 1912, *New York Herald*, February 18, 1912.

51. Chandler to Moses, May 24, 1912, in Box 2, File 11, Moses papers.

52. "Appeal of the New Hampshire Progressives," signed broadside in 1912 material, Bass papers, and in Churchill papers; Clinton McLane wrote Bass insisting that the primary disproved the idea that "Roosevelt and N.H. Progressivism are the same," April 25, 1912, Bass papers.

53. Bass to James Colby, March 4, and to John Gile, April 11, 1912 (quoted material in latter); Bass to Clinton McLane, May 6, 1912, Bass papers.

54. To Lyford, February 15, 1912, Box 2, File 7, Lyford papers. On January 15, Gallinger had said, "I do not propose to remain quiescent and allow that crowd to run over us in another campaign." To Lyford, ibid. Chandler wrote Moses in May that the old guard had been meeting since the fall to organize their effort to control the 1912 nominations. May 24, 1912, Box 2,

File 11, Moses papers. Several days before Bass's announcement, Lyford participated in a Boston meeting to plan strategy and select delegates for the Republican National Convention, none of whom would be members of the progressive wing. Lyford speculated that Bass could come out for Roosevelt, a move he believed would be harmful to the governor. Lyford to Gallinger, February 7, 1912, Box 2, File 7, Lyford papers.

55. Chandler to Moses, May 24, 1912, Box 2, File 11, Moses papers. Taft to Gallinger, February 7 and 13, 1912; Gallinger to Taft, February 10, 1912, File 6, Box 3, Gallinger papers; Lyford had been urging Gallinger to request Streeter to push Pillsbury onto the Taft bandwagon. To Gallinger, February 7 and 14, 1912, in Box 2, File 7, Lyford papers. Gallinger had been wishing in January that the party could "throw off the incubus of Kimball and Streeter." He said that everytime Kimball said the railroad was through with Streeter, the corporation brought him back. To Lyford, January 31, ibid. Gallinger never fully respected Taft as a politician. In 1910 he had wondered how the president could be "attending baseball games" while his legislation headed for "everlasting smash." As far as the senator was concerned, Taft did not have "the least conception of politics." To Lyford, May 6, 1910, Box 2, File 5, ibid. Gallinger to Charles Marseilles, April 10, 1897, in Marseilles File, Box 2, and to Lyford, February 12, 1905, Box 1, File 8, Gallinger papers; Agan, "New Hampshire Progressive Movement," p. 248.

56. Gallinger to Lyford, February 27, 1912, and Lyford to Gallinger, April 8, 1912, Box 2, Files 7 and 8, respectively, Lyford papers.

57. Gallinger to Lyford, April 4 and 20, 1912, Box 2, File 8, Lyford papers.

58. Bass to Pinchot, March 15, 1912, Series 4, Box 153, Pinchot papers; Bass to Roosevelt, March 13, 1912; Allen Hollis wrote Bass on March 9 about the disorganization that marked the Roosevelt effort; the Bass papers have a number of letters charging fraud, e.g., Leon Verrill (Rochester) to Bass, April 25, 1912, Harry Ayers (Enfield) to Bass, May 23, 1912, and Robert Manning (Manchester) to Bass, October 7, 1912; also memo in John Bass papers charging the use of Democrats in the voting in several cities, n.d. Chandler suspected fraud as well, e.g., to Willis McDuffee, May 2, 1912, Box 45, File 1, Chandler papers. Agan, "New Hampshire Progressive Movement," pp. 249–55.

59. Bass to Oscar Strauss, May 3, 1912; on March 25 Bass wrote Charles Sumner Bird that "the outlook here is very doubtful for us. . . . whether we can overcome the odds against us is problematical in the extreme." Typical of the "take heart and rejoice" letters was Albert Beveridge to Bass, May 20, 1912; all in Bass papers.

60. Wyman to Bass, February 27, 1912; Bass to Charles Sumner Bird, March 6, 1912; for examples of criticism of Roosevelt's Columbus speech, Wilfred Smart to Bass, February 21, 1912, and Harry Torrey to Bass, n.d., bemoaning Roosevelt's "radical views," and the need to explain "his really conservative reasons" for this position. Bass had trouble getting financial support from the Roosevelt campaign. He wrote Joseph Dixon at Roosevelt headquarters, "I have borne practically the entire expense to date myself"

(Mar. 28, 1912). All in Bass papers. Gallinger comment to Lyford, February 22, 1912, Box 2, File 7, Lyford papers.

61. Bass to Clinton McLane, May 6, 1912; also Bass to Arthur Eaton, April 3, 1912; John Staples to Bass, April 30, 1912, and Albert Dolloff to Bass, May 25, 1912; Bass papers.

62. Gallinger to Lyford, April 26 and 29, 1912, Box 2, File 8, Lyford papers.

63. Gallinger to Lyford, January 17 and 18, 1912, in Box 2, File 7, Lyford papers.

64. Harold Blake wrote to many of the state's progressive Republicans on January 26, 1912, to solicit their preferences for candidates; Bass was the clear favorite. Blake file in 1912 Bass papers. Daniel Remich was very suspicious of Bass and of the Worcester candidacy; Remich reported to Churchill that he had run into Bass on the Boston train and they had dinner together; Bass noted that Worcester was being pushed by Gallinger and "that element." Remich to Churchill, November 27, 1911, and December 5, 1911, Churchill papers; Worcester to Bass, January 12, 1912, asked if Bass wanted "another election & intend to make a campaign of it." Bass papers. Gallinger letter in *Nashua Telegraph*, February 18, 1912.

65. Lyford to Quinby, May 3, 1912, Box 2, File 7, Lyford papers.

66. Agan, "New Hampshire Progressive Movement," pp. 255–57; Rublee and John Bass both worked for the Roosevelt forces at Chicago; Theodore Roosevelt to Rublee and Sen. John Dixon to John Bass, n.d., copies in Bass papers.

67. Churchill to Bass, August 5, 1912; on July 4 Bass's secretary had written Clarence Clough asking his opinion on Bass's refusal to join national progressives in a call for a convention; Bass papers.

68. Bass to Churchill, August 1, 1912, and Churchill to Bass, August 5, 1912, Churchill papers; for enthusiasm of delegates returning from Progressive convention in Chicago, see, e.g., Willis Buxton and Oliver Hussey to Bass, August 10, 1912, Bass papers. "Reminiscences of George Rublee," pp. 96–97.

69. Minutes of the meeting (Robert Johnston, secretary pro tem) in Churchill papers; also Churchill to Robert Manning, August 15, 1912, ibid.

70. Agan, "New Hampshire Progressive Movement," p. 261; on September 6 Musgrove resigned as chairman of the Republican State Committee with a blast at Senator Gallinger, Musgrove file, Bass papers; Churchill to Edward Gallagher, September 10, 1912, Churchill papers.

71. Bass speech in 1912 "Speeches," Bass papers.

72. State of New Hampshire, *Manual of the General Court, 1913* (Concord, 1913), pp. 77–84.

73. Bass to Agnes Jenks, December 1, 1911, to Witter Bynner, January 2 and 6, 1912, to Mary Chase (president of the New Hampshire Woman Suffrage Association), January 3, 1912, Bass papers; Mary Chase to Churchill, thanks "for joining our ranks," October 23, 1911, Churchill papers; Bass speech in 1912 "Speeches," Bass papers. Still, in September 1912, Bass was cautious if not equivocal. He wrote Musgrove that he agreed to a proposal

to put women on the Progressive State Committee, provided they could identify the "right" women, i.e., ones who were willing and whose "method of procedure is such as will not arouse the active antagonism" of the anti-suffrage people, or "lay them and ourselves open to ridicule." Bass to Musgrove, September 23, 1912, Bass papers. A good survey of some of the activities and the individuals is Ida Husted Harper, *The History of Woman Suffrage*, vol. 6 in a series (New York, 1922), chap. 28.

74. Bass to his mother, Clara, August 27, 1912. She provided $10,000 and Bass $5,000; other state progressives joined to contribute $10,000, and Knox raised $25,000. For earlier efforts to make William Chandler's *Independent Statesman* a progressive semiweekly, see, for example, George Carpenter to Bass, December 7, 1911; for continuing designs on winning the allegiance of Pillsbury's *Union*, see Charles A. Perkins to Bass, June 6, 1912; Bass papers.

75. Gallinger to Chandler, September 24, 1912, in Box 45, File 1, Chandler papers. On Taft meeting, Gallinger to Lyford, June 26, 1912; also Lyford to Buffum, September 9, 1912, and to Chandler, September 13, 1912, Box 2, File 9, Lyford papers.

76. Chandler to Moses, May 24, 1912, Box 2, File 11, Moses papers, and to Gallinger, May 3, 1912, Box 45, File 1, Chandler papers.

77. Chandler to G. J. Diekema, October 26, 1912, in vol. 163, p. 21,252, to Nelson Aldrich, December 20, 1912, vol. 163, pp. 21,291–92, to Charles W. Eliot, March 14, 1910, vol. 160, pp. 20,621–23, in Chandler papers, Library of Congress. Chandler to Churchill and Bass, September 2, 1912, Box 45, File 1, Chandler papers. Chandler's conciliatory tone did not totally hide his anger; he counseled Lyford only to convince Gallinger and others "to refrain from severely punishing anybody until after November. We have other work to do." To Lyford, August 28, and September 11, 1912, Box 2, File 9, Lyford papers. Chandler's specific examples of "betrayal" referred to Roosevelt's failure to act against U.S. Steel expansion and against the New Haven acquisition of the Boston and Maine.

78. Gifford Pinchot to Bass, October 5, 1912, and Bass response drafted on the back; Allen Hollis to Churchill, September 4, 1912, and to Bass, November 2, 1912, Bass papers.

79. Robert to John Bass, n.d., and John reply, October 5, 1912: "I believe I would subject myself to severe criticism, under the circumstances, should I drop every thing here [Midwest campaign, primarily Chicago] after the fight that has been going on, and go to New Hampshire." 1912 File, Box E, John Bass papers. Burns file (1912) in Bass papers. On December 6, 1912, the agency sent a bill for "services on the last Election" to Robert Bass and Frank Musgrove, Bass papers.

80. Robert Manning to Bass, November 11, 1912, Bass papers.

81. Roosevelt to Churchill, November 14, 1912, Churchill papers; Oscar Strauss wrote Bass that "no one has done more to advance the Progressive Cause than you, who has been one of the wise and fearless pioneers." November 16, 1912, Bass papers.

82. Chandler to "Richard," December 6, 1912, vol. 163, p. 21,282, Chandler papers, Library of Congress.

6. "The Last Act of the Drama"

1. *Message of Governor Robert Perkins Bass to the General Court, Thursday, January 2, 1913* (n.p., n.d.), p. 13; Churchill to Bass, December 24, 1912, Bass papers.

2. Moses to Chandler, December 13 and 16, 1912, and January 3, 1913, Box 2, File 11, Moses papers.

3. Leonard D. White, "A Study of the New Hampshire Legislature of 1913," master's thesis, Dartmouth College, 1914, chap. 5; Agan, "New Hampshire Progressive Movement," pp. 270–72; Musgrove to Bass, November 11 and 13, 1912, Bass papers. I have used White's number of fourteen progressives in the house, although there is some dispute about this. Musgrove thought there were forty-five; Moses's estimate was eighteen, although he admitted that no one really knew, to Chandler, January 8, 1913, Box 2, File 11, Moses papers; Agan says fourteen is only "superficially" true (n. 9, p. 342). The latter is certainly the case; the "progressives" were no more a uniform and consistent bloc here than they had been on other occasions.

4. Bass to Roosevelt, January 30, 1913; also Roosevelt to Bass, January 28, 1913, and Chandler to Bass, January 11, 1913, in Bass papers. Edith Bass was not well in 1913, and clearly her well-being was of primary concern. In later years, Mrs. Bass would express regret and a sense of guilt at having perhaps deflected Robert from politics; Mr. Bass never indicated that he shared this interpretation (discussions with Perkins Bass, the eldest child of Robert and Edith Bass). For Pillsbury interest, see his letter to Bass, May 27, 1912, Bass papers.

5. To Chandler, January 27, 1913, Box 2, File 11, Moses papers.

6. To Lyford, January 27, 1913, Box 2, File 10, Lyford papers.

7. Moses to Chandler, January 3, 1913; other reports, January 8 and 15, February 10, 15, 17, and 24, Box 2, File 11, Moses papers.

8. Roosevelt to Bass, January 28, 1913, Bass papers. Bass statement, "To the Progressive Members of the Legislature," January 30, 1913; William Savacool to Bass, January 13, 1913, Robert Johnston to Bass, February 28, 1913, Robert Manning to Bass, April 5, 1913, and Bass to Winston Churchill, May 17, 1913, Bass papers. Chandler to Moses, January 16, 1913; Chandler said he had arranged for Roosevelt to press Bass to stay; clearly the ex-president's letter expressed different motives than Chandler had in mind. In Box 2, File 11, Moses papers. Also Chandler to Moses, January 9, 1913, suggesting a deadlock if all else fails, and to Bass, on the same date, and on January 7, Box 45, File 3, Chandler papers. On March 6 Chandler wrote railroad attorney Jack Kelley a "strictly private" letter suggesting that he, Chandler, might be the only unity candidate that could stop the Democrats from winning. He conceded that the entire situation was "quite ludicrous." Ibid.

9. Gallinger to Lyford, April 30, 1913, in Box 2, File 10, Lyford papers. See Arthur Link, *Wilson, The New Freedom* (Princeton, 1956), pp. 436–41.

10. Leonard D. White, the historian of governmental organization and administration, spent 1913 observing and questioning legislators and fol-

lowing newspaper coverage of the session as research for his master's thesis. White, agreeing largely with the newspaper editors whom he quoted, was quite critical of the legislator's behavior and of Democratic partisanship. There is no indication that he studied previous sessions for the purpose of comparison. "A Study of the New Hampshire Legislature of 1913," *passim*. See, as well, Pillsbury, *New Hampshire*, vol. 3, pp. 767–68: "the second longest session in the history of the State, and in some respects the most unsatisfactory."

11. *Session Laws of the State of New Hampshire, 1913;* White, "A Study of the New Hampshire Legislature of 1913," chaps. 4 and 5.

12. Analyses based on *Journal of the House of Representatives of the State of New Hampshire, January Session, 1913* (Concord, 1913); the twelve who voted for Bass on the final roll call included House Speaker William J. Britton; he did not vote on the regular roll calls.

13. Bass to Lawrence Davis, September 27, 1912, Churchill to Bass, November 6, 1912, and Roosevelt to Bass, November 14, 1912, all in Bass papers.

14. Wicker to Bass, n.d. (summer of 1913), Bass papers.

15. Bass speech on July 3, 1913, "Speech" File; Wicker to Bass, June 2, 1914; both in Bass papers.

16. Knox to Churchill, June 20, 1913, Churchill papers. Knox to Bass, April 30, 1913; "Leader Publishing Company" File; Bass to James Remick, July 8, 1913, and to Remick and Robert Manning, October 11, 1913, all in Bass papers. Norman Beasley, *Frank Knox, American: A Short Biography* (Garden City, N.Y., 1936), pp. 88–97. George H. Lobdell, "A Biography of Frank Knox," Ph.D. dissertation, University of Illinois, 1954, pp. 142–43.

17. Knox to Churchill, January 22, 1914, in Churchill papers.

18. Manning to Bass, n.d. (Sept. 1914), and Hollis to Bass, June 9, 1915, Bass papers. Lobdell, "Frank Knox, pp. 150–52.

19. Churchill to Bass, January 13, and February 20, 1914, in Bass papers.

20. Churchill to Bass, June 19, 1914; Robert Manning to Bass, June 3, and July 24, 1914; Rublee to Bass, July 23, 1914, and Bass to Rublee, July 28, and September 19, 1914, Bass, "Suggestions for Progressive Party Platform," n.d. (Sept. 1914); all in Bass papers. Rublee had negotiated an arrangement with Postmaster General Albert S. Burleson to accept Allison's resignation as postmaster and then leave the position vacant so that Allison could be reappointed following the election. For a good discussion of national Progressive party confusion, see George E. Mowry, *Theodore Roosevelt and the Progressive Movement* (Madison, 1946), chaps. 11–13; John A. Gable, *The Bull Moose Years: Theodore Roosevelt and the Progressive Party* (Port Washington, N.Y., 1978), chaps. 8 and 9.

21. State of New Hampshire, *Manual for the General Court, 1915* (Concord, 1915), pp. 134–36; *Manchester Union*, October 3, 1914.

22. Frisbee to Bass, October 3, 1914; Bass to George Rublee, August 17, 1914, to Clarence Clough, September 19, 1914, and to Congressman Stevens, September 22, 1914; Bass received some assistance from the *Collier's* editorial staff in compiling Gallinger's voting record; M. Farmer to Bass, September 9, 1914. All in Bass papers.

23. *Manual for the General Court, 1915,* p. 127; Bass to Henry Allison, October 8, 1914. Agan, "New Hampshire Progressive Movement," pp. 283–84.

24. Gallinger to Chandler, October 1, 1914, Chandler to Knox, October 3, and Knox to Chandler, October 3, 1914, Box 46, File 3, Chandler papers; Lyford to Moses, September 16, 1912, in Box 3, File 1, Lyford papers; *Manchester Union,* October 1 and 9, 1914; Clough to Bass, September 14, 1914; Bass to Musgrove, September 19, 1914. Bass papers.

25. Bass to Musgrove, September 19, 1914, Bass papers.

26. Bass to Allison, October 8, 1914; among other reports, see George Rublee to Bass, November 2, 1914. Rublee had helped arrange for Bass's trip, including obtaining from Secretary of Interior Franklin Lane a request that Bass report back on Indian tribes in the Southwest. Rublee to Bass, August 6, 1914. All in Bass papers. Robert Bass's son Perkins has advised me that while his mother suffered from tuberculosis, his father did not. Churchill campaign letter in *Manchester Union,* October 15, 1914.

27. Streeter to Moses, November 10, 1914, Box 2, File 12, Moses papers; Knox to Chandler, November 5, 1914, Box 46, File 3, Chandler papers. Roosevelt to Meyer Lissner, November 16, 1914, in Morison, *Letters of Theodore Roosevelt,* vol. 8, p. 845.

28. To Moses, March 15, 1915, emphasis in original, Box 2, File 12, Moses papers.

29. Manning to Bass, November 12, 1914, Bass papers.

30. Bass to Churchill, February 8, 1916, in Bass papers.

31. Bass to Roosevelt, June 30, 1915, to William Savacool, August 27, 1915, and to William Plumer, October 8, 1915, all in Bass papers.

32. Roosevelt to Robert Bass, July 28, 1916, letter in File E, John Bass papers. The letter is available in Morison, *Letters of Theodore Roosevelt,* vol. 8, pp. 1094–96.

33. Roosevelt to Churchill, August 4, 1915, in Morison, *Letters of Theodore Roosevelt,* vol. 8, pp. 958–59; Churchill, "Roosevelt and His Friends," *Collier's,* July 8, 1916; Gable, *Bull Moose Years,* chap. 10.

34. Bass to Robert La Follette, June 7, 1915, and to Benjamin Greer, same date, on his pessimism about the "reactionary" GOP; in Bass papers.

35. Gallinger to Moses, March 4, 1915, Box 2, File 12, Moses papers. This fight really flared following the election; see the exchange of correspondence between Lyford and Gallinger in December 1916 in Box 3, File 5, Lyford papers, e.g., Gallinger to Lyford, December 15, "I have endured the insults from Knox as long as I propose to."

36. Gallinger to Moses, March 4, 1915, in Box 2, File 12, Moses papers; Lyford to Gallinger, November 11, 1914, Box 3, File 1, Lyford papers; Dorothy Ann Pettit, in "An Analysis of the 1916 Presidential Election in New Hampshire," M.A. thesis, University of New Hampshire, 1968, on pp. 56–59 discusses reaction to Gallinger stopping the Rublee appointment.

37. Pettit, "Analysis of the 1916 Presidential Election," pp. 60–74; see, as well, Bass to Hapgood, September 16, 1916, and Musgrove to Bass, October 17, 1916. Bass's alienation was not a recent thing; on October 8, 1915, he had written to Progressive national chairman Victor Murdock that "I

have not been at all active during the past two years and feel personally very much like a man without a party." All letters in Bass papers. Lyford to Churchill, October 10 and 16, 1916; Churchill to Lyford, October 11, 1916, Lyford to F. H. Buffum, October 24, 1916, Box 3, File 5, Lyford papers. In the latter Lyford decided the best person to send out would be John Benton, who recently had not been reappointed to the public service commission.

38. Gallinger to Lyford, October 6, 1916, in Box 3, File 5, Lyford papers; Pettit, "Analysis of the 1916 Presidential Election," chap. 4; for example of difficulty of old Progressives in the GOP, see Louis Wyman to Bass, November 9, 1916, Bass papers.

39. December 4, 1916 (apparent; date unclear), Churchill papers.

40. Churchill attorney Herbert Lakin to Churchill, July 19, and December 20, 1910, April 16, 1913; Lakin to group of opponents, April 22, 1913, all in Churchill papers.

41. Churchill to Bass, June 12, 1917, Bass papers. For a good study of Churchill, see Robert W. Schneider, *Five Novelists of the Progressive Era* (New York, 1965), chap. 5.

42. Quoted in Schneider, *Five Novelists of the Progressive Era*, p. 210.

43. The Bass correspondence for the period 1914–20 is filled with references to these activities.

44. For superficial surveys of the war era in New Hampshire, see Squires, *Granite State of the United States*, vol. 2, chap. 25; and Pillsbury, *New Hampshire*, vol. 3, pp. 791–908; see also Richardson, *William E. Chandler*, pp. 729–34.

7. The Progressive Yankees

1. Text of speech in John F. Bass papers. The *Chicago Sunday Tribune*'s summary headline of the speech was "More Brains, Less Clubbing Urged for Reds" (Feb. 15, 1920). A good description of the New Hampshire events is David Williams, "'Sowing the Wind': The Deportation Raids of 1920 in New Hampshire," *Historical New Hampshire* 34 (1979), pp. 1–31. For national context, Robert Murray, *Red Scare: A Study in National Hysteria* (Minneapolis, 1955).

2. The Remick statement is reprinted in *Miscellaneous Writings, Speeches, Experiences, and Philosophy of James W. Remick, For his Family and Descendants*, privately printed (Concord, 1934), p. 432.

3. In this regard and in the discussion that follows I cannot dispute Peter Filene's argument that there never was a true progressive "movement"; on the other hand this seems to suggest more about the imprecision of our descriptive categories than it warrants the conclusion that the progressives were of little consequence. Filene, "Obituary for 'The Progressive Movement.'"

4. Any listing of key New Hampshire Republican reformers in this period would include, in addition to Bass and Churchill, Frank Musgrove, Clarence Clough, Robert Manning, John Benton, James Colby, Allen Hol-

lis, James Remick, Daniel Remich, Louis Wyman, Sherman Burroughs, and Edmund Cook.

5. *Monitor,* January 10, 1911; Pillsbury, *New Hampshire,* vol. 3, p. 729.

6. Lyford to Streeter, January 31, 1902, File 4, Box 1, Lyford papers. A good discussion of the "System of 1896" in American politics is by Walter Dean Burnham, *Critical Elections and the Mainsprings of American Politics* (New York, 1970), chap. 4.

7. This decline in turnout was not nearly as sharp as that which Burnham observed in a more classic example of a one-party state, Virginia. Burnham, *Critical Elections,* p. 80.

8. Wyman to Bass, July 11, 1910, Bass papers.

9. Lyford to Gallinger, September 21, 1910, Box 2, File 5, Lyford papers.

10. *Boston Journal,* September 7, 1912. Wyman to Bass, September 19, 1914, Bass papers.

11. McCormick, "Discovery That Business Corrupts Politics," is an important essay that seems appropriate to an explanation of the origins of Granite State progressivism; see as well McCormick's *From Realignment to Reform: Political Change in New York State, 1893–1910* (Ithaca, 1981), especially chap. 7.

12. Chandler to Churchill, October 1, 1907, Churchill papers.

13. The following correlation coefficients measure the relationship between the 1912 vote for Theodore Roosevelt, with voting on liquor license in 1910, and with voting on constitutional amendments in 1912 (voting yes on referenda): liquor license, −.20; corporation tax amendment, −.04; inheritance tax amendment, .06; strike *Protestant* amendment, −.01; basic tax amendment, .02. None of these values are statistically significant. Republican and Democratic presidential voting in 1912 showed the same relationships to these issues, except the Wilson vote related marginally more significantly (0.25) with the 1910 vote on liquor licenses.

14. Thomas Agan, "The New Hampshire Progressives: Who and What Were They?" *Historical New Hampshire* 34 (1979), pp. 32–53. While I did not attempt to replicate Agan's analysis, my impression is that he is correct. I believe the progressives may have been slightly more Congregationalist than the old guard, which his data confirm as do the voting patterns in 1912. The variation is marginal: the top Congregational towns (the top quartile) voted 22.1 percent for Roosevelt, 37.4 percent for Taft, and 38.6 percent for Wilson; the mean town vote for each of these candidates was 20.5 percent, 37.0 percent, and 40.4 percent, respectively.

15. Rollins to Bass, November 23, 1910, Bass papers.

16. See Lyford, *Life of E. H. Rollins,* pp. 303–14. Rollins also believed that the liquor issue contributed to this defeat.

17. *Message of His Excellency Charles A. Busiel, Governor of New Hampshire, to the Two Branches of the Legislature, January Session, 1895* (Concord, 1895), p. 3.

18. The accompanying table shows the vote for each major party's gubernatorial candidate as a percentage of the same party's presidential vote; for

Table for Note 18

Year	GOP	Democratic	Year	GOP	Democratic
1880*	99.18	100.06	1900*	98.34	98.50
1882	85.72	90.50	1902	76.85	95.36
1884*	98.30	101.26	1904*	94.48	104.00
1886	87.39	95.39	1906	74.92	110.56
1888*	98.01	101.78	1908*	83.97	122.97
1890	92.91	97.57	1910	84.49	112.13
1892*	95.66	98.62	1912*	98.72	98.50
1894	101.82	80.70	1914	140.96	96.98
1896*	84.23	133.20	1916*	104.97	88.74
1898	77.87	167.61			

*Indicates presidential election year.

nonpresidential years, the figure is each party's gubernatorial vote in that year as a percentage of its presidential vote two years earlier.

19. *Manchester Union*, October 10, 1904; Carr to W. Guy Colby, November 2, 1908, Box 10, Carr papers.

20. George Mason to Carr, October 29, 1908, and Daniel Remich to Carr, November 5, 1908, Box 10, Carr papers.

21. *Monitor*, April 23, 1900.

22. Bass to Charles Sumner Bird, October 21, 1913, Bass papers.

23. Hollis to Churchill, June 3, 1907, Churchill papers.

24. Churchill to E. Snell Smith, National Organizer of League of Taft Clubs, October 10, 1908, Churchill papers.

25. I find conceptually useful the work of Robert Wiebe and Samuel P. Hays in understanding community-local-parochial values, on the one hand, and society-cosmopolitan values, on the other. This framework does not "explain" New Hampshire progressive politics; it elucidates some of the themes. See Robert Wiebe, *The Search for Order, 1877–1920* (New York, 1967); several provocative Hays essays are conveniently available in his *American Political History as Social Analysis: Essays by Samuel P. Hays* (Knoxville, 1980).

26. Churchill continued to express an interest in Cornish politics; in 1908, prior to the local school meeting, he attempted to organize a group to attend this session and vote for members of the board. Churchill could not participate because of an "engagement elsewhere." Churchill to Philip Littell, March 11, 1908, Churchill papers.

27. Lyford to Frank Currier, February 17, 1908, Box 2, File 1, Lyford papers.

28. Moses to Chandler, November 30, 1906, Box 1, File 9, Moses papers.

29. Bass to Mr. Gilman, May 31, 1912, Bass papers.

30. F. H. Buffum to Bass, July 25, 1912, ibid.

31. Hollis to Churchill, September 4, 1912, Churchill papers.

32. Roosevelt to Bass, March 16, 1912, Bass papers.

33. McLane to Churchill, August 27, 1912, Churchill papers.

34. Remich to Churchill, August 26, 1912, ibid.

35. Musgrove to A. D. Felch, September 23, 1914, "Gallinger" File, Bass papers.

36. William H. Sisson to Churchill, September 5, 1908, Churchill papers.

37. Churchill to Burroughs, May 28, 1910, ibid.

38. George Ellison to Bass, September 7, 1910, Bass papers; also Ellison to Churchill on the same date, Churchill papers. See Burroughs campaign emphasis in *Manchester Union*, August 12, 1910.

39. This and the following discussion of changes in the state law in this period is available in William Chase and Arthur Chase, *Supplement to the Public Statutes of New Hampshire (Chase Edition, 1901) Giving All Amendments Made by the General Courts for the Years 1901 to 1913, Inclusive, Together with a Combined Index of the Public Statues (Chase Edition) and This Supplement* (Concord, 1914). The volume is well indexed and cross referenced, with annotations; I will not make specific references to it.

40. Theodorou, "Conservation in New Hampshire," chaps. 2 and 3.

41. Bishop, *Development of a State School System*, p. 75, and chaps. 6 and 7. School laws are summarized in New Hampshire Department of Public Instruction, *Laws of New Hampshire Relating to Public Schools, Compiled from Public Statutes and Session Laws of 1891–1913* (Concord, 1913).

42. See 1911 File, "Veto Durham College Appro. Letters," Bass papers; exchange of correspondence between the governor and college president W. D. Gibbs, Gibbs to Bass, April 26 and May 2, Bass to Gibbs, April 21 and 29, 1911, Bass papers. The galling issue to supporters of the college, and especially to its students, was that Bass had not vetoed the bill providing for the annual appropriation of state funds to assist Dartmouth College. For Bass on education, see, e.g., speeches at Colebrook Academy (Nov. 7, 1911) and to Philips Exeter Alumni (Dec. 9, 1911) in 1911 "Speech" File, ibid. Sackett, *New Hampshire's University, passim*.

43. See the 1911 "Robert Barrett" File in Bass papers; see also speech to White Mountain Board of Trade, August 11, 1911, and to State Grange, December 19, 1911, in "Speeches"; see as well Bass correspondence with Charles Hoyt and H. C. Hill in 1911; all in Bass papers. For discussion of the legislation, in addition to the details in the Chase volume, see Pillsbury, *New Hampshire*, vol. 3, pp. 719–20.

44. Chase and Chase, *Supplement to the Public Statutes*, pp. 35–36.

45. *Message of His Excellency, Chester B. Jordan, 1901*, p. 41.

46. *State of New Hampshire Manual for the General Court*, 1901 and 1913 numbers, provide accessible summaries of state officials. What these sources do not summarize are the total number of state employees.

47. These figures and those in the table of expenditures gathered from *Report of the State Treasurer of the State of New Hampshire, for the Year Ending May 31, 1900* (Manchester, 1900); *Report of the State Treasurer of the State of New Hampshire for the Fiscal Year, Ending August 31, 1912* (Concord, 1912); and State of New Hampshire, *Report of State Auditor for the Year Ending August 31, 1912* (Concord, 1912).

48. *Report of State Treasurer, 1900,* and *Report of State Treasurer, 1912.*

49. Gallinger to Lyford, June 11, 1912, Box 2, File 9, Lyford papers; Mabel Churchill to Lyford, November 18, 1916, and Lyford to Mrs. Churchill, November 20 and December 23, 1916, Box 3, File 5, Lyford papers.

50. School board membership calculated from *Report of the Superintendent of Public Instruction, 1912* (Concord, 1912), pp. 407–21; the top progressive towns were those consistently in the top quartile of support for Bass in the 1910 primary, and for the Progressive candidates in the 1912 and 1914 gubernatorial elections and the 1912 presidential election.

51. Speech on May 13, 1915, "Suffrage Folder," Bass papers.

52. *Manchester Union,* February 2 and 5, 1912; Bass to Rev. James Smith, February 13, 1912, Wyman to Bass, December 2, 1912, "Free Speech Hearings," Bass papers.

53. Bass to Tucker, October 11, 1913, Bass papers. For book order, Little, Brown and Company to Bass, March 14, 1911, ibid.

54. "Political Situation" drafts in 1915 "P Carbons," Bass papers.

55. September 30, 1910; anger over Boisvert's defeat (he was an incumbent) continued through the fall, see, e.g., *L'Avenir National,* September 29, October 19, 21, and 27, 1910.

56. November 9, 1910. The newspaper had editorially supported Patrick Sullivan, pointing out to readers that at least he spoke French; November 2, 1910.

57. Chandler to Bass, December 12, 1911, Bass papers. This continued to be a concern; in 1916 Knox was worrying about the "tendency of the French-American population of the state to become democratic." To Chandler, November 13, 1916, Box 46, "Oct–Nov 1916" File, Chandler papers.

58. August 4, 1911. See other editorials with this same complaint, e.g., May 15, 1911.

59. Manning to Bass, October 13 and 15, 1911, in Bass papers. Emphasis in original.

60. See Remich to Bass, May 15, 1911, and Bishop Guertin to Bass, May 5 and 22, 1911, in Bass papers. Bass reappointed the bishop's choice, John Kivel, to the license commission; he did not appoint Guertin-recommended William Starr to the public service commission.

61. This is not inconsistent with the model developed by Samuel P. Hays, "The Politics of Reform in Municipal Government in the Progressive Era," *Pacific Northwest Quarterly* 55 (1964), pp. 157–69. I do not find the reform to be part of an upper-class effort, as he did.

62. Carr to Frank Musgrove, May 5, 1909, "N.H. Gen Ct Corr. Concerning, 1909–10," Box 10, Carr papers.

63. Ayres to Bass, May 1, 1917, Bass papers.

64. Tobey to Mr. and Mrs. Robert Bass, December 26, 1913; Bass to William Plumer, October 8, 1915; Churchill to Bass, June 27, 1914; all in Bass papers.

65. For the seminal work on the activities of the progressives after the

war, see Arthur Link, "What Happened to the Progressive Movement in the 1920's?" *American Historical Review* 64 (1959), pp. 833–51.

66. Moses to Lyford, February 25, 1924, and Lyford to George Carpenter, March 12, 1924, in Box 3, File 11, Lyford papers. Files 10 and 11 have information on the legislative battles and the primary skirmishing. The "Moses-Coolidge" File in the Bass papers provides correspondence describing Bass's tactics, e.g., Bass to William King, February 20, 1924. See as well Bernard Bellush, *He Walked Alone: A Biograph of John Gilbert Winant* (The Hague, 1968), pp. 62–68. Lobdell, "Frank Knox," pp. 199–204.

67. Bellush, *He Walked Alone*, p. 68.

68. Bass campaign material for 1926, in Bass papers; see for example, "Announcement of Ex-Governor Robert P. Bass" (Dec. 7, 1925), and campaign newspaper, "The Primary, Facts for New Hampshire Voters." Bellush, *He Walked Alone*, pp. 77–79; Symonds, "George Higgins Moses," chap. 7.

69. Quoted in Otis L. Graham, Jr., *An Encore for Reform: The Old Progressives and the New Deal* (New York, 1967), p. 94. Graham identifies Bass as one of the old progressives who opposed the New Deal (p. 192).

70. Letter to the editor in Lebanon, New Hampshire, *Valley News*, August 4, 1960.

Bibliography

Primary Material
Manuscripts
John Foster Bass Papers. In Possession of John F. Bass III, Englewood, Florida.

Robert P. Bass File. Harvard University Archives.

Robert Perkins Bass Papers. Special Collections, Dartmouth College Library.

Clarence Carr Papers. Special Collections, Dartmouth College Library.

William E. Chandler Papers. Manuscript Division, Library of Congress.

William E. Chandler Papers. New Hampshire Historical Society.

Winston Churchill Papers. Special Collections, Dartmouth College Library.

Class of 1896 "Reports." Harvard University Archives.

Freewill Baptists, New Hampshire Yearly Meeting of, 1866–1914. Concord Office of American Baptist Churches of New Hampshire.

Jacob Gallinger Papers. New Hampshire Historical Society.

James Lyford Papers. New Hampshire Historical Society.

Charles S. Mellen Papers. New Hampshire Historical Society.

George Moses Papers. New Hampshire Historical Society.

Frank Musgrove Papers. Dartmouth College Library.

Ernest Fox Nichols Papers. Presidential Papers, Dartmouth College Archives.

Parish Census and Annual Reports. Archives Department. Roman Catholic Diocese of Manchester.

Gifford Pinchot Papers. Manuscript Division, Library of Congress.

William Jewett Tucker Papers. Presidential Papers, Dartmouth College Archives.

Government Documents
Canaan, Town of. *Annual Report of Selectmen and Other Town Officers of Canaan, N.H. for the Year Ending February 15, 1897.* Canaan, 1896 [sic].

Chase, William M., and Arthur H. Chase, comps. *The Public Statutes of the State of New Hampshire and General Laws in Force, January 1, 1901.* Concord, 1901.

————. *Supplement to the Public Statutes of New Hampshire (Chase Edition, 1901) Giving All Amendments Made by the General Courts for the*

Years 1901 to 1913, Inclusive, Together with a Combined Index of the Public Statutes (Chase Edition) and This Supplement. Concord, 1914.

Claremont, Town of. "Annual Report of Selectmen and Other Town Officers, 1901." Claremont, n.d.

Franklin, City of. "Sixth Annual Report of the Municipal Government of the City of Franklin for the Financial Year, 1900." Franklin, n.d.

Journal of the House of Representatives of the State of New Hampshire. 1901–13.

Journal of the Senate of the State of New Hampshire. 1901–13.

Manchester, City of. "Fifty-Fifth Annual Report of the Receipts and Expenditures of the City of Manchester, New Hampshire, for the Fiscal Year Ending December 31, 1900." Manchester, 1901.

New Hampshire Department of Public Instruction. *Laws of New Hampshire Relating to Public Schools, Compiled from Public Statutes and Session Laws of 1891–1913.* Concord, 1913.

New Hampshire General Court. "Report to the House of the Committee on Retrenchment and Reform." Concord, n.d.

New Hampshire Manual for the General Court. 1891–1917.

New Hampshire, State of. *Annual Reports.* 1890–1914.

———. Commissioner of Bureau of Labor. "Special Report on Summer Boarding Business and Resorts in N.H., 1899." Manchester, 1900.

———. Commissioner of Bureau of Labor. "Special Report on Summer Business, 1900."

———. *Messages of the Governor.* 1890–1914.

———. "Report of the New Hampshire Tax Commission of 1908." Concord, 1908.

———. *Session Laws of the State of New Hampshire.* 1909–1913.

U.S. Department of Commerce and Labor. Bureau of the Census. *Decennial Census Reports,* 1880, 1890, 1900, 1910, and 1920.

———. Manuscript Schedules for New Hampshire, 1880 and 1900.

———. *Special Reports: Central Electric Light and Power Stations, 1902.* Washington, D.C., 1905.

———. *Special Reports, Religious Bodies: 1906.* Washington, D.C., 1910.

Newspapers

L'Avenir National
Boston Herald
Boston Transcript
Concord Monitor
Concord Patriot
Granite State Free Press
L'Impartial
Manchester Union

Autobiographies, Collections, and Reminiscences

Hapgood, Norman. *The Changing Years: Reminiscences of Norman Hapgood.* New York, 1930.

Jackson, Robert. "Recollections of Winston Churchill's Campaign for the Republican Nomination for Governor of New Hampshire in 1906." Typescript. Darmouth College Special Collections.

Lyford, James. *Life of Edward H. Rollins: A Political Biography.* Boston, 1906.

Miscellaneous Writings, Speeches, Experiences, and Philosophy of James W. Remick, for His Family and Descendants. Privately printed. Concord, 1934.

Morison, Elting E., and John M. Blum, eds. *The Letters of Theodore Roosevelt.* 8 vols. Cambridge, Mass., 1954.

Old Home Week Addresses by Governor Frank Rollins, 1900. Concord, n.d.

Pinchot, Gifford. *Breaking New Ground.* New York, 1947.

Rublee, George. "Reminiscences." Oral History Research Office. Columbia University.

Tucker, William Jewett. *Public Mindedness: An Aspect of Citizenship Considered in Various Addresses Given While President of Darmouth College.* Concord, 1910.

Urofsky, Melvin I., and David W. Levy, eds. *Letters of Louis D. Brandeis.* 5 vols. Albany, N.Y., 1971–78.

Contemporary Published Material

Anderson, Thomas F. "Our New England Alps as a National Health Resort." *New England Magazine* 38 (1908).

Annual Conference of the New Hampshire Methodist Episcopal Church. *Official Journal.* 1896–1914.

Annual Convention of the Protestant Episcopal Church of the Diocese of New Hampshire. *Journal of the Proceedings.* Concord, 1890–1914.

Ayres, Philip W. "Is New England's Wealth in Danger?" *New England Magazine* 38 (Mar.–June 1908).

Baker, Ray Stannard. "Is the East Also Insurgent? Signs of Revolt in Republican Strongholds." *American Magazine* 69 (Mar. 1910).

Bar Association of the State of New Hampshire. *Proceedings.* 1900–1916.

Beatty, Jerome G. "The Rescue of New Hampshire and the Rise of a New Figure in Our Public Life." *Collier's* 47 (May 6, 1911).

"Biographical Sketches of the Governor, Councilors, and Members of the Senate and House of Representatives of the New Hampshire Legislature." In *The Brown Book,* various compilers. Concord, 1881–1913.

Chandler, William E. "Free Competition versus Trust Combinations." *Munsey's Magazine* 22 (Oct. 1899–Mar. 1900).

———. "The Growth of the Use of Money in Politics and of Railroad Power in New Hampshire." Concord, N.H.: Rumford Press, 1899.

———. "Jethro Bass Unreal." Concord, 1906.

———. "Merger Will Destroy Competition." *New England Magazine* 38 (May 1908).

———. "Methods of Restricting Immigration." *Forum* 13 (Mar.–Aug. 1892).

———. "National Control of Elections." *Forum* 9 (Mar.–Aug. 1890).

————. "Shall Immigration Be Suspended?" *North American Review* 156 (1893).

Churchill, Winston. *Coniston*. New York, 1906.

————. *Mr. Crewe's Career*. New York, 1908.

————. "Roosevelt and His Friends." *Collier's* 57 (Sept. 8, 1916).

"The Churchill Reform Movement, The Appeals of Bishop Niles and William E. Chandler to Welcome the Churchill Movement, Reform the Republican Party and Liberate the State from Slavery to the Boston and Maine Railroad and Free Passes." Concord, 1906.

Dole, Charles F. *The American Citizen*. Boston, 1892.

"The Fight against the Machine in New Hampshire." *Outlook* 90 (Oct. 3, 1908).

"For the Square Deal." *Outlook* 96 (Oct. 22, 1910).

General Conference of Freewill Baptists. *The Free Baptist Register and Year Book*. 1891, 1899, 1911.

"Governor Bass a Real Governor." *Outlook* 97 (Mar. 25, 1911).

"Governor Robert P. Bass." *Granite Monthly* 43 (Feb.–Mar. 1911).

Grand Lodge of New Hampshire, Independent Order of Good Templars. *Proceedings of the . . . Annual Session*. 1880–1900.

Johnson, Stanley. "A Novelist and His Novels in Politics." *World's Work* 17 (Dec. 1908).

Lucier, A. J. *The Machine: A Political Satire*. Boston, 1908.

Metcalf, Henry H., ed./comp. *One Thousand New Hampshire Notables*. Concord, 1919.

————. "A Prosperous Industry and Its Manager." *Granite Monthly* 28 (1900).

Minutes of the General Association of the Congregational and Presbyterian Churches of New Hampshire. 1880–1913.

Minutes of the New Hampshire Baptist Anniversaries. Nashua, 1893–98, 1900, 1904–9.

"Mr. Churchill's Virtual Victory." *Outlook* 84 (Sept. 29, 1906).

"New Hampshire and New Jersey." *Outlook* 98 (May 13, 1911).

New Hampshire Medical Society. *Transactions*. Concord, 1888–1912.

"New Hampshire Republicanism." *Outlook* 96 (Sept. 17, 1910).

New Hampshire State Grange. *Journal of Proceedings*. 1888–1917.

New Hampshire Universalist State Convention. *Minutes*. Manchester, 1892–1914.

New Hampshire Woman's Christian Temperance Union. *Minutes of the . . . Annual Meeting*. 1896–1912.

New Hampshire Young Men's Christian Associations and Evangelical Churches of New Hampshire. *Annual Convention*. 1882–90.

"The New 'Summer White House.'" *American Review of Reviews* 48 (July 1913).

O'Reilly, Mary Boyle. "The Daughters of Herod: A Plea for Child-Saving Legislation in New Hampshire." *New England Magazine* 43 (Oct. 1910).

Putnam, Frank. "What's the Matter with New England? New Hampshire: A Study in Industrial Vassalage, Political Medievalism, and the Aristocratic Ideal in Public Education." *New England Magazine* 36 (Aug. 1907).

Remick, James W. "Winston Churchill and His Campaign." *Outlook* 84 (Sept. 1, 1906).
Rollins, Frank W. "New Hampshire's Opportunity." *New England Magazine* 16 (July 1897).
Society for the Protection of New Hampshire Forests. *Annual Report.* 1901–14.
Strother, French. "A City without Strikes." *World's Work* 15 (Nov. 1907).
Sullivan, Mark. "The Way of a Railroad." *Collier's* 37 (Aug. 11, 1906).
Whitelock, William Wallace. "Mr. Winston Churchill." *Critic* 40 (Feb. 1902).
"Winston Churchill." *Arena* 36 (July–Dec. 1906).
"Winston Churchill." *Harper's Weekly* 43 (Aug. 26, 1899).
"Winston Churchill and Everett Colby." *Outlook* 90 (Sept. 19, 1908).
"Woman Suffrage in New Hampshire." *Outlook* 73 (Feb. 21, 1903).

Secondary Material
General

Abrams, Richard. *Conservatism in the Progressive Era: Massachusetts Politics, 1900–1912.* Cambridge, Mass., 1964.
Anderson, Donald F. *William Howard Taft: A Conservative's Conception of the Presidency.* Ithaca, 1973.
Baker, George P. *The Formation of the New England Railroad Systems: A Study of Railroad Combination in the Nineteenth Century.* Cambridge, Mass., 1937.
Beasley, Norman. *Frank Knox, American: A Short Biography.* Garden City, N.Y., 1936.
Blackford, Mansel G. *The Politics of Business in California, 1890–1920.* Columbus, Ohio, 1977.
Blum, John M. *The Republican Roosevelt.* Cambridge, Mass., 1954.
Buenker, John D. "The Progressive Era: A Search for a Synthesis." *Mid-America* 51 (1969).
Buenker, John D., John C. Burnham, and Robert M. Crunden. *Progressivism.* Cambridge, Mass., 1977.
Burnham, Walter Dean. *Critical Elections and the Mainsprings of American Politics.* New York, 1970.
Caine, Stanley P. *The Myth of a Progressive Reform: Railroad Regulation in Wisconsin, 1903–1910.* Madison, 1970.
Cartwright, William J., and Richard L. Watson, Jr., eds. *The Reinterpretation of American History and Culture.* Washington, D.C., 1973.
Clubb, Jerome M., and Howard W. Allen. "Collective Biography and the Progressive Movement: The 'Status Revolution' Revisited." *Social Science History* 1 (1977).
Coletta, Paolo E. *The Presidency of William Howard Taft.* Lawrence, Kans., 1973.
Cooper, John Milton, Jr. *The Warrior and the Priest: Woodrow Wilson and Theodore Roosevelt.* Cambridge, Mass., 1983.
DeWitt, Benjamin P. *The Progressive Movement: A Non-partisan, Compre-*

hensive Discussion of Current Tendencies in American Politics. New York, 1915.

Ebner, Michael H., and Eugene Tobin, eds. *The Age of Urban Reform: New Perspectives on the Progressive Era.* Port Washington, N.Y., 1977.

Filene, Peter G. "An Obituary for 'The Progressive Movement.'" *American Quarterly* 22 (1970).

Flint, Winston Allen. *The Progressive Movement in Vermont.* Washington, D.C., 1941.

Gable, John A. *The Bull Moose Years: Theodore Roosevelt and the Progressive Party.* Port Washington, N.Y., 1978.

Galambos, Louis. "The Emerging Organizational Synthesis in Modern American History." *Business History Review* 44 (1970).

Gould, Lewis L. *The Progressive Era.* Syracuse, 1974.

———. *Reform and Regulation: American Politics, 1900–1916.* New York, 1978.

Graham, Otis L., Jr. *An Encore for Reform: The Old Progressives and the New Deal.* New York, 1967.

Grantham, Dewey W. "The Contours of Southern Progressivism." *American Historical Review* 86 (1981).

Harbaugh, William H. *Power and Responsibility: The Life and Times of Theodore Roosevelt.* New York, 1961.

Harper, Ida Husted. *The History of Woman Suffrage.* Vol. 6. New York, 1922.

Hays, Samuel P. *American Political History as Social Analysis: Essays by Samuel P. Hays.* Knoxville, Tenn., 1980.

———. "The Politics of Reform in Municipal Government in the Progressive Era." *Pacific Northwest Quarterly* 55 (1964).

———. *The Response to Industrialism, 1885–1914.* Chicago, 1957.

Hobson, Wayne K. "Professionals, Progressives and Bureaucratization: A Reassessment." *Historian* 39 (1977).

Hofstadter, Richard. *The Age of Reform: From Bryan to F.D.R.* New York, 1955.

Holli, Melvin G. *Reform in Detroit: Hazen S. Pingree and Urban Politics.* New York, 1969.

Holt, James. *Congressional Insurgents and the Party System, 1909–1916.* Cambridge, Mass., 1967.

Jensen, Richard. *The Winning of the Midwest: Social and Political Conflict, 1888–1896.* Chicago, 1971.

Kennedy, David M. "Overview: The Progressive Era." *Historian* 37 (1975).

Key, V. O., Jr. *American State Politics: An Introduction.* New York, 1956.

———. "Secular Realignment and the Party System." *Journal of Politics* 21 (1959).

———. "A Theory of Critical Elections." *Journal of Politics* 17 (1955).

Kirby, Jack Temple. *Darkness at the Dawning: Race and Reform in the Progressive South.* Philadelphia, 1972.

Kirkland, Edward C. *Men, Cities, and Transportation: A Study in New England History, 1820–1900.* 2 vols. Cambridge, Mass., 1948.

Kleppner, Paul. *The Cross of Culture: A Social Analysis of Midwestern Politics, 1850–1900.* New York, 1970.
————. *The Third Electoral System, 1853–1892: Parties, Voters, and Political Cultures.* Chapel Hill, N.C., 1979.
La Forte, Robert S. *Leaders of Reform: Progressive Republicans in Kansas, 1900–1916.* Lawrence, Kans., 1974.
Leary, William M., Jr., and Arthur S. Link, comps. *The Progressive Era and the Great War, 1896–1920.* 2d ed. Arlington Heights, Ill., 1978.
LeBlanc, Robert G. *Location of Manufacturing in New England in the 19th Century.* Geography Publications at Dartmouth, no. 7. Hanover, N.H., 1969.
Levy, David W. *Herbert Croly of the New Republic: The Life and Thought of an American Progressive.* Princeton, 1985.
Link, Arthur S. "The Progressive Movement in the South, 1870–1914." *North Carolina Historical Review* 23 (1946).
————. "What Happened to the Progressive Movement in the 1920's?" *American Historical Review* 64 (1959).
————. *Wilson: Confusions and Crises, 1915–1916.* Princeton, 1964.
————. *Wilson: The New Freedom.* Princeton, 1956.
Link, Arthur S., and Richard L. McCormick. *Progressivism.* Arlington Heights, Ill., 1983.
McCormick, Richard L. "The Discovery That Business Corrupts Politics: A Reappraisal of the Origins of Progressivism." *American Historical Review* 86 (1981).
————. *From Realignment to Reform: Political Change in New York State, 1893–1910.* Ithaca, 1981.
McSeveney, Samuel T. *The Politics of Depression: Political Behavior in the Northeast, 1893–1896.* New York, 1972.
Margulies, Herbert F. *The Decline of the Progressive Movement in Wisconsin, 1890–1920.* Madison, 1968.
Maxwell, Robert S. *La Follette and the Rise of the Progressives in Wisconsin.* Madison, 1956.
Mowry, George. *The California Progressives.* Berkeley, 1951.
————. *The Era of Theodore Roosevelt, 1900–1912.* New York, 1958.
————. *Theodore Roosevelt and the Progressive Movement.* Madison, 1946.
Murray, Robert. *Red Scare: A Study in National Hysteria.* Minneapolis, 1955.
Nichols, Roy F. *Franklin Pierce: Young Hickory of the Granite Hills.* Rev. ed. Philadelphia, 1958.
Nye, Russel B. *Midwestern Progressive Politics: A Historical Study of its Origins and Development, 1870–1950.* East Lansing, Mich., 1951.
Olin, Spencer C. *California's Prodigal Sons: Hiram Johnson and the Progressives, 1911–1917.* Berkeley, 1968.
Rodgers, Daniel T. "In Search of Progressivism." *Reviews in American History,* 1982.
Rosenthal, Alan, and Maureen Moakley, eds. *The Political Life of the American States.* New York, 1984.

Russell, Howard S. *A Long, Deep Furrow: Three Centuries of Farming in New England.* Hanover, N.H., 1976.

Schneider, Robert W. *Five Novelists of the Progressive Era.* New York, 1965.

Sewell, Richard H. *John P. Hale and the Politics of Abolition.* Cambridge, Mass., 1965.

Thelen, David P. *The New Citizenship: Origins of Progressivism in Wisconsin, 1885–1900.* Columbia, Mo., 1973.

———. "Social Tensions and the Origins of Progressivism." *Journal of American History* 56 (1969).

Wade, Mason. "The French Parish and Survivance in Nineteenth-Century New England." *Catholic Historical Review* 36 (1950).

Wesser, Robert R. *Charles Evans Hughes: Politics and Reform in New York, 1905–1910.* Ithaca, 1967.

Wiebe, Robert. *The Search for Order, 1877–1920.* New York, 1967.

Wilson, Harold D. *The Hill Country of Northern New England, Its Social and Economic History, 1790–1930.* New York, 1936.

Woodward, C. Vann. *Origins of the New South, 1877–1913.* Baton Rouge, La., 1951.

Wright, James. "The Ethnocultural Model of Voting: A Behavioral and Historical Critique." *American Behavioral Scientist* 16 (1973).

New Hampshire

Agan, Thomas. "The New Hampshire Progressives: Who and What Were They?" *Historical New Hampshire* 34 (1979).

Allison, Hildreth M. "Hassle for the Top Spot: The Republican Gubernatorial Convention of 1906." *Historical New Hampshire* 36 (1981).

Armstrong, John B. *Factory under the Elms: A History of Harrisville, New Hampshire, 1774–1969.* Cambridge, Mass., 1969.

Bellush, Bernard. *He Walked Alone: A Biography of John Gilbert Winant.* The Hague, 1968.

Bellush, Jewel. "Reform in New Hampshire: Robert Bass Wins the Primary." *New England Quarterly* 35 (Dec. 1962).

Bishop, Eugene A. *Development of a State School System: New Hampshire.* Contributions to Education, no. 391. Teachers College, Columbia University. New York, 1930.

Blodgett, Geoffrey. "Winston Churchill: The Novelist as Reformer." *New England Quarterly* 47 (1974).

Blood, Grace. *Manchester on the Merrimack: The Story of a City.* Manchester, 1948.

Brown, William R. *Our Forest Heritage: A History of Forestry and Recreation in New Hampshire.* Concord, 1958.

Child, William H. *History of the Town of Cornish, New Hampshire with Genealogical Record.* Concord, n.d.

Cole, Donald B. *Jacksonian Democracy in New Hampshire, 1800–1851.* Cambridge, Mass., 1970.

Creamer, Daniel, and Charles W. Creamer. *Labor and the Shut-Down at the Amoskeag Textile Mills*. Works Progress Administration, National Research Project. Philadelphia, 1939.

Daniell, Jere R. *Experiment in Republicanism: New Hampshire Politics and the American Revolution, 1741–1794*. Cambridge, Mass., 1970.

Ermenc, Christine. "Economic Give-And-Take: Farmers and Aesthetes in Cornish and Plainfield, New Hampshire, 1885–1910." *Historical New Hampshire* 39 (1984).

Frizzell, Martha McD. *Second History of Charlestown, N.H.: The Old Number Four*. Charlestown, N.H., 1955.

Gates, Paul W. "Two Hundred Years of Farming in Gilsum." *Historical New Hampshire* 33 (1978).

Hanlan, James. *The Working Population of Manchester, New Hampshire, 1840–1886*. Ann Arbor, 1981.

Hareven, Tamara K. *Family Time and Industrial Time: The Relationship between the Family and Work in a New England Industrial Community*. Cambridge, England, 1982.

Hareven, Tamara K., and Randolph Langenbach. *Amoskeag: Life and Work in an American Factory City*. New York, 1978.

Jager, Ronald, and Grace Jager. *Portrait of a Hill Town: A History of Washington, New Hampshire, 1876–1976*. Concord, 1977.

Kinney, Charles B., Jr. *Church and State: The Struggle for Separation in New Hampshire, 1630–1900*. New York, 1955.

Lyford, James O., ed. *History of Concord, N.H. From the Original Grant in Seventeen Hundred and Twenty-Five to the Opening of the Twentieth Century*. 2 vols. Concord, 1903.

Macey, Barry A. "Charles Sanger Mellen: Architect of Transportation Monopoly." *Historical New Hampshire* 26 (1971).

McKinney, Gordon B. "The Hazen Bill of 1887 and the Ascendency of the Boston and Maine." *Historical New Hampshire* 38 (1983).

———. "The Politics of Protest: The Labor Reform and Greenback Parties in New Hampshire." *Historical New Hampshire* 36 (1981).

Morison, Elizabeth Forbes, and Elting Elmore Morison. *New Hampshire: A Bicentennial History*. New York, 1976.

Morison, George A. *History of Peterborough, New Hampshire*. Rindge, N.H., 1974.

New Hampshire, University of. *History of the University of New Hampshire, 1866–1941*. Durham, N.H., 1941.

Pillsbury, Hobart. *New Hampshire: Resources, Attractions, and Its People, A History*. 5 vols. New York, 1927.

Richardson, Leon Burr. *History of Dartmouth College*. 2 vols. Hanover, N.H., 1932.

———. *William E. Chandler: Republican*. New York, 1940.

Robinson, Maurice. *A History of Taxation in New Hampshire. Publications of the American Economic Association*. 3d series. New York, 1902.

Sackett, Everett B. *New Hampshire's University: The Story of a Land Grant College*. Somersworth, N.H., 1974.

Sanborn, Frank B. *New Hampshire: An Epitome of Popular Government*. Boston, 1904.

Scheiber, Harry N. "Coach, Wagon, and Motor-Truck Manufacturer, 1813–1928: The Abbot-Downing Company of Concord." *Historical New Hampshire* 20 (1965).

Schott, John. *Frances' Town.* Francestown, N.H., 1972.

Sherman, Rexford. "The New Hampshire Grange, 1873–1883." *Historical New Hampshire* 26 (1971).

———. "One Year on a New Hampshire Farm, 1888." *Historical New Hampshire* 32 (1977).

Somers, A. N. *History of Lancaster.* Concord, 1899.

Squires, James D. *The Granite State of the United States.* 4 vols. New York, 1956.

———. *Mirror to America: A History of New London, New Hampshire, 1900–1950.* Concord, 1952.

Straw, William P. "Amoskeag in New Hampshire—An Epic in American Industry." Newcomen Society Address. Princeton, 1948.

Taishoff, Sue. "New Hampshire State Politics and the Concept of a Party System, 1800–1840." *Historical New Hampshire* 31 (1976).

Taylor, William L. "The Nineteenth Century Hill Town: Images and Reality." *Historical New Hampshire* 37 (1982).

Turner, Lynn. *William Plumer of New Hampshire, 1759–1850.* Chapel Hill, 1962.

Wade, Hugh Mason. *A Brief History of Cornish, 1763–1974.* Hanover, N.H., 1976.

Whitcher, William. *History of the Town of Haverhill, New Hampshire.* N.p., 1919.

———. *Some Things about Coventry-Benton, New Hampshire.* Woodsville, N.H., 1905.

Williams, David. "'Sowing the Wind': The Deportation Raids of 1920 in New Hampshire." *Historical New Hampshire* 34 (1979).

Young, Allyn A. "The Birth-Rate in New Hampshire." *Quarterly Publications of the American Statistical Association,* September 1905.

Unpublished

Agan, Thomas. "The New Hampshire Progressive Movement." Ph.D. dissertation, State University of New York at Albany, 1975.

Cima, Ronald P. "The Emergence of Winston Churchill, New Hampshire Author of Progressivism." Honors thesis, Dartmouth College, Department of History, 1975.

Hammond, David. "New Hampshire Gold Democrats." Seminar paper, Dartmouth College, Department of History, 1975.

Hokans, James. "Railroad Combination in New Hampshire, 1835–1900." Honors thesis, Dartmouth College, Department of History, 1974.

Lobdell, George H., Jr. "A Biography of Frank Knox." Ph.D. dissertation, University of Illinois, 1954.

Munyon, Paul G. "A Reassessment of New England Agriculture in the Last Thirty Years of the Nineteenth Century: New Hampshire, A Case Study." Ph.D. dissertation, Harvard University, 1975.

Pettit, Dorothy Ann. "An Analysis of the 1916 Presidential Election in New Hampshire." M.A. thesis, University of New Hampshire, 1968.

Sholl, Robert K. "Critical Elections and Political Paradigms: A New Hampshire Case Study." Senior Fellow project, Dartmouth College, 1977.

Symonds, Merrill A. "George Higgins Moses of New Hampshire: The Man and the Era." Ph.D. dissertation, Clark University, 1955.

Theodorou, Nicholas. "Conservation in New Hampshire: A Bald Grab for Power?" Honors thesis, Dartmouth College, Department of History, 1979.

Theriault, George F. "The Franco-Americans in a New England Community. An Experiment in Survival." Ph.D. dissertation, Harvard University, 1951.

Vicero, Ralph D. "Immigration of French Canadians to New England, 1840–1900: A Geographical Analysis." Ph.D. dissertation, University of Wisconsin, 1969.

White, Leonard D. "A Study of the New Hampshire Legislature of 1913." Master's thesis, Dartmouth College, 1914.

Index

Page numbers followed by "t" denote tables; page numbers in italics denote illustrations; page numbers followed by "n" denote Notes.